LEARNING RESOURCES CTR/NEW ENGLAND TECH

W9-DCL-232

ENDLESS PROPAGANDA:
THE ADVERTISING OF PUBLIC GOODS

Paul Rutherford

Is there any public discourse left, or has advertising, with its aggressive sales techniques, usurped the role of democratic, civil debate? Beginning in the 1960s, there was a proliferation of social, political, and corporate advertising in affluent, developed nations that spoke to the 'public good' on everything from milk to family values. Surveying over 10,000 advertisements from the past 40 years, *Endless Propaganda* underscores the presence of advertising rhetoric, even in the context of apparently non-partisan collective health issues such as cancer.

The public sphere, argues Paul Rutherford, has been transformed into a huge marketplace of goods and signs. Civil advocacy has become a special art of authority that subjects politics, social behaviour, and public morals to the philosophy and discipline of marketing. Without suggesting that there is one simple way to understand the transformation that democracy has undergone because of this phenomenon, the author introduces and applies the cultural theories of several important philosophers: Habermas, Gramsci, Foucault, Ricoeur, and Baudrillard. The reader is thus given the necessary tools to critically examine the examples at hand and many others that exist beyond the pages of this study.

PAUL RUTHERFORD is Professor in the Department of History at the University of Toronto.

PAUL RUTHERFORD

Endless Propaganda:
The Advertising of Public Goods

NEW ENGLAND INSTITUTE
OF TECHNOLOGY
LEARNING RESOURCES CENTER

UNIVERSITY OF TORONTO PRESS
Toronto Buffalo London

b-oo   #43283653

© University of Toronto Press Incorporated 2000
Toronto Buffalo London
Printed in Canada

ISBN 0-8020-4739-4 (cloth)
ISBN 0-8020-8301-3 (paper)

Printed on acid-free paper

Canadian Cataloguing in Publication Data

Rutherford, Paul, 1944–
    Endless propaganda : the advertising of public goods

    Includes bibliographical references and index.
    ISBN 0-8020-4739-4 (bound)   ISBN 0-8020-8301-3 (pbk.)

    1. Advocacy advertising – United States.   2. Advocacy advertising.
    3. Television advertising – United States.   4. Television advertising.
    5. Advertising, Public service – United States.   6. Advertising, Public
    service.   I. Title.

    HD59.3.R87 1999   659.1′042   C99-932562-0

University of Toronto Press acknowledges the support to its publishing
program of the Canada Council for the Arts and the Ontario Arts Council.

This book has been published with the help of a grant from the Humanities
and Social Science Federation of Canada, using funds provided by the Social
Sciences and Humanities Research Council of Canada.

University of Toronto Press acknowledges the financial support for its
publishing activities of the Government of Canada through the Book
Publishing Industry Development Program (BPIDP).

In memory of Shan

Contents

Figures

Acknowledgments

Research for this book was made possible by funding from the Social Sciences and Humanities Research Council of Canada (SSHRC), that marvellous government agency which deserves much praise for the way in which it has assisted a myriad of academic projects. I also received a small grant, which again derives from the monies of the SSHRC, through the Department of History at the University of Toronto to complete aspects of the project. I am very grateful for this assistance.

The SSHRC funds enabled me to hire Kathryn Scharf, then a graduate student, as an assistant who performed, and performed very well, a variety of research and bibliographic tasks in the early months of the project. These funds also supported a number of trips to libraries and depositories in North America and Europe. I especially wish to thank the staff of the National Museum of Photography, Film and Television, in Bradford, England, who went out of their way to ensure that their visitor got the most out of a week's effort. Further, the SSHRC monies financed the purchase of a lot of tapes of television commercials from around the world so that I could conduct my research at home. Here I want to express my special thanks to Mark Morton, in 1994 video supervisor at the Television Bureau of Canada, who arranged for the duplication of a considerable number of foreign commercials held by the bureau.

Once more I was fortunate to have Virgil Duff as my editor. He and his assistant, Siobhan McMenemy, worked hard to speed the manuscript through the process of review, acceptance, and publication. This makes the fourth book I have published at the Press with Virgil's assistance.

PAUL RUTHERFORD
April 1999

Illustration Credits

I am grateful to the following for permission to reproduce images in the text:

Office of Public Affairs, California Department of Health Services, for permission to reproduce the anti-smoking ad (p. 102)

Benetton for permission to reproduce four ads (p. 160)

W.R. Grace & Co. for permission to reproduce four photographs from *The Deficit Trials, 2017 A.D.* (p. 188)

AT & T for permission to reproduce two photographs from their '*You Will*' ads (p. 195)

Greenpeace Canada for permission to reproduce three photographs from their ad *Air Supply* (p. 219)

Respect for Animals for permission to reproduce four photographs from *Dumb Animals* by Greenpeace then Lynx (p. 222)

Preface

This book investigates how advocacy advertising colonized the political, social, and moral realms of the public sphere in the affluent democracies during the past three decades. My account concentrates on the experiences of the United States, to a lesser degree those of Canada, Britain, and western Europe, and, on occasion, explores happenings in the rest of the world. It pays the most attention to what was aired on television. The text is organized into five parts that track the emergence, the expansion, and the genres of what I will call 'civic advocacy,' up to the end of the century. Each part is introduced by a theory essay (identified in the text by an asterisk) in order to establish the vocabulary and the approach that is employed in the succeeding chapters. The numbered chapters dwell upon particular collections of ads – drawn from health or political advertising – and some passages are heavy with examples, in order to determine the character and the profusion, and occasionally the effect, of this advocacy. I try to bring together the disparate strands of these explorations and commentaries in the book's conclusion, where I probe the ways in which the prominence of civic advocacy has affected the practices and even the character of democracy.

I have included in nearly all the chapters special subsections that concentrate usually on a single advertisement, sometimes on a group or a series. These subsections are set in smaller type than the regular text and introduced by an italicized title. The focus on specific examples is an attempt to provide a rough kind of justice for the individual artifacts of this propaganda. There might seem a contradiction here. How can any verbal description replicate the experience of viewing a commercial that sells, say, anti-smoking or recycling or Bill Clinton? It cannot. Rather, the very task of translating the audiovisual expression into a written document produces a text that lends itself to assessment, comparison, and discussion. Put another way, the focus constitutes a descriptive sign: it is a translation into prose which allows the reader to identify what an actual ad signifies. I have varied the style of these 'translations' to avoid too much uniformity.

The book belongs to that amorphous school sometimes called the New Cultural History. My account emphasizes the crucial importance of language or, more properly, of language as it is actually used in the form of discourses which express relations of power and bodies of knowledge. This history reverses the common-sense proposition: instead of accepting that we use language, which is correct but insufficient, it presumes as well that language shapes us (or speaks, makes, uses us – the verbs get ever more bold). For it is through an assortment of symbolic practices, meaning here 'talk,' 'text,' and 'image,' that language constructs people, often in ways which suit the needs of authority: language fashions our worlds, our desires and fears, our identities, and our enemies. That presumption justifies a close attention to the career, the styles, the imagery, the messages, and so on, of advocacy advertising as a specific technology of power.

Endless Propaganda draws upon cultural theory to explore the history and assess the phenomenon of civic advocacy. Theory poses questions, names concepts, establishes frameworks. Consider this book a modest exercise in applied theory: I draw from that collection of insights where a framework serves to organize an argument and a concept might better explain some happening or circumstance. I have leaned most heavily upon the works of Jürgen Habermas and Antonio Gramsci, both of whom wrote out of the Marxist tradition, plus three of that extraordinary (and very unMarxist) generation of French philosophers who have so mesmerized scholars in recent decades, Michel Foucault, Paul Ricoeur, and Jean Baudrillard. Habermas and especially Foucault have a presence throughout the whole book. All five of the major theorists are represented here because they worried a lot about discourse, signs, and power.

Occasionally, I offer criticisms or suggest revisions, though none of this amounts to a sophisticated critique of theory. I doubt that the theory will surprise any specialist in the field, at least not those scholars who know all five authors, though the applications might. The theory essays are meant for readers, rather than for specialists. I have tried to present these authors' views free from the specialized kind of terminology – jargon, if you like – which seems inevitable in this field of study. I have presumed that the works at issue are not well known (or that not all of them are known) to most readers of this book, who need to understand what, say, Gramsci or Baudrillard claimed, where it fits into the general realm of theory, and how it can be used to help understand, and appreciate, the import of terms like 'hegemony' or 'simulacrum.'

As I noted above, the theory essays serve to establish the framework of understanding for the chapters grouped in each part, a structure which gives the book the character of a mosaic. This oddity reflects the presumption that social truth is a multiple, that there are many truths which arise out of different subject positions, and, hence, that analysis ought to employ different approaches. The presumption did not always please the assorted experts who initially appraised the book in manuscript form. Some found the concepts alien, the essays familiar, and the apparent lack of a single, decided thesis disturbing.

In fact, my stance is more common in literary studies than in history. In an essay entitled 'A Vast Unravelling' which appeared in the *Times Literary Supplement* (26 February 1999), professor Michel Chaouli noted that many of his fellow scholars of literature had shed 'the traditional idea of method' to explore how 'various vocabularies of description make different aspects and tonalities of the world accessible to us.' So the aim was not 'to anchor' an 'argument in Truth' but to employ a 'lower-case truth' in order to pose certain kinds of questions. Out went any claim to objectivity. The approach now worked 'to put into relief or even to call into being the object it describes.' That is roughly what I have done in *Endless Propaganda*: the layering of various brands of theory has worked, I trust, not only to sketch the definition of civic advocacy, but also to provide an appreciation of its many-sidedness as both a symptom and an agent of the postmodern condition.

In any case, there is an argument in *Endless Propaganda*. The argument works off an existing model of democracy, authored by the philosopher Jürgen Habermas, where the quality of talk determines the merits, indeed the virtues, of any public action. Here is an abbreviated outline of that argument:

1 The public sphere is a utopian space where, to paraphrase Habermas, private people gather to discuss shared concerns. Ideally, what should prevail here is rational discourse.
2 The instruments of colonization were corporate, social, issue, and

political advertising, publicity that dealt with behaviours, feelings and beliefs, policies and parties and politicians, a phenomenon named 'civic advocacy.'

3 Although such publicity had antecedents reaching back to the early years of the twentieth century, the process of colonization took off after the mid-1960s in the United States and spread rapidly, especially in the 'First World.' Its spread was closely linked to the advance of television.

4 This propaganda worked to fashion and to popularize a dizzying array of new public goods (such as clean air, family values, the healthy body, women's rights) – as well as to warn against a collection of social risks (such as drug abuse, AIDS, environmental disaster, lung cancer).

5 Civic advocacy was and remains an instrument of élites who have the money or the connections to hire experts as well as to secure time or space on the mass media. The ads have been sponsored by governments and corporations, parties or churches, non-profit and non-governmental organizations, and, occasionally, a well-off individual.

6 Overall, whatever its content, civic advocacy constitutes a discourse which represents the world of affairs as a gathering of problems, products, and solutions, always to suit the purposes of selling, though some realities (such as war, labour's plight, or poverty, at least before the spread of homelessness) are rarely or never performed in its grand theatre of display.

7 This propaganda has created a special art and rhetoric of authority, often grounded in a moral logic or point of view, that has conditioned the behaviours of actors in the public sphere.

8 The boom in civic advocacy has worked to subject politics, social behaviour, and public endeavour to the philosophy and discipline of marketing.

9 That boom has also expanded the domain of the political: civic advocacy has penetrated the inner sanctums of the body, the mind, and the soul.

10 The result has transformed an enlarged public sphere into a huge marketplace of goods and risks, especially in postmodern communities, where citizens act as consumers and where participation (or non-participation) expresses, in varying degrees, an aesthetic response.

ENDLESS PROPAGANDA

Introduction:
Advertising as Propaganda

The little messages are scattered all over our memories.

Consider these incidents from life in and around big cities during the nineteen-nineties. The walls of London subway stations one summer day in 1994 sport a poignant plea to help find a cure for multiple sclerosis. An electronic sign on a highway to Florence (August 1998) urges Italians not to abandon their pets; street posters in Paris (also August 1998) tell walkers, in English, 'Better off alive with it than dead without it,' referring to a condom. The advertisements in a Toronto subway car call upon riders to get involved with community policing. Walk down a street in Ottawa and you might see a pro-life poster, complete with an illustration of a living heart and a promise of help if you phone a 1-800 number. Try to fly out of Canada and you may spy in the airport lounge a sad photograph of a girl, asleep in jail: the text warns youth not to use drugs overseas. Go into a bank and you face a collection of requests to donate petty cash to the victims of Alzheimer's, cancer, or hunger; the boxes are stationed next to the tellers to make it easy to indulge any generous impulse. A note in a hotel bathroom urges patrons to reuse the towels, reduce pollution, protect the environment – how easy it is to be virtuous. The mails bring a polite request from a foster parents' plan to sponsor a deprived child, or perhaps a plea to save the dogs of the Philippines from the tastes of locals. One side of a milk carton announces the utility of the Kids Help Phone to those children and teens who just 'need to talk.' Open up a package of Hanes Silk Reflections, a brand of stocking, and find an insert that explains how you should, and shows how you can, examine your breasts once a month for signs of cancer. Strangest of all is a brief slogan on a piece of rubber strategically located at the bottom of a urinal: 'Don't

Do Drugs!' What once was private space is nowadays a place for public admonitions.

The best channels of delivery are the mass media. A London newspaper carries a full-page ad about saving farm animals from cruel treatment; an ad in a New York daily calls upon people to 'be less productive at the office' by saving paper, turning off lights, using mugs, and so on. A radio station in Antigua warns against the dangerous link between diabetes and blindness. The pre-show commercial in a Canadian moviehouse is a surreal display of the many doors that will close in the face of any youngster foolish enough to drop out of school. Especially in North America, the television set brings a stream of corporate ads, unpaid public service announcements (PSAs), and, in season, political and issue ads. A visitor to Florida in 1990 witnessed so many ferocious commercials that he decided the country was 'paranoid about drugs and alcohol.'[1] Nor is the World Wide Web exempt: a visit to the AT & T Web site in 1996 allowed you to view a series of commercials depicting the marvels of an imminent future shaped by the company's engineers.

1 Public Goods / Social Risks

Each of these brands of advertising sought to sell a particular kind of commodity known as a public good, and sometimes to warn against a common risk or public bad as well.[2] The term 'public goods' is derived from the discipline of economics where these commodities are usually given a negative definition to emphasize their contrast to what is normal, namely, private goods such as chocolate bars or automobiles.

A 'pure' public good, such as the national defence system, has two basic attributes. First, the good is 'non-deductible' or 'non-rival,' meaning that use by one person does not diminish the utility for other consumers. Likewise, the cost of the public good does not grow as use increases. Economists recognize that in history few, if any, commodities are 'pure' in this respect. Virtually every good is subject to some form of congestion if use increases exponentially – a phenomenon all too obvious on the crowded urban highways of North America. But, in relative terms, the common benefits to street life of police patrols, for example, better approach the crucial state of 'indivisibility' than do those of hotdog stands.

Second, the good is 'non-excludable,' meaning that it is impossible to prevent any person from enjoying this social product. The difficulty thus arises of preventing 'free riders,' those who use a good without paying for that good, whether by not making a voluntary contribution or by avoiding taxes or by accident (as when so much of the 'Free World' apparently benefited from American nuclear might in the years of the Cold War). This is why economists talk about 'market failure,' the inability of private provision to supply most public goods.

The discussion of public goods has become an area of modest controversy. In some formulations it is not rational for persons to assist the joint supply of a public good, because that entails monetary or psychological cost but no extra advantage. In others there is resistance to the notion that government must compensate for the presumed failure of private provision. A third group of economists emphasizes that television programs or the Internet are as much 'impure' public goods as are publicly delivered services like sewers or courts.

Whatever we may honour – a gender, a class, a minority, an age, a nation, a continent, the world – that community will gain or lose from the consumption of these jointly supplied commodities. A public good becomes a means to a generally esteemed and mutually beneficial end: a drug-free America, social justice and public health, a united Canada or a sovereign Quebec, economic progress, unspoiled nature, world peace, crime-free streets, and on and on. These benefits promise to result from the widespread use of a particular object, the adoption of some policy, or perhaps the election of one individual, and commonly nowadays each is presented as a branded product: a government-approved condom or seat-belt, a policy such as deficit reduction, the election of a Margaret Thatcher or a Bill Clinton, the practices of safe sex or sober driving, named donations to feed famine victims, wheelchair access. The numbers of ends, means, and sponsors have exploded over the course of the past generation, especially in affluent countries. But so, too, have their negations: the list of social risks (newly perceived as commodities, but not necessarily new as issues) includes water pollution, radiation poisoning, political corruption, torture, AIDS, hunger, homelessness, and other spectres of an imminent dystopia. They are the consequences of an assortment of sins like selfishness or hedonism, persistent evils born of waste or intolerance, and occasional villains, whether the nuclear industry or the tobacco companies. No wonder that the task of social improvement often involves unselling, as much as selling, a particular attitude or behaviour.

This boom in public goods and social risks is not the only major break with the past, however. The other important change has been the entry of these special commodities into the blessed realm of the marketplace.

The discipline of marketing has been applied to the demand and the supply side of the political economy of public goods. How appropriate, then, that a writer in *Advertising Age* (28 November 1988) would describe the launch of George Bush as a 'line extension' of the presidency of the renowned Ronald Reagan.[3] True, we are dealing here as much with the analogy as with the reality of the market. Public goods are rarely put on sale. Nor do people necessarily treat them as they do ordinary commodities. Indeed, public goods often have a moral dimension that is lacking in their private rivals: their consumption can involve sacrifice, such as paying more taxes or giving up some cherished behaviour, which is why these commodities often reek of virtue. That said, public goods are subject to the same rigours of the famous 'four Ps' (product, pricing, promotion, and placement): they are pretested and positioned; they are packaged to suit disparate tastes; and they are targeted at specific market segments.

Consider the case of a thirty-second commercial sponsored by Hong Kong's Committee on Education and Publicity on AIDS in 1992 to reach out to that most vulnerable of populations, the sexually promiscuous. The camera showed a semi-naked woman who apparently put a condom on her companion (the action was suggested, not displayed). As the couple made love, a voice-over delivered the message: 'For those times when you decide to go all the way together, using a condom can form a gentle, but effective barrier against AIDS and other infections. For safer sex, always use a condom.' The urgency of the crisis was the justification for drawing upon the imagery of erotica: the risqué character of the PSA would surely attract the attention of high-risk folk, or so its apologists argued. The hope was that people would come to recognize that wearing a condom was no obstacle to extraordinary pleasures.[4] The use of the sexual sell was unusual in the story of anti-AIDS marketing, although there were some equivalents in the Scandinavian experience. But the ad illustrates the way in which a particular product might become a public good. And it highlights the attention that advocates paid to such issues as market segments, packaging, and psychological costs.

There is another way in which the analogy of the market fits. The new public goods came to prominence in a particular kind of intellectual space. That hoary old slogan of 'the marketplace of ideas' has been rejuvenated in postmodern times, except now it might better be called a marketplace of signs. The tumult of the sixties left behind a disturbed hegemony and a fragmented public sphere, particularly in the United States, and this condition spread to Europe and beyond, into the Third World and the post-Communist lands. Increasingly, politics invaded more and more areas of everyday life, even though since 1980 the authority of government has been circumscribed and sometimes privatized.

We have, in the words of Zygmunt Bauman, a 'tribal politics' of self-constructed identities, a 'politics of desire,' where agencies vie for scarce resources, balanced by a 'politics of fear' that seeks to forestall the lethal risks generated by the industrial machine, even a 'politics of certainty,' where experts offer proof and people seek confirmation to assuage anxiety.[5] Some of the cacophony can be put down to the birth or rebirth of a range of social movements, fundamentalisms as well as nationalisms, and rights crusades which challenged the way things were or are. These in turn provoked a renewed activism from established authorities, notably political parties and major corporations, which moved to counter the threat or capture the public. Meanwhile, the diminished state remained active as an agent pushing the new wealth of public goods. The result was an enormous burst of publicity and promotion as a variety of organizations sought that most valuable (because most scarce) of commodities, public attention.

2 Defining Propaganda

All of this publicity and promotion is part of propaganda today – though it is rarely recognized as such. Another of the ironies of the postmodern age is that this most persistent and ubiquitous barrage has gone largely unnamed in general or academic discussion.[6] Instead, aspects are called social or political marketing, public-information campaigns, public relations, issue advertising, and so on. Nothing names the single phenomenon. Why? Part of the reason lies with the term itself. 'Propaganda' is one of those problem words that do not lend themselves to easy definition. It used to be that propaganda was something the other fellow did, the Nazis in World War II or the Communists in the Cold War. It was the intellectual equivalent of mugging: propaganda meant lies and lying, the misinformation the enemy manufactured to persuade its victims and the unwary. That notion persists in ordinary conversation. But recently, at least in scholarly circles, propaganda has become a synonym for all kinds of mass persuasion.[7] The more sophisticated definitions often highlight self-interest, manipulation, irrationality, and especially intention: propaganda is a conscious act – an accidental propaganda is an oxymoron.[8] These definitions manage to avoid some of the confusion between propaganda and education or propaganda and news that bedevilled earlier efforts. But they leave propaganda without a distinct identity in the wider realm of promotion. So it is no accident that trendy souls in the popular arts have come to use 'propaganda' as a catchy and stronger term than publicity.

Missing from such explanations is the crucial focus on politics. What distinguishes propaganda from other types of publicity is not deceit, élitism, or authoritarianism, although one might make a case for any of these qualities. Above all, propaganda tries to determine happenings in the public sphere.[9] Whatever its particular shape, propaganda constitutes an intentional and sponsored message, a deliberate kind of 'symbolic practice' that seeks to persuade the body politic, or some significant constituency within the public sphere. It normally addresses or 'constructs' the model person: the teacher talks to attentive pupils, the cleric to believers, the advertiser to happy consumers, and the propagandist to good citizens.[10] In a much more pointed sense than its rivals, propaganda is both the language and the instrument of power.

Just about every institution and organization could be counted a vehicle, as well as a source, of propaganda. It is the equivalent of radiation in this promotional age. All kinds of intellectual objects – paintings, photographs, books, cartoons, press conferences – can emit propaganda. Political parties have always spread tales of woe and villainy and promise. There is some virtue to the infamous 'propaganda model' of the news media popularized by Noam Chomsky and his colleagues, although his arguments dismiss the reality of that 'vital arena of acceptable controversy' constructed by the press.[11] Recent times have seen the massive growth of a 'bureaucratic propaganda,' apparent in a host of reports by all sorts of organizations (and, notably, government agencies) that hope to influence public policy.[12] The orderly sequence of spectacles on display in museums is clearly fashioned to persuade visitors of the veracity of some preferred version of history.[13] Corporate headquarters try to evoke feelings of awe because they are meant to be the visible embodiments of the power and wealth of their residents.

But none of these forms of propaganda is so common in our times as a species of advertising I will call 'civic advocacy,' most especially the television version. Since 1965, this type of advertising has become, increasingly and ordinarily, the chief mode of propaganda in everyday life throughout the affluent world. The barrage of propaganda encompasses many different types: PSAs, government ads, charity appeals, corporate-image campaigns, issue advertising, many religious messages, social ads, political spots, counter-ads, and cause-related publicity. Its chief sponsors are the state, the corporations, and voluntary associations, variously known as non-profits or non-governmental organizations, although in theory anyone with sufficient money – such as a Ross Perot – can publish or air advocacy, always assuming the compliance of the media. At bottom, the prominence of civic advocacy reflects one of the attributes of postmodern culture: the ubiquity of publicity.

That ubiquity is yet another reason why this propaganda is rarely recognized as such: labelled advertising, a commonplace phenomenon, the anti-abuse commercial or the corporate ad or the charity appeal seems to be just one more piece of promotion in a world inundated with ads. In the early 1980s an especially active Canadian government went to great pains to deny that its policy advertising attempted to persuade, since that smacked of propaganda. Neither the opposition nor the press was convinced. During the mid-1990s the *Wall Street Journal* ran a series of print ads in *Advertising Age* that offered testimonials from business and marketing people to explain why corporate ads were another tool of sales, just like normal brand ads, except that in the right magazine they could be very effective. Heaven forbid that individuals might realize they had a political objective as well. A mystique surrounds the PSA, at least in agency circles: the AIDS message or the anti-drug commercial is advertising in the public interest, an honour, an accolade, maybe even compensation for all the soap ads, and so on, that are the bane of the 'creative's' existence (the 'creative' being that soul who designs the ad). The fact that it is propaganda remains 'the dirty little secret' of this whole business.

But civic advocacy does not simply produce a replica of regular advertising. Corporate-image campaigns, for example, might boast the upbeat tone of most consumer commercials. By contrast, health advertising has employed a distinctive kind of fear appeal, and environmental ads specialize in horror and apocalypse. That is because the crucial purpose of an anti-fur or a safe-driving ad is to unsell a bad habit. When the election campaign gets tough, political spots in the United States often go negative. The notorious attack ad has been widely stigmatized as a symptom and an agent of the decline of American democracy. By the 1990s, industry apologists lamented that political spots were giving advertising a bad name: Ketchum Communications actually ran an ad headlined 'DON'T CALL IT ADVERTISING.'[14]

The differences go well beyond the issue of style, moreover. Advocacy

Figure 1: Some Properties of Advertising

1 *compression*: the use of a compacted style of presentation, which involves short bursts of information.

2 *stimulus*: the use of words, images, and sounds to grab or hold attention, often in the form of jolts.

3 *practicality*: the offering of apparently realistic solutions to common problems.

4 *parasitism*: the appropriation of and/or embedding in other discourses, thus seeking credibility and employing camouflage.

5 *stereotyping*: the use of the commonplace, clichés, archetypes, and accepted motifs, to ease understanding.

6 *symbolism*: the extensive use of poetic devices, metaphors, and images to represent, associate, and evoke.

7 *playfulness*: the inventive, ambiguous, or parodic use of signs, whether linguistic or pictorial, that break the rules.

8 *hyperbole*: the use of an exaggerated, inflated, or overdone style of expression, though at times from an ironic standpoint.

9 *repetition*: the reiteration of slogans, images, motifs, and logos within an ad, over a campaign, or across a sequence of campaigns.

10 *intertextuality*: the constant reference to existing documents, broadly defined to include all sorts of written and audiovisual artifacts, including other ads.

11 *juxtaposition*: the practice of putting very different signs together, often ripped free from their original contexts. These signs may be organized as contrasts in a simplified and bold arrangement of oppositions to guide understanding or as associations linking one sign to another so as to extend a halo effect over one of them.

12 *direct address*: the attempt to personalize, notably by using (in English) the word 'you' and employing eye contact (on television), to create a false sense of intimacy.

---

advertising is normally an instrument of domination in a much wider apparatus of disciplinary power. The exceptions to this rule, the examples of counter-ads or culture jamming (in which rebel types construct ad parodies or deface existing ads), are rare. Most messages express the wishes of the powerful. During the early summer of 1998, for example, the American tobacco industry poured tens of millions of dollars into television ads as part of a successful campaign to stop the passage in the Senate of a bill that aimed to curb teenage smoking. Meanwhile, halfway across the world, a desperate Indonesian government filled outdoor boards in the capital city of Jakarta with pleas 'to buy local products, support the besieged rupiah, and try to save money and live modestly' to offset the financial disaster of the times.[15] Propaganda usually presumes, and confirms, hierarchy: it is typically a monologue originating on high (from experts, officials, politicians, managers, and the like) but directed below (to young people, adult citizens, minorities, etcetera). Civic advocacy links leading corporations, elected governments, and established non-profits in a common alliance to condition the imagination and discipline the bodies of the citizenry. But that does not mean that authority has always succeeds in realizing such ambitions.

3 Impacts

How do we know that any of this propaganda has produced any effect on its intended targets? At one level that question is unanswerable. 'We will never know if an advertisement or opinion poll has had a real influence on individual or collective wills,' Jean Baudrillard once pointed out, 'but we will never know either what would have happened if there had been no opinion poll or advertisement.'[16] The cognitive sciences offer some guidance as to how any message may work on the minds of receivers. From their standpoint, people appear as collections of schemata and scripts, derived in large part from past experience: the schemata are bodies of generic knowledge about behaviours, settings, and situations, while the scripts amount to plans of action aimed at securing particular goals.[17] Messages work best when they build upon those schemata, particularly when they offer believable scripts that promise some resolution of the social problem or moral ill. A clever ad slogan, for example, can even use what is in a target's memory to foster inferences, to make people 'jump to conclusions.'[18]

Much of the earlier analysis of communications posited a model of persuasion that was so complicated you might wonder how anyone could ever change her mind.[19] John Cacioppo and Richard Petty, however, argued the case for two distinct 'routes to persuasion.'[20] The central route presumed that the receiver not only paid close attention to the message but actively processed the information to understand its meanings. That more traditional brand of persuasion might operate in cases where, say, a person listened intently to a lecture or carefully read a book. It did not necessarily apply to advertising, which often waylaid its victims while they were watching television, reading a magazine, or driving from work. The peripheral route, by contrast, assumed that the receiver was not engaged, was perhaps lazy or preoccupied or unwilling to elaborate an argument. Such a 'cognitive miser'[21] might still be stimulated by vivid pictures, loud sounds, the credibility of the source, or the cogency of the performance. Here an emotional appeal – using fear or disgust, causing surprise, or evoking guilt – might be much more telling than any overtly rational approach.[22] Indeed, experimental research on mental processing has discovered how visual signals can not only activate the emotions before the mind comes into play, but also can continue to condition what we think afterwards.[23] The resulting impact, even though shallow, the persuasion ephemeral, could none the less be significant, especially if that effect is accentuated by repetition or other means. It is this more insidious brand of persuasion that makes civic advocacy seem sinister: somehow the propaganda works to program the mind of the unaware, or unwary, soul.[24]

But what if the viewer actually did pay attention: he screened out distractions and focused on the ad? In that case, consuming advertising, especially viewing commercials, could take on some of the attributes of 'the aesthetic encounter,' to borrow from the vocabulary of Mihaly Csikszentmihalyi and Rick Robinson. 'The aesthetic experience occurs when information coming from the artwork interacts with information already stored in the viewer's mind,' they argued. 'The result of this conjunction might be a sudden expansion, recombination, or ordering of previously accumulated information, which in turn produces a variety of emotions such as delight, joy, or awe.'[25] Or, as in the case of many a social ad, I could add shock, fear, and perhaps revulsion, among other negative emotions. The authors explored four distinct responses that could characterize the experience (here translated to suit my purposes): 'perceptual,' a reaction to the look and the feel of the commercial; 'emotional,' the result of both the stimuli embedded in the ad and 'personal associations' evoked by these stimuli; 'intellectual,' a response which focuses on the claims made in the ad; and 'communicative,' perhaps the most important, where the viewer employs the ad as a lens through which to understand issues, events, or his culture.

That last response might be rare indeed. Only a very few commercials were a smashing success. One such instance was the famous *Chief Iron Eyes Cody* of the early 1970s from the Advertising Council and Keep America Beautiful Incorporated: the grand lament over the pollution of America remained well known for years afterwards. Its powerful script, its production values, and its lead character captivated viewers. But other ads in the same campaign were soon forgotten. Individual spots are always unique performances – of talent, artistry, and technical wizardry – all to win attention. People may try to avoid these messages. People do discount ad claims. Still, that resistance can sometimes be overcome by creativity. And some performances do generate an aesthetic encounter.

4 Functions

Consider the number of different roles played by advocacy, particularly the audiovisual variety, in the public sphere.

a) Distillation

Overall, this propaganda amounts to a potent exercise in public art and public rhetoric, making images and fashioning slogans that turn the ordinary into the extraordinary. Civic advocacy assembles spectacles that work on and with the popular imagination, spectacles that envisage, and sometimes propagate, basic hopes and collective fears. Put another way, the ads distil or purify, shearing away unnecessary baggage, to present these hopes and fears in as bold a fashion as possible. So, in 1988 during a California referendum campaign over a proposed twenty-five-cent tax on a package of cigarettes, Ailes Communication created ads for the tobacco industry (officially 'Californians Against Unfair Tax Increases') which identified Proposition 99 as a tax scheme meant to funnel monies to rich doctors and likely to encourage smuggling and exacerbate crime. These ads exploited a distaste for special privilege and a fear of crime that had been revealed by polling voters to see how best to shape the anti-Proposition 99 message. By some accounts the packaging was working and support for the proposition did drop, but only until the pro forces retaliated by revealing that a supposed cop appearing in another ad was also a part-time actor, a point that immediately raised the issue of integrity.[26] The Ailes presentation lost its credibility, in short, when tainted by the evidence that it was phoney.

b) Vehicle

Civic advocacy carries much more than an individual message. Spots and campaigns transmit ideas and agendas, sometimes an ideology, that reflect the ambitions of a particular group. In the United States one of the most controversial ads of the mid-1980s, *Deficit Trials, 2017 A.D.*, sponsored by W.R. Grace, a major corporation, embodied a belief widespread within the business community that big government and big spending threatened the American future. The same performances may also presume, and less often represent, as in this case, a utopia or a dystopia, an alternative to the present social and political arrangements. It is these visions that connect with the yearnings for a better self and a better world, and the fears of loss, decline, or catastrophe, all of which persist in the body politic.

c) Catalyst

Where advertising shines is in its ability to reach so many people and to repeat so often its simplified messages. Civic advocacy attempts to enact power: to assert and deny, to confirm or change, to intensify or rebut, to silence as well as to produce, and nearly always to exert a form of intellectual closure. Sponsors and critics are most interested in the effects of propaganda. But, at best, advertising is only a weak force: it lacks the raw impact of other, more immediate instruments of power, notably money and guns. Rarely does a spot or a campaign act alone upon the audience. More often the campaign constitutes part of a marketing mix, a general kind of assault which makes it difficult to identify the actual consequence of the propaganda. Anti-smoking ads usually work well only with other agents, notably legal bans and price increases, to bring about any substantial change in habits. A special series of 'PSAs for criminals' in Cleveland, Ohio, in 1985 served to reduce the frequency of gun crimes, because they publicized a new mandatory eight-year jail term if a gun was used in a robbery.[27] One definite limit on ad power is the presence of other views, other propaganda, in the marketplace of signs. For that reason, the Clinton campaigns of 1992 and 1996 used rebuttals to counter any attack ads put out by the Republicans. Still, civic advocacy, on its own, can and does leave a mark: it names issues, shapes how we understand these issues, diverts as well as focuses popular attention, masks special agendas, assigns blame or praise, identifies heroes and villains, destroys reputations, offers solutions, and creates excitement.

d) Signal

At one level, however, a spot may be significant in itself as a display of interest, of priorities, or simply of authority. In Britain, in the mid-1980s, the Labour-dominated Greater London Council signalled its determination to survive by launching a major ad effort against Prime Minister

Margaret Thatcher's plans to get rid of it.[28] In Canada, in the mid-1990s, an anti-smoking campaign was presented as evidence of the good intentions of the Liberal government. The sponsor offers the message to demonstrate commitment to a public goal, especially when other means such as legislation or regulation are deemed inappropriate. Sometimes the hidden purpose of a campaign is to suggest action, to pretend that the sponsor (often the government but also corporations) really is trying to tackle a social problem; that seems especially the case with anti-drug efforts in the United States during the early 1990s. This type of advocacy treats the public sphere as a common theatre, a site for a show.

e) Discourse

Civic advocacy transforms both its domains of concern and its audiences. Even the ambitions of the leading players are influenced by its presence. It propagates a distinct vocabulary, a way of speaking about objects, and a repertoire of images. By the 1990s the lingo of marketing had thoroughly infected the ordinary language of political handlers and journalists. Witness this headline from a story by a Canadian reporter, Susan Delacourt, on the eve of a federal election in 1997: 'Tories strut their stuff in Charest label. Party's new television commercials designed to follow trend of touting brand assets.'[29] Civic advocacy fashions a world full of problems but also full of solutions, a place where social issues are individualized and personal agency is celebrated. Leaders can become retailers, citizens appear as buyers. Answers lie in the mass consumption of public goods.

Not only do leaders merchandise goods, and risks; they themselves become products. One excellent example of such a presentation was George Bush as politician. Unlike Ronald Reagan, Bush lacked a compelling vision, however simple or mundane. His persona was the result of a process of self-marketing, backed by ad magic. Witness this critical comment from Jay Rosen:

> George Bush is a dangerous man on the campaign trail because, lacking a political self, he is willing to say anything. Reducing his campaign to a package of stimuli disturbs him not at all ... With no self to reveal, he can have others, more gifted with language, strike the right chords with the audience ... The 'Education President,' the 'Environmental President' – Bush seeks these labels the way Barry Manilow seeks the right chords for a new song he's writing. Manilow's songs are never really 'new.' They track over

the memory of his previous songs. When you hear one for the first time, you think that maybe you're remembering it ... This is the way Bush plays politics: He tries to hammer out the chords that will resonate with enough voters to keep him in office. It's not even correct to say that he's a man without principles, for he believes in a principle that reduces 'reality' to a quaint concern of the weak-minded.[30]

Dangerous or not, of course, the skill of Bush's handlers was insufficient to win him re-election in 1992.

Allow me to borrow and extend the meaning of a very useful term coined by Andrew Wernick: the 'promotional sign.' A sign is a triadic unit composed of a signifier (the vehicle), which conveys a signified (the concept), that links to the referent (the actual object). But in the realm of publicity the relations usual among the three parts are fundamentally altered. 'A promotional message is a complex of significations which at once represents (moves in place of), advocates (moves on behalf of), and anticipates (moves ahead of) the circulating entity or entities to which it refers.'[31] Consequently, the boundary between the signifier and its referent (Wernick prefers to use 'sign' and 'object') is blurred. In advocacy advertising this process goes one step farther. We are faced here with the phenomenon of the illusory referent: the object does not exist as a public good until its symbolic meanings are constructed and transmitted by propaganda. The signifiers, the words and images, actually come to create that to which they refer. A public good cannot be outside of its context of promotion.

This highlights a crucial effect of this advertising in the political culture of recent times: the new propaganda has carried marketing, as philosophy and as discipline, throughout the public sphere. This statement ought not to be taken as a claim that a particular 'discursive formation' (à la Michel Foucault) has triumphed.[32] The actual success of marketing owes much to other factors, notably the technique of polling and, more recently, the arrival of the computerized database. Civic advocacy shares significance in the public sphere with other kinds of discourses, particularly news, its twentieth-century rival. But in practice, advertising as propaganda normally organizes fears and desires (whereas consumer advertising reverses that ranking) among target populations in order to construct and sell a range of social products. So the PSAs, the political commercials, the corporate ads, and the rest, together constitute one formation that has worked not only to build public truths but to reshape liberal democracy.

PART I: BEGINNINGS

*HABERMAS'S LAMENT

Now for the first time there emerged something like modern propaganda, from the very start with the Janus face of enlightenment and control; of information and advertising; of pedagogy and manipulation.

Jürgen Habermas, 1962[1]

Habermas defined the problem. Or, rather, his book on the public sphere did. Jürgen Habermas matured in the Marxist tradition of western Europe, specifically that associated with the Frankfurt School of Critical Theory (he once referred to himself, a bit ruefully, as feeling like 'the last Marxist').[2] By then (1989), Habermas as philosopher had moved far away from any recognizable Marxism to articulate a vision of an egalitarian order that rested upon the act of speech. His heresy was apparent early on. He wrote a postdoctoral thesis, rejected by his Marxist supervisors, that became *The Structural Transformation of the Public Sphere*, first published in West Germany in 1962.[3] According to one later critic, his purpose was to explain how the Federal Republic of Germany had gone badly wrong.[4] If so, the result was of much wider relevance, for the book probed the rise and fall of public opinion in the practice of representative government throughout the history of western Europe. It has proved one of the most fruitful contributions to democratic theory in recent times, and that is why it continues to provoke scholarly discussion.[5]

Central to Habermas's vision of a radical democracy was the notion of the public sphere. This we might now term a virtual or imagined community, since it did not necessarily exist in any definite space: he once defined the sphere as 'made up of private people gathered together as a public and articulating the needs of society with the state' (176).[6] These private persons were citizens, not subjects, whose act of assembly and acts of discussion generated views which served to check and guide the state. The parallels with the reawakened desire of the 1990s for a civil society of voluntary associations and energetic citizens should be obvious. So, too, are the parallels with Tocqueville's praise of the American passion for organized togetherness. The public sphere, in short, was and remains the source of that public opinion which must legitimate authority in any 'real' democracy.

This public sphere had a double nature, as both utopian promise and historical artifact. Its success depended upon the extent of access (as close to universal as possible), the degree of autonomy (the citizens must be free of coercion), the rejection of hierarchy (so that each might participate on an equal footing), the rule of law (particularly the sub-ordination of the state), and the quality of participation (the common commitment to the ways of logic). What Habermas called 'rational-critical' debate was a compendium of many different virtues: rationality, equality, openness, critique, dialogue, exchange, and argument. 'I think what attracted me to Habermas, really,' mused Zygmunt Bauman later, 'was his ideal of a society shaped after the pattern of a sociology semi-nar; that is, that there are only participants and the one thing which matters is the power of argument.'[7] Habermas saw rebuilding the public sphere as the means whereby the project of the Enlightenment could be completed in the realm of politics.

The ideal had never been attained. What had been realized was the bourgeois public sphere, initially a collection of property-owning, educated males whose comfort and prestige rested upon the workings of the marketplace and the family. In the Middle Ages 'lordship was some-thing publicly represented' (7) before the people, a way of making visi-ble the authority of the ruler. A public sphere emerged, largely during the eighteenth century, because of the growth of coffee houses and literary societies, the appearance of voluntary associations, and the oper-ations of the press. Parliament and like institutions became the instru-ments of this public sphere in its efforts to discipline the state. Public opinion had become a force to be reckoned with, especially in Britain and France, by the early nineteenth century. Habermas's view of this achievement may seem excessively sanguine, especially for a Marxist, one reason why he was later charged with the sin of romanticism.[8]

Slowly, during the course of the late nineteenth and early twentieth centuries, the exclusions of class and gender were broken down, and the public sphere approached the ideal of universal access. How sadly ironic that reform should coincide with the beginnings of the deforma-tion of the public sphere. Or so Habermas argued. The immediate agents of decay were the advance of the social-welfare state, the growth of a culture industry, and the competition of large-scale private interests (although he did not stress corporate authority itself). A new set of big newspapers, devoted first to profit, turned the daily press into an instru-ment of manipulation: 'it became the gate through which privileged pri-vate interests invaded the public sphere' (185). Habermas pointed to a number of crucial transformations – he was a great fan of binary logic: the citizen became the client, culture was reduced to entertainment, popular participation gave way to mass consumption, public debate was replaced by élite negotiation, public opinion lost out to 'nonpublic opinion' (236). He even talked about a 'refeudalization' of power whereby the public sphere existed, or was briefly recreated, only to give sanction to the decisions of leaders. All in all, the final chapters of *The Structural Transformation* have a deeply pessimistic cast which would shortly seem at odds with the course of events in the 1960s.

Habermas saved some of his most savage criticisms for publicity. It was not that he disdained publicity *per se*. Far from it. Habermas looked upon 'critical publicity' as a creative force that had once given substance to the public sphere and significance to public opinion. By publicity he meant oral and written speech, whether the lecture or the pamphlet or the editorial, which announced the results of reasoned thought to the wider world. 'Originally publicity guaranteed the connection between rational-critical public debate and the legislative foundation of domination, including the critical supervision of its exercise' (177–8). Habermas's description of the operations of the public sphere emphasized the verbal and the aural. It was the practice of speech which guided his account. The public sphere worked best as a debate where people could give voice to their opinions in a general discussion that proceeded most properly in the form of a dialogue.

But in recent times a malignant type, which he usually called 'manipulative publicity' (178), had become all too common. 'Even arguments are transmuted into symbols to which again one can not respond by arguing but only by identifying with them' (206). Such propaganda managed views, fostered political theatre, and conveyed 'authorized opinions' (245). That was why it became an agent of 'refeudalization,' presenting and representing authority to supine groups of clients and consumers. 'Publicity imitates the kind of aura proper to the personal prestige and supernatural authority once bestowed by the kind of publicity involved in representation' (195). Habermas now resorted to visual metaphors to describe the deformation of democracy, especially to variations of the phrases translated as 'showy pomp' (195) and 'staged display' (206). In effect, Habermas treated visual communication as a mode whereby authority asserted its dominance over the people, whether medieval subjects or modern masses.

Habermas was not alone in his worries about public discourse. In the same year (1962) in which he published *The Structural Transformation,* Jacques Ellul released his *Propaganda: The Formation of Men's Attitudes.*[9] He was even more virulent in his denunciation of propaganda than Habermas. Ellul focused his attention upon something he called the

'propaganda of integration' (for example, biased newscasts, misinformation, political education) that worked over time to engineer the individual to suit the needs of social mechanisms. 'It is a long-term
propaganda, a self-reproducing propaganda that seeks to obtain stable
behavior, to adapt the individual to his everyday life, to reshape his
thoughts and behavior in terms of the permanent social setting.'[10] All
too much of his argument was asserted, never proved, and some of his
claims bordered on the ludicrous.[11] Ellul's reading of psychology had
convinced him that propaganda created zombies: the victims were soon
addicted to constant doses of propaganda that destroyed their capacity
to function as independent souls. More effectively, Ellul made clear that
propaganda had become a 'necessity' in a democracy. 'Propaganda is
needed in the exercise of power for the simple reason that the masses
have come to participate in political affairs.'[12] The 'propaganda state'
was here all right, and not just in the Soviet Union or Communist
China, but in western Europe and North America.[13]

Likewise, in 1964, Herbert Marcuse published that extraordinarily
successful work of critical polemic *One-Dimensional Man: Studies in the
Ideology of Advanced Industrial Society*, which would become, for a while, a
text much admired by the New Left.[14] Among much else, Marcuse here
disclosed an authoritarian style of language that he claimed had fast
attained dominance in the public discourse of the affluent democracies.
If the voice of command had originated in the world of advertising, it
was now deployed by all sorts of authorities, 'the time-keepers and managers, the efficiency experts and the political beauty parlors,' always to
manipulate individuals increasingly unable to generate their own ideas.
'It is the word that orders and organizes, that induces people to do, to
buy, and to accept,' he wrote of this language. 'It is transmitted in a style
which is a veritable linguistic creation; a syntax in which the structure of
the sentence is abridged and condensed in such a way that no tension,
no "space" is left between the parts of the sentence.' This speech and
this publicity had had a positively hypnotic effect: the abridged syntax,
an emphatic 'concreteness,' the constant use of 'you' or 'your,' and the
endless repetition lodged 'fixed images' in people's minds which served
both to intimidate and to glorify. And what was the end result?: the
denial of the possibilities of 'protest and refusal,' or in other words the
inculcation of 'one-dimensional thought.'[15] The propaganda state, in
Marcuse's formulation, had virtually eliminated the chances of any resistance, a bizarre observation given the explosion of dissent that was just
around the corner.

Habermas, Ellul, and Marcuse drew in different ways upon mass society theory, an intellectual fashion particularly influential in the 1950s. That theory was closely associated with such European luminaries as Theodor Adorno and Max Horkheimer (Habermas's initial supervisors) as well as leading American intellectuals such as David Riesman and C. Wright Mills (each quoted by Habermas).[16] One chapter of Mills's *The Power Elite*, for example, assessed the tragic conversion of the American public into a mass in terms similar to those of Habermas.[17] Mills also warned that 'the public of public opinion has become the object of intensive efforts to control, manage, manipulate, and increasingly intimidate.'[18] That, too, was commonplace: typically, mass society theorists laid a heavy burden of blame on the logic of mass communication and the practices of the mass media.[19]

But what gave Habermas's account a special cachet was his attention to the expanding and malignant role of advertising. One section of a chapter on politics carried the evocative phrase 'The Public Sphere as a Platform for Advertising' (181). The practices of 'public relations' (193) and 'political marketing' (216), he argued, had extended the sway of advertising far beyond the bounds of the economy, a phenomenon that originated in the United States. Habermas had no doubt that the discourse of advertising was inimical to any form of rational-critical debate. 'For the criteria of rationality are completely lacking in a consensus created by sophisticated opinion-molding services under the aegis of a sham public interest. Intelligent criticism of publicly discussed affairs gives way before a mood of conformity with publicly presented persons or personifications; consent coincides with good will evoked by publicity' (195). That might have seemed exaggerated when he wrote it. But it certainly was prophetic.

1

The Imperialism of the Market: The United States, 1940–1970

In the summer of 1943, so the story goes, an English visitor was struck by the signs of 'normality' everywhere as he flew over the state of Nebraska – 'hundreds of miles of it and not a sight or sound to remind one that this was a country at war.' But when his lunch arrived, he received a small jolt: there, stamped on his pat of butter, was the command, 'REMEMBER PEARL HARBOR.' 'Of course they knew there was a war on,' commented George Will. 'However, Americans believe that a bit of advertising never hurts.'[1]

1 The 'Market Revival'

The term 'market revival' featured prominently in the introduction to the second revised edition of the classic *The Affluent Society*, published in 1970.[2] Its author, John Kenneth Galbraith, discussed the revival chiefly as an ideological phenomenon of the postwar years. A series of conservative-minded academics had articulated a new defence of the marketplace to protect America from the ills of socialism; their defence swiftly captured the fancy of business editors, who spread the word far and wide across the country. The renewed gospel praised 'the social efficiency of the unmanaged market' and warned against any form of interference, most especially the intrusion of the state.[3] That challenged the prevailing practices of Keynesian fiscal policy in the governance of the United States.

The popularity of the gospel suited well the economics of the times: an extraordinary boom commenced in the mid-1940s and persisted, almost uninterrupted, through the 1950s and 1960s. Eric Hobsbawm has fittingly described this era as the Golden Age of Capitalism, when the industrial machine directed an ever-increasing array of products to larger and larger numbers of consumers, first in North America and soon in western Europe.[4] These were the years of unquestioned American economic dominance in a world where the U.S. dollar was the tool and the symbol of fiscal stability, when U.S. 'capital stock' produced half of everything in the advanced countries.[5] Seemingly, the market had delivered on its promise of abundance for the many, at least in the lands where capitalism was entrenched.

One of the signs of the market revival was the growth in advertising: ad expenditures in the United States rocketed from $3.3 billion (or around $24 per capita) in 1946 to over $15 billion (more than $76 per capita) by 1965.[6] In the mid-1950s the historian David Potter decided that advertising was the American innovation *par excellence*, the great institution of his land of plenty.[7] Galbraith was hardly pleased by the prominence of advertising, however: he regarded this discourse as a way of unbalancing the American democracy. 'Advertising operates exclusively, and emulation mainly, on behalf of privately produced goods and services. Since management and emulative effects operate on behalf of private production, public services will have an inherent tendency to lag behind.'[8] Its influence threatened to undo the advances made during the Depression, transforming the republic into a thoroughly selfish society. But what Galbraith did not explore, even in the 1970 edition, was how advertising had also invaded the public sphere.

2 The Advertising Council

Civic advocacy first boomed during World War II. There had been many preliminaries, of course. As early as 1908, AT & T began corporate advertising to persuade the public of the merits of its control of the country's telephone service. During the previous war, the head of America's Committee on Public Information, the former publicist and promoter George Creel, saw his tasks as selling war and selling America, tasks he celebrated in a later book called *How We Advertised America* (1920). After some prewar experiments, Metropolitan Life started in 1922 an ongoing campaign to sell the virtues of healthy living to Americans, and especially to policyholders. Public relations enjoyed its first boom in the interwar years: its great pioneer was Ivy Lee (as Habermas noted) and its first philosopher was Edward Bernays (who wrote a book entitled *The Engineering of Consent*). Guided by the advertising genius Bruce Barton, giant corporations like General Electric, General Motors, Du Pont, and U.S. Steel sponsored campaigns to identify themselves as public institutions. During the Depression the National Association of Manufacturers, among others, mounted a heavy-handed campaign to sell business, tarnish labour, and ward off government.[9]

The newest wave of civic advocacy was part of an effort by corporate America to renew its prestige.[10] The reputations of business and of advertising had suffered badly during the Depression: advertising, in particular, seemed like a dangerous waste of money to New Dealers, and the industry was threatened with tax changes and new regulations even when the war emergency broke. Still, the onset of the war offered a golden opportunity for both business and advertising to redeem themselves in the public mind. Unable to market their normal products, because these were no longer available, individual corporations poured money into institutional ads (up from $1 million in 1939 to $17 million in 1943)[11] that sold 'the American way' and damned foreign regimentation – sometimes domestic as well. More immediately, such ads worked to associate the corporation's name, whether the Pennsylvania Railroad, General Motors, or Coca-Cola, with the courage and victory of American warriors. The postwar implications of such messages were obvious: business might thereby encourage a better environment for free enterprise, once the struggle ended.

Even more important, at least in the long run, was the creation of the Wartime Advertising Council in 1942, the result of an initiative by the advertising agencies, although it included representatives from the media and advertisers. The council worked closely with Washington (especially the Office of War Information) to coordinate the volunteer efforts of the agencies to help the war effort by preparing and placing all sorts of propaganda. This gave a special meaning to the term 'public service,' since the plan was conceived as part of a public relations endeavour to prove the national worth of advertising – indeed, to exploit wartime patriotism to protect an anxious industry. Council campaigns sponsored the sales of war bonds, the creation of victory gardens, many kinds of conservation, the recruiting of nurses, and blood donations. It has been estimated that something around $1 billion worth of advertising was contributed through the council during the three and a half years of war.[12] The result?: a host of posters full of warnings, pitches, and admonitions (for example, 'A SLIP OF THE LIP WILL SINK A SHIP') supported by simple, bold images (say, a determined young woman flexing her muscle), some heroic, some fearful. Whatever their effect on the war effort itself, these good works heightened the self-respect of ad men (there were precious few ad women then), fostered public goodwill (or so polls suggested), and impressed politicians. Even the reform clamour of times past was momentarily stilled. The propaganda was a resounding success.

There was no reason to dismantle such an effective apparatus at the close of the war: instead a refurbished Advertising Council was created, still intimately associated with the federal government but now linked even more closely to corporate America.[13] The Ad Council became one of those places where representatives of élites, in this case government, business, and communications, met to determine (or rather to try to determine) the course of national affairs. The council approved campaigns, assigned a coordinator, found agencies, and sought media, sometimes in strange places: Stone Container Corporation supported nine Ad Council causes by printing symbols and slogans on its cartons![14] In 1951 alone, council activities secured approximately four billion 'listener impressions' on radio.

One of the main tasks was social advertising. The Ad Council sponsored campaigns for a wide assortment of worthy groups and causes, such as Religion in American Life, Better Schools, forest conservation, highway safety, Savings Bonds, CARE, the Armed Forces, and so on, all of which were calculated to win friends and buttress authority. They were safe causes: none threatened to upset the social order. Sometimes these campaigns did have an impact. The National Safety Council claimed that its 'Stop Accidents' campaign had saved a whopping 550,000 lives on the highways over twenty years; the National Citizens' Council for Better Schools thought its advertising had helped build 670,000 new schoolrooms over twelve years.[15] A combination of radio spots, a TV cartoon, poster ads, kits, merchandise, and even a Virginia licence plate made Smokey the Bear, the spokescritter of America's forests, a household name across the United States – and, purportedly, saved $1 billion in fire damage.[16] But more often the initiatives were not especially effective. A verbose campaign for the United Nations in Cincinnati in 1946 failed dismally, despite the use of radio, newspapers, pamphlets, and speakers.[17] In 1948 Paul Lazarsfeld and Robert Merton concluded that the odds against 'propaganda for social objectives' were very steep: success required some combination of monopoly (no challenge), canalization (acting on existing values), and supplementary personal contact.[18] No wonder most campaigns stumbled.

Figure 2: American Posters from World War II

The second task was more obviously ideological. In the immediate postwar years, American capitalism seemed overcome, once more, with a deep desire to speak its Truth, and not just to the world outside but to the American public in particular. During the 1940s and well into the 1950s, there was fear in the business community over the spreading infection of socialism and Communism. The urge to proselytize was especially compelling because of the ideological dimension of the Cold War. The purpose of what was sometimes called 'economic education' was to remedy the lamentable ignorance of ordinary Americans about the virtues of free enterprise and the villainy of alternatives. That inspired two Ad Council initiatives in the late 1940s, the first to inoculate the public against Communist propaganda and the second to tout free enterprise. All of this blended into a much more diverse range of corporate projects to sponsor right thinking, at an estimated cost of $100 million in the early 1950s.[19] Not even the boom of the fifties ended the desire to re-educate: the council worked with corporate and government leaders to launch 'The Future of America' (1954), 'People's Capitalism' exhibits (1956), and 'Confidence in a Growing America' (1958). Ads for the last campaign ran in seventy-six national magazines, more than one thousand newspapers, and on television, purportedly receiving one billion impressions.[20] Clearly, the volume of propaganda bore out Habermas's fears about the ways in which élites worked to control public opinion: here was a species of 'psychological warfare,' to use a contemporary term, directed against the home team.

Did any of this matter, however? Maybe. The American Medical Association mounted a huge effort in 1949–50 to forestall 'socialized medicine'; the national health insurance scheme did not pass, although this defeat was likely whatever the propaganda.[21] An advocacy campaign by the A & P grocery chain seemingly improved sales and increased public

---

Figure 3: Smokey the Bear. The Forestry Service has been the sponsor of what is arguably the most famous postwar poster campaign in the United States. The campaign to protect America's forests from fire began in 1942. Smokey appeared a few years later to become the renowned spokescritter of conservation. In the early years, Smokey was sometimes a young bear who was saved by humans from the ravages of fire. But the most famous representation became Smokey as a grandfather figure who watched over all the trees and creatures of the forest and constantly admonished Americans to behave properly. In short, Smokey became a moralist.

1. The First Smokey, 1944

2. A Praying Smokey, 1963

3. Smokey Bear Stamp, 1984

support, a result which may have helped the company stave off the full effects of an anti-trust suit.[22] But the most resounding and expensive failures were all those designed to sell 'people's capitalism.' A *Fortune* editor, William Whyte, brutally mocked the free-enterprise promotions. The campaigns never established a reason to trust the message, never bridged the gap between the sponsor and the audience, never grappled with the realities of the actual workplace (preferring instead nostalgic stories of a small-town America), and never listened to ordinary Americans, only told them the Truth.[23] Although such propaganda may have soothed edgy capitalists, there was little evidence that it changed the minds of the public.[24]

3 The Rise of Paid TV

Contrast that failure with the effects of political advertising. Admakers had long been part of the game of politics. The first political spots date back to the 1928 election, when the Republicans financed brief radio talks.[25] But it was the use of television that turned advertising into a potent instrument for marketing politicians.

That became clear in 1952 when Rosser Reeves, one of the leading admakers of his generation, masterminded the television campaign of the Republican candidate, Dwight Eisenhower. [26] Reeves first used poll results, some from George Gallup, to discover that ordinary Americans were most concerned about ending the Korean War. He then created ads to position Eisenhower, meaning to control the perceptions of this brand relative to the competition. Forty spots were produced in one day, each introduced as 'Eisenhower Answers the Nation!' in which the candidate delivered a short, snappy response (an early soundbite?) to a prepared question from a standard-issue American. Perhaps the most remarkable success was to convert the general, a man of war, into a leader who would bring peace with honour: that was the message of a sixty-second 'bio,' *The Man from Abilene*, which portrayed Eisenhower as a leader with the experience and talent to bring to an end the wearisome Korean War.

Here was a positive ad, a prototype for many later promotions of one candidate or another. Twelve years later, its opposite, the attack ad, reigned supreme. The 1964 contest between the Democratic incumbent, Lyndon Johnson, and the Republican challenger, Barry Goldwater, was among the most bitter elections in recent times. According to one count, the percentage of negative ads was higher in 1964 than in any other election from 1960 to 1988.[27] Perhaps the harsh tone was the result of Goldwater's hard-right views which represented a challenge to the prevailing liberal ethos of the day. Goldwater's ads emphasized the man's tough stands on the issues of Communism abroad and immorality at home. The Johnson campaign proved much more imaginative, however, drawing upon Goldwater's own past comments to label him a wild cowboy (he did come from the West). One ad suggested that his pro-nuclear views could mean that children would be poisoned by strontium 90 or cesium 137 (this attached to an image of a girl licking an ice cream cone!). Another had him receiving support from the Ku Klux Klan (who were shown in their notorious regalia). A third sawed the eastern seaboard off the map of the United States, a visual demonstration of the disdain Goldwater had expressed for this section of the country.

Daisy: But none of these compared with the infamous *Daisy* spot, otherwise known as *Peace, Little Girl.* The purpose of the commercial was to bring to mind the danger implicit in Goldwater's declared willingness to employ what he referred to as 'tactical' nuclear weapons in small-scale wars, perhaps the kind emerging at that moment in Vietnam (which, by the way, was an issue generally avoided during the campaign).[28] The result was an attack ad that scared and offended some viewers. The initial idea was supplied by the creators of the Volkswagen campaign, Doyle Dane Bernbach, the most famous agency of the 1960s, which had signed on to handle the Democratic account. But the crucial refinements came from Tony Schwartz, a freelancer who suggested the addition of a little girl pulling the petals off a daisy. It was that touch which gave this sixty-second, black-and-white ad such poignancy.

The spot opens on a pastoral scene, a field in the countryside somewhere (in fact, the shot was from 'the Henry Hudson Parkway north of New York City'),[29] with the sun shining, birds singing in the background, and a cute blonde girl playing with a daisy. Here was an image of innocence and vulnerability, of peace, something to warm the heart of the viewer. It might evoke actual memories or ersatz memories, the kind put in place by movies, television programs, and other ads. The girl is clearly happy, absorbed in her play, unconcerned about her surroundings. She slowly, a bit unsteadily, counts up to nine.

Suddenly a harsh male voice blasts through the peace of the scene, counting down steadily from ten, each number enhanced with a slight echo. At this point the girl looks up and the image freezes: she seems startled, as well she might. The camera moves rapidly forward to target on her eye. When the countdown reaches zero, the camera seems to push through her pupil to display the most feared of all sights, an atomic explosion (complete with the requisite sound of the blast), leaving the impression that the little girl and her world have been obliterated.

The last half of the commercial furnishes a succession of images of the explosion: it glows, roils, a mix of dark clouds, white light, and strange lines of force. While the horror unfolds on the screen, we hear in the background a portion of a speech given by Lyndon Johnson on the perils of the time. 'These are the stakes: to make a world in which all of God's children can live ... or to go into the dark. We must either love each other, or we must die.' That selection was inspired. When the final graphic, the admonition to vote for Johnson, comes on screen, a sombre-voiced announcer repeats the message and adds, 'The stakes are too high for you to stay home.'

The spot was an extraordinarily interesting piece of propaganda, full of contrast and symbolism, easy to understand, and packed with emotion. Above all, *Daisy* played out that role of the 'distillation': it had staged a display of the ultimate horror of these years, nuclear holocaust, a spectre ever present in the Cold War era. It was addressed to parents, adults, and citizens – indeed, making voters into citizens of the world. The fear it evoked was then directed into the presidential contest. Resolution was possible; the horror could be avoided simply by voting for Johnson. There was no doubt about the impact of the ad, even though the party paid for only one showing during an evening movie on 7 September. The excitement was such that the other networks ran it on news shows as well, which strengthened its credibility and expanded its audience. Calls flooded the White House switchboard. There was the inevitable story of the little girl who 'went to bed in tears after seeing it.'[30] Republican leaders expressed outrage. Yet nowhere in the ad was Goldwater's name actually mentioned. That did not seem to matter. Indeed, in later years, people recalled having heard Goldwater's name or actually having seen his face. ('Talking to us,' claimed Edwin Diamond and Stephen Bates, 'Rosser Reeves misremembered it as showing a mushroom cloud coming from behind Goldwater's head.')[31] In his 1973 book, *The Responsive Chord*, Schwartz pointed out that the ad had connected with an existing anxiety, something already in people's heads. They did worry about whether Goldwater was trigger-happy.[32]

The passage of time has exaggerated the significance of *Daisy*: 'the spot has been credited with poleaxing Goldwater's Presidential bid,' according to one later comment on Schwartz's career.[33] In fact, Goldwater's candidacy was a lost cause from the beginning, barring some unforeseen event or mishap that might have rocked the Democrats. One big concern of the Johnson forces was to get the vote out, so sure were voters that the

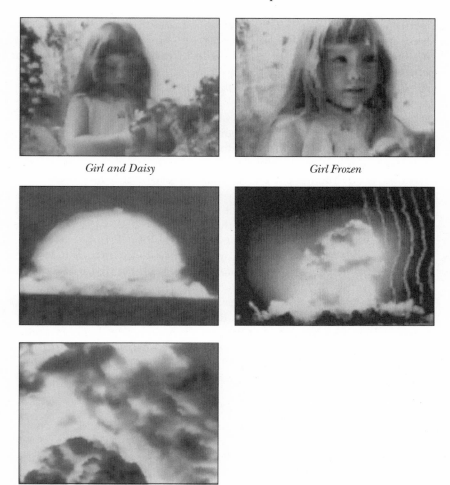

Girl and Daisy   *Girl Frozen*

The Unfolding of the Nuclear Explosion

Figure 4: Scenes from *Daisy*

incumbent would win, a priority evident in the final words of wisdom from the announcer. *Daisy* was an aesthetic intervention, a sensational one, which served to confirm an existing trend: the commercial was an accessory to the 'murder' of the Goldwater candidacy. It positioned the Republican challenger as a threat to peace and to humanity – a dangerous man, in short. In any case the significance of *Daisy* was not so much what it did as what it showed. Thereafter, activists of all kinds, and not just in politics, would point to the example of this spot as evidence of the artistry and power of television propaganda.

It really was not until 1968 that political advertising and the overall apparatus of marketing played a crucial role in deciding the presidential race. The core team of Richard Nixon's campaign contained advertising types who were well aware of the ability of paid TV to shape media and popular agendas. Nixon also had the money to realize their ambitions; his rival, Hubert Humphrey, did not. In broadcasting expenditures alone, the Republicans spent $12.6 million, double the amount spent by the Democrats. According to Edwin Diamond and Stephen Bates, the Nixon team waged the first 'high-tech' campaign, complete with extensive polling, attitudinal surveys, pretesting of commercials, focus groups, demographic targeting, and so on. Repackaging positioned the Republican candidate as a man of principle, a New Nixon, and that commodity squeaked out an electoral victory over the Democratic brand.[34]

The trouble was the cost, not just of victory but of competition. According to one contemporary estimate, overall campaign costs had risen from $140 million in 1952 to $250 million in 1968.[35] The escalating significance of television threatened to make elections a millionaire's game – either the candidate's millions or those of his (occasionally her) backers. The result was the passage by a Democratic Congress of the Campaign Broadcast Reform Act of 1970, which set caps on the amounts that candidates could spend.[36] By one estimate the new law would have restricted the Nixon campaign in 1972 to $5.1 million, a lot less than had been spent in 1968. No matter: Nixon vetoed the bill on the grounds that it favoured incumbents and limited freedom of speech.[37] Money would continue to fuel the advance of political marketing.

4 Progressive Crusades

Another zone of activity opened in the decade of the 1960s when liberal and left advocates turned to advertising, and television, to advance their causes. Early on, the Advertising Council responded to the new mood of change sponsored by the White House to fashion a message of reform, though a reform in which authority clearly lay with existing leadership.

John F. Kennedy: Consider a 1962 spot for the Peace Corps, a government agency set up the year before to channel the idealism of American youth into the task of saving the world. Volunteers were expected to use their knowledge and skills in various parts of the developing world. The commercial boasts high production values: a nice mix of visuals and sound; a careful sequencing of photos that make for a kind of moving collage; a soft, almost poignant melody playing in the background; plus gripping images of men, women, and children. It opens with a series of black-and-white photographs of young people that resolves into scenes of helping. Then we hear the president's voice, as he delivers a message extolling the role of youth in the Peace Corps. It is a demonstration of 'the American spirit' which shows 'our desire to live in peace, our desire to help.' These volunteers are 'serving a large cause: the cause of freedom and a peaceful world.' The president's words justify a succession of shots of young and old victims of misfortune, plus some images of suffering children ('who may live in poverty and misery' – it is their eyes which best display this sorry fact) of a kind which will become a staple in the ad coverage of the Third World. Then Kennedy himself appears on the screen, saying 'there can be no greater service to our country.' The ad ends with a Washington address to which interested viewers can write for more information.[38]

John F. Kennedy was a fine example of the kind of work that onlookers would claim had signalled the arrival of a 'creative revolution' in American advertising during the 1960s. It exhibited many of the features that would become standard in the realm of propaganda during the course of the next three decades. There was a special trajectory to the advocacy ad, an ongoing dynamic which worked to attract, involve, and eventually sell the viewer. *John F. Kennedy* aimed to play the role of both the 'catalyst,' to win new recruits, and the 'signal,' to display the government's concern. It attempted to celebrate volunteers and mobilize American youth by offering a positive spectacle of people helping people, a saga of triumph. Even if the opening images had not won attention, the voice of the president would have signified to the casual viewer that here was a message worth noticing. His words not only hailed the viewer but defined that viewer as an American, and so someone committed to certain ideals of belief and conduct. He had exercised the moral gaze, bestowing his blessing, and thus the nation's blessing, on the young men and women who worked so hard to help others. The youthful volunteers were represented as Ameri-

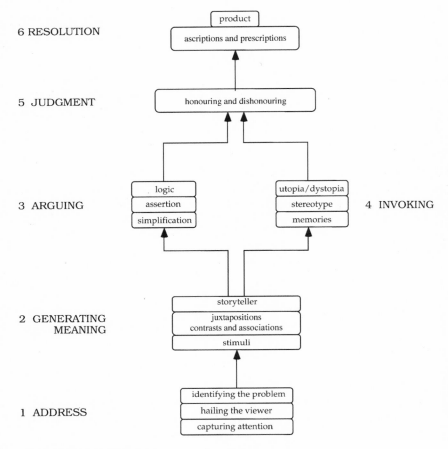

Figure 5: The Trajectory of Civic Advocacy

ca's best and brightest – that is, as social heroes who had devoted their efforts to serving their country (patriotism) and helping the less privileged (altruism). Indeed, their activities became a source of pride (nationalism) for Americans as a whole, a visible demonstration of America's moral worth. A later recruitment appeal called *Beach* (1965) used images of a lazy couple tanning themselves at the seaside to flay youth who avoided engagement.[39] Here the moral gaze dishonoured. But *Kennedy* didn't scold, at least not directly. Altogether the ad invoked the dream of togetherness: it might recall religious dicta about sharing, memories of neighbourliness, moral tales of charity, perhaps images of service. Its mix of firmness and poignancy and its use of the president's own words (Kennedy was still a credible leader) gave the commercial an aura of sincerity.

But read again the description of *John F. Kennedy*. In hindsight, it is all too easy to reinterpret its message, or rather to detect what may have been an unrecognized assertion of authority. It can be readily identified as a 'vehicle' of American imperialism. How ominous that phrase 'our desire to help' can sound: Kennedy's speech may be seen as an excellent demonstration of the way in which the Peace Corps fitted into the dynamics of America's projection of power. The visuals show white Americans helping the black Other, a symbolic expression of the leadership role the United States had taken up in its battle to make the world safe for its kind of democracy. A third Peace Corps ad, *Politics* (*circa* 1967), actually confronted this slur: the screen shows a baby asleep, a happy mother, a pleasant female teacher, and a young boy – 'If you told these people that the Peace Corps is the hypocritical extension of an imperialistic establishment's military-industrial complex,' declares the voice-over, 'they would think you crazy – and you would be.'[40] The trouble is that the images emphasize once again the contrast between white power and black dependence.

A different kind of ambiguity haunted the propaganda that was used in the War against Poverty. At the end of the 1960s, groups like Religion in American Life, the National Alliance of Businessmen, and the National Urban Coalition called upon white America to recognize its moral duty to the black underclass of the United States. In 1968 the Advertising Council took on what its president called 'the most massive project ever mounted by this organization during its 26-year history,' to focus attention on the problems of African-Americans in the cities.[41] But one of the results, *No Children* (1968), conveyed an impression of menace, a collection of black youth ready to visit revenge upon a white society that offered them no jobs and no hope. The motif of despair was even more evident in *Slumlord* (also 1968), part of the 'Give a Damn' campaign in New York: 'we' became 'them' – the camera put us in the place of a young black man who took the tour of a dingy and dirty apartment.[42] The most ballyhooed commercial, aptly entitled *Love*, the centrepiece of a campaign that supposedly garnered $30 million in free air and print exposure, turned out to be no more than a slick celebration of racial harmony.[43] A collection of celebrities, male and female, mostly white and black, stood and clapped and sang 'Let the Sun Shine In' from the musical *Hair*, demonstrating a sense of community that could overcome all barriers. The simple lesson?: 'Love. It comes in all colors.' That sad effort for the National Urban Coalition had substituted a vision of togetherness for the scenes of poverty and hopelessness proffered in other ads. Saving America would require much more than this kind of mushy propaganda.

More controversial were the initiatives of individual admakers. In 1967 two staffers at Doyle Dane Bernbach produced an ad that featured a large picture of a rat and a request: 'Cut this out and put it in bed next to your child.' The execution was so striking that the ad 'was shown on television, read on radio, and reproduced as news in newspapers and magazines,'[44] making it an early beneficiary of the phenomenon of the media echo. It was credited with forcing Congress to pass a Rat Extermination Act it had previously rejected. By contrast, the next year a widespread campaign in favour of gun laws, occasioned by the assassinations of Robert Kennedy and Martin Luther King, Jr, and backed by *Advertising Age*, proved much more difficult. One of the scare ads featured a shadowy figure and the headline, 'The man behind you is thinking of blowing your brains out.' But some media outlets refused to carry this and other ads, perhaps because of the opposition of the National Rifle Association. Congress listened, eventually passing the Gun Control Act of 1968; but Congress did not endorse that simple proposition of *Advertising Age*, 'Guns Must Go.'[45]

In 1971 Ira Nerken, a twenty-year-old student at Yale University, inspired a project to unsell the Vietnam War. He and other volunteers mobilized admakers to produce and distribute a series of anti-war ads (including a spot called *Apple Pie* that won a Clio Award in 1972). The most striking image appeared in a print ad featuring a bandaged and tired Uncle Sam, his hand outstretched, and the statement 'I WANT OUT' – in short, a parody of the famous recruiting poster. That plea, of course, could easily be taken as an admission of defeat, and it was no wonder papers refused to publish it.[46] The campaign failed.

Already radicals had begun to generate propaganda that focused on the ills of the consumer society. Indeed, hindsight would give credit to dissent for fostering a surge of propaganda.[47] Reputedly, the well-known admaker Howard Gossage launched the first major environmental campaign in 1966, when his agency helped the Sierra Club resist efforts to dam the Colorado River and thus inundate the Grand Canyon. Late in 1967 ads in the *New York Times* and the *Washington Post* told readers, 'While you're eating dinner tonight, 417 people will die from starvation':

the ad was placed by a group concerned about the population explosion and world hunger.[48] The most dramatic challenges on the national scene were the anti-smoking commercials of 1969–70, which came about because the Federal Communications Commission (FCC) supported the Fairness Doctrine complaint of John Banzhaf, III: television stations were required to carry counter-ads to balance cigarette commercials, because smoking was deemed a major health hazard.[49] Later, Action for Children's Television sent out three PSAs which demanded better programs and fewer commercials on television: one of these did receive airtime on ABC and NBC.[50] In 1972, the Stern Concern, a Los Angeles group, attempted to get the networks – to no avail – to carry spots, narrated by the actor Burt Lancaster, that were critical of Chevrolet and various painkillers.[51] Also in 1972, the People's Lobby used a range of print and broadcast ads to fight for the California Environment Act Initiative, ads that attacked big business and championed nature, though in the end its propaganda and its cause were overwhelmed by the opposition.[52] In short there had been a lot of sound and fury but little actual gain.

5 The Birth of Social Marketing

A partial legacy of these progressive crusades was what shortly became known as 'social marketing.' That phrase burst on the scene in the late 1960s and early 1970s. Professors of marketing, and some practitioners, began to claim that their discipline was one of the crucial tools that could redeem the escalating social crisis in America's big cities and in the Third World. Out poured speeches and articles – one whole issue of the *Journal of Marketing* (July 1971) was devoted to social marketing, soon followed by edited collections and, eventually, full-blown textbooks. A cynic might decry the whole enterprise as an act of self-promotion. Perhaps so: a new profession soon makes claims to moral worth. But social marketing was very much a technology of power, a method of meeting social challenges and managing social change.

The touchstone document (if later citations are any indication) was 'Social Marketing: An Approach to Planned Social Change,' written by Philip Kotler and Gerald Zaltman, which appeared in the aforementioned issue of the *Journal of Marketing*. Kotler, the more senior author, was then a named professor in management at Northwestern University and a director of the American Marketing Association; the younger Zaltman, an associate professor of behavioural science in Northwestern's Department of Marketing, had specialized in social change and the diffusion of innovations. The authors expressed their gratitude to the 'Educational Foundation of the American Association of Advertising Agencies' for some unspecified support 'which permitted activities leading to many of the ideas expressed in this article.' Consequently, the piece, or at least its authors, had a kind of official sanction from one of the institutions of marketing.

Consider 'Social Marketing' as a special kind of semiotic exercise – a sequence of textual operations bent on producing signs and generating meanings to serve a political purpose. The article was a monologue, packaged in the rhetorical style common to the social sciences: it featured one clear, authoritative voice; differing viewpoints were cited but contained; and a particular hypothesis was honoured, its worth accredited by a series of examples and footnotes. The chief task was to map out the new domain of social marketing, and that involved the use of definitions and comparisons, efforts to name and classify, both ordering and mystifying, and always justification. Marketing emerged first as a facilitated and administered exchange, which made it 'a fundamental aspect of both primitive and advanced social life.' That established marketing as natural, historical, and inevitable. But what distinguished this philosophy from sales was the emphasis 'on discovering the wants of a target audience and then creating the goods and services to satisfy them.' The fiction – that marketing presumed consumer sovereignty – served to bolster its democratic pretensions. The existing vocabulary of marketing, and especially the famous 'four Ps,' were tailored to suit social ends. In this way the world was organized around problems, products, and solutions. The scheme was tested against the experience of a variety of endeavours, including an Indian government's project of family planning (flawed) and the promotional efforts of the American Cancer Society (praised). Using the right language was not enough, however: the authors made abundantly clear that the application of the concepts, the techniques of research and planning, and the discovery of target markets all required sophisticated and skilled personnel. This last activity highlighted the significance of a professional management which could administer the all-important details of any project.

In the end what social marketing promised was efficiency. It was a way in which existing institutions, identified as 'change agents,' could regain command of the future. In short, élites now had available a philosophy and a technology to manage innovation, to make the social machine operate better, through seduction rather than coercion. Accentuate the rewards: 'The main point is that social marketing requires that careful thought be given to the manner in which manageable, desirable, gratifying, and convenient solutions to a perceived need or problem are presented to its potential buyers.' Indeed, this mix of strategy and tactics could serve as a paradigm for nearly all forms of propaganda.

6 The Soap Analogy

'Why can't you sell brotherhood like you sell soap?' G.D. Wiebe asked in 1952.[53] Twenty years later, the answer seemed simple: you could. You could sell just about any policy or behaviour, idea or politician – as long as you employed the technology of marketing. 'There's nothing more American than selling and we're selling an idea,' claimed one political consultant.[54] Not that this was always a cause for rejoicing. Even Kotler and Zaltman noted the concern over the increase of manipulation and, in a deft phrase, over the amount of 'promotional noise.'

Most of the worry centred on politics. In 1969, newspaperman Joe McGinness caught the public's fancy with *The Selling of the President 1968*, where he skewered the Nixon campaign. His exposé of the skill and cynicism of the handlers who had made the 'New Nixon' built upon considerable public unease. Right from the beginning, participants and observers had argued that marketing converted a candidate into a packaged good like toothpaste, cereal, or soap. Both Eisenhower and his opponent, Adlai Stevenson, found television advertising undignified. After a session filming commercials, Eisenhower said ruefully, 'To think that an old soldier should come to this.'[55] In 1960, a Kennedy backer noted how the Democrats always charged that 'the GOP tries to "sell" its candidate to the country the way Madison Avenue sells soap.'[56] The entertainment section of the Sunday *New York Times* in 1980 carried a story entitled 'The Art of Selling Politicians like Soap on TV.'[57] 'Politicians have become the ultimate consumer product,' wrote a Canadian observer in 1992. 'Just like a box of soap, a can of soup or a carton of cornflakes, they require marketing strategies, promotion campaigns and plenty of spin to grab that all-important market share.'[58]

What underlay the soap analogy was a mixture of disdain and fear. Political marketing committed a category error: it converted a person into a commodity. The act of transformation created a public good which could be consumed by the electorate. In 1954 a team of analysts, including Seymour Martin Lipset and Paul F. Lazarsfeld, argued that 'the decisions that a modern Western man makes every four years in the political arena are similar to those he makes every day as a consumer of goods and services.'[59] But marketing also demeaned democracy, or at least what people normally believed to be the ethos proper to a democracy. An important boundary had been crossed. Soaps, cereals, soups, these were among the most trivial things in our daily routine. Politicians, ideas, policies, these belonged to a much more significant realm of our lives. Treating both the same, indeed treating leaders like soaps, packaging social reform like cereals, this was a form of transgression. It folded politics and ethics into commerce. Civic advocacy, and especially political marketing, could awaken a kind of moral horror over the consequences of this brand of progress. 'The use of advertising to sell statesmen is the ultimate vulgarity,' wrote the admaker David Ogilvy in 1963.[60] The sense of wrongness, however, would eventually wane among the wider public as this kind of propaganda became standard practice.

PART II: AUTHORITY'S WORK

*GRAMSCI: HEGEMONY

The work of hegemony, so to speak, is never done.

Ralph Miliband, 1982[1]

At bottom, 'hegemony' means rule via persuasion. But its articulation is much more complex than such a modest formulation suggests. For hegemony is grounded upon an apparent contradiction between inequality and consent. And the very process of securing consent conjures up the spectre of conspiracy.

We owe the concept of hegemony to the *Prison Notebooks* of Antonio Gramsci (1891–1937), an Italian Communist leader who produced a formidable body of writings during the many years he was incarcerated by the Fascist regime.[2] The *Prison Notebooks* were no ordinary collection. They included thoughts, notations, drafts of essays, reconsiderations, musings, much of this provisional or incomplete and sometimes ambiguous.[3] Gramsci used the term 'hegemony' to evoke a cluster of related meanings such as rule, dominance and predominance, popular consent, power, cultural and moral authority, leadership, and empire or the projection of empire.[4] He talked, sometimes vaguely, about a 'ruling class' and a 'historical bloc' which in 'the moment of hegemony' might secure dominion.[5] His more extended reflections emphasized the importance of ideology as a determining factor in constituting political rule, which implicitly ran counter to the earlier Marxist emphasis upon the means of production.[6]

The consequence of his imprecision was that later generations of theorists could give the concept of hegemony their own special twists to suit the changing circumstances of the times. One of the most successful elaborations was that produced by the English Marxist Raymond Williams. Williams turned what was meant to be a tool of revolution into a technique of explanation. He argued that 'hegemony' referred to an all-encompassing process of class rule, to a 'predominant practice and consciousness.'[7] 'For hegemony supposes the existence of something which is truly total, which is not merely secondary or superstructural, like the weak sense of ideology,' Williams wrote, 'but which is lived at such a depth, which saturates the society to such an extent, and which, as Gramsci put it, even constitutes the substance and limit of common sense for most people under its sway, that it corresponds to the reality of social experience very much more clearly than any notions derived from the formula of base and superstructure.'[8] This kind of interpretation proved very popular with the emerging school of Cultural Studies, perhaps because it could be used to justify their fascination with the artifacts of popular culture – studying soap opera and other everyday representations of life also meant studying hegemony.[9]

Unfortunately Williams's definition and its offshoots explain too much. Even Williams worried about 'the totalizing tendency of the concept':[10] hegemony becomes something gargantuan that encompasses domination, ideology, practice, and culture. Indeed the effort to understand how a 'sense of reality'[11] may have come about, or what a particular action signifies (so John Fiske theorized the import of peeing in one's pants!)[12] can take the analyst far away from the domain of politics, which was Gramsci's initial and ultimate focus of attention.

The brief definition that opened this essay is an attempt to promote a more restricted version of the concept. (Or, to be more exact, a return to a pattern of usage present in *Policing the Crisis*, a formidable work of polemic and analysis by activists of the British school of Cultural Studies in the late 1970s.)[13] My approach looks upon hegemony as a deformation of that public sphere which Habermas idealized and lamented.[14] Hegemony is not just about power, but about power that is routine, institutionalized, organized, and generally accepted – in short legitimate power or authority. Its two dimensions are legitimation and governance: hegemony involves the use of cultural means to command the political resources of society. A hegemonic regime avoids the use of physical force, except for normal police work, because it does not need to coerce compliance. That said, the threat of official violence still lurks behind the institutions of authority.

Hegemony presupposes hierarchy, a substantial gap between the high and the low, which manifests itself in relations of domination and subordination. The owners and managers of capital, the top politicians and state bureaucrats, generals and admirals, media magnates, and the heads of organizations, though not necessarily in any unified fashion, all seek control over the means of producing and distributing public goods, the very substance of politics nowadays. These élites work through alliances with professionals, artists, and intellectuals – call them licensed agents – who operate the means of persuasion and display, and are rewarded with money and status, even a share of power, for their efforts. Together, they strive to perpetuate their leadership by determining the plethora of signs, meanings, and practices that operate in the public sphere.[15] Success requires the submission of the vast majority of the public not only to this conspiracy but to inequality. The ordinary folk must accept authority: they are complicit in their own subordination, becoming the consumers of the public goods made and sold by their superiors. The consent of the governed is often passive rather than active, reluctant or temporary or even cynical, a combination of both belief and disbelief which is a common feature of (at least) postmodern times.[16] Indeed, success is rarely total, most especially when there is an overproduction of public goods.

That leads to a widely accepted dictum: hegemony is never finally achieved; it must always be renewed.[17] Occasionally, élites accommodate some of the demands of subordinate groups, though not those which promise to overturn such 'ideological sentinels' as 'the national interest' or 'the sanctity of property' or 'law and order.'[18] Challenge is constant. Where these challenges come from remains a matter of debate. The existence of inequalities (of wealth, power, and status) and of distinctions (sometimes called identity and lifestyle politics) gives rise to opposition. What these factors do not foster, novelty may, whether in the form of a new technology (such as television) or a new outlook (such as environmentalism). No less significant is the issue of efficiency: the inefficient exercise of authority will itself foster challenge – witness the ways in which the Vietnam War provoked civil unrest in the United States. Such challenges appear part of the very circulation of power, following Michel Foucault: the extension of power seems to provoke resistance, which, in turn, warrants a further exercise of power.[19]

Consequently, hegemony is productive as well as repressive. Authority must constantly seek to universalize a set of values, to explain and to justify, to maintain legitimacy, which is why it encourages a proliferation of discourse.[20] Authority must also try to determine what is permissible, eccentric, or transgressive, what can be said or shown, even how the permissible will be expressed. The obverse of this is equally important: hegemony normally involves a process of silencing or rendering invisible, a series of prohibitions, and it is here that the element of repression enters the picture. The purpose of policing is to ensure that 'subordinate groups lack the language necessary to conceive concerted resistance,' in the words of the historian Jackson Lears.[21] Little wonder that one of the headquarters of hegemony is the mass media.

'Every relationship of "hegemony,"' Gramsci argued, 'is necessarily an educational relationship ...'[22] The necessity of intellectual labour explains the importance of propaganda in the social and political equation. 'Ideas and opinions are not "born" spontaneously in the brains of each individual; they have had a centre of formation, of radiation, of propaganda, of persuasion, a group of men or even a single individual who has elaborated and presented them in their actual political form.'[23] A sudden spurt of propaganda could indicate a crisis of hegemony, be that a social emergency or a moral panic, where the persuasion of the public appeared crucial to any solution. More often, though, propaganda was one of those 'modes of incorporation' that Raymond Williams asserted served to transmit meanings to the populace.[24] It then amounted to a tool of élites employed in the creation of an administered society.

So, at its worst, propaganda remained the intellectual equivalent of mugging. This suggests a much darker picture of hegemony than Gramsci had imagined. After all, he believed that agitation and effort would eventually lead to the moral and intellectual leadership of the Marxist vanguard. Instead, the power of capital and its allies in the West, in part because it has changed its character since the 1930s, proved far too great to surrender easily to challenges from below. There was no way, for example, that Gramsci could appreciate the kind of semiotic power at the disposal of a form of rule organized around the philosophy and the technology of marketing.

2

Restoring Order:
Nixon's America, Etcetera

Order in the United States: 'So I pledge to you: We *shall* have order in the United States.' The single word 'NIXON' zooms out of the centre to fill the top half of a screen which has now turned blue. That ends one of Richard Nixon's campaign ads of 1968. It is a masterpiece of what has been called 'propositional editing':[1] a sequence of bold visuals are juxtaposed to underline a sharp contrast between radical dissent and law and order. The ad mixes still photos of destruction (a burning building, a trashed street, a broken machine), angry youth (two bearded men, one yelling, an injured man running, bloodied victims), police weaponry (a tear-gas gun being fired, a hand gun, a sinister close-up of bayoneted rifles), and policemen (who look as though they are dressed for war). In the background plays a harsh but rhythmic music, with a slight echo, suggesting turmoil and disorder. Here indeed is violence on television. And the voice-over is none other than the candidate himself. In measured tones he admits that dissent is 'a necessary ingredient of change.' But that does not justify the resort to violence. 'Let us recognize that the first civil right of every American is to be free of domestic violence.' Hence the pledge.[2]

The authoritarian menace of the ad is obvious. 'THIS TIME VOTE LIKE YOUR WHOLE WORLD DEPENDED ON IT' – that apocalyptic slogan appeared on many a Nixon spot. The Republicans were trying to promote and exploit fear among ordinary Americans. Angry youth, the New Left, violence in the streets, riots and lootings, all were presented as signs of the breakdown of law and order.

In fact these were symptoms of a hegemony in trouble, a crisis but not a collapse of legitimacy (there never was a revolutionary moment), because the prevailing élites were no longer able to negotiate differences effectively and thus sell a consensus. The sources of that crisis?: striking evidence of incompetence (the Vietnam War) as well as the renewed perception of inequality (notably racism and poverty). In particular, a sense of alarm afflicted the licensed agents of authority, the journalists, admakers, entertainers, and intellectuals who staffed the apparatus of culture. On another level the crisis reflected the emergence of an adversary and a counter-culture, popular among youth and especially university students, whose most radical exponents, the New Left, dreamed of an alternative hegemony. The authority Nixon won in the election, and more broadly the legitimacy of the 'establishment' of the day, needed reinforcement.

The ad spoke a deeper truth than anyone at the time could realize: the leitmotif of the next decade was restoration, at least from the standpoint of authority. The necessary work was begun under Nixon; it was not completed until after he had been forced from office. But it was completed – order was restored in America.

1 The Ideology of Order

The Nixon White House soon orchestrated an assault on dissent, the adversary culture, even an unruly media, employing a whole host of measures, including the use of force. Propaganda was part of this reaction. Vice-president Spiro Agnew became notorious for his effusive denunciations of all sorts of enemies. Perhaps because ad men were prominent in its ranks (H.R. Haldeman, Dwight Chapin, and Ronald Ziegler had been employed by the J. Walter Thompson agency), the administration was particularly attuned to the need for television advocacy. The liberal priority of the War on Poverty fell by the wayside. Instead, the White House worked closely with the Advertising Council to advance a host of campaigns, against drugs and crime as well as for voluntarism and energy conservation.

The chief domestic commodity the Nixon White House sought to merchandise to the American public was law and order. That goal could justify a collection of public goods, from more police on the streets to a gun-control law to stricter prison sentences. But in the hands of Nixon and his team, law and order symbolized a lot more than any such relatively modest proposals. In 1969 Nixon listed the ills of the times: 'drugs, crime, campus revolts, racial discord, draft resistance' – 'on every hand, we find old standards violated, old values discarded, old principles

ignored.' He told his college audience that the counter-culture endangered 'fundamental values' and threatened 'the process by which a
civilization maintains its continuity.'[3] Ensuring order meant returning to
a mythic land, an idealized version of life in the fifties, an America before
the troubles of the late 1960s, when streets were safe, whites went unchallenged, young people obeyed, work was valued, and so on. Here was the
first attempt to market the utopia of America Past, an America that
supposedly existed before the 1960s, an enterprise that would become
commonplace in presidential politics during the rest of the century.

Nixon and his team had not originated this ideology. The signs were
already present in some of the spots put out by the ill-fated Goldwater
campaign in the 1964 presidential race. At one point, the Republican
team had assembled a half-hour film which portrayed the moral decay of
Johnson's America: urban riots, a woman in a topless bathing suit, and so
on. That film the candidate rejected as too risky. But the ad called *Choice*
made the point that crime, smut, and corruption were eating away at the
soul of America.[4] Besides, other Republican leaders had given voice to
the yearning for order: according to Edward Jay Epstein, Nelson
Rockefeller established a crucial link between drug abuse and violent
crime in his effort to reunite the moderate and extreme wings of the
party during his gubernatorial contests in New York.[5]

What the Nixon team did was to fashion issues or appeals which
promised to mobilize the so-called silent majority and win support from
Democrats. The idea was to split the liberal camp away from dissent, to
reconstruct a common front of mainstream progressives and conservatives, whether in the top echelons of politics or in business and the
media. That strategy was particularly evident during the 1972 presidential race in the 'Democrats for Nixon' ads that painted the Democratic
candidate, George McGovern, as a dangerous radical. The anti-war
McGovern was the nominee of a mixed bag of progressives and dissenters
who had briefly shifted the Democratic party at the national level towards
the left. So an ad made out that he would designate almost one in two
Americans as eligible for welfare. The Republicans focused particularly
on McGovern's attitude towards the war and towards defence. John
Connally, former Democrat, former governor of Texas, former Nixon
secretary of the Treasury, spoke in one spot about how 'insane' the
McGovern defence budget was. 'It would end the United States' military
leadership in the world,' he warned; 'it would make us inferior in
conventional and strategic weapons to the Soviets.'[6] But the most common and lasting effort was a child's nightmare of playing war.

McGovern Defense Plan: Nixon's admakers wished to demonstrate just what impact a McGovern victory would have on the country's war machine. They borrowed a spot from one of McGovern's rivals, Hubert Humphrey (then out of the race), which had warned that McGovern would cut 'our defences back to the level of a second-class power.' Except that the Nixon team decided to add images of toys to show just what this meant.

The spot was simple and graphic. A military drumbeat played behind the action: while the camera focused on toy soldiers and equipment, the announcer told how McGovern's plan would eliminate one-third of the Marines and the Air Force, one-fourth of Navy personnel, one-half of interceptors and one-half of the navy fleet, plus reduce the carriers from sixteen to six. As these statistics were mentioned, hands came out to remove the toys. That established, the announcer quoted Humphrey on how severe this cut was, before switching to Nixon aboard a naval vessel (music: 'Hail to the Chief'). Nixon, we were told, believed in 'a strong America to negotiate for peace from strength.' The spot ended with the listing of its sponsor: 'Democrats for Nixon.'

McGovern Defense Plan was both an attack ad and a scare ad: it sought to reaffirm fears about McGovern's intentions in a way similar to the more dramatic *Daisy*. Unlike *Daisy*, however, *McGovern Defense Plan* used facts backed by pictures, adopting the form of a 'reason-why' appeal. The ad embodied that ideology of order which prevailed in White House circles: maintaining power abroad was the accompaniment of restoring authority at home. That meant ensuring America's might against all comers, something Nixon promised to do. The success of the spot depended on the currency of a cluster of words, images, and symbols that constructed a world organized around the titanic confrontation between democracy and Communism. In this world, the U.S. defence establishment was constituted as a crucial public good. A strong defence evoked anti-Communism, and patriotism, and machismo, three of the components of that Cold War nationalism which gave America an international identity even when détente was in the air. For that Cold War vision identified America as the leader and guardian of the Free World of non-Communist states. Reducing national defence, inevitably, threatened the cause of civilization.

The anti-McGovern propaganda was potent: that doughty old Democrat, AFL-CIO president George Meany, at one point claimed that McGovern had 'become an apologist for the Communist world.'[7] Nixon won a resounding victory in the November election, with 60.7 per cent of the vote: clearly he had captured the support of some erstwhile Democrats. Still the contest persuaded just over half (55.7 per cent) of the electorate to cast their ballots, evidence of considerable apathy and disenchantment.[8]

2 The First War on Drugs

In retrospect, the most crucial of the Nixon campaigns was the war on drugs (1969–73), mounted by elements inside and outside the White House. The project played out a variety of political purposes in the cause of hegemony. The reason lay in the symbolic potency of recreational drugs such as marijuana, hashish, heroin, LSD, and barbiturates and amphetamines. The drug problem, as it swiftly became known, was closely identified with youth and, more specifically, with the counter-culture, where taking drugs had become emblematic of liberation. The civic advocacy sought to awaken a kind of hysteria, what has been called a 'moral panic,' among the adult population by focusing public attention upon a radical evil (and away from social reform).[9] This necessitated the practices of both simplification and typification to transform a social phenomenon into a moral ill. The addict became the requisite 'folk-devil,' the object of fear and loathing. In the process, these civic ads worked to dishonour the being, and so the politics, of the counter-culture. They propagated images of its perverted lifestyle, where filth and disease and tragedy reigned supreme, a lifestyle that served as a contrast to the virtues of a 'normal' way of life. They rooted crime in a disgusting practice rather than in poverty or injustice. Propaganda made easier the task of labelling radical critics as delinquents, that is, as social pariahs who must be watched, policed, and quarantined by regiments of helpers and guardians to ensure that their contagion did not spread to corrupt families that were still clean.[10] The war on drugs aimed at saving not just individual bodies or even a generation of young people; it was a vital act of containment to protect the social body as well.

Here was a crusade that could command the support of all sorts of people and, in particular, the makers of culture whose loyalty to the existing regime of ideas was disturbed. Liberals as well as conservatives could agree that drugs were a scourge. It was a way of unifying the political class behind a cause that bolstered rather than threatened the existing structures of authority. The state played the key role, of course: the project was implemented or coordinated at all levels of governance by law-enforcement bodies, special agencies, and existing departments. Governor Ronald Reagan of California joined the fray early, in 1969, when he authorized a special effort against drug abuse. The White House formally jumped into the war by announcing in 1970 a three-year, all-media campaign which involved the departments of Health, Education and Welfare, Justice, and even Defense (concerned about the drug habits of GIs). The White House also initiated a special conference to bring television producers and advertisers on side, so that entertainment programming would carry the new message about the danger of drugs. There were similar efforts to sensitize key personnel in radio and newspapers, to win over church leaders, and to foster special events such as Drug Abuse Prevention Week and the National Drug Alert. The hysteria was fuelled all the more when federal agencies released to the media bigger and bigger numbers that purportedly counted both the population of addicts and the crimes they committed.[11]

The project could call upon the talents of leading agencies such as Young and Rubicam, Grey Advertising, Compton Advertising, and Wells, Rich, Greene.[12] Both football and baseball organizations aired anti-drug spots, featuring their own stars. Even students were enlisted in one imaginative enterprise that planned to use their creative material to ensure that the crusade was written in a language youth would find believable.[13] A wave of propaganda rolled over America: the airwaves were, for a time, full of radio and television PSAs (some designed specifically for African Americans and Hispanics); newspapers and magazines also carried the anti-drug messages, as did outdoor poster and transit ads. People were told to send for a series of booklets ('Pot Primer for Parents' was one example), and they could even phone a Heroin Hotline should they wish to turn in a pusher.

The propaganda had to be very careful about what it dishonoured, however. It was essential to draw clear distinctions between abuse and use, dangerous drugs and licensed remedies. So in *Yo-Yo* (1969), the National Institute of Mental Health told people to obey their doctors when using amphetamines and barbiturates. In any case, a lot more consumer commercials advocated the virtues of over-the-counter drugs than PSAs warned of their complications.[14] The propaganda also had to avoid allowing the label 'narcotic' to spread to other kinds of substances or pleasures. Liquor interests exploded with fury when some Blue Cross advertising suggested that alcoholism was the most severe drug-abuse problem facing the nation.[15] The war was against youth drugs, not the so-called legitimate products of the pharmaceutical, liquor, or tobacco industries.

The declared goals were specified in a news report about one Illinois effort started in 1970. 'Called Project Straight Dope, the campaign is designed to deglamorize narcotics, warn youngsters away from the perils of drugs, give them support against their peer groups which may endorse drugs, and get them to think for themselves.'[16] The aim was precisely *not* to 'get them to think for themselves' – the campaign hoped to program youth.[17] But one purpose of this and other initiatives certainly was to deglamorize drugs.

In his book *The Symbolism of Evil*, Paul Ricoeur identifies the leading symbols of evil as defilement, sin, and guilt. The first term, 'defilement,' connotes a stain or a blemish, a fatal act of transgression which brings in its wake both sin and guilt. The best of the anti-drug spots built their images around this motif of defilement. Doing drugs, consuming the impure, made the sinner the legitimate target of contempt and hostility who must suffer and ultimately die.[18] So in *Haight Ashbury* (1970), Jack Webb of *Dragnet* fame used a roving camera to take the viewer on a quick tour of the legendary home of the flower children, now transformed by speed, heroin, and LSD into a horror of trash and dirt, empty shops, alleys clogged with garbage, violence and crime, and everywhere broken people.[19] Likewise the spooky *Ten Little Indians* (1971) displayed the hell house lived in by a group of addicts: the words of the children's song are changed to emphasize how each of the junkies is done in. The lucky one goes to jail while the rest die, some painfully; and all this is shown on screen.[20]

Animal (1972): By contrast, this commercial concentrated on one victim/villain. *Animal* was created by Young and Rubicam for the Mayor's Narcotic Control Council in New York City. The sixty-second spot is shocking but realistic, the grainy appearance and the documentary style conveying authenticity: it tracks the degradation of a white youth, about eighteen years old, named Joey. He is driven by his habit to plead for drugs from a youthful pusher, then to try to steal money from his mother and his brother, and finally to rob a woman on the street. At one point his body is so racked with pain that he vomits beside a row of parked cars. The voice-over explains what these images mean. 'This is a drug addict. Unlike a man, he has no sense of right and wrong, no use for reason. He only feels, and what he feels most of the time is fear. He runs away from reality because reality is what scares him most of all. He lives off human beings because he's afraid to live like a human being. He's alive, but you couldn't call this really living.' At the end of the commercial he is shown in a cold alley, amidst litter, taking his dose of heroin. Superimposed on this picture of sin is the admonition: 'DON'T JOIN THE LIVING DEAD.'

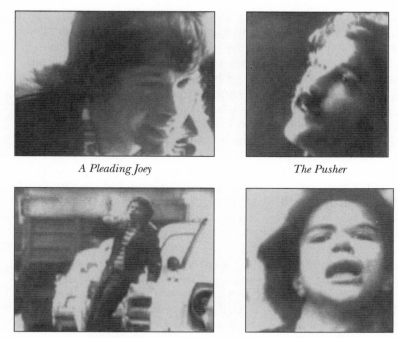

A Pleading Joey

The Pusher

A Sick Joey

The Fleeing Animal

In the Alley

Figure 6: Scenes from *Animal*

Animal demonized the addict. He had been 'othered,' cast out of decent society, represented as an object of loathing.[21] Joey was stripped of the attributes of manhood: he lacked reason, affection, even the ability to control his own body. He was both predator and victim, much like the vampire of horror fame, subject to the implacable demands of his appetite. He was not really human anymore: instead he had become a monstrosity, a creature surviving in his own personal hell, a world of fear and filth and crime. Joey was an offence against humanity. There was a lot of emotional overkill in this message, but little rational argument. The ad did not explore; it only denounced. Viewers were being asked to despise the addict, not to pity him. In short, *Animal* presented few verifiable facts, offered a one-dimensional view, and worked to provoke revulsion. It served to build or confirm people's prejudices by what critics would call 'blaming the victim.' Like other exemplars of this first war on drugs, *Animal* best expressed the fear and loathing of an official morality.

There was little evidence that such propaganda impressed the youth of America. According to a Young and Rubicam vice-president, research had found that youngsters thought most of the claims 'ridiculous.'[22] The athletes as anti-drug proponents were not believable, the scenarios did not match actual experience, the ads were too preachy, and so on. A series of later investigations by social scientists confirmed that the propaganda had little discernible impact upon the behaviour of its reputed targets.[23] But such findings hardly negated the political significance of the anti-drug campaigns. In the public sphere they had acted as a 'catalyst,' though in this regard their target had been the wider citizenry, the respectable majority of ordinary Americans. Here the aim had been to vilify. 'The generation of fear had succeeded,' argued Edward Epstein later: 'even in cities which had few, if any, heroin addicts, private polls commissioned by the White House showed that citizens believed the drug menace to be one of the two main threats to their safety.'[24] More to the point, the advocacy advertising and the attendant apparatus of marketing the crusade had attached a stigma to the counter-culture and its ways. In this case a 'symbolic' victory was also a 'real' victory. The campaign could wind down after 1973, not because the drug problem was solved but because the act of containment was concluded.

3 The Revival of Corporate Advocacy

The third front in the struggle to restore order was opened by that other concentration of authority, big business. Beginning around 1970, a number of corporations began to use print advertising to harangue one public or another. Management was worried about polls that showed a waning trust in business[25] and a growing faith in regulation,[26] about Ralph Nader and consumerism, about the booming popularity of environmentalist causes, about the economic ignorance and apparent animosity – 'accusatory journalism' said one executive[27] – of the media, above all, about the regulatory powers of the federal government and its bureaucracy. Corporate America wanted a way to speak out, loud and clear.

By 1975 the advertising executive John O'Toole, among others, had named the phenomenon 'advocacy advertising' in a fashion that clearly identified its role as propaganda: 'an advocate for the system and for individual corporations within that system.'[28] Even firms that avoided direct advocacy began to shape their normal advertising to reflect public concerns. A 1975 survey by the Association of National Advertisers of '114 large companies found that about 30% of their corporate advertising centred on questions of the environment, energy, and private-enterprise economics.'[29] By one guesstimate, advocacy and 'grassroots lobbying' was costing corporate America roughly $1 billion a year at the end of the decade.[30] Among the players were Big Oil, the forestry industry, the Caterpillar Tractor Company, Union Carbide, Bethlehem Steel, Du Pont, and the Chase Manhattan Bank. But no one was sure just how to re-market free enterprise to a doubting public, so sponsors pursued different strategies to turn business into a public good.

Unquestionably, the most famous example of advocacy was the ongoing project started by Mobil Oil at the beginning of the decade. Initially, the company used ads on the Op-Ed page of leading newspapers (an innovation of the *New York Times* in 1970) to communicate its views at length on a variety of issues, usually associated with the oil and gas industry. Boring, fact-filled, tendentious? – perhaps so: yet the wordy ads were an attempt to pursue a coherent line of argument, to publicize a position in a fashion suited to the dictates of rational discourse. Whether the advertorial persuaded anyone, the very style of presentation conveyed the message that Mobil Oil was a responsible and reasonable player in the marketplace of signs: the ads were a 'signal' of the corporation's concern. In 1975 Mobil began to supplement these advertorials with a lighter fare, called 'Observations,' appearing in Sunday newspapers.[31] A purpose of this advertising was to keep a close watch on the news media and government, to correct what Mobil considered were errors and biases in their positions. The need for fair play was a constant theme in its advertorials. Mobil wished to establish a public presence and a public voice as the moral expression of capitalism.[32] It certainly succeeded in establishing a presence.

Mobil engaged its readers in discussion. The American Electric Power Company tried to enlist them in a war. In 1974 the company, then one of the largest and most profitable producers of electricity, launched a major campaign to shape a national energy policy, particularly to press the virtues of coal, and locked horns with the Environmental Protection Agency (EPA). The company's ads (labelled racist by some critics) made infamous the image of two cartoon sheiks (as the stand-in for the oil-rich Arab countries) who prospered because of America's unwillingness to exploit its own enormous coal resources.[33] The text of the thirty-six ads hammered home the scary message that America faced stark choices now which would shape its destiny forever. The campaign worked to concentrate and focus an already-existing set of fears awakened by the oil crisis of the seventies: listen to the environmentalists and their allies in government and America would suffer disaster (though the Middle East would get rich); listen to the voice of reason, meaning the company, and America would progress. Judging the impact of such a campaign proved impossible, though it did excite the news media and upset the EPA. At the very least it was a 'catalyst,' and there was a postponement of certain provisions of the Clean Air Act which the utility had objected to. The campaign certainly demonstrated the machismo of the company's managers, which may well have been its chief, though unstated, virtue.[34]

The Californians Against the Pollution Initiative (CAPI) campaign of 1972, orchestrated by the public relations firm Whitaker and Baxter for a state referendum, represented the most aggressive form of corporate advocacy. It came about because a left advocate called the People's Lobby had acquired sufficient signatures on a statewide petition to bring a proposed Clean Environment Act to a vote. CAPI was a front organization of esteemed citizens financed by corporations, particularly the petroleum and chemical industries, threatened with a host of controls and prohibitions on pesticides, fuels, energy development, and so on. CAPI generated an enormous quantity of propaganda: 1.6 million copies of two booklets, lots of transit posters, a blitz of radio and television ads (1,788 TV placements alone) in the last three weeks of the campaign, and a final statewide advertising surge in newspapers. Especially towards the end, CAPI attempted to frighten Californians by warning of 'severe power shortages,' massive job losses, a halt to 'virtually all train and truck transportation,' even a plague of mosquitoes that could 'bring back malaria.' The sponsors of the initiative were represented as weird folk, unrealistic and dangerous, committed to absurd ideas. The campaign certainly did mobilize popular opposition. The initiative was defeated by a two-to-one margin at the polls.[35]

Even if all this agitation was novel, its style was usually not. Corporate advocacy in its purest forms was generally confined to newspapers, financial papers, and magazines. Print offered a dignified environment for a traditional mode of persuasion. The ads were often verbose, logical arguments requiring some mental investment by readers to extract the meaning. Typically, management – and corporate advocacy was invariably decided by senior management – wanted to speak not so much to the general public as to target audiences: shareholders and customers, journalists, Washington politicians, and a vague group sometimes called 'influentials,' meaning the educated and affluent citizenry. One of the key purposes of corporate advocacy was to discipline the news media, a mission first taken up by Mobil using advertorials and rebuttals to ensure that what it considered inaccuracies or calumnies never went unanswered. Print was a cheaper and better vehicle for such a purpose than television.[36] Besides, broadcasters had placed a ban on controversial advertising (outside of referenda and the like).

Despite this ban, the example of corporate advocacy did come to shape a kind of capitalist propaganda on television. Some of the advertising of Big Oil argued the virtues of a public good: so Exxon touted the need to develop coal and Chevron the virtues of conservation.[37] Much more significant were a series of public service campaigns, organized under the auspices of the Advertising Council and the federal government, that set out to universalize the values of competition, profit, productivity, and abundance that were part of American capitalism. They marked the return of that ghost of advocacy past, the notorious efforts to sell business of the 1940s and 1950s. Except now the chosen vehicle was the much more potent medium of television.

The effort to boost capitalism showed through in a number of Ad Council campaigns. The jobs programs, technical education and training, and rehabilitation projects of the early seventies all sought to improve and expand the labour pool. According to one team of researchers, Consumer Information 'could be construed as a public relations pitch for business.'[38] President Ford's bizarre WIN (Whip Inflation Now) campaign of 1974–5 earned considerable business support because it laid the responsibility for inflation on the individual consumer.[39] Indeed, the initiative inspired such ad marvels as 'McWin,' a five-cent rollback on sandwich prices at some McDonald's franchises in Cincinnati.[40] Much more obvious, however, were the two efforts at re-education – yes, once again, the American public was thought to be steeped in economic ignorance – the National Productivity campaign (1973–6) and the American Economic System campaign (1976–8). The White House was involved in the inception of both of these.

The productivity campaign was designed, in the grandiose rhetoric of one champion, 'to change the thought of an entire nation.' It was, strange as it may sound, a business–government exercise in semiotics which grew out of the worry that the efficiency of the American industrial machine was falling behind foreign competition. Apparently, Americans treated productivity as a 'dirty word,' a sign which they believed signified 'speeding up the production line.'[41] But that was not so with this 'noble cause,' according to Jack Powers, the president of McCann-Erickson, the agency that masterminded the campaign: the purpose was to 'generate an emotional uplifting of the national spirit,' to get people to work better, not work harder or longer hours.[42] The initial effort on television was a piece of cuteness entitled *Sign Your Work* (1973). The ad showed the operator of a hotdog stand, a car repairman, and a street cleaner, all of whom somehow left their names on their work. Voice-over: 'What if we all had to sign the work we do? We'd do it better, just out of pride.' The advantages would be to give better service and make better products and keep jobs in America. How to ensure this: 'Just do the work you'd be proud to put your name on.' It was an example of how easily humour could become silly. The campaign soldiered on for another three years.

Selling free enterprise turned out to be a bigger project that demonstrated, even more, how propaganda could turn into farce. What sparked concern was the results of an opinion survey suggesting that many Americans had little faith in free enterprise, and even less in corporate America.[43] A secretary of Commerce got the ball rolling with a speech to the Ad Council urging 'nothing less than an effective campaign to improve public understanding of our American economic system.'[44] About $2 million was raised overall, a small portion from the Department of Commerce and the rest from industry, and eventually around $50 million was donated in space and time to distribute the ads. The centrepiece of the project was a booklet entitled *The American Economic System – and Your Part in It*, which became an instant hit when business organizations and firms ordered quantities in bulk.[45] Public service announcements were supposed to entice viewers to order their own copies.

But even before the PSAs aired, the campaign had become controversial. Benjamin Rosenthal, a Democratic congressman, charged that the re-education was no more than a species of propaganda for the administration and big business, made all the worse by the transfer of government funds to assist the plot. Early in 1976, Jeremy Rifkin, the head of the People's Bicentennial Commission, began a counter-attack (through press releases and paid print ads) to promote 'economic democracy': he wanted equal time on television to push his own booklet, *Common Sense II*, which explained how corporations were the source of all manner of political and economic ills. Later in the year yet another critic, this time a liberal coalition of mayors and unions and the like, also used the Ad Council effort to grandstand – they had a commercial in which rich people got upset while reading a booklet that raised questions about the economy. Meanwhile, the networks fussed over the PSAs because they seemed to advocate a position and thus breached the no-controversy rule. That occasioned the return of Congressman Rosenthal, who praised the networks and released a report which damned the booklet as an empty collection of Madison Avenue clichés about the economy that would not enlighten anyone, though it might deceive or disappoint.[46]

Eventually the campaign got off the ground, although apparently only NBC aired the initial spots. The next year's series mocked well-dressed Americans with low 'E.Q.'s' (Economic Quotients), presumably to attract more viewers to send for the booklet. After the campaign ended, Barton Cummings of Compton Advertising was more than willing to brag to *Advertising Age* (27 November 1978) about the successful education of America. An estimated nine million copies of the booklet did go out, one and a half million as a result of individual responses. That sounded like a grand success. Except that surveys of Americans afterwards revealed that on average they knew less about the economy, or at least less about what the promoters deemed significant, than they had before the whole fiasco began. The humorous ads of the second year may even have convinced some viewers that it was 'socially acceptable' to have a 'lack of economic knowledge'![47] In fact, the propaganda of this and other brands of economic re-education was at best clever, at worst inane, and rarely memorable. The norms of democratic practice simply would not justify using the airwaves to express in a fervent or dramatic fashion the virtues of capitalism.[48]

These and other findings might be taken as evidence of failure. Surveys of the level of confidence Americans had in business leaders were very gloomy: a high confidence rating in 1966 of 55 per cent had plummeted to 27 per cent in 1972. It rose slightly to 31 per cent in 1974, only to fall again to 16 per cent in 1980. But surveys did not plumb the extent of both acceptance and accommodation among the public. What was crucial was not just the messages of corporate propaganda but the presence of this propaganda in newspapers and, particularly, on the airwaves. It was a display of power, a 'signal,' which dissent could never match. Indeed, the significance of this presence was enhanced by the growing silence and invisibility of opposition. That absence was not by choice, however.

4 The Apparatus of Control

Critics, reformers, dissidents, cranks, and adversaries all wanted access to television. The purpose was not necessarily to engage in debate. One dissident, Edwin Koupal of the People's Lobby, said flatly that his rule of campaigning was 'Never debate.'[49] Instead, advocates wished to assert: the prospect of sending a clear and compelling message to millions upon millions of viewers was extraordinarily appealing. That was the way to turn one's cause – whether it was abortion rights or energy conservation or non-smoking – into a public good. Relying on the free publicity of the news was hardly a satisfactory alternative: as the San Francisco Women for Peace once argued, the 'straightforward manner' of news delivery could never induce 'the psychological effect' possible with advocacy ads.[50] Journalists mediated and interpreted the experiences and the opinions they covered. The task of reporting was subject to a series of codes and conventions that contributed to the maintenance of the existing hegemony. Dissent found its views marginalized, trivialized, simplified, stereotyped, sensationalized, miscast, or simply neglected. Even a movement as potent as the New Left had been unable to escape the frames of the news media, and that failure had contributed to its eventual demise.[51]

There were significant obstacles preventing any form of dissent from ever getting on television to promote its views. Going the PSA route, at least on a national scale, usually meant dealing with the Advertising Council. Its blessing virtually ensured a measure of success: the campaign would be designed by a volunteer agency (leaving only production costs to the sponsor), the council would see to the distribution of the ads, and television stations were much more likely to air spots bearing the imprimatur of the council. Yet the Ad Council was the guardian of the status quo, called by one veteran critic a 'corporate front that hides propaganda and advocacy under the guise of neutrality.'[52] Indeed, the presiding board was full of company vice-presidents, media managers, and ad executives.

In practice, the Ad Council consistently acted as a mechanism of authority. It got into hot water when it endorsed a 'Write Hanoi' campaign, including a radio spot entitled *Message to Hanoi* (1972), partly sponsored by the Red Cross, that called on Communist forces to open up their camps to neutral observers and provide a list of the names of prisoners of war – the purpose was, of course, to dishonour the anti-war movement. It favoured mainstream causes that conformed to the core values of the dominant classes: one of the most successful launches in the early 1970s was the United Negro College Fund campaign that saw white charity, not legislation, as the route to black advancement. By contrast, the Ad Council avoided endorsing anti-smoking counter-ads (late 1960s); it neutered birth-control messages for Planned Parenthood (early 1970s); and it actually rejected ads desired by no less than a federal agency (mid-1970s). The rules against controversy and partisanship were consistently wielded to block any form of critical propaganda.

The clash between the council and the Federal Energy Administration (FEA) was the most interesting example of censorship. The agency had wished to use PSAs to dishonour Big Oil in the campaign to get Americans to save energy. The intent was to evoke xenophobia, to direct the patriotic sentiments of the public against the Middle Eastern producers of oil and the American firms that delivered the oil. 'The Hand' (1974) was one of the Federal Energy Administration's first suggestions. 'The earlier proposed spot showed the Statue of Liberty standing alone at one end of a chessboard,' claimed a journalist. 'A sinister-looking hand, rings and cufflinks sparkling, enters the picture and surrounds the statue with pieces shaped like oil derricks while the voice-over says: "America is a weakened giant caught in a global game of power ... and you are paying for it with your dollars."' But that spot, and a less heated version, were both vetoed by the Ad Council and its chosen agency, Cunningham and Walsh. The Ad Council president, Robert Keim, claimed that the 'FEA was pushing for "alarmist" advertising, unsupported by "national and international events."' The FEA wanted sufficient funding (one proposal was for $50 million) to mount a paid campaign.[53] That did not happen. Nor did this campaign appear.

Going to the networks directly was no less frustrating. Typically, their spokespeople answered that controversial issues were best dealt with in news and public affairs programming. The networks were loudly opposed both to counter-ads and to paid advocacy, which, so it was claimed, would require allowing time to offended parties to respond under the Fairness Doctrine. That conjured up the horrible vision of a 'Tower of Babel' in which television would be taken over by a welter of competing voices.[54] Over the years, the networks rejected proposals from anti-war groups, critics of Big Oil and nuclear power, consumer advocates, and Mobil Oil, as well as Jeremy Rifkin. Turning down a corporation like Mobil was touted as proof of the evenhandedness of the networks. Indeed, the ban on advocacy was represented as a democratic measure that prevented monied interests from buying network time. In fact, the television authorities rejected the notion of a marketplace of ideas, refusing to surrender their fundamental power to determine what kinds of claims and counter-claims would be allowed prominence in the public sphere.

That left dissidents little choice but to petition the Federal Communications Commission (FCC). Over the years, the FCC had developed the Fairness Doctrine to assess the public performance of radio and television. The doctrine required a broadcaster to devote a reasonable amount of time to the discussion of matters of controversy. It also mandated 'fairness': a television station, for instance, had to allow opponents an opportunity to express their views when it aired the opinions of an advocate. The famous Banzhaf decision on cigarette advertising (1968) opened up the possibility of extending the Fairness Doctrine to enable a much wider range of controversy on TV. In 1966 the commission had received a mere 509 fairness complaints; in 1970 it received more than 60,000.[55] During the early 1970s, Business Executives' Move for Peace (BEM) insisted that a radio station sell airtime for anti-war advocacy, environmentalists took issue with two Esso commercials that purportedly advocated an Alaskan pipeline, peace groups challenged military recruitment ads while the Vietnam War continued, and the Friends of the Earth (FOE) demanded the right to answer commercials for automobiles and gasolines.[56] Only one commissioner, Nicholas Johnson (1966–73), endorsed the notion of enforced access, via either paid advocacy or counter-ads. Others feared that any significant extension of the Fairness Doctrine would change the whole shape of television broadcasting. So the FCC said no – the actual operation of the Fairness Doctrine was patently *unfair*.[57]

Some of the petitioners then took their cases to the courts. The

Washington, D.C., Court of Appeals proved sympathetic. In the FOE case (1971) the court ruled that there was no substantial difference between the health hazards posed by gasoline commercials and those posed by cigarette commercials, and the judges required that the FCC reconsider the merits of the complaint.[58] Had this decision held, the scope of the public debate would suddenly have been expanded to encompass the promises and the claims of consumer advertising. Advertisers might well have begun evacuating television if faced with the prospect of counter-advertising, or so went the speculation. In any case, the FCC put forward a clarification of the Fairness Doctrine in 1974 that specifically repudi-ated the Banzhaf decision and removed consumer advertising from all doctrine obligations. Just as serious was a favourable ruling (1971) on the BEM claim (and a related case brought by the Democratic National Committee) that the networks' ban on paid advocacy violated the First Amendment. The consequence?: a redefinition of the permissible that would have offered an opportunity for a much wider range of opinion. What saved the day against a sudden excess of democracy – or, more properly, of marketing – was the Supreme Court's reversal (1973) of the Court of Appeals ruling. Not only did Chief Justice Warren Burger affirm the wisdom of the Fairness Doctrine, he argued that unfettered access would favour the rich and erode the 'journalistic discretion' of broad-casters.[59] The door was closed on dissent.

It was not closed on corporations, though. The practice of corporate advocacy had always been regarded with suspicion by a few Democrats in Congress. In 1975 a delegation that included Senator Birch Bayh and Representative Benjamin Rosenthal appealed, unsuccessfully, to the Fed-eral Trade Commission to act against the 'misleading claims' of image and advocacy ads, print and broadcast, sponsored by a variety of energy companies.[60] In 1978 the Supreme Court ruled in the *First National Bank of Boston v. Belotti* that Massachusetts (and so eighteen other states) could not prohibit companies from participating in referenda campaigns. In-deed, the decision extended the embrace of the First Amendment to cover the whole of corporate advocacy, which now became a species of free speech in the public interest.[61] That was the only substantial change in the right of access in the 1970s. A decade later, moved by the deregulatory craze of the late 1980s, the FCC itself rescinded much of the Fairness Doctrine and, soon afterwards, the networks began to accept paid advocacy. By this time, of course, the adversary culture of the late 1960s and early 1970s was just a historical memory.

5 A Legitimacy Crisis?

Was hegemony restored? Order certainly was restored – but things were not quite the same as before. In *The Confidence Gap* (1983), Seymour Martin Lipset and William Schneider pondered whether there was 'a legitimacy crisis' in the United States. The concern grew out of a series of polls illustrating a dramatic decline in the levels of confidence people had in the leaders of major institutions. Not only had confidence levels tumbled in the late 1960s, they had fallen even farther in the case of government and business during the course of the 1970s. The authors also noted a substantial growth in what they termed 'anti-business sentiment' (reaching a peak of 61 per cent in 1979) and 'anti-government sentiment' (which peaked at 67 per cent in 1980). But running counter to such trends were findings that indicated that the same Americans (in, for example, a February 1981 poll) who condemned leaders still rated the political and business systems 'basically sound' (or, rather, two-thirds of them did). Similarly, another poll (1978) found that almost three-quarters of respondents expressed 'a great deal of confidence in this country.' All of which led Lipset and Schneider to conclude that America suffered a crisis neither of confidence nor of legitimacy but rather of 'competence,' driven by events, particularly political troubles.[62]

Even the authors, however, admitted that the legitimacy of the institutional élites was in tatters: what people distrusted were the 'concentrations of power and the cynical, self-interested abuse of power by government, business, and labour leaders.' Clearly the efforts to re-legitimize authority, of which economic re-education was only one, had not overcome the shocks of the late 1960s. But a lot of civic advocacy had not aimed, at least not directly, at legitimacy. Rather, it was a species of attack propaganda: the Nixon ads, the anti-drug commercials, the business assaults on government, referenda campaigns, these sought to trash the left and any liberal allies. They were primarily concerned with dishonouring, with provoking and marshalling fear against radical change. The import of this attack advertising, moreover, was enhanced by the restrictions placed upon adversary politics. What authority stifled was dissent: it sought to silence the voices of criticism and to render invisible their imagery. Increasingly, as the seventies marched on, the élites regained their command over the shape of the symbolic universe which constructed politics. That deprived Americans of one discourse of resistance, especially those Americans on the bottom of the social ladder – many of whom would not bother to vote. By default it favoured that other ideology of change, the 'neo-conservatism' of the New Right (which should have been labelled neo-liberalism, at least in philosophical terms) that became so prominent in the politics of the 1980s. For this ideology would allow the haves in society to articulate their disenchantment with big government.

'By negation, order reaffirms itself,' wrote Paul Ricoeur.[63] What happened in the United States in the 1970s was ample demonstration of that proposition.

3

Governing Affluence:
The First World in the Seventies

Searching: Imagine a journey through a real house of horror. You are the camera. The door opens into a darkened interior, charred by fire and smoke. Water dribbles down the walls. You hear the sound of heavy breathing as you walk up the mutilated stairs. Names are called out – parents cry out for their children, children cry out for mummy and daddy – and these names echo through the empty, devastated halls and rooms. You pause briefly at some scene of ruin: burnt food, the charred remains of a closet. Always there are the sounds of heavy breathing and the echoing names. You do not know whether anyone escaped the blaze. The ad invites us to assume the worst. Then the camera stops its journey, and from one edge the screen 'burns off,' revealing what a voice-over repeats: 'KEEP MATCHES AWAY FROM CHILDREN.'[1]

Searching (1975) was an instance of shock advertising, sponsored by the British government, probably appearing courtesy of its Central Office of Information (COI). What the Americans had started spread to other parts of the advanced world (and sometimes beyond) in the course of the 1970s. There were differences. Corporate advocacy never reached the same proportions outside of the United States, though by the early 1980s it was sufficiently prominent in Canada to justify a special public affairs conference of luminaries from business, government, and academe.[2] Britain prohibited the brand of broadcast political advertising that the United States had come to accept as normal. But the tone of British propaganda on matters big and small (such as the hazard of matches) was often much more hard-hitting. In any case, civic advocacy, whether sponsored by public or private authorities, established itself as a common technology of governance across the so-called First World and even began to spread into the less advantaged places outside this privileged zone.

1 The Propaganda Boom

The popularity of civic advocacy marked a new interest in persuasion, rather than regulation or direction, as a mode of governance. The practice of 'public communication campaigns,' to use an American euphemism, seemed better suited to the formalities of a democratic polity.[3] That resulted from a convergence of factors.

The most obvious was rooted in technological change, a commonplace in the story of the twentieth century, in this case the arrival of television as the dominant mode of communication in affluent countries. The small screen was so important not just because television was the chief vehicle for civic advocacy, though it was that; or even because it privileged the visual over the verbal and, to a lesser extent, the emotional over the rational, though again these were significant consequences of television; but also because the triumph of television had important effects upon the reputation of the mass media in country after country. It was not only a Marshall McLuhan who got excited by the possibilities. According to Lawrence Wallack, a later critic, there emerged the belief 'that almost any given social or health problem can be adequately addressed if the right message could be communicated to the right people in just the right way at the right time.'[4] What fuelled this 'mass media fallacy' was the prospect of reaching huge numbers of people on the cheap: 1984 figures showed a cost of $102 to reach one American in person, twenty-five cents to use direct mail, but a mere three cents via mass communication.[5] The fact that such a statistic was around indicated a particular cast of mind which reduced communication to simple contact. In any case, the triumph of television provided not only the opportunity but an excuse to propagandize.

A second factor was the new sophistication of the television commercial as a tool of persuasion. Civic advocacy had not been totally reshaped by that 'creative revolution' which transformed the ways Madison Avenue sold private goods.[6] Public communication campaigns often retained the mood of earnest enthusiasm, a didactic tone, a liking for demonstration, the hard sell, and such other characteristics prevalent before the mid-1960s. Few advocacy ads employed the ironic or sexual sells, rebel talk, and talking young that had enlivened the mainstream of advertising. The serious, 'official' purpose of civic advocacy militated against humour and sex and rebellion. But admakers were able to translate many of their techniques, notably special effects and clever photography, to fashion a more effective propaganda. The emphasis on visuals came through in efforts to jolt viewers with harsh or startling images: a boy playing Russian roulette with a pistol, a drowning man, another walking around with smoking dynamite strapped to his body, a woman hit by a drunk driver.[7] Instead of the signs of affluence or beauty, admakers tried to evoke pity, guilt, or shame with the signs of suffering: frustration, sadness, despair, crying, violence, mutilation.[8] What they developed, then, was a dark aesthetic which offered up visions of peril and pain. Although not always present, certainly not in corporate advertising, that dark aesthetic became a trademark of much civic advocacy around the world.

The next factor was the spreading acceptance, and knowledge, of how to sell public goods. This occurred across two dimensions. Initiatives pioneered in the United States were soon emulated in other places. Take the example of political advertising. Saatchi and Saatchi, that most aggressive of British ad agencies, successfully imported American styles and ploys to market the newly chosen Conservative leader, Margaret Thatcher, in 1978 and 1979 as the saviour of a Britain suffering from a myriad of social and economic ills.[9] Its best-known effort was a pre-election poster entitled 'Labour Isn't Working': the agency photographed a group of unemployed (not 'real' unemployed, though, and that caused an uproar) who appeared as a long queue disappearing into the horizon – the poster was placed in choice outdoor spots around the country and was reprinted in many a newspaper.[10] At about the same time, Venezuelan political parties were hiring American political consultants to tell them how to spend their money to win an election. One of the oldest veterans, David Garth (he had worked for Adlai Stevenson in the 1950s), was credited with introducing 'biting advertising' on behalf of an opposition party, a style that, critics claimed, 'foments social division' – meaning exploits class tensions.[11]

The other dimension grew out of the expanding register of civic advocacy. What were called 'marketing principles' were applied to more and more causes in an increasing variety of countries. Consider the extraordinary range of behaviours which became the target of particular commercials during the 1970s.[12]

Eating: In *Cookie Monster* (U.S.A., 1974), that child celebrity of the television program 'Sesame Street' reveals that he eats meat and fish, vegetables, fruit, and milk, in addition to tons of cookies. In *Aging Man* (U.K., 1977) poor Jimmy/Jim is a victim of excess, his mouth stuffed with food by mother, wife, and self, until he ends up in the hospital. Both ads play with the idea that 'you are what you eat.'

Drinking: In *The Hang Over* (Finland, 1976) we see the pain of a man who has drunk too much. A cute spot from Ontario's Ministry of Health, *Drinking Bird* (1975), tells viewers, 'Why let others push you into drinking more than your limit? How much you drink isn't up to them ... it's up to you.' In each case the agent of sin is excess. One of the more amusing attacks on excess, though, occurred in France, where a moderation campaign sponsored by liquor manufacturers told consumers, 'Count your drinks. Seven drinks a day – never more'!

Sex: In *V.D. Is for Everybody* (U.S.A., 1974) Americans are told how dangerous it is to indulge in unprotected sex. *The Surprise* (Sweden, 1979) urges youth to use a condom to avoid an unwanted pregnancy. Both label a pleasure a peril. Perhaps the most famous image to come out of the birth-control campaigns was the picture of a pregnant man that made Saatchi and Saatchi famous in 1970.

Exercise: The people in *Get off Your Rocker* (U.S.A., 1976) are admonished to stop relaxing and get active. The overweight male in *Walkies* (U.K., 1977) is taken out for a walk to the park, on a leash, by his wife. Lazing around becomes a public sin.

Speech: What we say and how we say it is the target of public scrutiny, and obloquy, in the anti-racism message *Faces* (U.S.A., 1975) from the Anti-Defamation League of the B'nai B'rith.

Cleanliness: In *How Could I Tell You* (Hungary, 1980) we watch how the dirtiness of a young man – his messy room, his smoking, his unwashed body – disgusts his sweetheart. Here intimate space has been turned into a public stage.

Leisure: Even the couch potato is warned that he is a slave to mental domination. In *Who's Master* (Japan, 1981), we see the TV set taking a man, again on a leash, for a walk, in that bizarre ad.

Advertising, of course, was only one part of a marketing strategy that might also involve personal advice or special clinics or even rituals of exercise. This combined approach was evident in one of the most celebrated American campaigns of the decade, the Stanford University Heart Disease Prevention Program, launched in three cities in 1972.

The last factor was the existence of an eager group of sponsors. All kinds of institutions wanted to cajole the public. The Construction Safety Association of Ontario made *Bucket* to tout the need for workplace care, a com-

Would you be more careful if
it was you that got pregnant?

Figure 7: The Pregnant Man. The ad was actually completed before Saatchi and Saatchi existed. It was prepared by employees of a consultancy known as Cramer Saatchi for the Health Education Council. But Charles Saatchi so heavily publicized the effort to the industry and the media that it became closely associated with the newly created agency. Since then it has entered the annals of health promotion as one of the most celebrated posters of all time.

mercial that actually captured the public fancy and even secured the top spot as the Gold Bessie in Canada's annual advertising awards festival of 1968. The Society for Crippled Civilians, also Canadian, took to TV in 1973 to explain the plight of the disabled to 'ordinary' viewers. McDonnell Douglas sponsored ads in the United States positioning the United Nations as an instrument of world peace, part of a corporate image campaign as well as a sign of its commitment to public service.[13] Similarly, Esso ran a campaign on West German television in 1974 and 1975 to sponsor energy conservation.[14] Also in Germany, a huge automobile club used bumper stickers and magazine ads to champion 'driving freedom' ('Freie Bürger fördern freie Fahrt') against a government poster campaign to promote speed limits on the autobahns.[15] And in 1977 Japan's Advertising Council offered *Egg*, a commercial urging food conservation ('There is a limit to food resources.' 'Are you sure you're not wasting food?').

The single most active sponsor was the state through its many agencies. The turmoil of the 1960s had provoked a sense of political crisis in the affluent world. 'We know that among huge minorities in the western countries, there is a new, profound and widespread disaffection with the pretensions of government,' admitted a government task force in Canada in 1969.[16] Some years later, a report for that élite body the Trilateral Commission worried about 'the governability of democracies' in an era when populations were much less docile.[17] These presumptions had already set the stage for a new wave of propaganda. Since the Nixon years, Washington had made extensive use of public service announcements (it sponsored ten of the twenty-five major campaigns endorsed by the Advertising Council in 1972–3), and its additional spending on publicity stood at $146 million in 1979 (ranking it twenty-eighth among all advertisers). In 1975 a series of major campaigns on conservation ('Save It'), inflation, and the referendum on the European Economic Community turned the Labour government, briefly, into the single largest advertiser in Great Britain. But the most enthusiastic convert to civic advocacy was unquestionably the Canadian government. By the end of the decade, Ottawa consistently ranked as the top sponsor in the country, and its efforts were supplemented by some provincial governments, notably Ontario and Quebec: state expenditures reached roughly $160 million in 1980, or $6.66 per person.[18]

The enthusiasm of the Canadian state was overdetermined: there were many reasons why its politicians and bureaucrats would see in advertising a way to guide democracy. The practice of state intervention had always been much more common in Canada than in the United States, partly because of the constant need to reinvent a nation that shared the continent with a gigantic neighbour. The Liberal government of Pierre Elliott Trudeau that took office in 1968 and dominated political life until 1984 (apart from one brief interlude) was especially sympathetic to the idea of social and cultural engineering. Trudeau presided over a substantial expansion of the apparatus of the federal government and, so, its civil service. During the early 1970s his administration funded Information Canada, nicknamed 'The Ministry of Truth,' to coordinate the public communications of the state. Government agencies and departments, working with health professionals, came increasingly to rely upon advertising campaigns to modify what they deemed bad behaviour, whether that was smoking too much or exercising too little. One of the triumphs of the times was the Participaction campaign, meant to get Canadians to work out regularly, which became famous because it trumpeted as fact what was, apparently, a lie: that the average sixty-year-old Swede was in better shape than a thirty-year-old Canadian.[19] After a separatist victory in Quebec in 1976, the Canadian Unity Information Office, nicknamed 'Propaganda Canada,' was launched (and would spend about $32 million) to mastermind the selling of a new constitution as well as to counter the popularity of sovereignty in Quebec.[20] (Its efforts were partially answered by opposing campaigns from the provincial government of Quebec, controlled by the Parti Québécois.)

At the beginning of the new decade, Canadian ministers went public over the issue of advocacy advertising: that instrument, or something like it, was essential to supplement news coverage, to combat anti-Ottawa sentiment, to inform the public, to improve life and health, to sell public policies, even to enhance the credibility of government.[21] 'Our constitutional ads were a low-key attempt to offset this negativism, to emphasize some of the things we did agree on ...' asserted Jim Fleming, then minister of state for multiculturalism, who explained that the government had to boost public morale in the ongoing, never-ending constitutional squabbles. 'Our ads didn't push the federal government's specific position, they stressed unity and pride of country. All they tried to sell was a positive attitude.'[22] A critic added that state advocacy was also essential to mask inaction: all too much of government advertising was part of a game of smoke and mirrors, cheaper than actually funding reform yet useful to pretend concern or claim success.[23]

The most infamous of these advocacy campaigns sought to convert constitutional reform into a public good – never an easy sell, because of the boredom factor – by reminding Canadians of the virtues of being Canadian. In one case that meant shots of natural beauty and marvellous geese while the voice-over talked about freedom and the like. One opposition politician, Bob Rae, had this disgusted comment: 'I'll never be able to look at Canada geese or a beaver in quite the same way again. I'll see them as Liberals in disguise.' Provincial leaders, then locked in a battle with Ottawa over money and power, apparently regarded the campaign as an attempt to soften up the country to accept a unilateral constitutional reform.[24]

However extreme, the Canadian example highlights what was becoming standard throughout the western world. First, the necessity of constant propaganda to push the agendas of governments in a public sphere where other state authorities, interest groups, corporations, and political parties struggled for local ascendancy. Second, the desire to use advertising to escape dependence on the news media as a mode of constructing public opinion. Third, the utility of this advertising as an instrument of management to administer the attitudes and behaviour of a wayward population. The new wave of television commercials was only the most visible component of a much larger, usually unrecognized complex of propaganda: position papers, task force and commission reports, statistical surveys, questionnaires, polling results, pronouncements, speeches. Some originated with politicians and bureaucrats, but others were authored by their private allies on specific issues such as heart disease, nature conservancy, or drinking and driving. Here was a mechanism of power displayed in its full splendour. A vast tide of words, figures, and images washed over the publics of the affluent democracies, creating a special kind of intellectual context to condition the practices of each and all.

2 Semiotic and Other Labours

It would be possible to give advocacy ads a postmodernist reading: to subvert the text, decentre prevailing values, give presence to what is absent, and all the other manoeuvres this strategy of interpretation employs.[25] That is more or less what some viewers do. But advocacy ads do not invite such treatment: usually they are not intended as playful texts, and they certainly were not in the 1970s. Rather, this propaganda conformed, and continues to conform, to a modern or, to be more exact, a 'neo-modern' design, despite the fact that the television commercial itself has been celebrated by some critics as the vehicle of a novel sensibility.[26] Civic advocacy usually seeks to fix meaning and close off interpretation on behalf of governance.

Even so, the postmodernist's toolbox supplies some useful ways to understand the construction of signs, differences, and meanings – in short, the kind of semiotic labour that the advocacy ad endeavours to carry out.[27] This requires a movement across the three levels of the propaganda: the individual exemplars, the overlapping genres (of corporate ads, charity appeals, and so on), and the category itself (civic advocacy in general). The last two, of course, are 'supertexts,' the fictional results and mechanisms of analysis. The focus of attention is upon the three processes of totalizing, interpellating, and privatizing, themselves the consequences of a cluster of textual operations, which seek to transform the consciousness and behaviour of the viewer.

Keep in mind these points. While the examples are all drawn from the testing times of the 1970s, in fact each of these processes would persist, becoming a part of the permanent repertoire of advertising as propaganda. What I describe here, consequently, is one way of looking at the basic structure of civic advocacy – as an instrument of hegemony – at any time and in any place. Second, a vital element left out of my brand of 'ideology critique'[28] is the utopian aspect of certain kinds of civic advocacy, notably corporate and 'green' advertising (see Part IV where I remedy this deficiency). Third, the critique deals only with the various exemplars and the phenomenon, not with the results of propaganda – that is, with the objectives of the sponsors and the admakers rather than the responses of the target populations.

a) Totalizing

This term refers to the ways in which an ideology expresses its will to power and its assertion of control over a text, an act whose success gives any message a definite and homogeneous meaning.[29]

Particularly in the seventies, advocacy ads were almost invariably constructed as unified monologues, so as to avoid both ambiguity and dialogue. Consider the resolutely upbeat anti-smoking ad *Skateboard* (1977), sponsored by the Comité Français d'Education pour la Santé and aimed at France's teenagers. It presented three separate vignettes in the space of half a minute. In each case one teen offers a smoke to another: the offer serves as a sign of esteem, of friendship, of completion. In each case the other teen takes the cigarette and crushes it with panache and pleasure, an act of joyous destruction. The text at the end tells us: 'Une cigarette écrasée c'est un peu de liberté gagnée.' The aim was to dishonour smoking and honour abstinence. The ad tried to define the rejection of smoking as a positive act of will, a rebellion against the expected that signified freedom and thus potency and energy. Put another way, the ad used the technique of reversal, identifying a negative as a positive. It constructed the good teen, the model citizen, as clean-living and energetic. The presentation, however, was too bold, too didactic, too simplified, yet another case where the process of 'distilling' the essence of an ideal type did not work. Neither the adolescents nor their behaviour rang true. Instead, a kind of moral hype had rendered the message unbelievable. Such happy and obedient teens could exist only in a dreamworld.[30]

Propaganda worked both to 'universalize' (make eternal) and to 'naturalize' (make commonplace): that is, the sponsors sought to centre their cause by wedding the message to one of the prevailing values or myths of society.[31] David Paletz and his fellow investigators noted how often America's PSAs promoted their public goods in terms of shared values such as hard work, temperance, thrift, self-help, family life and togetherness, and consensus.[32] Political ads in the United States from 1968 onwards had candidates moving forward at a fast pace, sometimes pointing, all to suggest such widely esteemed qualities as energy, direction, and leadership – the visual cliché of the moment. Anti-smoking campaigns and other brands of health promotion constantly evoked the ideal of the perfect body, an ideal that presumably all could cherish whatever their class or race or gender. Corporate image advertising made much of the virtues of progress and prosperity as a boon to humanity. Corco of Puerto Rico used animation in *Plasticine* (1975) to show how the company's refinery would bring jobs, industry, and affluence by sponsoring a petrochemical boom: we 'see' clothes, tires, telephones, hoses, toasters, and so on appear out of Corco's pipelines.[33] What was ignored, of course, was any possible link between development and exploitation or between progress and pollution. Establishing a presence also meant creating an absence.

A final operation of 'closure,' both 'textual' and 'ideological,' occurred within each ad. Here the purpose was to provide an ending, to offer a resolution.[34] It was not always possible to achieve a full closure, especially not if the problem was too great. But a collection of visual and verbal cues might build a coherent illusion that would satisfy the need to provide a single, unified meaning.

Cy Banash (U.S.A. 1971): Here is an instance of a charity appeal which falls into the camp of liberal advocacy – it is a 'vehicle' for that brand of activist, engaged, urban liberalism associated so closely with the Kennedy clan of the 1960s. Much of the ad is frenzied, full of jerky motions, clipped language, sharp sounds, and sometimes anger. That's because it recounts a sad story of hard times in the big city. Towards the end a voice-over tells us, 'When poor people are in trouble they come to legal aid, a thousand a day.' The focus of attention isn't so much the poor as a middle-aged, white lawyer, rumpled and balding but also active, aggressive, and, of course, caring. He interviews a victim on the phone (and orders a cheeseburger from a black colleague), instructs a non-Anglophone on how to behave (complete with the wagging finger of authority), tells a new arrival to take his wounded buddy to a hospital ('I'm a lawyer, not a doctor'), and reams out a young client who's lying until he realizes the now weeping man is starved (so he hands over his cheeseburger). His is a noble work. But it needs funds:

'OK, we'll get an investigator over   *'Did you eat today?'*
right away.'

Figure 8: Scenes from *Cy Banash*.

'The poor can't pay; somebody's got to; give money,' exclaims the voice-over. 'You can't call a lawyer if you haven't got a dime.'

Cy Banash had enacted closure in a variety of ways. It was an ad which worked the contrast between the top and the bottom. It had defined the poor as objects and victims, never the agents of their own salvation: they were people with no power and little hope who could not secure justice without assistance. They definitely were not like 'you,' the viewer. They were on the bottom of society. On the top of that society, the white lawyer was also unlike 'you' – he was akin to those heroes of the professional sagas that had graced American television screens in the 1960s: a doctor like Ben Casey or a teacher like Mr Novak, a dedicated man who gave his all to secure justice in a flawed world. This appropriation of a particular look and style, also known as 'intertextuality,'[35] was supposed to convey an assortment of meanings about power and life. Along the way, masculinity, whiteness, and expertise were all honoured. So, too, was that Kennedyesque brand of liberalism where the privileged strove to help the down and out. Naturally, the notion of hierarchy, of a sharp distinction of power, was assumed, or rather normalized.

Even so, *Cy Banash* could not promise a final resolution. It left the impression, as did the professional sagas, that the cycle of problems would never end. Underlying it was that age-old maxim, 'The poor will always be with us.' But the point was that your money could enable the continued, effective management of these problems. The civic-minded were shown a way in which they could contribute to both social justice and social peace in their community.[36]

b) Interpellating

The term 'interpellation,' otherwise known as 'hailing,' was coined by the French semiotician Roland Barthes and popularized by the French Marxist Louis Althusser. It refers to the process whereby a message tries to position individuals, to define their subjectivity, even to provide a social identity.[37] Hailing serves, above all, to satisfy people with an illusion of autonomy and centrality that suits the purposes of ideology.

One of the most obvious ploys is the practice of direct address which works to capture the attention – to hail – the prospective viewer. Direct address employs the word 'you' and its non-English equivalents, eye contact between on-screen characters and the viewer, and both the imperative and the querulous modes of expression. The purpose of this 'personalized language,' as Herbert Marcuse once mused,[38] was to make familiar, to promote a brief moment of empathy so that the public as individuals would identify themselves or their actions with people and behaviours appearing in the spectacle created by the admakers.

The 'Clunk, Click' campaign (early 1970s): This famous British initiative relied on the television celebrity Jimmy Savile to cajole viewers to use seat-belts when driving. Savile, a slim, mature man with a handsome mane of white hair, appears well-dressed in a suit or some smart, casual outfit. He speaks directly to the camera; his tone is caring, and his voice carries conviction. He is usually twinned with an accident victim who would explain why he or she was injured. In Max, a young man in a wheelchair tells us how his negligence brought about this sad fate; in Carol, we look into the hurt eyes of a disfigured fifteen-year-old girl who did not buckle up.[39] Savile, of course, is the friendly face of authority. His gaze establishes Max or Carol or Mr Reader or Myrtle Searle as a case. He identifies what is the cause of her/his mutilation. He works to put us in their place, to remind us, gently but surely, that we must obey as well. Carol and the rest were authentic examples of an anonymous mass of past, present, and future victims. These narratives of pain allow Savile to deliver the slogan: 'Clunk the car door, click the seatbelt, and do it every trip.' In its day, 'Clunk, Click' became a household expression.

There were variations, of course. Recall that Searching put us in the place of the camera. Likewise, the Canadian warning Impaired Driving (1972) was shot from the viewer's perspective.[40] A voice-over explained what would happen to us from the moment we were picked up by the police, particularly the shame and embarrassment of being treated like a criminal. The admakers employed a host of visual tricks to hold our attention: jerky or slow motions, panoramas and close-ups, muting and glows, facial distortion and fuzzy lights, grainy and abstracted displays, even angle shots. 'We' are invited to take up the place of the absent sinner. Similarly, 'we' are asked to take the place of the disabled in *It Isn't Fair* (U.S.A., 1978), where a college is organized to suit wheelchairs, the blind, and the deaf and dumb.[41] Try on these identities, such ads invite, and see what it is like to experience life in a different kind of world.

The advocacy ad was also capable of supplying both recognition and motivation.

Folks Like Us: Americans are told just how incompetent they are to deal with the problem of youth drugs in *Confrontation* (*c.* 1972), where an 'ordinary' – meaning middle-class – family falls apart because parents and teenager cannot bridge the generation gap.

The Self-Interested Man: British Gas offered two variations in 1980, *Good Housekeeping* and *Uncle Joe*, in which 'common' folk – working-class people, in short – learn to save money through energy conservation. The use of a north country patter serves to speed the recognition.

Patriots: The Exxon Bicentennial campaign (1975) asks viewers to define themselves as proud Americans who live in a land that gave birth to Mark Twain, Helen Keller, and Dizzy Dean.

Consumers: Contrast that campaign with the identity celebrated in Brazil's 1979 *Brand Labels (Tiger)*, where we learn how advertising has made all those playful people so happy.[42]

There was, then, a wide variety of identities tailor-made by propaganda, perhaps greater than those present in consumer advertising. No matter: they all served to position viewers as apparently free subjects of authorities that worked to construct them. The success of hailing depended on the misperception of the individual. That made people complicit in their own subordination.

c) Privatizing

This term evokes the practice of turning public enterprises into private companies, a commonplace of government during the late 1980s and early 1990s. Except here it pertains not to enterprise but to ideas. It might best be seen as a specialized version of the power to name, label, or 'frame' something or someone.[43] The unrestricted ability to name can be awesome: it enables its master to determine essence, to establish what can and cannot be said about an object and how that object should be approached, understood, treated, solved, or eliminated. Privatizing usually lacks such a scope since it involves issues that were or are already present in the public sphere. But it does work a transformation. The process entails a double manoeuvre: the conversion of the collective crisis into a personal problem and of the social issue into a moral ill.

Civic advertising must simplify and stereotype if it wishes to reach large numbers of people in a short time. The difficulty is that such an operation will necessarily focus attention on one aspect of an issue in order to offer some concrete solution. This reduction normally results in other kinds of operations that are implicitly, and sometimes explicitly, political: the search for analogies, a need to decontextualize or to trivialize, and the avoidance of controversy (depoliticization).

Analogies: The British government in its ad *Swimming Pool* (1978) compared the plight of unemployed youth to untrained swimmers drowning in a pool, until 'saved' by the adults (read employers) standing around the edges. The images are striking, dramatic, and, of course, misleading – they say nothing about the actual nature of unemployment.

Decontextualizing: Consider the way an ad can exclude crucial dimensions of a social disaster. Pro Matre, a Brazilian organization, announced the forthcoming International Year of the Child with *Dolls* (1978). In it the announcer explains how thousands upon thousands of children in Brazil will 'die of hunger, of diarrhoea, of measles, of tetanus, of smallpox, of tuberculosis ...' The screen pans over a mound of broken and discarded dolls. A dirge plays in the background. Nowhere does it allude to the factors of class, race, or poverty – to the roots of this story.

Trivializing: The constraints on what a sponsor thought should be said at times produced suggestions that were ludicrous, given the scale of the problem. *Grandpa's Oil Lamp* (1977) features just that, an old oil lamp. The voice-over explains, 'When Grandpa's lamp was running out of oil, Grandpa did this. [The flame is reduced.] Now the world is in the same situation. It's running out of oil. So we have to do this.' Such was the suggestion of a way to solve the world's energy crisis from the Finnish Broadcasting Company.

Depoliticizing: Gulf Oil of Canada offered the soothing *Spoon* (1975), which explained that there was a lot of oil now, that there would be an oil shortage if no new reserves were found, and that Gulf was investing millions in seeking additional deposits. The long-winded ad couldn't resist the observation that Canadians were privileged beings: 'We've had a silver spoon in our mouths up to now here in this country.' But it did avoid all mention of the possibility of rationing, price controls, or government direction.[44]

In one way or another, all of these examples practised avoidance, masking or neglecting or absenting some dimension of a problem which might upset the sponsor or authority in general. The other side of privatizing was a kind of 'displacement' whereby the significance of something, such as what causes smoking, was transferred from one agent – say, a corporation – to another agent, the individual smoker.[45] The advocacy ad endeavoured to make problems personal and moral, ensuring that any blame stuck to the individual so that any solution depended upon individual action.

Censoring: A kill-joy of an ad, *National Drinking Game* (U.S.A., 1972), warns that some party animals are actually flirting with alcoholism. A group of people are having fun drinking and laughing and talking. But they are under surveillance, and the unseen voice begins to question them about their habits: When do they drink? How much do they drink? Why do they drink? What happens when they drink? By the time the voice has finished the interrogation, the party's also finished. The questioner's moral gaze has altered the meaning and significance of good times.

Blaming the Victim: Another common ploy was to blame the victim for his or her own plight. That was especially evident in anti-drug ads in the United States, but it could apply in many health campaigns. *The Two Georges* (1977), a British spot, contrasts a young George and an old George, who happen to 'meet' in a bar. The sad state of the old George is the result of eating and drinking far too much – and exercising nothing more than his mouth.

Blaming Mother: One particularly nasty piece of work is *Sewing Machine* (1971) from Britain's Central Office of Information. A preoccupied mom forgets about her bored child, who is playing outside in the yard. The child wanders onto the sidewalk, sees a friend (but not an onrushing car), runs out into the street, and ... we hear the impact. All the time authority, in the form of a voice-over, explains how a mother must always, always supervise her children, or disaster will result.

Assuming Responsibility: In any case, 'you' had to admit your responsibility to correct the problem. A track star instructs Americans in *Jim Ryun* (1974) on the need to 'Pace yourself or lose' in the race to conserve energy. A fake Will Rogers tells viewers in *Merry-Go-Round* (1979) that they must curtail their demands if they wish to correct inflation.[46]

3 The Anti-litter Campaigns

All of these operations found expression in the robust effort to keep the affluent world clean and tidy. The leading agency in America, where the anti-litter campaign went on television in the early 1960s, was an organization called Keep America Beautiful, Inc. (KAB). KAB sponsored local projects which involved citizens and especially youth in the practical task of keeping their neighbourhoods clean and attractive. But at another level, KAB was, or became, a corporate front to displace the blame for pollution from business to the consumer. At times the organization was funded by Pepsi-Cola, Philip Morris, Ford, the American Can Company, the United States Brewers' Association, and the Glass Containers Manufacturers' Institute. In the mid-1970s, KAB opposed legislation requiring returnable bottles and containers, an action that led the Sierra Club to resign from its advisory committee. KAB's slogan in the seventies was blunt and simple: 'People Start Pollution, People Can Stop It' – in short, the slogan privatized this environmental issue. KAB worked with the Ad Council in the 1960s and 1970s to make Americans conscious of their moral duty. One of its spokespeople offered a revealing comment on the purpose: 'The whole campaign is directed toward the individual. We wish to stimulate a sense of individual responsibility for environmental improvement. This is a more positive approach than pollution control.' That was not a position endorsed by prominent environmental associations.[47]

Anti-litter ads embody an ideal of cleanliness that was once particularly associated with a bourgeois outlook on life, perhaps because it was the middle classes who first made such a fetish of cleansing the body. But picking up litter had now become a sign of the good citizen – making the landscape clean was universalized as a public good.[48] Trash, grime, or graffiti were signs of disrespect and disorder.[49] Indeed, they signified that public space had been appropriated by individuals, or perhaps even taken over by criminals: consider how often shots of dangerous places (alleys, social housing, ghettoes) featured dirt. That justified efforts to dishonour the litterbug whose actions endangered the commons.[50] So cleaning up the environment meant ordering that environment, a mark of civic pride and good habits.[51] The tidy city symbolized a well-regulated and a well-disciplined populace, à la Singapore.

The American campaign produced one superb exemplar of public art, an expression that transcended ideology and moved into the realm of utopia. Working for KAB and the Advertising Council, the Marsteller agency created the most famous PSA of the 1970s.

Chief Iron Eyes Cody (1971): The focus is on the travels of a majestic Indian chief across modern America. We see him first in his canoe, shot from the side of the river, through an opening in the trees. Then begins the dramatic music, mostly drums but soon trumpets. We get various shots of the chief paddling. Then, in one shot, the first signs of litter: newspapers, cans, scum, floating on the water. He travels past a bridge, a dock, a large ship, smoke. His image is superimposed on what looks like a derrick and a refining plant, giving off clouds of something evil. Back to the canoe and the refuse. He beaches the canoe on a shore full of litter. The music changes, becoming softer.

Finally a voice-over gives guidance: 'Some people have a deep, abiding respect for the natural beauty that was once this country.' The camera focuses on the noble face of the chief. He walks to the edge of the highway. A woman in a car tosses out the window a bag of garbage. The bag lands at his feet. 'And some people don't.' The focus returns to the chief's face, he turns, the camera moves in, and we see a tear falling from his right eye. 'People start pollution. People can stop it.' We move to a shot of a pamphlet, ''71 Things You Can Do to Stop Pollution,' and an address. 'Write for pollution booklet ... (address on screen and repeated by voice over).' The final panel has the mention of the sponsor, Keep America Beautiful, plus the Ad Council logo.

The ad was a condemnation of modernity. The unnamed chief represented the noble savage, a famous American character. His body and his bearing proclaimed a singular reverence for nature – indeed, he becomes the instrument of nature. His gaze exposed the anti-utopia. He was the witness to what had been done to a once-beautiful America, a land trashed by industry, trade, and so many uncaring, unthinking people. Progress had a terrible cost. His tear expressed the sense of sadness at the loss of beauty, innocence, and reverence. His story conveyed an extraordinary sense of moral outrage at the failure of American society. America had been judged and found wanting.[52]

Chief Iron Eyes Cody was aired many, many times until it sank deep into the popular consciousness: by one estimate, it received $750 million

Figure 9: Chief Iron Eyes Cody. Here is the face that throughout much of the 1970s symbolized a distressed nature. It was a face that seemed to fit the age-old stereotype of the noble savage: a strong, wise, experienced man who, *as an Indian*, instinctively had a deeper understanding and love of the American land-scape than any white person could match. It is an interesting example of a case where someone the culture labelled 'Other' was, for that reason, useful to cast shame upon the dominant public for their misdeeds.

worth of free airtime, and 'several billion viewer impressions,' in its long run of over a decade.[53] No wonder it was well remembered as a favourite, not only among PSAs but among the top advertisements of all time (ranking thirty-eighth out of fifty in one 1997 poll).[54] Whatever the criticisms of the overt message, and there were some, the commercial was so effective that the 'crying Indian' (for his name was not widely known and that anonymity may well have been a blessing) became a symbol and a metaphor of environmental horror. It resonated: for *Chief Iron Eyes Cody* had performed an anger born of a multitude of green movement tracts, news reports, and television images. It gave a special, powerful, moral shape to this anger. The ad had transcended its origins.

4 The Constant Chatter

Consider one sign of the times taken from the referendum experience of Quebec in 1980 when voters were asked to decide (for the first but not the last time) whether their province should become a separate nation. Because Ottawa wished to get out its message about how important the Canadian connection was to the welfare of all Québécois, all manner of government ads filled television screens, sometimes as many as nine in a single broadcast hour.[55] The point was to keep the presence of Canada and of Ottawa before the voters. It would have been hard for an ordinary TV viewer to avoid all this promotional noise.

This was by no means just a Canadian strategy, of course. When governments in the affluent zone grew worried about energy, they endeavoured to market the practice of conservation among the populace, not only through numerous ads and slogans, demonstrations, and pamphlets, but also through taxation. Britain's Electricity Council showed adults in *Child's Play* (1980) how a sweet little girl saved energy and money by playing in the attic (where there was insulation), using a bowl to collect water (rather than running the tap), taking a shower (because a bath was much more wasteful), and so on.[56] Israeli authorities had a television host urge viewers to turn off their lights while a camera focused on the gauges of the electric company, which soon registered a dramatic fall, as part of a 1980 campaign that purportedly reduced electricity consumption by 6 per cent over an eight-month period.[57] Here was public communication in action.

The sponsors of propaganda took the opportunity to represent themselves, their ambitions, their performance, and their allies in a very favourable light. David Paletz and his fellow investigators discovered that America's PSAs persistently proclaimed the integrity of officials, the competence of institutions, and, above all, the stereotype of a helpful state. An especially funny British spot called *Outside Loo* (1977) had a poor bloke struggling to go to the bathroom at night outside in the cold simply because he had not contacted his friendly local government for a state-funded home improvement grant.[58] Corporate advertising was forever telling people how this or that company was bent on serving them, their community, or their nation. Consider one example, *Light On* (1978), from the German firm Osram, the maker of light bulbs: a visual extravaganza of lights entertained the eyes while a song celebrated Osram's conquest of darkness.[59] Even non-profit organizations played this game. Amnesty International established its proprietary claims over the problem of political prisoners in one Danish spot.[60] This was an example of the staging of authority theorized by Jürgen Habermas.

Less and less heard were cries of 'participatory democracy' and all those other radical-sounding shibboleths of the late sixties. Instead of dialogue, there was more monologue: the chattering classes, not the popular classes, held sway. 'A dominant power may legitimate itself by *promoting* beliefs and values congenial to it,' argued Terry Eagleton; '*naturalizing* and *universalizing* such beliefs so as to render them self-evident and apparently inevitable; *denigrating* ideas which might challenge it; *excluding* rival forms of thought, perhaps by some unspoken but systematic logic; and *obscuring* social reality in ways convenient to itself.'[61] These strategies of ideology were all played out in the practices of propaganda, whether in North America or western Europe, wherever authorities endeavoured to recover their grip on public life.

PART III: CAMPAIGNS OF TRUTH

*FOUCAULT: DISCIPLINE

The personal is the political.

Feminist slogan, 1970s

At the moment of his death, the philosopher-historian Michel Foucault (1926–84) was the premier theorist, at least in the western world, of those human sciences he had so often criticized.[1] His books, essays, lectures, interviews, and musings, many published or republished in a variety of editions and collections after he died, had challenged orthodoxies, fostered controversy, and inspired innovation in a range of disciplines.[2] There was a quality of the perverse about his views: he seemed to delight in arguing the contrary. The past became a topsy-turvy realm where that bright march of progress might now be revealed as the sinister expansion of control. He fashioned, with the help of translators and fans, a vocabulary of fabulous concepts that could both excite and puzzle, if not infuriate, because the terminology mixed novelty and familiarity, specificity and ambiguity: 'discontinuities' and 'ruptures,' 'archaeology' and 'genealogy,' 'episteme,' 'discursive formations' and 'non-discursive practices,' 'surveillance' or 'the gaze,' 'the micro-physics of power,' 'truth-telling,' and on and on.[3] The terms and the definitions multiplied as the master shifted his interests and his focus over the years.

That applied especially to Foucault's theory of power (which, strictly speaking, is a misnomer, because he denied he had produced such).[4] The kind of power which fascinated Foucault was active, creative, persistent, and omnipresent. 'What makes power hold good, what makes it accepted, is simply the fact that it doesn't only weigh on us as a force that says no, but that it traverses and produces things, it induces pleasure, forms knowledge, produces discourse,' he once claimed. 'It needs to be considered as a productive network which runs through the whole social body, much more than as a negative instance whose function is repression.'[5] There was no outside to power, no way of escape: 'power is co-extensive with the social body; there are no spaces of primal liberty between the meshes of its network ...'[6] Humanity was in a box.

The crucial brand of power in modern times he initially called 'discipline,' a term made notorious in *Discipline and Punish: The Birth of the Prison,* his best-known book in North America.[7] Here Foucault argued that the prison and similar total institutions, such as the asylum or the military camp, were the initial models for the exercise of power in the nineteenth and twentieth centuries.[8] Foucault found his metaphor and model in Jeremy Bentham's conception of the ideal prison, called the Panopticon, where an unseen guard stationed in a single high place could watch all the prisoners, unbeknown to these objects of his gaze. This process of surveillance rendered its world transparent. The 'new type of power,' he believed, was 'one of the great innovations of bourgeois society.'[9] He was particularly intrigued by the everyday, small tyrannies of a liberal order.[10] He posited the growth of a disciplinary society (but not, he once added, a 'disciplined society')[11] where people were constantly observed and systematically categorized; their bodies constrained, drilled, and directed; their behaviour examined and regulated – where, in short, authorities acted always and in detail on the individual subject. 'The perpetual penality [sic] that traverses all points and supervises every instant in the disciplinary institutions compares, differentiates, hierarchizes, homogenizes, excludes. In short, it *normalizes*.'[12] This power had broken free from its origins, something he called 'the swarming of disciplinary mechanisms,' to enable the expansion of a host of 'flexible methods of control' which gave society a 'carceral texture.'[13]

Later works added to, and sometimes modified, this intensely bleak presentation of the disciplinary society. What was translated as volume one of *The History of Sexuality*[14] talked about the emergence of a system of 'bio-power,' where the techniques of disciplining the body were parallelled by 'a bio-politics of the population.' This bio-power took command of the life processes of the individual and the social body, seeking to define the right to happiness as well as to determine the satisfaction of needs.[15] These notions were extended in a series of lectures Foucault gave at the Collège de France in 1978 and 1979 around the theme of 'governmentality,' in which politics became 'the conduct of conduct' or 'the government of one's self and others.'[16] Crucial to the workings of what he also called 'political rationality' were the twin effects of an 'individualizing' and a 'totalizing' power, where the arts of government were directed at each and at all.[17] Foucault emphasized that authority was exercised not only, or even mainly, by the state, but rather by an 'ensemble formed by the institutions, procedures, analyses and reflections, the calculations and tactics that allow the exercise of this very specific albeit complex form of power.'[18] By now Foucault also argued that the companion to the mechanisms of discipline were 'apparatuses of security' which managed whole populations. Still, if the terminology was more refined, and more exotic, the basic vision of a social tyranny remained.

Meanwhile Foucault had been exploring the relations between structures of power and bodies of knowledge. A social tyranny sponsored as well as expressed a semiotic tyranny. Put simply, the exercise of power always fostered knowledge, and these bodies of knowledge justified authority. Foucault was especially intrigued by one aspect of this relation, the production of truth. 'Each society has its régime of truth, its "general politics" of truth: that is, the types of discourse which it accepts and makes function as true; the mechanisms and instances which enable one to distinguish true and false statements, the means by which each is sanctioned; the techniques and procedures accorded value in the acquisition of truth; the status of those who are charged with saying what counts as true.'[19] Foucault believed that the engines of truth were the institutions and discourses of the sciences, notably medicine and psychiatry (his *bête noir*) but also economics, politics, and, ultimately the whole range of human sciences. He identified the schools and universities, writing, the army, and, of course, the media as the chief agents of the dispersion of truth to the wider population. Success was never guaranteed, however: the manufacture and distribution of truth always remained a source of 'political debate and social confrontation.'[20]

All of which raises the crucial issue of management. One of the outstanding phenomena of the past generation has been the proliferation of managerial discourses of health, welfare, rights, and citizenship. These specialized vocabularies, political narratives, and politicizing rhetorics express the will to power of doctors, lawyers, educators, charity activists, social workers, civil servants, sometimes clerics – indeed, all manner of specialists. Such discourses embody both a sense of mission and a special agenda. A portion of this intellectual energy has found fulfilment in the missives of the governing bureaucracies, in the activities of what has sometimes been called 'the nanny state.' But by no means all. There has been an extraordinary growth across the affluent world of a third sector, neither corporate nor state, made up of non-profit and non-governmental organizations.[21] A small but none the less crucial segment of that vast body – whether Mormons, a heart-and-lung association, Planned Parenthood, a disability rights group, Amnesty International, Mothers Against Drunk Driving, Save the Children, or the Partnership for a Drug-Free America – has sought to exercise power over the ordinary lives of individuals and populations, and for their own good. The project can easily be lauded: the efforts to improve and to civilize the community, whether that means enhancing the public's health or eliminating domestic violence, seem patently worthwhile. Even so, these are also another expression of the constant struggle for dominion, both intellectual and social, this time mounted by a kind of moral élite, or rather groups of bourgeois professionals who seek such a status. In the process, more and more aspects of what was once deemed private, from smoking to family life to charity, have become matters of public notice.

The network of non-profit organizations constitutes yet another material condition for the 'discursive practice' called civic advocacy. Propaganda is by no means the only way in which these voluntary associations have made their mark. The professions have established centres (say, for women's studies or health promotion) and departments (such as public administration), sometimes even faculties (for example, social work), in universities where they can produce and reproduce their brands of knowledge, which in turn have spread into the curricula of public and private schools. The non-profits have tried to shape the news through press conferences, reports, and other forms of what has been called 'media advocacy.'[22] They have lobbied governments to secure new legislation or strengthen existing regulations: indeed, they have won important allies within the bureaucracies of the welfare states, some part of which the expert professions have staffed, which then advance their special agendas. They have forged links with corporations to win funds and jointly sponsor projects. They have established clinics, sponsored talks, sent out canvassers, organized marches and boycotts, built community networks, and so on, to achieve a direct contact with the public. But the most visible techniques were and are the vigorous and insistent campaigns of truth, sometimes assisted or even orchestrated by the state, sometimes aided by corporations, used to demonize, to celebrate, and to beatify; to manufacture villains, heroes, and victims; and, always, to champion a proliferating array of public goods. Truths have become commodities made by a few organizations, competing in a general marketplace, and sold to a huge collection of consumer-citizens.

The process of packaging transformed the nature of the message: the makers of propaganda boasted their own type of truth-telling, which reshaped rhetoric and art into moral spectacle. The archive of social advertising is overstuffed with tales of excess and indulgence, stories of sin and evil, melodramas of seduction or resistance, promises of redemption, and threats of retribution. Here are some of the best examples of propaganda as sermon: the moral pose seemed necessary to justify the intrusion into people's personal lives. The one-minute commercial – even more, its thirty-second offspring – might be much too short to deliver a carefully reasoned argument to viewers, whether or not it adopted the guise of the editorial or the news story. But that time was (and is) more than sufficient to deliver evidence of right thinking and right feeling and right doing to these same viewers. In particular, the social ad could excel at that moral game of honouring and dishonouring, itself a variation of the power of naming. Television advertising would present objects of pity or empathy, concrete instances of sin, villains as well as heroes, spectres that provoke anxiety or solutions that evoke awe, examples that occasion guilt or shame, altogether turning the ordinary world into a stage where good struggled with evil. The appeal was to the emotions, especially fear, as well as to the intellect. Here we have an instance of both universalizing and marketing: translating the agenda of a group or coalition not only into a species of information that has much wider appeal but also into a collection of stimuli that promises a greater impact. The moral translation, in short, could better serve the needs of potential managers than any straightforward presentation of the pros and cons of a policy or practice, especially in a day and age when the attention span of the public has contracted.

The advertising industry was eager to assist. No awards collection of advertising art seemed complete without examples of stunning commercials made to assist a good cause. 'You work on a lot of advertising to make somebody a little richer. Public service is a chance to make a difference,' declared Kirk Souder, art director at David Deutsch Associates, New York.[23] The rhetoric of public service was such a commonplace that it might be taken as the admakers' gospel of civil responsibility. By the late 1980s, Ruth Wooden, president of the Advertising Council, would claim this idealism and voluntarism as proof that the sixties generation had finally come of age and secured control of advertising agencies.[24] Doing good was a form of compensation, a source of professional self-esteem, proof of social worth. 'If anybody has an image of the marketing and advertising community as being people who don't care about social issues,' claimed one Canadian anti-drug crusader, 'that's a total myth.'[25] At times the zeal of this community seemed motivated more by a definite self-interest: when, for example, America's National Association of Broadcasters began to work closely with advocacy associations on an anti-drinking and driving campaign to forestall congressional action against beer and wine advertising.[26] But, whatever the motive, the advertising industry in the 1980s and 1990s did lend its apparatus and its skills to the task of civic advocacy on behalf of a new assortment of truths.

Foucault never paid much attention to propaganda as such. The operations he wrote about were the time-table, drills, the examination, the medical gaze, panoptical systems, all of which might serve to construct docile bodies. Yet the propaganda of his times did amount to an attempt to realize discipline by other means.[27] 'Discipline "makes" individuals,' according to Foucault; 'it is the specific technique of a power that regards individuals both as objects and as instruments of its exercise.'[28] A rapidly expanding wave of social advertising defined the individual as a citizen who consumed, and populations as markets that bought, public goods. It, too, sought the construction of 'docile bodies,' programmed to suit the agendas embedded in assorted languages of management.[29] In practice, it became – more properly, social marketing became – a progenitor of public neuroses that sought to control the behaviours of populations.

4

Healthy Bodies, or the New Paranoia

Consider this litany of alarm. Smoking now kills more than '3 million people per year.' Since 1950 cigarettes and the like have brought death to 'more than 60 million people in developed countries alone.' Tobacco use produces 'a global net loss of U.S.$ 200 billion per year.' In three or four decades the death rate should hit '10 million per year.' These estimates came from a Web site of the World Health Organization (WHO) devoted to promoting World No-Tobacco Day, 31 May 1997. They justified the director's declaring 'a global public health emergency,' and calling on governments and activists worldwide to take swift action.

Typically, the arithmetic of truth generates these big numbers: missing is the logic or the evidence that might serve to validate the scare. Why bother?: a special calculus of peril serves to create the desired sensation. Certainly, the WHO site did not offer anything so mundane as proof. WHO relied on its own credibility plus decades of anti-smoking propaganda to persuade. Indeed, the vilification of the tobacco companies, now widely regarded in the affluent world as 'merchants of death,' must count as a cardinal success of health advocacy. But the tobacco industry was by no means the only target of the discourse of public health.[1]

1 The Return of Public Health

In retrospect, the release of the report of the Surgeon General's Advisory Committee on Smoking and Health on 11 January 1964 marked a turning point. It launched a major revival of the public health crusade, first in the United States but soon elsewhere in the affluent zone. A sign of the new times was the arrival during the mid- and late 1970s of a body of knowledge called 'health promotion,' soon to prove a powerful engine of dogma and truth.[2] The discourse explicitly challenged the prevailing 'biomedicine' because it focused attention on the social roots of health. The aim of health promotion was to forestall illness and death by ensuring that individuals and communities lived in a healthy fashion. The approach first found official expression in Canada in the Lalonde Report (1974), named after the then minister of Health and Welfare, a report that was initiated in part by a desire to slow the escalating costs of health care in Canada's medicare system. In 1979 came the American equivalent, the surgeon general's *Healthy People*, which ascribed about half of the nation's deaths to 'culturally sustained behavioral and life-style factors.'[3] Apparently, Great Britain was a laggard, not getting into 'the prevention business' until well into the next decade.[4] By then a succession of papers, meetings, symposia, an international conference (in 1986, in Ottawa, co-sponsored by the federal government, WHO, and the Canadian Public Health Association), even a world charter had given health promotion intellectual momentum. Advocates now talked about the need for a 'healthy public policy,' in which every law, every action of government, would be judged according to the imperatives of health. Such grandiose dreams were typical of the managerial discourses.

The proper meanings of health promotion were always contested. A radical element believed that health promotion must tackle problems of poverty and housing, perhaps seek out capitalist villains, work with social movements such as feminism or environmentalism, even 'empower' ordinary people to determine their own fate.[5] That proved a fruitful source of criticism of the many crusades of the new public health. For, in practice, health promotion was only occasionally democratic. The definition which prevailed, at least outside academe, focused instead on getting ordinary people to change their unfortunate ways. The Lalonde Report described health promotion as a 'strategy aimed at informing, influencing and assisting both individuals and organizations so that they will accept more responsibility and be more active in matters affecting mental and physical health.' According to one government source in the United States, health promotion 'begins with people who are basically healthy and seeks the development of community and individual measures which can help them to develop lifestyles that can maintain and enhance their state of well being.'[6]

That emphasized the role of specialists, whether inside or outside of government, who would guide, direct, and control. No wonder the people who pushed health promotion in Ontario, the wealthiest of Canada's provinces, were 'public health workers, educators, social workers, civil servants, community developers, social scientists, and health administrators.'[7] They constituted a network of professionals whose very jobs encouraged a 'social activism' to realize a shared vision of a healthy land. These 'professional social reformers' gained status and authority as instruments of public health. This mix of altruism and self-interest – or, rather, the predominance of a particular agenda – was another common feature of the managerial discourses.

The mainstream definition of health promotion also encouraged an approach which critics soon labelled 'blaming the victim.' The refashioned public health was both the child and the scold of affluence. It was born in wealthy societies, rich in medical services and health professionals, where the increased longevity of the populace subjected people to the threat of disability and death from an avoidable range of accidents, at home or at work, and non-infectious diseases such as heart trouble or lung cancer. The surgeon general's report on smoking, followed by the initial anti-drug craze, raised political questions about the pleasures of affluence. The wave of safety issues in the 1970s – workplace safety, fire prevention, seat-belts, impaired driving – highlighted the wrong choices people made in their daily lives. During the late 1980s the general panic over AIDS (which, unlike most other diseases of note, was infectious) focused critical attention on promiscuity, the celebration of sexual excess. None of these causes – or 'wars,' as the crusaders were wont to describe them[8] – were ever completed, ever won, because there was always a new generation of potential victims. Saving the kids from ills like teenage pregnancy, drug and alcohol abuse, and smoking became a great cry of the 1990s, especially in the United States. Indeed, the health crusade promised to go global: by the late 1990s WHO was warning of a future catastrophe because the advance of life expectancy meant that the people of the developing countries would suffer the same kinds of ills as the citizens of the affluent world. The answer everywhere and always was to force a change in lifestyle.

That required not only the continuous surveillance of the habits of the population by health professionals (Foucault's panoptics); it demanded re-education so that individuals would police their own behaviour (promotional signs). Enter social marketing. Consider the case of Canada's Health Promotion Directorate.[9] By the early 1990s it was an enthusiastic proponent of the so-called neutral methodology of marketing, so enthusiastic that its leading professionals were eager to tout the virtues of this technology throughout the world.[10] The directorate was responsible for two major campaigns, the anti-smoking 'Break Free' and the anti-drug 'Really Me,' both aimed primarily at adolescents.[11] These campaigns relied upon the assistance of many other organizations: provincial addiction agencies, the Non-Smokers' Rights Association, the Canadian Medical Association, even a corporate body such as the Concerned Children's Advertisers Association. The campaigns secured a host of 'private-sector partners,' companies such as Pepsi-Cola Canada or Marvel Comics or the Canadian Broadcasting Corporation, about eighty firms in all, which contributed the equivalent of roughly $40 million over a five-year period (1987–92). Whereas society's 'heavies' were well represented, the target population was not. Instead, the teens were classified: the directorate commissioned a special psychographic survey which divided the youth market into seven strangely named tribes: 'Thank Goodness It's Friday' (the self-indulgent), 'Passive Luddites' (the down-to-earth), 'Big City Independents' (the self-interested, success-oriented), and so on. Supposedly, this bizarre typology enabled the directorate to better tailor its messages to the differing attitudes and behaviours of teens.

Scads of booklets went out, and anti-smoking and anti-drug videos were distributed, if less lavishly; displays and contests sought to involve families; a Spiderman comic book warned of the evils of drugs; there were national non-smoking weeks; and special broadcasts worked to boost teen self-esteem. But the key was ads, and especially television commercials, which were needed to reach teenagers and their parents and to heighten public consciousness of the evils of tobacco and drugs. The commercials adopted a particular style then common in made-in-Canada consumer advertising. Because the officials believed scare did not work, the ads were gentle, upbeat, reasonable – soft sells of 'positive lifestyles.'[12] In 1992 the directorate employed national tracking surveys to show that youth was aware of all this activity. These findings it linked to data about attitudes (such as how many teens, and in what tribes, agreed that 'doing drugs is cool') and behaviours (such as that 28 per cent of passive Luddites smoked 'daily, at least on occasion'). How sophisticated it all seemed.

In fact one of the campaigns, 'Break Free,' soon embarrassed the government. According to the *Globe and Mail* (2 March 1994), surveys showed that the campaign only fostered contempt. 'Teenagers see the commercials as an example of the government "talking down to them ... as if they were gullible, ill-informed and naive ..."' The health minister terminated 'Break Free.' Yet she and her colleagues remained committed to the mechanism of advertising because the rise of smuggling had forced a dramatic decrease in the tax per package of cigarettes. A few months later a new advertising campaign, much more hard-hitting than before, was in the works, designed to reach all sorts of Canadians, especially young women.[13]

2 Fighting Indulgence

Health advocacy was always a difficult task. Whatever the cause, it had to fight against the main currents of popular culture. 'Television is the pusher,' claimed Nicholas Johnson, a onetime Federal Communications Commission (FCC) member, in 1974.[14] The kind of health American TV favoured was clearly biomedical, where the heroic doctor, assisted by the best machines and the right drugs, was the source of good care.[15] Television entertainment glamorized sexual play, endorsed drinking, and treated food as fun. Witness the provocative headline of one Planned Parenthood ad: 'They did it 9,000 times on TV last year. How come nobody got pregnant?'[16] Advertising on television and elsewhere was the worst offender, because marketing campaigns fostered drinking, wild driving, smoking, drug dependence, overeating, poor nutrition, and above all the panacea of consumption.[17] The mismatch of resources was ludicrous: the *Guardian* (7 April 1986) pointed out that the alcohol and tobacco industries each had roughly £100 million a year to spend on promoting bad habits, while the Department of Transport could assign only £3.9 million to the drink/drive campaign and the Health Education Council £1.75 million to anti-smoking. The self-righteous tone of the outcry was itself evidence of how sour the attitude of health promoters was towards the prevailing mass culture.

The crucial weapons, by necessity if not choice, were televised PSAs, since they could reach a very large audience, and an audience which might otherwise avoid any health message.[18] But there were always problems with the PSA. The PSA was usually an unpaid advertisement, depending on the goodwill of the broadcaster to receive exposure and placement. The health promoter was more likely to meet with success than rivals, at least in the United States: one survey in 1973 discovered that more than four in ten PSAs broadcast dealt with health or safety issues, presumably because their importance to the ordinary viewer was obvious.[19] But PSAs might run anywhere on the schedule, to fill what unsold time a station had, so they could air in the late evening and early morning, provoking the comment that the acronym really stood for 'people sound asleep.'[20] The advocacy was subject to censorship by networks and stations, a problem that particularly affected efforts to market contraceptives: Britain's Independent Broadcasting Authority banned one PSA in 1983 because it 'might appear to condone promiscuity.'[21] Even when the PSA ran at a decent time, it was usually buried in a cluster of consumer ads whose overall message touted exactly that indulgence and excess which health advocacy abhorred.

The most serious problem became a time shortage, at least in the United States. First a PSA overload emerged at the end of the 1980s, when the blitz of the Partnership for a Drug-Free America (PDFA) stole time away from other crusades.[22] That receded. But by the mid-1990s the American networks were replacing PSAs in prime time with more self-promotion, sometimes linking an entertainment star to a worthy cause, much to the disgust of the Advertising Council.[23] The anti-smoking forces in California avoided this problem because the state government used paid media (financed by an extra tax on a pack of cigarettes) to battle the tobacco industry. Elsewhere, governments typically purchased some of their time and space: in 1995 Health Canada sought one bonus spot in return for one paid spot for its anti-smoking effort.

In style, the PSA also had problems. The public goods that advocates might push, such as seat-belts, smoke alarms, exercise, or condoms, lacked appeal and pizzazz. In 1989, for example, the Comité Français d'Education pour la Santé felt it necessary to sponsor a series of television shorts (a mere eight seconds long) to mock male worries about the condom: such as that women did not like it or it was difficult to put on or it ruined sex.[24] In fact, very often advocates lacked any tangible public good other than the overall boons of a healthy body and cheap health. That drove them to fashion 'public bads,' and so to moralize about the risks involved in indulgence and excess. 'We are approaching the problem posed by the $110 billion illegal drug industry from a marketing point of view,' claimed Tom Hedrick, the man in charge of the PDFA. 'What we're doing is competing with drug pushers for market share of non-users.'[25] Health promoters were unselling, or demarketing; that is, they trashed private goods such as cigarettes, recreational drugs, alcohol, and rich foods – toxins all of them – and denounced pursuits such as smoking, getting high, or being promiscuous that brought people much pleasure. Practise restraint. Limit indulgence. Avoid excess. Shun vice. It is little wonder that the health advocate came across as a puritan.

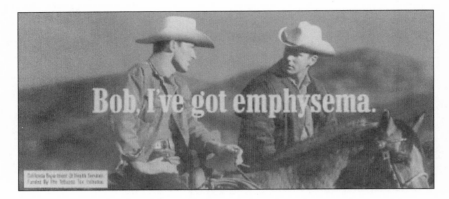

Figure 10: Mocking Stereotypes. Even health ads can indulge in a bit of black humour. This outdoor board for the California Department of Health Services in the late 1990s is an excellent example of the use of satire in social advertising. It was part of the state's ongoing war against smoking and the tobacco industry. The ad recalls the famed campaigns for Marlboro cigarettes once mounted by Philip Morris. Here are two cowboys, out on the range in that legendary west where men roamed free and proud. Except one of the cowboys now turns to his compatriot and admits, 'Bob, I've got emphysema,' or, 'I miss my lung, Bob.' The cowboy now speaks the 'truths' of anti-smoking.

Time and again admakers tried to avoid the stigma of preaching, even though that is exactly what they were doing, because of the worry that people would discount the message. For this reason, creatives sought to appropriate the idiom and the images of the target, most especially youth. So New York's Ketchum Communications employed 'devilishly attractive models, reverse psychology and even rap music to cut through the aura of permissiveness that pervades today's pop society' in one campaign to reduce teenage pregnancy. In 1992 the Ontario Ministry of Health used 'lifestyle images of gays and sexually active teenagers' plus the slogan 'No glove, no love' to push condoms. More vulgar was a French slogan, 'Condoms: F... AIDS,' since the word 'fuck' was part of 'the youth idiom.' Too often, the attempts at plain speaking, and especially at youth talk, seemed just plain phoney.[26]

Sometimes the ingenious admaker even tried a weird variant on the sexual sell. Was it the intention of the Asociación Española Contra el Cancer to emulate the eye of the peeping Tom when it sponsored *Dos*

Pechos (1994) in a Spanish campaign against breast cancer? The commercial was full of shots of young, attractive, and startled women who struggled to cover their bare breasts revealed by the prying camera. 'If you feel ashamed about showing your two breasts,' asserted the voice-over, 'imagine showing just one?' Or consider *Stay* (1988), a spot from Britain's Health Education Authority in the campaign against AIDS. The setting was a young woman's residence, just after the couple had completed dinner. What comes next?: sex, or at least the promise of sex. The camera suddenly acts out the male gaze, displaying the women as a sexual object: we see a close-up of her legs revealed by the miniskirt, of her cleavage, and of her welcoming lips. This promise of passion is cast as dangerous because, as the voice-over explains, the brief moment of pleasure can bring infection and eventual death if you do not practise safe sex. What justified such presentations was the conversion of the sexual display into a moral spectacle.[27]

There was a prurient appeal endemic in the health spectacles. These promotional signs hailed the viewer as a voyeur who was engaged by the presence of sin and evil, suffering and tragedy. The taste for a dark aesthetic lay at the heart of the experience. According to one British source, 'research has shown that young men want to see a great, violent crack-up in drink and drive advertising.'[28] Scare and fear were the mainstay of health advocacy, even though there was considerable debate over their impact. The most effective scare required that people also receive a promise of resolution, a practical remedy that would reduce or eliminate the threat. In assorted experiments fear worked on different kinds of people in very different ways: it might foster action or provoke flight, and that depended not only on such demographic factors as sex or age, income or education, but also on the psychographic profile of the subject, issues of mood, self-esteem, and so on.[29] Too much scare could so upset people that they either avoided the message or hardened their attitudes. It might even boomerang: in one Canadian test of a so-called 'tombstone' ad, a smoker claimed that the anxiety it caused was so intense that she 'just wanted to have a cigarette.'[30] On a grander scale, according to the *Guardian* (5 June 1989), the flood of 'health scares' over AIDS, smoking and cancer, allergies, and high blood pressure had 'prompted the British nation into defiance.' But a lighter touch usually meant a dose of black humour. Shock and fright, however packaged, so often prevailed because, sponsors hoped, they could win attention and activate self-interest. The key to success was the overall quality of the performance.

The Driver   The Sweetheart

The Tragedy

Figure 11: Scenes from *Country People Die*

3 Impure Lives

Three stock characters reappear across the many performances of health advocacy. These represent people whose moral compass has gone awry. You will find other personae – even, for example, the occasional saint. But the stories of the sinner, the monster, and the villain serve as object lessons and warnings of how we, too, may become victims. They are 'distillates,' what this brand of advertising collects from the broad span of human experience.

a) Sinners

Country People Die ... (Safe Driving, Australia, 1994): It's nighttime and four youth are in a car, chatting happily – a recipe for disaster. The driver, Mark, takes his eyes off the road to kiss his sweetheart, who has just said she'd rather stay in the country with him than work in Melbourne. The car wanders out of its lane, Mark swerves to avoid a threatened head-on collision, the car goes off the road and rolls, though it turns right side up. Everyone seems okay, except for the sweetheart who's unconscious and has a thin stream of blood running down the side of her face. Then the horror: the car catches on fire, we briefly (and mercifully) hear only some of their screams, ended by an explosion of flame. Cut to the morning where two farmers are talking about the accident, which Jake blames on city kids. Except it's not city kids. Suddenly Jake's wife calls him. She weeps: 'It's Mark, there was an accident ...' Cut to a black screen and white lettering: '7 out of 10 people who die on country roads live in the country.' 'Why us?' she moans. Cut to a second screen: 'Country people die on country roads.'[31]

Most especially *young* people die. The ad expressed one of the persistent themes of health advocacy, namely that youth is a time of danger – in marketing terms, a problem that requires a series of solutions. Whether the issue be drugs or cigarettes, AIDS or alcohol, teens and young adults are more often featured as victims than any other age group. Kids are not yet disciplined, they are prone to rebel and to experiment, and they are too confident of their own immortality. Health propaganda sought to smash this illusion of invulnerability by showing how easily the body of youth could be maimed or wasted.

Country People Die ... was sponsored by the Transport Accident Commission, an Australian agency that had won international notoriety for its species of terrorist advertising on behalf of road safety. By the mid-1990s its example had begun to influence practise in Ontario, for instance.[32] In fact, the slice of life had always seemed especially well-suited to safety commercials because it emulated the style of action/adventure drama, except for the tragic ending. Usually the ad started with shots of the ordinary: say, a couple escaping the city (U.K., *Honeymoon,* 1972) or a mother driving to pick up her son at school (France, *Use Your Seat Belt,* 1985). Inevitably there came a moment of inattention, perhaps an act of carelessness (like smoking in bed). Then disaster struck: the accident, fire, sometimes the blood and gore, and the anguish. A South Korean ad, called *The Evil Effects of Drinking* (1990), started at the scene of death and worked back to its source, drinking in a bar. The final warning?: 'THE FILM CAN BE REVERSED, DEATH CANNOT.' The overall message?: this was a perilous world where harm and death were ever-present.[33]

The motif of vigilance was central to anti-AIDS campaigns. No one could see whether a person was infected unless the victim was in the final stages of the illness. So West Germany's Ministry of the Family alerted citizens to their peril with *Prevention* (1988), which followed poor Thomas through four sexual adventures until he ended up barely moving in a hospital bed, complete with a nurse at his side. Sometimes the creatives tried to emphasize the threat by giving HIV a visible mark, a red dot in one British spot (*Tracing*, 1988), a purple froth in two American ads (*Car* and *Roof*, 1990). One Italian nightmare, ironically named *Love* (1987), used darkened shots, close-ups of faces and hands, and a rising crescendo of music to suggest two people making love, with a sudden reversal at the end when the music turns sinister, a cold blue infects the scene, and the woman's face and the man's head take on aspects of a skull. The purpose of these spots was to show sex as dangerous. It was a classic attempt at repositioning, to turn what was once a private good into a social risk.[34]

Anti-smoking promoters had a liking for testimonials from past sinners. In the mid-1980s the famed actor Yul Brynner was made to speak from the grave: he did a spot for the American Cancer Society that was all the more poignant because it aired after he had died from cancer. The Massachusetts Department of Public Health sponsored two similar ads about a decade later. In one, *Truth: Sackman*, a handsome woman with a ruined voice explained how as a model in TV ads she had sold cigarettes, but now as a victim she warned of cancer. In the other, *Truth: Reynolds*, the grandson of R.J. Reynolds informed viewers, 'the last thing the tobacco companies want is for you to know how many poisonous chemicals there are in cigarettes.' Sackman and Reynolds hoped to redeem themselves, or, in Reynolds's case, his family. We are in the presence of truth-tellers, and their warnings carry conviction, a moral weight.[35]

None of these efforts compared with the sad spectacle of an emaciated heroin addict in the PDFA commercial *Lenny* (1996). This was an extended interview (two and a half minutes in one version) in which we see and hear clips of Lenny telling us about himself, how he started, what he feels, what he has suffered (vomiting, sores), what he hopes (success in the new year – 'And I'll bet my life on it'). Clearly, the ad was a collection of the best bits, meaning the more gruesome and the most poignant, excerpted from at least one long session with the addict – yet another 'distillation.' Lenny was cast as the classic loser, one of the most despised creatures in American society. At the end comes the unsell: 'Heroin. Want Some?' The award-winning ad was a horrible invasion of privacy, demonstrating in a way that seemingly could not be faked just what drugs will do to the human being.[36]

b) Monsters

Smoking Baby (American Cancer Society, 1984):[37]

Video	Audio	Text
This is one continuous shot. The image of a foetus moves into focus from the left side, its body coloured a distressing orange. Its thumb is in its mouth. It looks down.	An organ playing vaguely sacred music.	
The camera moves out and away, as the foetus removes its thumb and slowly turns away from the viewer. Then we see in its tiny hand a long cylindrical object, which it now draws towards its mouth.	The sound of a heart beat that will continue throughout the performance.	Female voice-over: 'Would you give a cigarette to your unborn child?'
The whole foetus is now on display (even the umbilical cord is shown), covered by a luminous outline of a blue egg shell, presumably representing the womb. The infant-to-be puts the cigarette in its mouth and proceeds to suck. Its head draws back and a little puff of smoke is released from its mouth.	The music changes slightly, moving from the sacred to the sinister.	'You do. Every time you smoke while you are pregnant.'
The screen goes to black. On screen comes the title 'American Cancer Society,' plus its logo.	Now the music has gone but the heart beat remains.	'Pregnant mothers: Please ... don't smoke.'

The producer of *Smoking Baby*, Joseph Vogt, exclaimed, 'This is what America needs right now – to be punched in the gut with this stuff.'[38] Neither NBC nor CBS agreed: both networks refused to run the PSA, the first because the spot was 'potentially offensive' and the second because it was 'too graphic.' Indeed *Smoking Baby* did offend pro-choice activists because it depicted a foetus as a completed infant.[39] But it also impressed: Britain's Anti-Smoking Quitline ran its own version of *Smoking*

Baby (1992), in which the swollen belly of a naked smoker moves in and out, expelling the smoke from her naval.[40] Yet another version appeared a few years later, this from AvMed, a Florida-based health-management organization (HMO), which featured a baby compelled to smoke a cigarette attached to the nipple of a feeding bottle. Dramatic, graphic, revolting, whatever the label, the image of the puffing baby was transgressive: it violated cultural assumptions about the purity and innocence of new life. At one level, the original *Smoking Baby* conveyed the simple message that the nicotine 'you' consume, or, rather, that the future mother consumes, will contaminate her unborn child. But at another level, the spot worked because it showed how a smoking mother betrayed her infant, how she poisoned the baby she should love.

Perversions, or monsters, make for striking images. They stun with their wrongness. They immediately evoke the moral faculties, because they call to mind what is right and proper. The viewer is expected to be shocked, perhaps disgusted, so that he or she will be more receptive to the unsell. The motif of transgression could be played out in all sorts of ways. An emaciated, slightly crippled, and ugly male witch constantly blows smoke into the crib he is tending in what must be a nursery out of hell (U.K., *Baby*, 1985). A young man, the victim of a car accident, or rather of drinking and driving, is reduced to a baby who must be fed by his grieving mother (U.K., *Dave*, 1995). A father offends all expectations by declaring how happy he was when his son, the drug addict, died (Norway, *The Dive*, 1993). A user is represented as a puppet, 'moving at the rhythm commanded by drugs,' one of many reflections on the theme of enslavement (Spain, *Marionette*, 1985).[41]

One spectacular variation was the notorious *Grim Reaper* (1988), which sought to fuel the anti-AIDS hysteria in Australia. The ad deployed the metaphor of a gigantic bowling alley where grisly spectres of death rolled balls at collections of human beings, singles and families, women and children.[42] Critics charged that the images would terrorize children.[43] A test of this little horror, in the bland language of academe, 'produced significantly more tension and energy, and less calmness and fatigue,' among a collection of American college students than did a more reasoned discussion of condoms.[44] The great advantage of the striking image was its ability to break through all the ad clutter on TV. Nightmares like the *Grim Reaper* were bound to get noticed. And their very nastiness 'signalled' the enormity of the problem.

Sometimes creatives tried to drive home the message by actually showing how horrible the transformation was. In *Quick Time* (Ontario Ministry of Health, 1993) an attractive teen takes one puff and ... morphs: her face immediately ages, her eyes sink inwards, her skin bags, her hair becomes straight and stringy, and she emerges as an old coughing hag. We are in the presence of black magic of the postmodern variety, where a toxic agent like smoke writes its effects directly and immediately upon the face of the victim. The theme of decay was a natural for ads directed against the common vices of tobacco, alcohol, and drugs. Particularly vivid was an Argentine commercial, *One Is No One* (1986), where the various senses of an adult, male addict are shut down: we actually see the eyes, the nose, and the mouth close over and his hand become rigid. The PDFA offered *Faces* (1987) in which the beautiful face of a blonde teenager is ravaged by her devotion to drugs (her eyes turn a sickly blue) before she dies. Earlier, in 1985, two British spots, *Control* and *Dummy*, had graphically displayed the way a young man and woman moved from a state of assurance, even cockiness, to a condition of illness and suffering, all because they used heroin.[45] A related set of posters were styled according to 'the idiom of a cosmetics ad.' Ironically, they proved too attractive to some youth, who stole them to decorate their walls: the wasted look of the addicts appealed to their aesthetic sensibilities.[46]

These are, at bottom, tales of retribution which bear some resemblance to the story of Eve and the apple: the victims choose their own fate when they sample the forbidden fruit. Their sins are visited on their bodies, which become the visible proof of corruption. This scenario replays that motif of defilement that was so pronounced in *Animal* and the other efforts of the first 'war on drugs.'

c) Villains

The Doll (Anti-drug, U.K., 1987): The spot shows a young woman seduced, enslaved, and eventually killed by drugs, all in sixty seconds. Teenage women are not the only pawns of ill fate in the moral theatre of health advocacy – but it is surprising how often they figure as the archetypal victims of one vice or another. We first meet Liz putting on make-up in her room before joining a party. She discovers her boyfriend, Paul, smoking heroin with a bunch of other adolescents. He convinces her to try – 'Trust me,' he says. Then, rapidly, she gets hooked, her looks suffer, and she ends up sharing a dirty needle, again with Paul. Throughout, these events have been visited upon her doll, a small touch of reverse voodoo. At the end a needle pierces the doll's heart, and the doll falls to the floor. On-screen: 'SMACK ISN'T WORTH IT.'[47]

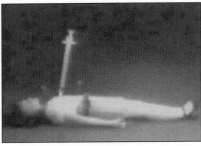

One Victim   *The Pusher*

Figure 12: Scenes from *The Doll*

This 'seduction most vile' shifts some of the blame onto the pusher. Now we are in the presence of evil, but a hidden evil which is commonly shown with a benign or charming face – like Paul's. For the pusher must act in a way which saps our moral resolve. America's anti-drug advocates have run a couple of these ads about pushers: a smooth-talking Michael J. Fox (*Bad Guy / Good Guy,* 1988) who tries to con viewers, or an older youth (*Tricks of the Trade,* 1987) who trains a young teen how to seduce his peers.[48] Anti-smoking ads have occasionally blamed parents, whose example teaches kids to smoke or, more recently, whose habit poisons children with secondhand smoke.[49]

The true 'demon' of the 1990s was the tobacco executive, however. The process of vilification began when California launched its Tobacco Control Program in 1989, a key aim of which was to 'expose the predatory aspect of the profit-driven tobacco business and reposition tobacco marketers as part of the problem.'[50] In 1990, *Industry Spokesmen* caused an enormous fuss by portraying a collection of suits engaged in a conspiracy against the well-being of Americans. ('Every day, 2,000 Americans drop smoking, another 1,100 also quit. Actually, technically, they die. That means this business needs 3,000 fresh new volunteers every day.')[51] A later effort in 1994 used actual footage of company leaders testifying before a congressional committee, executives who, the ad insinuated, had lied about the addictive effects of tobacco in the past and now denied the harmful effects of secondhand smoke. The R.J. Reynolds Tobacco Company threatened libel action against television stations running the spot, which was eventually withdrawn by order of Governor Pete Wilson.[52] To little avail. Others took up the same cause. *Happy*

Birthday, made for the Massachusetts Department of Public Health, won a Clio Award in 1996 for its depiction of a victim who sang 'Happy Birthday' to the tobacco companies through the hole in his throat. These and similar spots finally realized a purpose of the radical wing of health promotion: they identified big business as the source of mass death. The anti-smoking campaign now emphasized how big tobacco had targeted kids, thus exploiting the renewed panic over children which had caught hold of public thinking in the mid-1990s.[53]

4 The Question of Effects

Over the years much energy has been spent to determine the effects of health advocacy. All too often the answers have been meagre. Social science did not offer much solace, though some sponsors invested heavily in polls and surveys that generated lots of figures. Much favoured were statistics of advertising recall, aided or unaided, sometimes linked to a survey of attitudes or behaviours. The 'Country People Die on Country Roads' campaign, for example, registered a 90 per cent recall among rural drivers. But the fact that recall stats were also used to demonstrate the effectiveness of Canada's 'Break Free' campaign suggests how pointless the enterprise could be.[54] In a few cases sponsors could employ the same sort of measures used by commercial marketers. The Comité Français d'Education pour la Santé reported that because of an assault on drinking (in 1985) 'wine and beer consumption fell by 10% in the year following the campaign, while mineral water sales took off.'[55] Similarly, the Centers for Disease Control asserted (in 1988) that calls to their AIDS hotline had risen from 20,000 a month to 190,000 over the course of the campaign.[56] Or a sponsor might take credit for what was really a social trend: an executive of Canada's famous Participaction project noted how the percentage of people 'into fitness and health' had risen from 5 per cent in 1971 to 25 per cent or 30 per cent twenty years later.[57] Then there were self-reports. Admaker Mike Lublow, creator of the 'Learn Not to Burn' campaign, proudly recounted the kudos he had received from around the world because the information his campaign dispensed had saved lives.[58] The most outlandish, though, were PDFA boasts: 'We can legitimately take some of the credit for the 25% decline in illicit drug usage since our program was launched.'[59] What one journalist called 'phantom numbers,' based on dubious estimates and wishful thinking, were so prevalent in the war on drugs that few claims could be easily verified.[60]

Still, in the 1970s, two assaults on heart disease, Stanford's project and the Finnish North Karelia experiment, demonstrated that heavy media promotion could bring about significant improvements in individual attitudes and actions.[61] The later Quit for Life efforts in Australia showed some decline in smoking as a result of media pressure, especially when supplemented with community activities.[62] During the early 1990s, the combination of police surveillance and heavy advertising employed by the Transport Accident Commission was credited with dramatically reducing the toll of death and injury on the roads of Victoria, Australia.[63] One of the few, very clear examples of propaganda's ability to change behaviour in the desired direction came out of the California experience. An intensive anti-tobacco campaign, at a total cost of $28 million, was launched in April 1990 using television and radio and, shortly afterwards, print and billboards as well. The campaign lasted roughly a year before tailing off and disappearing in June 1991. Although per-capita consumption of cigarettes had been increasing prior to April 1990, these figures fell by over 12 per cent in the next year, and then levelled off. That was paralleled by a considerable increase in the numbers of smokers who made a 'quit attempt' during the early months of the campaign. No other aspect of the Tobacco Control Program was up and running in this time period. In short, health advocacy worked its promised magic here.[64]

But there has been much more evidence of apparent failure, or only temporary success. A close study showed that the seat-belt campaigns of the early and mid-1970s in the United States were, as one critic put it, a definite 'flop.'[65] Britain's famous 'Clunk, Click' campaign of the mid-1970s did increase the use of seat-belts, though when the 'propaganda pressure' went off, public concern and public usage waned as well – 'legislation was the only answer.'[66] An 'anatomy' of a public information project directed against drinking and driving discovered little change in behaviour.[67] Anti-smoking and anti-drug efforts had a boomerang effect on certain populations, fostering defiance and hardening attitudes or bestowing a dark glamour on the vices that was especially appealing to youth.[68] The 'Just Say No' projects of the late 1980s against drugs and, in some measure, against early pregnancy and against AIDS became the target of all sorts of criticisms because they had no lasting effect on the conduct of their intended audiences. Once the 'media weight' behind the PDFA campaign waned, so too did its ability to affect the attitudes of young people. Media and politicians were much exercised in the mid-1990s over the fact that American teens were returning to drugs (though by no means at the rate of the early 1970s). After all the moralizing, teenage pregnancy remained extremely common in the United States: close to a million cases a year. The extraordinary efforts to banish unsafe sex from the gay community in the United States ultimately failed. Many, especially younger homosexuals, just were not listening to the anti-AIDS messages: a 1991 study estimated that 'more than half of the nation's 20-year-old gay men will contract HIV during their lifetime, if current trends continue.'[69]

Such findings led critics to dismiss the whole thrust of health promotion, and especially health advocacy. Writing in the *New York Times Magazine* (15 September 1996), Jesse Green quoted some of these sceptics in 'Flirting with Suicide':

Lloyd Johnston, program director, Institute for Social Research, University of Michigan: 'These things can become jokes very quickly. Remember the fried egg campaign? *This is your brain. This is your brain on drugs.* It was only a slogan, and the best you can say for a slogan is that it may work for a little while. This one did. It definitely spoke to kids, at least for a time; then it lost its persuasive power and maybe even became negative. In a way, the more successful these things are, the shorter their shelf life.' (41)

Gloria Feldt, president, Planned Parenthood Federation of America: 'Moralistic slogans and intervention programs based unrealistically on no-sex vows do *not* reduce teen pregnancy or sexual activity. In fact, there have been studies that show they may actually *increase* the desire of teen-agers to experiment: to find out what it is they've been told to say no to.' (41)

Walt Odets, Berkeley psychologist and gay activist: 'Most prevention efforts have been based on risk-elimination rather than risk reduction ... If you say to a man, "In order not to get H.I.V. you are never going to have sex again without a condom," his response would be that that seemed impossible. But there's a difference between going out with a guy you've never met whose status you don't ask about, and a friend you've known 10 years who tells you he's negative. Education has refused to allow gay men even to *think* about that difference ... It's a very old story, telling gay men how to have sex; publicly they're complying, privately they're doing something else.' (45)

The last comment points to the wider social import of health promotion. Its brand of marketing seeks to produce or to confirm public fears, sometimes paranoia and terror as well. The body has emerged as one of

Figure 13: 'Drugs Kill.' This 1987 message highlights the motif of violence. The visual is simple but clever. You sniff cocaine, you may as well blow your brains out. Doing drugs is equated to committing suicide.

the major obsessions of postmodern times: the body as a site of pleasure and power, an arena of struggle, an object of care and work, a source of torment.[70] That last definition was and remains central to the whole project of health advocacy. Life was threatened by habits, whether smoking or tanning, drinking or overeating, which persisted because they satisfied the sensual urges of the body. The contradiction between the body as victim and the body as villain induced an extraordinary level of hysteria in the early years of the AIDS scare. *Family*, a British scare ad of 1986, asserted that 'We're all at risk' and warned that 'there will be no tomorrow,' unless people took preventive action. *Don't Die for Love* (U.S.A., 1986) told viewers, 'AIDS isn't just a gay disease, it's everybody's disease, and everybody who gets it dies.'[71] Time and again, creatives sought images that evoked the fear of violence to the body: the 'bodybag' posters of an Ontario assault on drinking and driving, the gun motif of anti-drug propaganda, morgue shots in all kinds of campaigns. The PDFA won an award in 1997 for a gruesome *Ashley–Teeth*, aimed at teens: an attractive young woman carefully removes her earrings, eyelashes, makeup, lipstick, eventually her teeth, all to reveal the ugly face of the drug addict.[72] The practice gave explicit expression to a hysteria that infected health advocacy at all times. Advocates use fearful imagery and scare copy only in part because it cuts through ad clutter and commands attention. Such images and such rhetoric best express a sense of panic that lies at the foundation of the new wave of public health concern. The one crucial purpose of the health spectacles is to convey that same mood to the wider public.

There is little wonder that all this propaganda adds its bit to what one scholar has called 'low-level fear – naturalized fear, ambient fear,' which has become a part of the atmosphere of living, especially in North America.[73] Health advocacy is, in this sense, a 'catalyst' provoking dread. A particular fear might be awakened when a smoker develops a sore throat, a sexually active person becomes ill, a youth is sickened by trying heroin. The imagination has been conditioned. The ambient fear may manifest itself in a brief panic over some general threat to the body: for example, the supposed cyanide poisoning of Chilean grapes set off hysteria in North America in March 1989, which led to the trashing of Chilean fruit by grocers and consumers in both Canada and the United States.[74] The public mood has been primed.

Both types of fear, personal and social, can have political effects. Fear can justify. The campaigns for seat-belts and against drinking and driving were indexes of their social significance that not only ensured their place on the public agenda but also conditioned the political environment for the laws and the regulations that eventually produced substantial changes in behaviour. Fear can silence. Whatever its impact on the prevalence of crack, cocaine, heroin, marijuana, and the like, the war on drugs helped to prevent public discussion of the merits of drug tolerance for at least two decades.[75] Fear can provoke. The mounting crusade against big tobacco during the 1990s served to delegitimize one of the most powerful of industries and paved the way for an escalating series of legal and legislative assaults in the United States. Promoting fear is another way of exercising power.

5

Charitable Souls:
The Practice of Altruism

These are no ordinary children. You can find them looking out from posters and billboards, in the pages of newspapers and magazines, sometimes on movie screens and on television. They may be infants or teens, a boy or a girl, with different skin colours, and of any age up to about twenty. They can be forlorn, injured, starving, abused, neglected, frightened, disturbed, expectant, hopeful, happy, or sometimes thankful. They do share one characteristic: they are disadvantaged – by race, class, gender, health, situation, or other circumstances. They are meant as objects of pity. They plead with us – as caring adults, privileged people – to enrich their lives with money, time, effort, love. Their presence should trigger our pity. Let me call them the Charity Kids. They are a visual cliché deployed in all too much of the propaganda designed by philanthropic agencies to mobilize support and donations.

1 The Charity Offensive

Charities have experienced something of a boom during the last third of the twentieth century. In Britain alone, around 155,000 distinct charities were registered with the state at the beginning of 1997. The incomes of the top two hundred had grown from approximately £597 million in 1980 to £2.8 billion fifteen years later. In Canada, more than one-quarter of tax filers together donated $3.4 billion in 1994, up from $1.79 billion ten years before. Americans were considered the most charitable of souls: according to the London *Times* (10 September 1989), the average U.S. household donated an amount five times greater than the £70 normal in the United Kingdom. Another source had Americans handing over almost 2 per cent of their income to the voluntary sector. In 1993 almost three-quarters of American households gave an average of $880 each, much of this to religious institutions. None of this necessarily made America the most generous country, however, since such statistics did not count the extent of tax support each state offered to social welfare and foreign aid. But the statistics did demonstrate the significance of charities and giving, especially in the United States.[1]

Not all the charities were alike. Consider the British case. A few, such as Save the Children, founded in 1919, were old and well-established. Many more were new – and ephemeral: some 3,225 names were added to the charity register, and 3,459 were removed, in the first five months of 1997. Seventy per cent of all the agencies had an income of £10,000 or less, whereas a mere 5 per cent of the top charities shared 85 per cent of the total annual income of £18 billion. Among the top ten fund-raisers in 1995 were Oxfam, the Red Cross, Save the Children, the National Society for the Prevention of Cruelty to Children (NSPCC), two cancer research bodies, the Salvation Army, and a group devoted to helping the aged. Two years earlier Save the Children alone had raised £112 million for its domestic and international projects. Oxfam's income in 1993–4 was close to £87 million, roughly 60 per cent of which came from public donations.[2] It was these charity giants, in Britain and elsewhere, that counted most in the public sphere.

There was never enough money to go around, of course. The charity boom had been driven first by an ever-increasing need. At home, a host of factors such as automation, stagnant or declining real wages, downsizing, and perhaps crime and what was called 'moral decay' had exacerbated the problem of poverty, even contributing to the apparent expansion of an underclass and to the visible spread of homelessness. Abroad, the combination of too many people, too much war and civil strife, political or economic catastrophe, rampant disease, and the mysterious workings of the global marketplace fostered immiseration in the Least Developed Countries plus a massive increase of the refugee problem. At the same time, the rise of neo-liberalism and, more important, a deficit crisis dictated the contraction of the welfare state and the reduction of foreign aid. Yet that credo (confusingly called neo-conservatism or the New Right in the United States) did not reign unchallenged. A welfare ethos persisted: affluent people and affluent countries retained a conscience, of sorts. Need, ideology, and conscience all nourished the charity offensive.

The big charities employed a particular vocabulary of aid to explain their activities. They talked what was colloquially known as 'the language of business,' promising efficiency and economy: 'Doing good fast and cheap' would be an appropriate slogan.

> City Harvest is efficient and cost-effective. An operating cost of less than 39 cents per pound of food is achieved by picking up and delivering food on the same day, thereby avoiding warehousing costs.

They spoke of the virtues of self-reliance.

> Oxfam works now in 80 countries worldwide with the aim of helping people to help themselves. For example, it supports a credit fund in Mali in Africa which helps poor women set up small businesses; supports training in organic gardening and tree planting in Bangladesh; and helps an organisation of tribal people in the Philippines keep land-grabbers off their ancestral lands.

Aid came in many different forms: relief, the immediate delivery of help to the needy and the stricken; development, where monies and expertise were invested in local projects so people could save themselves; and advocacy, the promotion of a worthy cause, whether housing for the homeless or debt relief for the Third World.

> Share Our Strength not only wants to feed hungry people (the short-term approach), they also want to equip them with the tools they need to change their lives through improved nutrition, medical support, and education (the long-term approach).

The underlying rationale was a narrative of common humanity, given a special inflection depending on the affiliation or the purpose of a charity. That narrative lamented the contrast between affluence and poverty, privilege and deprivation, which must somehow be overcome to ensure a good life for all. Witness this explanation from Britain's Catholic Fund for Overseas Development (CAFOD) in 1995:

> For development is much more than just aid. It is also about ensuring the world is made a fairer place, with just policies on debt and trade, where all are included and all have a chance. As we move towards the millennium, the divisions between First World and Third World, East and West, are becoming less distinct. At the same time, the divide within each nation between those who are included and those who are excluded is becoming

sharper. The gap between those who have a chance to participate in the benefits of development and those who are on the margins of society, scrabbling to eke out an existence, is widening and becoming more diffi-cult to bridge. Our Christian faith, our membership of a single human family, challenge us and demand that we do not simply accept this as inevitable.

The promise?: aid would work a revolution – of values, of lifestyles, of means – in which the poor at home and abroad would not only escape the cycles of war and famine, disease, hunger, and exploitation but would become productive, self-reliant citizens of a brave new world. The victims would cease to be.[3]

Agencies, big and small, sought aid from political and corporate organizations. That did not mean that the agencies were simply co-opted, though in the United States an agency accepting government funding could not easily engage in advocacy. Rather, the charities sought to construct limited alliances focused on specific goals which mobilized their expertise and outsiders' funds. Governments were eager to maxi-mize the effects of restricted funds by signing contracts with non-profit organizations to deliver services and implement social policies.[4] During the 1980s, USAID, for example, provided funds to charities such as Catholic Relief Services in Kenya or CARE and Save the Children in Somalia.[5] Refugee aid could swiftly mount up, and much of it was funnelled through non-profits: the United States contributed $338 mil-lion, the European Union $295 million, and Japan $151 million in 1995 alone.[6] At home, businesses were increasingly willing to assist worthy causes in a variety of ways. That could mean working with agencies to direct employees' charitable donations: an umbrella group called Ameri-ca's Charities, dating back to 1980, offered corporations a variety of choices and claimed that its members would receive the support of about ten million employees 'in workplaces nationally and abroad' by 1994.[7] More dramatic were such shared enterprises as Charge Against Hunger, mounted by American Express (AMEX) and Share Our Strength, which sought to combat the ill effects of poverty, homelessness, and hunger in America.[8] Sufficient money was generated via AMEX transactions that, so the boast went, 64,742,000 pounds of food were distributed and 3,868,981 people were helped, in 1994 alone. By the mid-1990s this kind of alliance was referred to as cause-related marketing where a corporation expected substantial returns in public prestige from its involvement with charity. One problem with cause-related marketing was whether the alliance might undermine the moral authority of the charity. 'It's like walking a tightrope,' admitted Timothy Shriver to the *New York Times* (23 June 1995) about selling marketing tie-ins for the Special Olympics. 'We don't want to lose the integrity of the cause. We're not just a commercial property. We're not just something that is up for sale.' Yet the attraction was obvious: corporate sponsorship of the World Games for mentally retarded athletes had risen to $28 million (from $21 million four years earlier), and the related spending on products and services had soared to $35 million (from $7 million). What has emerged, in the Anglo-American world at least, is a 'mixed economy of welfare' that incorporates the state, private enterprises, non-profits, and (as always) kinship networks.[9]

Inevitably, the charity offensive made the non-profits actual players in the public sphere. The news media paid attention to the views and reactions of leading charities. So, too, did politicians. Charities lobbied governments, legislatures, and bureaucrats, whether to retain or secure contracts, to protect specific programs, or to advocate a cause.[10] Their international brethren worked their way into the political process of that most Byzantine of forums, the United Nations: an assortment of child protection agencies proved a powerful force behind the shaping and the acceptance of the Convention on the Rights of the Child (1989).[11] By the 1990s the international aid agencies had a role in building support for armed intervention by western regimes into the chaos of Somalia and later, much more briefly, to protect the Rwandan refugee camps (before they finally dispersed) in a decrepit Zaïre. Overall, their exercise of power rested upon two rationales, social expertise and moral authority. The last was in some large part a function of propaganda.

2 Branding Altruism

It was crucial to capture public attention ('share of mind' in ad jargon) to buttress the integrity of the cause and the institution (secure 'goodwill' and 'build an image'). The major charities employed the whole panoply of techniques that together constituted mass marketing: targeted research, telephone appeals, direct mail, press releases and, eventually, video news releases (VNRs), news management, telethons, point-of-purchase material, even videos for nightclubs and trailers on film, as well as all sorts of advertising. Where possible, organizations used the latest advances in technology to deliver their messages. In 1995 one Canadian agency, the Canadian Catholic Organization for Development and Peace (CCODP), sent out a press release announcing that its three new PSAs could be downloaded from the Anik satellite by television stations.

The key instrument of persuasion was the television ad, although its dominance took time to emerge. Naturally, the United States led the way: the Red Cross used television as early as the 1950s. After 1970, major charities had come to rely heavily on the PSA, however flawed that instrument might be, because it could generate an awareness that might be exploited later by canvassers or direct mail. By the end of the decade the practice was usual in Canada as well: major charities such as the Crippled Civilians, UNICEF, and the Easter Seal campaign produced award-winning ads. In Britain, however, regulations severely limited what could be said or done. Although free PSAs had existed on independent television since 1978, and community service messages did appear on the BBC, it was illegal to appeal for funds or to sell an organization on any broadcasting medium. The lifting of these restrictions, and the end of a ban on paid charity ads, both in 1989, was very much in the interest of the majors, who had lobbied hard for the right to mount television campaigns, which of course would enhance their grip on the 'charity market.'[12] The Conservative government of the day hoped thereby to promote 'active citizenship,' claimed the *Sunday Times* (3 September 1989), meaning that people would be persuaded to give more time and money to charities. Indeed, the charity commercial was commonplace in Britain and on the continent during the next decade.

Mobilizing the public was never easy. Unlike health advocates, the charity promoters could only occasionally employ appeals to self-interest. The National Kidney Foundation in the United States used the warning 'It Might Happen to You' in the 1970s. A slightly sinister commercial for the Canadian Cancer Society in 1986 told smokers to contribute money now so that there would be a cure when they needed it. The Asociación Española Contra el Cancer (1992) used pictures of Pope John Paul II plus the news of his benign tumour to extract funds from viewers: 'We can't all count on that much of God's help.' In 1996 USAID offered a PSA in which it argued that foreign aid actually produced markets ('$46 billion in new trade') and jobs ('920,000 new positions') for Americans: 'By helping others, we help ourselves.' That last was a stretch, of course, which worked more to dishonour the claim that foreign aid cost the United States a huge sum of taxpayers' money without any return.

Another tactic was to try to build empathy so that the viewer could understand the gravity of the cause. Sometimes an effort was made to put the viewer in the place of the victim. The ALS Society of Canada sponsored the scary *Buried Alive* (1987) where 'you' are being interred: the announcer explains how when 'you' have Lou Gehrig's disease (amyotrophic lateral sclerosis), 'Muscle by muscle, nerve by nerve, your body shuts down. Your senses are alert as you watch yourself die.'[13] Sometimes the appeals used real people, ordinary folks. So an elderly schoolteacher in the Peace Corps spot *Retirees* (1990) spoke about the virtues of teaching the children of Belize, rather than wasting her time and skills frolicking on the beaches of Florida.[14] One of the most favoured ploys in the United States was to find a celebrity to deliver the pitch. Beginning in the late 1970s, the Red Cross featured Lucille Ball, Mike Douglas, Dionne Warwick, Bob Hope, and Bill Cosby in its 'Help Keep the Red Cross Ready' campaign.[15] By the 1990s movie stars would turn up in ads for all kinds of charities: Denzel Washington (Boys and Girls Clubs of America), Susan Sarandon (City Harvest), and Jeff Bridges (The Hunger CleanUp). Even the supermodel Cindy Crawford would appeal to Internet users to tune in for a live AIDS benefit called 'Maximum Exposure.' The presence of celebrities not only attracted the eye but carried conviction, or so it was thought. The stars of entertainment had acquired a kind of authority as truth-tellers, at least in the United States.

Everywhere the immediate task was to produce a branded product that would promise to solve some kind of problem. A partial transcript of the the NSPCC's *Christmas Gifts* (1992) demonstrates just how that could be done:[16]

> [On screen: 'Will you give £15 this Christmas?'] Will you give an abused child a gift of £15 this Christmas? Your £15 [on screen 'Your £15 will help pay for that vital visit.'] will help pay for the vital visit of a Child Protection Officer, your £15 will help keep our Child Protection Helpline open [on screen: 'Your £15 will help keep our Child Protection Helpline open.'] for anyone to call who suspects a child is in danger. And your £15 means [on screen: 'Your £15 will help us counsel more children'] we can counsel more children to help put their nightmares behind them. So this Christmas please imagine there's an extra child to buy a gift for, and call 0-800-444-230 now.' The voice-over repeats the number and says, 'We're waiting for your call.'

The charity kept repeating how a simple, modest donation could bring about all kinds of marvellous things. It constructed a token of altruism, a tangible public good which an ordinary person could purchase that would work some sort of magic.

Figure 14: Leila's Transformation. Here is visible 'proof' of the extraordinary effects of the branded product. The ad, sponsored by International Action against Hunger in France during 1994, showed just what 100F would do for a victim in Somalia. The first Leila was photographed when she arrived in one of the organization's aid stations, the second four months later. 'Your' gift and 'our' agency had miraculously turned a Hurt Child into a Bright Child.

These tokens came in all sizes and shapes. In the 1930s, Save the Children had pioneered the sponsoring of children: a donor received an actual child, or at least his or her photograph, as well as letters and cards and progress reports demonstrating how the child's existence was transformed by the monthly gifts.[17] Oxfam touted its 'Fairtrade Mark' on ordinary goods as 'a brand signature, to show consumers what's moral!'[18] Before it was undone by a tainted blood scandal in the mid-1990s, the Canadian Red Cross suggested that people gave the gift of life when they donated their blood. The National Literacy Hotline reminded potential volunteers that 'reading is power,' and that the time they donated could make an American citizen.[19] An AmeriCares commercial showed a plane taking off by tearing free from the restraints of red tape, all to symbolize the 'can do' spirit of that emergency relief agency.[20] CARE U.S.A. made much of the promise of self-sufficiency in a corporate campaign in 1988 that focused on work in Asia, Africa, and Latin America: 'CARE – we're helping people to learn to live without us.'[21] There was, in short, a marketplace of charity goods: the donor could choose from a wide variety of brands to express pity and assuage guilt.

3 Visions of Hell

In Britain in 1990 there was a gathering outcry over the character of charity advertising. 'Wherever you look these days, there's an advert for a charity, and it's probably none too pleasant,' claimed Stephen Cook in the *Guardian* (17 September 1990): 'a gruesome description of the diffi-culties of eating for someone with severe multiple sclerosis, a picture of a child being smothered by a pillow, or an account of the Brazilian police raping, mutilating, and murdering a young woman.' Nor was that the end of the horror. Consider these items: a pile of dead dogs in a poster by the Royal Society for the Prevention of Cruelty to Animals (RSPCA), and later a Christmas TV ad in which a puppy ends up in a nasty mantrap; the recounting of stories of sexually abused children under the headline 'A Bedtime Story' (The National Children's Home), which drew a rebuke from the Advertising Standards Authority; a picture of a surgical drill being used in an operating theatre (Conway Seymour Leukemia Fund) – 'Donating bone marrow hurts like hell. Donating money is absolutely painless.' Then there was a series of commercials pushing relief for the Third World: pictures of suffering, starving, and dead children (*Ken Livingstone*), black-and-white footage of emaciated Jewish corpses being shoved into a mass grave linked to coloured pictures of starving children (*Concentration Camp*), and a little white boy who goes down to the under-ground toilets to get a drink of water (*Toilet*).[22]

Blame was laid at the feet of a Tory government which had cut back on 'public provision,' at 'more competition' for the public's pound, and at the victory of 'advanced marketing techniques.' All these claims were correct, but the basic fact was that sponsors and admakers believed shock worked. Back in the mid-1980s the NSPCC had managed to boost dona-tions substantially with a new Saatchi and Saatchi campaign called 'The faces change, the bruises don't.' 'There were posters of children covered in burns and whip marks, children covering their faces in despair ...,' noted one journalist in the London *Times* (12 June 1985), yet even the letters of outrage often contained a donation as well. And not only the

British believed in the value of shock. 'We used the dark side of the situation to motivate people to give blood, time and money,' claimed Wallace O'Brien, president and chief executive officer of J. Walter Thompson, the long-time agency for the American Red Cross.[23] Scary, ugly, disgusting pictures were a proven technique for manufacturing a wave of guilt.

The trouble was that charity advertising amounted to a privileged form of discourse about the Other. So often 'we' were hailed, once again, as voyeurs, looking in on the misery and suffering of another. Unlike consumer advertising, this propaganda was not about us, about somewhere we would like to be or someone we would like to emulate. 'We don't pay to join in, we pay to keep away,' wrote a slightly cynical journalist.[24] One Canadian commercial for the Red Cross in Quebec made that explicit. *Help* alternated text and pictures, the last a 'distillation' made up of personal horrors, before telling viewers to contribute to the 1991 campaign:[25]

Text	Pictures
'Right now, some people in Quebec are going through the worst nightmare of their lives.'	A man on fire, caught in flames, screaming as he falls.
'We know that if you could, you would help.'	A woman drowning, or at least gasping for air, in the water.
'But this TV show is simply too good to miss.'	A man running with a woman, wrapped in blanket, in his arms.
'That's why we're asking you to send money.'	An old woman, in anguish, wrapped in blanket, seemingly pleading to the sky, as she is comforted by a female Red Cross worker.
'So you can get on with your life.'	A male Red Cross worker administering heart massage to a man lying on the floor.
'And we can go on saving lives.'	

That at least was about other Québécois. But what about images of the homeless or of refugees? 'Some critics call it the "starving-baby syndrome"; others term it the pornography of relief because it captures people in their most exposed positions, defenseless to protest,' lamented one observer. 'Human beings are reduced to hollow shells, bloated stomachs, or empty gazes.'[26] The cumulative effect of all this dark propaganda was to construct or perpetuate compelling stereotypes whose cultural significance was far greater than was ever intended.

a) The Postmodern City

Imagine yourself standing on the sidewalk of a downtown street in a very big and busy city, anywhere in the affluent world. This is a city full of activity, life, pleasures. But not for you. You can see through the windows of stores all manner of goods and luxuries – but there is not a door which will allow you entry. You spy people at work in the bright offices – but they do not need the likes of you. You are hungry – but the gaudy restaurants require the money you do not have. So you survive off what the fortunate discard in garbage cans. There may be people all around you, yet still you are alone because they do not seem to notice your presence. Or if they do, it does not matter: a woman will stare and then avert her eyes, perhaps upset by your appearance or your smell or the shape of your body. You try to talk to a man in a business suit: if he hears, he does not understand. You speak different languages, and he does not care. Only if you are a child may he respond, except then you are in danger. You suddenly realize that you have nowhere to go, no family, no home, apart from the streets. The tall grey buildings curve at the top to close off the sun and the stars. You have no way out. You are trapped, impotent, poor, a pariah. Yours is a life of despair in the postmodern city.

That was a pastiche: no single ad incorporated all these horrors. I have created a kind of collective vision, inspired by the many fictions of charity advertising devised to address the ills of life in the affluent world. This kind of experience is played out in innumerable ads about the abused, the deprived, the distracted, the discarded, and the homeless. The postmodern city is a setting and a situation where admakers and promoters can play out their particular nightmares.[27]

Figure 15: The Postmodern City. *Lifestyles of the Homeless* was created by Chiat Day/Mojo of New York for the Coalition for the Homeless. It was a takeoff on a then-famous television series called *Lifestyles of the Rich and Famous*. The commercial tracked the daily existence of one of the homeless, a man called George. The spiel was full of ironic comment on the virtues of this 'life of complete independence.' This treatment of homelessness as though it were a lifestyle choice made the plight of its victims all the more poignant.

The Big City

George Enjoying His View

Mixing with the Power Elite

Grabbing a Bite to Eat

A Bedroom Sleeping Hundreds

Living Like There's No Tomorrow

Is There Anybody out There? (The Samaritans, U.K., 1985): One of these nightmares stood out. The Samaritans are a refuge of last resort where the unwanted
and distraught may find succour. This extraordinary cinema ad captured the
horror of isolation and hopelessness that was a leitmotif in reflections on the
postmodern city. The Board of Film Classification rated it 'only for persons
fifteen years and over.' The ad managed to get free airtime on both BBC and ITV
news programs. And it won a Gold Lion in the 1986 Cannes International
Advertising Film Festival.

Saatchi and Saatchi, that remarkably creative shop, had put together a very
simple performance, highly symbolic, an emotional rather than a rational sell,
which worked through metaphor and association. The admakers paired down
the dystopia to an essence (never *the* essence, since this truth was so much the
construction of its signs and its context). The commercial took its title from a
piece on the rock superhit of Pink Floyd, the album *The Wall,* released in 1979,
and that song plays throughout the performance. There is only one continuous
visual. The opening shot reveals what looks like a colour experiment of the
Abstract Expressionists: on the top and bottom are thin black borders which
highlight an enormous blue sheet, mottled with white blotches, that seems
stretched across the screen. And it is, either stretched rubber or plastic, for
almost immediately we see the imprint of open hands and then a face straining,
as if to escape the imprisonment, to break through this terrible wall. The
camera moves in slowly: sometimes the face appears to scream, the open mouth
outlined on the sheet, sometimes the face sags dejected, yet still the person
thrusts forward – all to no avail. Meanwhile, that ominous song plays on, its
sinister mood enhanced by a cough, by snippets of ordinary conversation,
sounds of exertion and then sounds of suffocation, squeals and shrieks, and
eventually long screams. The voice repeats the plea, 'Is there anybody out
there?,' once with a slight echo, later with a choral background. Then the
camera moves back, and superimposed on the screen is the word 'YES.' Who,
you might ask?: 'THE SAMARITANS.' The spectre, the imprints on the stretched
sheet, disappear.

Is There Anybody out There? was a layered performance. The mix of
visuals, sounds, and music was so compelling that the basic message of
alienation was obvious. This victim had no identity, no name, age, race,
or gender – the victim personified anonymity. But a fuller appreciation of
the commercial depended upon another work of art, the album itself,
and that text was an expression of a more general sense of malaise with
our times. *The Wall* was a meditation on the ugliness of (post)modern
life, how the innocent dreams and hopes of childhood soured when

family, school, and society operated on the young soul. People were
trapped behind a wall they had built: they were numbed, frustrated,
disciplined, punished – one of the last songs recounted a trial of the
victim who showed 'feelings of an almost human nature.' Above all
(post)modern 'man' could not connect: he knew, when he phoned,
when he asked, 'There'll be nobody home.' (A companion effort in 1990
called *Sarah* had an attractive young woman driven to despair because she
could not speak to us, the viewer, in clear English, indeed in any recognizable tongue.) It was here that the album and the ad evoked that sense
of loss, that yearning for community in a world full of goods but devoid
of ... what?: caring, sharing, hoping, friendship. The problem had been
the subject of much lament in academic and popular forums, among
conservatives and radicals, usually without any end or any remedy. But
because this was an ad, *Is There Anybody ...?* offered a solution to the
problem so neatly represented. And, unlike the album, the ad ended on
a happy note: The Samaritans are there when you need them.[28]

b) The Third World

Imagine yourself standing again, but this time by the side of a dusty road
baked by the sun. You are certainly not alone. All around, you can see
enormous numbers of men, women, and children, and perhaps some
animals, moving as one mass body down the road. Everyone is hungry,
thirsty, too hot, and there is not enough food or water to go around.
There are flies, buzzing loudly, many more than the people they torment.
You begin to notice individuals: a lame man, a woman carrying an infant,
the haunted eyes of a little girl – the mass body has faces, but they all
speak the same story of despair. Their home is no more – drought,
famine, war, civil strife, one intractable problem or another, has made it
impossible for the hordes to stay. For some people this place that is no
place is the end: you see the tiny misshapen bodies of starved children,
the exhausted adults, the people who can no longer walk. But the rest,
the masses, move on, doomed to a journey that will never end.
    This, too, is a constructed nightmare, the representation of the Third
World as hell, built out of many individual performances. It is a world
consistently defined by negatives: drought, war, violation, deprivation.[29]
What makes the Third World hell, then, is not just the absence but the
denial of all the ordinary virtues of existence (always the existence of the
affluent) in the West: abundance, health, peace, security, freedom, and
so on. 'Their' life is the obverse of 'ours.'

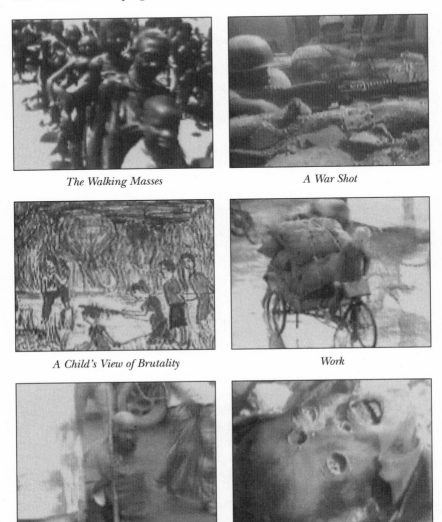

The Walking Masses

A War Shot

A Child's View of Brutality

Work

Street Life

The Dead

Bread for the World (Daikonishes Werk, Germany, 1992): How long does it take to teach people the 'Truth' about history? A mere sixty seconds? A Christian advocacy group set out to re-educate Germans in this extravaganza of visual stimuli: paintings, photographs, film clips, slowed imagery, overlays and blends, black-and-white inserts, quick cuts, all mixed with an ironic and dismal script, delivered against the background of what sounds like a dirge.

The ad takes us on a whirlwind tour of the relations between Europe and the Third World, a system of domination and subordination. It presents Europe as the villain which has despoiled, devastated, and enslaved the Third World. The undifferentiated indigenous people are shown working, suffering, dead, starved, at war. Fundamental is the notion that the Third World is *our* hell, ours in the sense that our ancestors and our rulers made it so.

Bread for the World breaks down into four propositions and a final command:
1 Paintings and sketches of conquest, discovery, dominance, the submissive populace – mostly single shots. Voice-over: 'Hundreds of years ago, Europeans conferred the blessings of civilization on the natives of the Third World.'
2 Images of toil, hardship, mutilation, death – moving pictures and some still inserts. 'They showed them how to work.'
3 Images of poverty, a cripple, a crowd, starved legs. 'They showed them what it means to stand on your own feet.'
4 Clips of war planes, weaponry, warfare, and death – modern scenes. 'And they provided them with the most up-to-date technology.'
5 'Let's give those people in the Third World what they really need: help to help themselves.' Sponsor: 'Brot für die Welt Postgiro Köln 500500-500.'

This was a postcolonial history, a politically correct history, a vision of truth that expressed the perspective of the victims and losers, not the

---

Figure 16: The Third World. Here are some scenes of the Third World as hell drawn from *Children's Drawings, Accompagnez-les jusqu'à la frontière,* and *Bread for the World.* Such images re-occur so often in charity and relief advertising that they have become symbolic. We see the image and we know it is the Third World. Of course, the images are not unique to advertising: most are derived from news and public-affairs shows. In July 1998, for instance, the Toronto *Globe and Mail* illustrated a front-page story of a famine in Sudan with a photograph of a starving mother and child, all the more striking because it evokes the cliché of Madonna and Child. Some days later the same photograph appeared in a World Vision Canada ad exhorting readers to rush aid to save lives (2.4 million imperilled) before it was too late.

winners, in the story of how the West won the world.[30] It 'signalled' the guilt of Europe, at least according to some of its citizens.

c) Hurt Children

Common in both visions of hell are threatened, injured, or dead children, the most important promotional sign that the charity offensive can deploy in its effort to provoke guilt.

Some of these are all too legitimate, as in an ad where, first, we hear the sounds of banging, then see an infant bashing its head against the bars of a playpen (*Rocking*, Hong Kong, Friends of Orphans in Rumania, 1993). The message?: 'THIS IS HOW 100,000 ROUMANIAN ORPHANS WILL ROCK THEMSELVES TO SLEEP TONIGHT.'[31]

Many other cases involve an element of camouflage, however. A flood of pictures of starving children was the signature of yet another African famine. So, in 1985, the Spanish horror *Etiopia* thrust sixteen pictures of dying kids into the faces of viewers, all to the sound of the tick of a clock: 'ETHIOPIA IS DYING BY SECONDS.' Africare told Americans in 1994 to donate old shoe boxes, since they did not want to part with money, so that aid workers could bury the babies dying because of the Rwandan crisis. A boy comforts his bruised and abused sister in one nasty presentation of life in the postmodern family (*Put Their Fears to Rest*, Saskatoon United Way, Canada, 1990); both children startle when the door opens and light strikes the fearful face of the sister. This was an ad to generate funds for a collective charity, the United Way. In *Gift* (1993), a British girl discovers that a gift box contains nothing: we learn that she has a tube stuffed up her nose and is waiting in hospital for the gift of life, an organ donation. The ad exhorted people to sign their donor cards, and tell their next of kin, in order to benefit everyone, not just a little girl.[32]

Images of hurt children can garner public sympathy where images of homeless men or sick women will not. That late-nineteenth-century villain the pauper has returned in a new guise a hundred years later: the dependent adult, whether a welfare mother or a permanent refugee, is looked upon in many circles as one of the sins arising from state and voluntary systems of social support. These folk can seem little better than parasites who feed off the taxes and generosity of the working citizenry. But the young boy or girl remains a generic icon of hope and innocence in the affluent world, an image less likely to polarize or upset the watching citizens. So the damaged child becomes a 'public bad,' one of those unwelcome commodities, that might lead these citizens to take the necessary action. The effort to cast all manner of appeals for aid, at home and abroad, in terms of children is a way of avoiding the problems of compassion fatigue and the rhetoric of anti-welfare that have eaten away at support for social democracy. We are faced here with a reality of propaganda that has become the official reality of welfare.

d) Invidious Comparisons

The Danish Red Cross sponsored one ghoulish ad in which a happy picture of a white mother and child, the child contented, is slowly transformed into a sad picture of a black mother and child, the child starving.[33]

The practice of invidious comparison has been widespread in charity propaganda, where it has served as a mode of critique that might push people into giving. The United Way was ready to tell Americans to *Remember All You Have* (1990) and Canadians to *Count Your Blessings* (1991), backed up by assorted pictures of deprivation. In 1994 the Salvation Army ran a campaign in Canada which juxtaposed the talk of some affluent and satisfied soul against images of homelessness (*Shelter*), cold (*Clothing*), and hunger (*Food*). But what the ads did not do was attempt to identify any of the causes of poverty, to suggest that our good luck might rest on their misery.[34]

The critique could be more pointed where the issue was aid to the Third World.

Bank Manager (U.K., 1994): The sponsor, the World Development movement, shows a well-dressed, older, white male, looking very much the privileged person, lecturing an unseen listener about the need to pay back an outstanding loan.[35] The manager has his book (the source of power), his plush seat (the seat of authority), and he rises and gazes out the window (at his domain):

> Look don't give me a hard luck story, I hear them every day, and quite frankly they bore me. The facts are simple: in 1973 this bank gave you a loan and you still haven't paid it back. Admittedly you paid back the initial sum, but not the interest, which to date amounts to nine times the amount originally borrowed. Nine times. So you better get your act together. Times are tough, and we're all having to clamp down. And don't look at me like that. This is a bank, not a charity.

Then the camera switches its angle, and we see in the chair the object of this tirade: a young black man, really a boy, with a ragged covering over one shoulder and part of his chest, looking a bit forlorn and insolent, and then just chastened and hopeless. What to do about this arrogance? 'Cancel the Third World Debt.' 'Move your account to a bank that's not involved.'

Even this parable was restrained, of course. The bank manager is hardly a well-loved character in contemporary popular culture, so the ad merely drew upon an existing resentment. Charity propaganda is rarely so forthright as *Bread for the World*. Too much censure might offend. In 1976 Oxfam dropped a planned commercial because of a ruling by a broadcast authority that its reference to the unequal distribution of wealth around the world amounted to a political statement.[36] Instead, sponsors and admakers preferred to hint at our culpability in ways that would awaken people's doubts or fears just enough to spark a sense of dishonour, and thus foster a guilty response.

e) Positive Images

It is not surprising that the dismal imagery provoked a reaction. People who were crippled, blind, deaf, or retarded objected to ads that identified them as 'The Disabled,' where the focus on what was abnormal othered and victimized the individual. The starving-baby image so common in the relief campaigns for Ethiopia and Somalia eventually came under fierce attack. 'This stereotyped image has come to represent a whole continent, when it is in fact only a small part of the story,' admitted Save the Children in the mid-1990s. 'Its over-use has offended Africans in particular.'[37]

There were always sponsors who chose alternative visions, or, rather, who used the soft sell rather than the shock approach. The lighter touch has been especially well done in Canada, where some charities have consistently chosen warm images of happy, active people. A different tradition of disability advertising has positioned people with handicaps as survivors and achievers, people who could do something rather than just wait passively for assistance. By the early 1990s big charities like Oxfam, UNICEF, and Save the Children began offering up stories of triumph which showed how Africans were breaking the cycle of hunger and poverty. But this approach could have a downside as well. *Pumps* (MetroHealth Center for Rehabilitation, U.S.A., 1992) pushed images of wheelchair athletes, engaged in a strenuous game of basketball, who were so super-abled that they evoked disbelief. The humour employed in a campaign for Presbyterian Support Services in New Zealand (*Polevaulter, Lulu,* and *Bragatos,* 1991) actually worked to create perceptions of seniors as fools and exhibitionists. Even Canadian ads were sometimes marred by highly sentimental portrayals of marvellously resilient victims, like the youthful and attractive mother in *Walk* (Canadian Paraplegic Association, 1984) who taught her child to toddle.[38]

What did not change was the emphasis upon children. However, instead of just hurt kids the propaganda now featured more bright children, like the thankful girl in *Chatterbox* (United Way of Dade County, U.S.A., Deafness, 1987) or the singers in *Cancer Kids* (Canadian Cancer Society, Ontario Division, 1991).[39] *Digger* (U.S.A., 1985), a spot for UNICEF Cards, ended with a shot of happy black kids playing with the abundant water that now (thanks to aid) blessed their village.[40] A poignant ad for the Special Olympics had one of the young athletes conquer life in an early morning run through the postmodern city.[41] The tactics might have changed; but the imperative of marketing remained.

4 Saviours

Accompagnez-les jusqu'à la frontière (France, 1984): The famed relief agency Médecins sans Frontières touted its virtues in this very sophisticated piece of propaganda. The commercial asks viewers to assist its noble tasks, presumably with a donation. The ad works the contrast between the calm and comfort of a flight aboard a passenger plane and scenes of hectic activity in various Third World sites. The featured character is a handsome, white, male doctor who recalls his past activities as he flies back home from a tour of duty. His patients have been a succession of black and yellow peoples, emaciated children, injured adults, crying women – in short, that mass body with the many faces of despair. So the most startling contrast is between the empowered white expert and the disempowered people of colour. The image of the white man as saviour seems little more than an updating of an older imperialist myth about the European as civilizer.[42]

In fact the commercial exhibited, albeit in an especially blatant fashion, a characteristic that has been common in charity propaganda. 'Advertisements portraying individual white aid workers as saviours of a helpless African community belie the fact that the overwhelming number of aid workers are black Africans,' claimed two British reporters. 'The central role that African villagers play in the improvement of their own lives is rarely, if ever, acknowledged by Western charity advertisements, newspapers or television newscasts.'[43] Time and again this brand of advocacy advertising represented its personnel, and so the sponsors, as social heroes whose moral devotion to the task of saving the Other made them agents of civilization.

The Red Cross: In *Love Story* (Spain, 1987), a volunteer's mouth-to-mouth resuscitation equates with the kiss of love and life. In *Unforgettable Visit* (Denmark, 1991) the efforts of another volunteer energize an enervated senior: he vibrates with pleasure and excitement. Over the years the Red Cross has liked to see itself as a helping hand, although the image of two hands joined has been used by many an agency.

Boys and Girls Clubs of America: Denzel Washington, the African-American movie star, praises Billy Thomas, the man who ran the club where Washington grew up. 'It's a positive place where thousands of people like Billy Thomas helped young people succeed. Does it work? It did for me.' (*Billy*, U.S.A., 1993)

The Parkinson Foundation: The eerie commercial *Puzzle* (Canada, 1980) has a victim, rendered nearly helpless by the disease, who is guided by a child, acting as the surrogate for the foundation, to complete a puzzle properly.

Oxfam: The arrival of Oxfam trucks bearing aid marks the turning point in *Break the Cycle* (U.K., 1990), from black-and-white scenes of typical Third World horror to images of work, achievement, and even pleasure.[44]

These are all examples of a rhetoric of management that is rife in the non-profit sector. Charity advertising is always an act of self-promotion, unless it hides its sponsor. That applies across the affluent zone, whether in North America or Europe, whatever the kind of organization in question. Sometimes an agency just helps, sometimes its work transforms; whatever the claim, however, the agency possesses the problem and orders the solution. It mediates between Us and Them. The charity becomes the crucial instrument of moral authority, exercising the power to construct Our guilt as well as Their need. It produces a diversity of 'products,' the public goods of assistance, which the affluent can purchase, thus soothing Our conscience; it distributes those 'products' to a wide variety of victims in the cities and the Third World, thus implementing Our pity. One can find masked in such assumptions and images a desire to command, both at home and abroad, to fashion a world in which the professional as expert administers a dependent population whose subjectivity rests on lack, on deprivation. It seems reminiscent of that much older narrative of empire which has waxed and waned in significance throughout the history of the West. It recalls, in particular, the Christian sense of mission that moved clerics to save souls in darkest London and deepest Africa, to civilize and discipline, over a hundred years ago. Count this propaganda a 'vehicle' for a postmodern brand of imperialism, soft rather than hard, friendly and caring rather than brutal and bloody.

6

Administered Minds, or Shaming the Citizenry

Smile (Singapore Tourism, 1988): The grumpy face of an Asian male fills the centre of the screen. He frowns when a female finger tries, unsuccessfully, to alter his expression. A tuba plays a familiar melody in the background. On screen comes a cue to explain why this might be worth watching: 'How to Make a Billion Dollars.' A male voice-over explains, 'Every year, tourism brings in four billion dollars to Singapore. And it's up to everyone of us to keep it coming.' While he speaks, the fingers reshape that grumpy face, now suddenly malleable: first one cheek is pushed up, then the second. 'Because it isn't just a smile that matters, it's an attitude.' Meanwhile, back at the face, the hands have plumped the cheeks, made the eyes friendly, and peaked the eyebrows. The once unwelcoming chap is now definitely smiling. 'And that's why we have the Singapore Tourism Awards' (the last phrase appears on screen with the addition of the numeral '88'). 'So next time you meet a visitor, give him your billion-dollar smile.' The woman's finger pulls down the man's lower lip. And, indeed, the compliant subject does exactly as ordered: we see (for the subject's voice is silent) him mouth a magnificent hello.[1]

Only in Singapore? Not so. *Smile* typified a common brand of propaganda – call it 'administrative advertising' – used throughout the affluent world of the 1980s and 1990s. It was part of a much wider effort at social engineering in which marketing was only one tool (legislation was equally, if not more, important) used in efforts to program affluent populations. Authorities, and not just the state, set out to construct or reconstruct the citizen – his behaviour, her attitudes, their conduct – in ways that suited some purpose or agenda. That priority inspired an assault upon the personal – or, rather, it turned private actions into matters of public record and accountability. Here propaganda set out to render visible hidden or secret things.

1 Shaming (and Praising)

There was an emotional signature attached to each of the campaigns of truth. Not to every performance, of course. But there were obvious and persistent preferences which prevailed even across time and place. Health advocacy promoted fear about the condition of the body: it was as much an instrument of social paranoia as of public health. Charity appeals generated guilt by contrasting the privileges of the affluent to the misery of the Other: here was evidence of what a guilt-ridden society the West had become. Administrative advertising sought to disgrace – sometimes to produce shame in the viewer, sometimes to stain, to vilify, even to banish a particular kind of person. This genre of propaganda acted as a contemporary expression of the ancient art of shaming.

Fear, shame, and guilt all threaten well-being. Shame and guilt can be especially close companions, since they both refer to that state of spiritual anguish caused by the violation of social norms. Years ago anthropologists contrasted what they called guilt cultures, notably those of the West, where internal sanctions reigned, and shame cultures, notably those of Asia, where external sanctions prevailed. That argument fell into disrepute, partly because it was so Eurocentric, partly because guilt and shame were present in all societies. But notwithstanding the thrust of recent scholarship, there was merit to a contrast of these two states of being. Guilt refers to the private self, to individuals who have sinned by acting, or not acting, contrary to their moral codes. Shame refers to the social self, to individuals who are condemned, or who think they will be condemned, for conduct or attributes that offend the community. What is crucial is the imagined or actual eye of another, an eye that judges and names. The social self is both the subject and the object, the villain and the victim in the equation of shame. He or she bears, in the words of Erving Goffman, a 'spoiled identity,' a deep and at times irredeemable imperfection, an unworthiness that reaches the soul. Shame manifests itself in a face that hides, a head held low, a body that cringes, a desire to disappear from the sight of others.[2]

Shaming means exposing. The act of shaming hails citizens first as voyeurs (of course!) but then as pupils, supposed to learn from the moral spectacle. The purpose is to attach to a type of person a moral stigma, a mark that signifies transgression. The stigmata are not usually visible, but rather manifest themselves in a person's conduct. Their presence serves to define the unworthiness of the subject. Thus the propagandist becomes the embodiment of the public eye who casts a moral gaze upon the offender. Consider one effort of the ad guru Tony Schwartz, of *Daisy* fame: he placed a small ad in the press announcing that New York's 'Lincoln Center Supports Addiction,' and urging the inquisitive to phone an 800 number where they could learn how this much-honoured cultural centre took tobacco money to assist its presentations.[3] Here the purpose was not only to stain but to make guilty. Attaching stigma might be achieved by ridicule, as in the case of anti-sexism, though not all causes suit this mechanism. A second approach was to evoke contempt, disgust, even revulsion, a common ploy in the battle against racism. Finally, there was the display of humiliation where the sinner suffered the fate of exposure, punishment, and above all pain. That closed the circle, since the display of humiliation falls within the realm of the fear message.

The theatre of shame could reverse itself. Sometimes administrative advertising would endeavour to praise a group, an occupation, or a people. The celebration still stereotyped, but now these marks were represented as virtues, not stigmata. We were expected to honour and to emulate these favoured folk, who acted as models of good citizenship, just as the victims of shaming acted as warnings. In each case, however, what was being sold was a particular set of social standards, an array of approved conducts, that were not only public goods but moral goods as well.

2 The Disciplinary Regime

We recall how Philip Kotler and Gerald Zaltman, those enthusiasts of social marketing, worried about the effects of a massive increase in 'promotional noise.' That increase occured in the 1980s when governments, in particular, spent lavishly on advertising (though the pace of the increase waned in the mid-1990s when states waged war on their deficits). During the Thatcher years, for example, ad expenditures increased by almost 300 per cent in a decade, moving the British government ahead of Unilever, the previous leader. That occasioned much the same kind of hand-wringing about government advocacy as had occurred a decade earlier in Canada.[4] Even municipal authorities got into the act: in 1992, Osaka sponsored the commercial *Carried Away* as part of a campaign against illegal parking, while Barcelona hoped *Dogs* would help to keep the streets free from dog dirt.[5]

The Osaka and the Barcelona ads were typical of much of this propaganda. They mixed information and persuasion, usually to achieve some modest end. But the cumulative effect of all this promotional noise had a greater significance. Consider the example of the Consumer Information Center in Pueblo, Colorado, a branch of the U.S. Department of General Services. For years it produced humorous ads designed to entice Americans to order its free catalogue of government booklets.[6] One oft-repeated promise was that the information took the threat out of living: 'You'll be better prepared for what life throws at you.'[7] Authority constantly warned of perils, new and old: radon gas, guns at home, illiteracy, personal debt, urban wildfires.[8] In obedience lay security. The list could go on *ad nauseam*: administrative propaganda was a normal practice in the ongoing effort to manage society.

The other significant task was to reconstruct citizens, to persuade and often to shame them into adopting some higher standard of public conduct. During the late 1970s and well into the 1980s, western-European governments urged employers to offer a helping hand to youth trapped by a lack of work. That provoked an excess of metaphor: drowning youth, a runner doomed to circle forever, a gaggle of people stuck on the wrong side of a bridge.[9] In the 1990s a more pressing concern was the tax evader and his ilk who refused to pay their way, an issue which inspired a series of efforts to represent taxes as a public good. During a campaign that sought to shame deadbeat dads, Ontario aired a spot about 'a young girl who watches helplessly as toys, clothes and food gradually disappear around her because support payments are not being made.' Peruvian sources even claimed a gigantic return of lost tax monies as a result of their campaign to bolster civic honesty.[10]

Perhaps the most fruitless project of the nineties, however, was an American effort to persuade voters to return to the polls they had deserted as their mass democracy decayed into a republic of 'haves.' One ploy was to equate voting with power – in short, to make this instrument both a private and a public good which people could use to exercise their will.[11] More common were the attempts to blame and to shame voters for their failure to do their duty. One spot contrasted the passions of East Europeans, ready to fight for the right to vote, with the indifference of Americans (*Harsh Conditions*). A second comparison showed young people stuffing themselves into a phone booth – 'Can you imagine what a difference it would make if the young people of this country had the same enthusiasm for the voting booth?' (*Phone Booth*). A companion spot pictured the deconstruction of the American flag, its stars, stripes, and colours removed because of the people who didn't vote (*Flag*).[12] The failure to produce much result merely underlines the fact that the disciplinary regime did not create a disciplined society.

But there was one campaign of shaming that apparently did work, at least in North America, so much so that it became a model for all sorts of administrative advertising. Drinking and driving had long been one of those crimes which were treated casually, as though a certain amount of this behaviour was expected. The result was carnage on the highways. During the 1980s, however, the trajectory of statistics suddenly and dramatically reversed. That success reflected a combined effort to control drunk driving: the actions of government agencies, the police, Mothers Against Drunk Driving (MADD) and like groups, television stations, the insurance industry, even liquor and brewing companies, had raised the priority of combating this evil. New laws stiffened the penalties for impaired driving, and better enforcement ensured their application. A wave of propaganda marketed the virtues of safe highways, harsher penalties, the concept of the designated driver, and so on. Such ads became a sign of Christmas when social drinking was so common. Motives might be mixed. MADD wanted to end the carnage. Anheuser-Busch, manufacturer of the famous macho brew Budweiser, wished, as well, to prevent the 'Don't drink' ad.[13] The television industry feared an effort to ban all booze advertising. The whole project nicely illustrated the workings of that ensemble of institutions, laws, practices, and purposes which, Foucault had theorized, constituted the mechanisms of governmentality. It also constituted an effort to change the practice of masculinity: time and again, the target was identified as an erring male who needed to be civilized.

Shaming was a crucial technique. One common motif was the virtue of surveillance: people must monitor what their guests or their buddies do. Mates looked after mates in an early Australian effort (*Card Game*, 1980), in which working-class males took care of one of their own who had drunk too much. 'When friends don't stop friends from drinking and driving, friends die from drinking and driving,' warned the U.S. Department of Transport in *Crashing Glasses* (1983). In *Michael* (1984), sponsored by the Insurance Bureau of Canada, a bereft woman tells the sad story of her fiancé, who drank too much and never made it back to his apartment: 'I should have tried to stop him. And I didn't.' A bit later *Mike* (U.S. Department of Transport, 1989) put another grieving girlfriend in a cemetery. 'Take the keys, call a cab, take a stand,' admonished the voice-over. We were all, and we were always, responsible for the well-being of siblings, spouses, neighbours, and friends.[14]

More dramatic was the persistent effort to disgrace the drunk driver. That really began in the early 1970s when the National Safety Council in the United States ran *Scream Bloody Murder* in which a female voice-over explained, 'It's not the drink that kills on our highway. It's the drunk, the abusive drinker, the problem drinker, the drunk driver.' In a different vein, the Motor Vehicle Branch in British Columbia, Canada, offered *Impaired Driving* (1972), a two-minute docudrama which took the viewer through the whole shameful process of arrest, the booking, a night in jail, and the inevitable notoriety when released. This particular script would be repeated nearly ten years later, again in British Columbia (*Caught*, 1983) and in California (*The Party's Over*, 1984). The American commercial added an extra bite: the upscale white offender was faced with the additional peril of spending a night with assorted low types in a common cell, a peril made manifest by his fright and their glee.[15]

Another favoured script focused on the torment suffered by the drunk driver, his family, or the family of his victims. The camera showed life in the aftermath of an accident (*Eyes*, U.K., 1992); the anguish in the emergency ward of a hospital (*The Girlfriend*, Australia, 1991); and the recriminations in a hospital room where his family visited the injured driver (*Kids*, Canada, 1994). Not even the home was spared: the centre-piece of a £1 million campaign, the poignant *Kathy* (U.K. 1991), concentrated on a crying girl while in the background the mother berates the husband:

> How can she forget about it? She can't even sleep. She heard a kid at school saying you were a murderer. I don't know what to tell her. How am I supposed to explain that you killed a little boy? I won't ever understand why you had to drive. Now everything's screwed up. Isn't it? Well, isn't it? Look at me.

The Independent Broadcasting Authority ruled that the ad could not play before 9:00 P.M., since it might disturb children.[16] In another British effort, *Fireman* (1987), an observer says of the drunk driver, 'I don't know how he'll ever live with himself.' In yet a third, *Drink-Drive* (1995), he is simply called an 'asshole.' An action once half-accepted had become anathema. Label the drunk driver a pariah.[17]

3 Re/Building the Community

One of the abiding features (and, some would add, ills) of postmodern times is a sense of personal and social incoherence, whether this means the dispersed self, multiple identities, or social fragmentation. This sense may explain another obsession, namely the constant effort to make or remake a community. Just as the siren songs of commercial advertising told consumers how they could construct their identities and change their lifestyles through the purchase of private goods, so the sterner voices of civic advocacy explained how citizens could build a better world through such public goods as varied as family love, civility, patriotism, equal rights, and the like. The key, as always, was to make the correct choice: here propaganda constituted both a theatre of shame and a theatre of praise for the ways of virtue.

a) Reaffirmations

Attention focused on certain zones of tension where identity was created or expressed. The first of these was the family, which seemed in a particular state of crisis (when had it not been?) because of divorce, working couples, neglected children, and forgotten seniors. That inspired a species of 'neo-traditionalism' (to employ one of those horrid, contemporary words) in which people were urged to talk, to listen, above all to love one another. The Mormon Church was an especially active champion of love and affection: just add this to your family, so the promise went, and all your troubles would go away (the actual performances, though, were much more effective than such a bald assertion).[18] But there were other proponents. One of Spain's child welfare agencies, supported by the government of Andalusia, worked a twist on the old symbol of the Madonna and child, showing the loving *Animals* (1990) – zebras, penguins, monkeys, lions – so that humans might learn how to parent properly. An agency of the British government could not resist a display of shamed relatives (1989), suffering the pangs of guilt, gathered together at the funeral of a neglected grandmother. The costs might well be higher, according to Brazil's *Chaplin* (1990): you, that is mother and father, could either make a Charlie Chaplin with love and affection or fashion an Adolf Hitler who would 'give back to the world ... hate and violence.'[19]

The second site was the pantheon of social heroes – the noblest of citizens whose achievement merited celebration and whose conduct deserved emulation. This is where propaganda constituted its most obvious theatre of praise. In fact there were all too many claimants to public honour: American soldiers, Californian and Australian veterans, Ontario farmers, South African miners, nurses, even journalists.[20] All of these claims contained a hefty dose of someone's self-interest, whether a government that wished to recruit, an industry trying to allay unrest, or professionals seeking recognition. More palatable were the ads honouring a Good Samaritan – the Mormons, again, offered a number of these spectacles[21] – and, in particular, the pleas for volunteers. Indeed, the retreat of the welfare state turned the volunteer into a public good vital to the well-being of society. In 1989 British Columbia's Ministry of Social Services and Housing ran three spots praising foster parents for their work in saving children. In 1990 the Points of Light Foundation, presumably named after an evocative phrase in U.S. President Bush's inaugural address, urged Americans to 'Do something good, feel something real.'[22] The most extravagant sell, however, came earlier (1987) in a testimonial by movie star Whoopi Goldberg:[23]

> Think about this. If everyone of us gave just five hours a week to the cause we care about, it would be like mobilizing twenty million full-time volunteers just to tackle the problems of our society. We could all but wipe out drug abuse, juvenile crime, illiteracy, all those things we keep hoping will go away without our help. Just five hours a week. But it has to start with somebody. So give five. What you get back is immeasurable.

A third area of difficulty was manifest in the nation itself. Canadians might be forgiven for believing that they were cursed by an overdose of patriotic propaganda because of their country's never-ending series of constitutional crises. A national birthday (such as the country's 125th anniversary in 1992), a constitutional wrangle, or some other spasm of public emotion would provoke a wave of ads. A few were sombre, including a couple of shaming ads, sponsored by the Council of Concerned Canadians, that told Canadians to stop building walls and practise understanding.[24] Most were upbeat celebrations of things Canadian – mountains, woods, birds, celebrities, or just plain happy folk. Early in 1992 one newspaper estimated that the government had spent $8.5 million in the first three months to air 'six spots featuring uplifting music – *For Love of This Country*, sung by a young Montreal girl – and footage of beautiful scenery and such famous Canadians as Terry Fox, Roberta Bondar and Paul Henderson.'[25] That did not always please:

> An angry fan went into his office the morning after one of the recent National Hockey League playoff games, during which there were many

showings of the Secretary of State's For Love of This Country campaign, and told his colleagues: 'If I hear that little girl singing "I love Canada" one more time, I'm going to throw something at the TV set.'[26]

Such ads inadvertently expressed a more fundamental 'truth' about the country: that a patriotic Canada existed only as a promotional sign, a floating signifier, an imagined and asserted quantity which served the varied purposes of élites, especially political authority in Ottawa and corporate authorities across the country, whose power and profit required some semblance of community.[27] Much of this propaganda, then, avoided the reality of a divided land.

The same illusory quality was attached to similar projects in other places, for Canadians were not the only sufferers. The values of harmony, understanding, tolerance, and civility were loudly asserted to combat the absence of community. A Brazilian bank sold the virtues of civility, instead of strife (*For a Better Life*, 1981): 'Men of today, there is still time for joy, for love, and to discover that life is a lovely fantasy that we live together.'[28] A department store in Argentina touted the need for reconciliation after the collapse of the military regime: in *Homecoming* (1983) we saw a young man reunited with his father, no matter what the angers of the past.[29] The Los Angeles riots of 1992 occasioned a host of proposals for PSAs to bridge the gap between black citizens and white by means of sermons on understanding, shared values, and the virtues of talking.[30]

Similarly, the end of apartheid in South Africa brought efforts to sell peace and harmony, two public goals previously in very short supply, at an estimated cost of $20 million in donated talent, time, and space.[31] A related ad, *Bushman* (South African Olympic Team, 1993), constructed a new symbol of unity and hope out of what it claimed was an old image of power and peace fashioned long, long ago.[32] It was an impressive act of creation masquerading as an act of discovery. At one level, the admakers were trying to invest a particular symbol with traditional meaning, to make it numinous. At another they were engaged in a national work of healing and renewal to create a sense of community. Here was a promotional sign twice over, one that could work only by creating its own referents.

b) Anti-Discrimination

How the tone changed when the focus shifted to the problems of discrimination, to issues of exclusion and inferiority centred on race and ethnicity, women, disabilities, age, and sexual orientation. At least in

Canada, multiculturalism did inspire positive ads (although in talking about a new project, one admaker proclaimed that his purpose was to avoid 'those happy-faces, everybody's wonderful campaigns. We've had those up to our yin-yang in Canada').[33] But much more dramatic, both here and elsewhere, was a species of attack propaganda which employed reason-why, ridicule, and denunciation to trash views labelled as bigotry or prejudice – racism, sexism, ableism, ageism, heterosexism, or homophobia – by the advocates of human rights. This propaganda was one of the most visible tools of a rights movement that, by the 1990s, had won considerable support from the leaders of the professions, organized religion, the state, and even the corporate sector.

There was, as usual, little attempt at debate in the marketplace of signs. The task of the attack propaganda was to make its targets appear as Untruth – that is, to transform them into social risks which people recognized as harmful to the community. Rights advertising constructed, once more, a theatre of shame. The ads sought to impose correct thinking, correct speaking, and even correct listening (one radio spot in Toronto told people not to listen to ethnic jokes), in short, a form of discursive tyranny. The commodity this brand of civic advocacy sold was none other than political correctness.

Ironically, the very effort to trash the creeds now labelled pernicious required the rights ads to incorporate, and thus draw attention to, claims they pronounced wrong or hateful. Consider this spot, created in response to a new wave of xenophobia in the Europe of the mid-1990s:

Racist (Cash TV, Switzerland, 1994): The racist in question is a beer-swilling tough who speaks directly to the camera. In the beginning he is able to express his bile. 'Foreigners ... there's over a million here. Too many for Switzerland ... Drugs and crime that's what they've brought us. And 200,000 unemployed. Who grabs those jobs? I'm no racist but there is a limit. The criminals and lazy bastards they should fuck off.' Then the sound, lights, and eventually the visuals are successively cut off, because the film crew is made up of immigrants, which aptly demonstrates the desire to silence and to render invisible the racist enemy. The overt message is that immigrants did in fact contribute to the economy, so much so that they are vital to its efficiency. 'Foreigners. Without them our economy will stand still.' A little creative misreading could easily give that message a sinister cast.[34]

Although it was and is impossible for rights advocates to deny the import of difference, it was thought that propaganda might remedy how people treated difference in the course of their daily lives. The source of discrimination became not some social or biological 'reality' but what has been termed 'social construction,' a notion especially suited to the postmodern mentality.

Elizabeth (Department of Community Service, Australia, 1981): A confident and effective person who has overcome the limitations imposed by her inability to use her hands in a normal fashion blames her mother for labelling her disabled. When her mother died, she came to life. Similarly, in *Sign Language* (U.K., 1987), the Royal National Institute for the Deaf admonished the hearing majority – a few of whose representatives are shown (but not heard – they have been silenced) making excessive gestures of contempt – not to presume that deafness means stupidity. 'SO PLEASE DON'T TREAT US LIKE IDIOTS.'[35]

Grandpa's Computer (Ontario Minister for Senior Citizens' Affairs, 1987): This humorous piece has two spry elders (there was even a hint of sexual activity) play out the role of slow, slightly dim, and always backward seniors to satisfy the foolish expectations of their now mature children. Similarly, in *Policeman* (Canada, Urban Alliance on Race Relations, 1994) we are shown the face of a youngish black male, while also on screen are typed a name and a list of his crimes – but at the end that black male is identified as the policeman who captured the social menace. The ad both presents and then refutes the prevailing stereotype, and fear, of 'tough, black youth.'[36]

Objects (Colectivo de Educacion No Sexista, Spain, 1989): This ad mocks assumptions that differences between men and women justify confining each sex to a separate realm of existence. Each object is shown as the voice-over delivers the ridicule: 'Clothes-peg: it doesn't bite, it doesn't attack men. Steam iron: non-allergenic, no dangerous side effects. Sewing needle: its sting isn't poisonous. In this country six out of ten men are unaware of these facts. Common vacuum cleaner: using it regularly won't cause impotence.'[37]

Likewise, the attack propaganda did not question the persistence of hierarchy – how could it? – but concentrated instead on emphasizing that these facts could never justify discrimination.

Nobody Is Better (National Association of Television Program Executives [NATPE], U.S.A., 1993): The screen is filled with quick cuts of various white or black athletes doing amazing things. The African-American celebrity Danny Glover explains: people may be 'bigger,' 'stronger,' or 'faster,' but 'absolutely nobody is better.'

Brains (European Youth Against Racism, U.K., 1995): We see a fake comparison of the brains of different racial types, showing no difference, until the smaller brain of the racist is displayed. That ad, intentionally or otherwise, reversed a whole tradition of race 'science' which had ascribed different intellectual abilities to whites, Asians, and blacks.

Anti-Discrimination (Coordinadora de Iniciativas de Minoria, Spain, 1991): The ad cited individual genius against mass prejudices. A selection of black-and-white shots of events and/or people was mixed with bigoted comments from male and female voices. Martin Luther King, Jr: 'Bloody black bastard.' Albert Einstein: 'Smart-arsed Jew boy.' Gabriel García Márquez: 'Grease-ball Spic.' Nadjib Mahfuz: 'Filthy Arab.' Federico García Lorca: 'Dirty queer.' Stephen W. Hawking: 'Useless cripple.' Carmen Amaya, a dancer: 'Fucking Gypsy scum.' Voice-over: 'Do you too really think any one of us is better than them?' 'Have some respect for others.' Yet once again the very act of denial required the repetition of these bigoted epithets.[38]

'You may think a little stereotyping is harmless. It's not. When you misjudge someone or they stereotype you, it hurts,' warned Geraldo Rivera in a 1996 PSA. 'It can lead to conflict. Worse, it can deprive someone of their basic rights. Don't stereotype. No matter what someone looks like or how they act, give people a chance.'[39] The most compelling arguments focused on the harm discrimination fostered at home and in the wider world. An appealing young lad in *David's Story* (1988) explained how being labelled 'Mongoloid' or 'retarded' imprisoned him in stereotype.[40] A Finnish ad (*Equality*, 1983) noted how sexism was the only reason why women received less pay and promotion than men.[41] Indeed, prejudice and discrimination kept kids apart, made our cities impassable for the physically disabled, doomed South African children (in the days of apartheid) to medical neglect, fostered gay-bashing and the suicide of homosexual teens, and on and on.[42]

Yet this wave of attack propaganda did not dispel the so-called evil of stereotyping; it may well have produced as much dissent and cynicism as agreement. For the targets were examples of what Foucault called 'subjugated knowledge,' widely held beliefs and information now apparently discredited by science.[43] Indeed, in the recent past racism, sexism, and homophobia had all enjoyed the support of some branches of science, so they retained a degree of intellectual legitimacy. Worse yet, the continued efficacy of these subjugated knowledges was confirmed by the daily experience of difference and hierarchy that shaped the context of living throughout the lands of affluence. They provided scripts, practical guides in an age of identity politics, multiculturalism, affirmative action, and competing entitlements. Besides, stereotyping was commonplace in all sorts of other calculations, from insurance risks to voting blocks, practised by the most respected of institutions. It is no wonder that the marketing of political correctness provoked widespread resistance, even mockery, outside official circles.

4 The Plague of Crime

No other ill revealed the limits of the disciplinary regime so effectively as the problem of crime, most especially violent crime, during the 1980s. All sorts of statistics displayed the stark fact that North America had become a much more violent society since the fifties. In the United States the problem was especially serious: the overall number of violent crimes increased from 288,460 in 1960 to 1,039,710 fifteen years later and then to 1,820,130 by 1990.[44] Such numbers provoked panic, especially among women and African-Americans, and promoted daily behaviour conditioned by the fear of becoming another victim of crime.[45] In early 1994, Gallup found that more and more voters were listing crime as their number one concern, even though, long before then, governments and other authorities had mounted a major offensive to restore 'law and order' in the streets and homes of America. That involved a host of measures: tougher laws, more police, better surveillance techniques, improved technologies, and, of course, more propaganda. Ironically, the escalation of public worry about crime coincided with a dramatic drop in actual crime rates, especially in large American cities, during the mid-1990s. Something, perhaps everything, had begun to work.

The mainstay of anti-crime propaganda was what came to be known as the McGruff PSAs, named after their continuing fictitious character, a so-called crime dog who had his debut in 1979. The PSAs' purpose was to mobilize a presumably dispirited population by showing how ordinary citizens could fight crime. So the introductory ad, *Stop a Crime*, had the animated dog, who appeared superimposed in a live-action setting, tell people – brilliantly capturing the arrogance of administrative advertising – 'It's my job to teach you to protect yourselves. It's your job to learn.'[46] What he told those first viewers was to lock their doors, light up these same doors, make windows secure, have a neighbour keep an eye on the house when they were gone, and use a timer to turn lights on and off. They were also urged to write to an address for more information about how to 'Take a bite out of Crime,' the campaign slogan. The campaign proved an instant hit, not just with anti-crime managers but with the general public: a later survey discovered a high rate of recall (over 50 per cent) and liking, as well as some action (including buying a guard dog, which was not advocated!).[47] McGruff went on in later years to tackle teen crime, drug abuse, domestic violence, and, inevitably, child abuse in the mid-1990s (the theme song: 'Where Have All the Children Gone?,' adapted by Peter, Paul, and Mary, a famous sixties folk-rock group, from one of their superhits). Another study, of anti-violence PSAs of 1991, found even higher rates of recall and attention among the public, and even greater satisfaction among anti-crime managers.[48] In 1995 the campaign received an estimated $54 million of donated time and space, ranking number three among the Advertising Council's thirty-five programs. By this time, of course, McGruff was just the most visible aspect of a massive marketing effort to sell crime safety via demonstrations and special training sessions, contact with schools, community activities, a crime prevention month (October), and, above all, the mailing of tons of printed guides and action kits. McGruff also had a lot of rivals, perhaps because his success had demonstrated the payoffs from anti-crime propaganda.

In the 1990s, the chief target was the young male, white and especially black, who was deemed all too likely to be violent and also more likely than ever before to be armed. Once again, many sponsors used propaganda to orchestrate a theatre of shame that might compel youth to listen. 'This is the time for psychological warfare' against 'the underclass adolescent,' argued Bob Garfield, the ad critic of *Advertising Age* (15 July 1991). 'It must sting him, embarrass him, shame him out of the twisted bad-is-good social order of the streets, while empowering him elsewhere to earn the respect of others and himself.' That was a tall order. Derrick Thomas, an African-American football star, tried to explain how aggression was fine in sports but violence was definitely 'uncool' elsewhere: 'Take it out on the field, not on each other.'[49] One Clio Award winner (1995), *Et Tu Brutus*, offered viewers jolts of violence and excitement, a chase and a confrontation, just like so much television drama, in an attempt to persuade youth that they were actually killing themselves. Yet the context seemed wrong, and the style too frenzied. The result had the potential to glamorize violence and accentuate the sense of power attached to both guns and gangs. Once again, the propaganda clashed with the dictates of a subjugated knowledge, a knowledge born of life in the streets and enhanced by the images of violence sold by the culture industries.

WHILE YOU'RE TRYING TO
FIND THE RIGHT WORDS, YOUR FRIEND
MAY BE TRYING TO STAY ALIVE.

Figure 17: The Anonymous Victim. The woman here has little individuality and no history. She has been stripped of what makes her unique so that she can represent a particular group: battered women. Such ads must deny context – that is, whatever situation, whatever factors brought about the violence. Even the absence of the male (we must presume that she has been hurt by her spouse or boyfriend) is important to the purpose of the message. That way, we can be held responsible for her condition. Her existence becomes our shame. But how long will such an image evoke the necessary sentiment? How much more shock, how much more damage, will be required to provoke next time?

The other grand concern was over violence in the home, and here American efforts were echoed in other parts of the affluent world. During the 1980s, news stories revealed that the home was not the sanctuary of peace once celebrated in bourgeois dreams. Instead it had become (or was it always?) a site of pain where parents abused children and men abused women. Sometimes the propaganda blamed distraught mothers; more often it was violent fathers; occasionally, the whole family was labelled dysfunctional. The result, as Britain's National Society for

the Prevention of Cruelty to Children (NSPCC) made all too clear in
Excuses (1991), was damaged children, an excess of hurt that could never
be excused.[50] The statistics of what was euphemistically called spousal or
partner abuse were even more startling. Viewers learned from *Furie*
(1987), 'Au Québec, plus de 200,000 femmes sont victimes de violence
conjugale.'[51] Things were worse in Britain, apparently, where one woman
in four would be a victim according to *Statistics* (1995).[52] Nor was the
United States any better: 'Every twelve seconds a woman in this country is
abused,' the announcer claimed in *Mark Russell* (ESPN network 1996).[53]
Who cared whether the statistics were accurate?

What made these and similar ads so nasty was their taste for the
graphic. *Furie* displayed the aftermath of a quarrel, the battered, bleed-
ing woman locked in the bathroom and the infuriated male hammering
at the door. *Statistics* actually showed a man brutalizing a woman: shov-
ing, punching, and kicking her, obviously relishing his moment of triumph. The Ontario Women's Directorate first simulated a rape and later
showed men hitting women in public.[54] Women's Aid in Britain mugged
the viewer by showing a series of pictures that focused on the damage
inflicted on various parts of women's bodies.[55] Playing throughout was
the song, 'Stand by Your Man,' an added and dark touch of irony. The
whole point was to get the crime out into the open, to push family,
neighbours, friends – and the abused themselves – to take action. The
milder *Mark Russell*, for example, flashed the name of an abuser (fictional, not real) on the video screen at a football game: this would show
just what sort of a man you were. There was evidence these tactics could
pay off: an outrageous campaign in Scotland provoked some 12,000 calls,
one-quarter purportedly from abusers. The thrust of the more extreme
ads was to blame masculinity, to shame men for waging war against
women and children. But a simple claim that men as men were at fault
was not popular: one American study found that people resisted 'framing' men as the enemy.[56]

If not men, then who was the enemy? Or, rather, what was the enemy?
One answer might be television. The baneful effects of television viewing
had been a staple of sociological research since the early 1960s. But only
in the mid-1990s did this brand of science begin to find expression in any
form of civic advocacy. And, strange as it may seem, the agitation was
sponsored by elements within the broadcasting industry. Britain's Independent Television Commission argued that it protected the public
interest, particularly children, against a wave of television violence.[57]
More often, the aim was to shift the moral gaze from the industry itself

onto the parent. The Canadian Association of Broadcasters showed in 1994 PSAs how violence depicted on television could reach children and stain your screen with blood, if you the parent did not take care.[58] In the United States, an industry organization told parents to supervise what their kids watched, associating television with other perils such as knives, medicines, and guns.[59] By contrast, PBS identified its service as a safe haven, telling these same parents that commercial TV worked on the premise that 'violence sells.'[60]

The fear was that TV violence threatened to educate a new, amoral generation of predators who, once they grew up, would produce a crime wave more vicious and terrifying than anything seen before. That prospect reflected the views of some criminologists, although these were more likely to cite 'fatherless households and fractured neighbourhoods.'[61] No matter: the fear was transformed into a warning about television by an extraordinary trio of ads from Südwestfunk (SWF), the public broadcasting corporation for South West Germany:

The SWF-TV campaign: These stunning commercials identify TV as the Evil Eye which spreads horror wherever it establishes its domain. There is no compromise here: this is evil and it is polluting our children. Hell has arrived, and it is featured every night on TV – and our children are watching it.

Storytime (1994): An Exercise in Incongruity. A gentle granny reads a bedtime story to a wide-eyed, cute girl, all snuggled in bed. Except the bedtime story is full of nasties: blood, gore, and body parts. The announcer's comment: 'Of course you don't tell your children bedtime stories like these. But they watch them. On TV, at night. Just think about it.'

The Gun (1994): A Surreal Display of Innocence Betrayed. A man loads what looks like a gun, turns, aims, and fires at us. In the course of the next forty seconds he will shoot again and again, and we will hear in the background sounds of alarm and pain. But the focus is on a series of dazzled or startled children, always watching. Attached to each is a factoid: '14 RAPES,' '44 TORTURES,' '526 MURDERS.' Back to the gunman, 'IN ONE WEEK,' focus on what he is fondling, a remote control device, 'WITH ONE WEAPON.' Voice-over: 'Protect your children from violence on TV. A flick of the wrist is all it takes.' When open, the remote discharges not batteries but bullets.

Idols (1995): The Barbarians Are Out. This dark fantasy takes us back to the postmodern city, now deserted but for children who reign over streets full of ugly buildings, graffiti, and broken windows. We're offered a collection of performances, each slowed, each violent, displaying otherwise ordinary children hunting and hurting other children. In one, a boy holds a knife to a girl's throat while his companion empties her pockets; in another, a bigger boy smashes his smaller victim with a lead pipe while a crowd eggs him on. Attached to each of these vignettes is a title, of a movie like *Rambo* or a TV series like *Power Rangers*. Between these horrors are brief glimpses of mesmerized children, each watching something that flickers ... the television. We hear sharp electronic sounds, heavy breathing, distorted voices, screams, the noises of hitting, gunshots, the sounds of pain. Superimposed on a black screen at the end is the ominous warning: 'Children look for role models. Give them a helping hand before someone else does.'

Each commercial ended with the same label: 'A recommendation of SWF Television.' SWF had attempted to unsell a social risk – violent, mostly foreign, programming – so that it could brand its own public good, a sanitized television.[62]

It was this purpose, however, which pointed to a new role for advocacy advertising, as a method of repackaging private and particular products for consumers.

7

Appropriations: Benetton and Others

A defining attribute of culture at the end of the twentieth century is the appeal of the eclectic, a penchant for hybrids, fusions, *bricolage*. And this attribute of the culture is reflected in its advertising. Consider events in the United States, always the home of experiment, in 1997 and 1998: the federal government adopted paid PSAs (for the census and for anti-drug campaigns), the Ad Council agreed to tailor PSAs to the network's promotional efforts, the Arthritis Foundation turned to an ad-supported infomercial to raise funds, and the Children's Television Network (purveyors of *Sesame Street*) proudly announced a new initiative – 'Play It Smart' – to 'grow' its brand. More intriguing, however, was the evidence of mutations in the other direction: the signs that social advocacy was shaping the practices of consumer advertising. The particular means fashioned by advocates to get their messages to a public through all the commercial clutter were now being appropriated by the friends and foes of consumer advertising to capture the attention of a jaded public. Indeed, some leading corporations had begun to mount their own campaigns of truth, hoping that a moral (dis)guise might add weight to efforts to sell their goods or their images. Let me state the obvious: this imitation is in itself evidence of the growing importance of advocacy advertising in the discursive universe of our times.

1 The Benetton Project

On 23 January 1994, an unusual exhibition of photographs came to the Joseph D. Carrier Art Gallery, at the Columbus Centre, a complex built for the Italian-Canadian community in Toronto. The collection was on an international tour sponsored by the Italian clothing manufacturer

Benetton. The next year, similar exhibitions were scheduled for the Museum of Contemporary Art in Lausanne, the Bienal de São Paulo, and other locations throughout Latin America. The photographs had been either taken or selected by Oliviero Toscani, an Italian photographer and Benetton's creative director, to use in the company's advertising – or, as it preferred to say, its communications. However, they were presented here as art, situated on a wall at the proper viewing height, offered without the familiar logo, 'The United Colors of Benetton,' that had accompanied the same images when they appeared in magazines or on billboards – sometimes to great hue and cry. A media kit gave a brief history of the advertising and provided copies of a few press responses, from the past three years, to what had been one of the most innovative and controversial campaigns of the early 1990s. The exhibitions were billed as a chance to revisit the images and relive the sensation.

The Benetton Group is one of those new, innovative, global enterprises that have captured the fancy of theorists, sometimes referred to as post-Fordists, who seek to explain how industrial society and the economy have been transformed in postmodern times.[1] The Benetton family founded the clothing manufacturer in Ponzano Veneto, near Treviso, in north-east Italy in 1965. The firm made its mark by producing brightly colored sweaters aimed at youth: its target market during the 1980s became people aged eighteen to thirty-four everywhere in the affluent world. Benetton focused on manufacturing: it employed a system of flexible production and speedy distribution in which the design and colour of goods could be swiftly altered (within ten days, according to one estimate) to respond to changes in demand detected at its outlets. Success turned it into the largest purchaser of wool in the world. The company's main centres of production were all in western Europe, notably Italy, France, and Spain, where it became the dominant clothing manufacturer. Gradually, the firm expanded its product line to include other clothes and accessories (eventually, watches, perfume, and condoms). All of these goods were sold through licensed outlets that reached well beyond the affluent world: by the mid-1990s it boasted 7,000 'points of sale' in 170 different countries, although its position in the key market of the United States had weakened considerably since the late 1980s. Benetton has been called (and the label was meant as a compliment) 'the McDonald's of the fashion industry' because of its ubiquity and its uniformity. Sales were estimated at approximately $2.055 billion U.S. in 1997, generating a net income of $164 million.[2] The family-owned Edizione Holding still controlled the

Benetton Group (roughly 70 per cent of it in 1999), which had gone public in 1986.

The company had advertised consistently only in Italy and France prior to the early 1980s. In 1984, at a time when it was expanding rapidly, averaging one store opening per day, it began to invest substantial sums in a new global communications strategy.[3] However, Oliviero Toscani was not out to sell product, at least not obviously: 'I take pictures, I don't sell clothes,' he proclaimed.[4] Rather, chief executive officer Luciano Benetton hired Toscani in 1982 and gave him the leeway – 'incredible freedom' Toscani once enthused[5] – to propose novel approaches and issues. The original idea was to generate images, largely free of text, which could speak the same way to consumers in very different parts of the world. Benetton hoped to overcome the tyranny of language.

Initially, Toscani offered striking pictures of unusual, often beautiful, young people, of different races, sometimes dressed in Benetton garb, to which he attached only the company name. These people looked processed, unnatural: they were ideal types, not ordinary folks. Toscani made abundant use of the semiotics of gesture and setting and artifact. His people were shot in particular poses, located in some special tableau, helped by props like a flag or the globe, all of which carried a hefty symbolic freight. 'Who is this Benetton anyway?,' Soviet leader Gorbachev had asked in 1986: Benetton had lined a route taken by French president Mitterrand and Gorbachev with posters of two black children, one in Soviet colours and the other in American colours.[6]

Consider just one of the ads from this first wave of Benetton messages:

Arab/Jew (1986): Two youthful males, a handsome Arab and a bespectacled Israeli, stand together, each with an arm on the other's shoulder, one hand touching a globe. The ethnic markings of the dress and the features are blatant, buttressed here by text written in Hebrew and Arabic. The two adolescents look out at us provocatively.

Toscani's images celebrated harmony, peace, multiracialism, and agency – that is, the individuals confront us as confident souls. More subtly, the photographs spoke of difference and identity, emphasizing the looks of youth, of race or nationality, and of gender. In short, they were about particularity. *Arab/Jew,* like others in this first wave, was a happy image, suggesting a future of bright promise brought to us courtesy of youth (and Benetton?).[7]

Then, beginning in 1989, Toscani created much more dramatic, some-

times playful, and often ambiguous photographs that were clearly designed to provoke. The product, Benetton's fashions, completely disappeared from the company's advertising. Instead, consumers saw the
handcuffed wrists of a black and a white male (*Handcuffs*, 1989), a priest
giving a passionate kiss to a nun (*Priest and Nun*, 1990), or simply a series
of crosses –one with a Star of David – marking the dead (*War Cemetery*,
1991), but always with that one addition, what had become the company's slogan and logo: 'The United Colors of Benetton.' Here is one of the
most outrageous examples:

Breastfeeding (1989): The ad featured the torso of a young black woman suckling
a lusty white infant. The woman's red cardigan was open to reveal her bosom,
one well-formed breast left bare and the other covered by the baby she cradled in
her gentle hands. It was supposed to signify, claimed a later blurb, 'that equality
goes beyond kneejerk reactions and conventional perceptions.'[8] Sex, race, and
class: an image that served up such an explosive mixture could suggest black
servitude just as easily as racial harmony.

The anger of some unspecified African-American organizations (*New
York Times*, 15 April 1991) convinced Benetton to withdraw the ad in the
United States. But elsewhere, in Austria, Denmark, Italy, and France, the
stylish and striking photograph won awards. Europe was cited to refute
America – this was art. In time, *Breastfeeding* won more awards than any
other single image Benetton used.

Later, Toscani admitted a grandiose ambition: to construct a new
common language of images that would undo the Babel of tongues
dividing humanity. Were his photographs intended to repair God's flawed
work, wondered the astonished reporter?[9] In fact, these campaigns demonstrated just how resistant culture was to a global campaign, at least of
the kind that Toscani had developed. Each of his carefully designed
images came without text, except for the logo. What intrigued or pleased
one group upset another. They divided as well as thrilled. The sight of a
nun and a priest kissing antagonized elements in Catholic Italy but won
an award in secular Britain. Muslim authorities found the display of three
children of black, white, and Chinese ancestry sticking out their tongues
not cute or even vulgar but plain obscene. A picture of coloured condoms floating in mid-air was vetoed by American media as 'pornographic,' though it was accepted elsewhere. A collection of marching
wooden puppets, Pinocchios, each with a long nose, evoked images of ex-
dictator Pinochet and his army in Chile. Neither Toscani nor Benetton

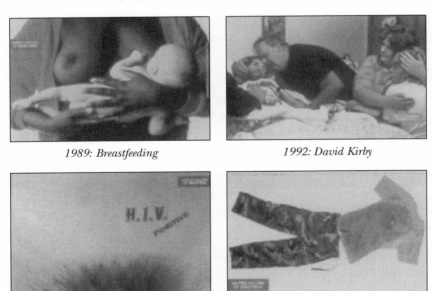

1989: Breastfeeding   *1992: David Kirby*

1993: Abdomen   *1994: Marinko Gagro*

Figure 18: Some Benetton Ads

could fix the meaning of their advertising, although they certainly tried to do so via press releases and interviews. In a way the mixed responses all confirmed a claim once made by Roland Barthes, that 'the meaning of an image is never certain' unless it is grounded by words.[10]

A different problem was that many of these photographs looked stylized, more like fashion shots or carefully arranged fakes. So a third wave of 'reality' images in 1992 answered this criticism by using actual photographs that had appeared elsewhere and could thereby claim authenticity – with the crucial addition of the company's signature, 'The United Colors of Benetton.'[11] Equally important, the campaign shifted to the negative: Toscani selected images that spoke of environmental disaster, violence, refugees, and child labour. But the transfer of the images from the context of news to the context of advertising caused upset. What was acceptable as a visual record of some horror or another became offensive as the vehicle of a sell. The series elicited charges that Benetton was trying to brand suffering and exploit misery. Britain's Advertising Standards Authority advised publishers to refuse virtually all the ads.[12] The

French ad watchdog, the Bureau de Vérification de la Publicité (BVP), also recommended a ban.[13] German courts deemed some of the images illegal under a special provision that prohibited competitive practices '*contra bonos mores*.'[14] Toscani would make no apology. 'We are focusing the interest of consumers on issues – on daily life, the human condition – instead of human consumption,' he said in Chicago.[15]

One of the 'real pictures' Toscani had appropriated (from *Life* magazine) dealt with the subject of AIDS:

David Kirby: The single most famous photograph of the 1992 series was a deathbed scene, in which an emaciated David Kirby, an AIDS activist, was surrounded by his loving family, who seemed, by contrast, unfortunately plump. Kirby looked almost Christlike: 'It's a religious allegory – a modern-day Giotto,' claimed one critic (*Adweek*, 17 February 1992). There were charges that Toscani had touched up the photograph (and in fact the picture was colourized). Not so, responded Toscani: 'Personally I call this picture "La Pietà," because it's a Pietà, which is real.' Unlike Michelangelo's Pietà, which, he suggested, 'might be a fake.'[16]

The next year Toscani pursued the subject with three ads showing portions of a human body tattooed with the label 'HIV positive.' These had a double meaning. First, *Abdomen* (the lower part), *Arm*, and *Backside* were supposed to suggest the access points HIV used to enter the body. Second, each was a metaphor meant to condemn, not condone, the social stigma attached to the unfortunate.[17] That was not the way some people read this propaganda. 'BENETTON AIDS AD BRANDED AS "NAZI"' shouted the business-page headline of the New York *Post* (17 September 1993). The company was successfully sued by a group of AIDS victims in France for defamation: the judge ruled the ads 'a provocative exploitation of suffering.'[18]

Meanwhile, Toscani's antics had outraged yet another special interest. In February 1994, Benetton began a campaign for peace in the former Yugoslavia by publishing a photograph of the bloodstained clothes of Marinko Gagro – this time with some extra text, albeit in Serbo-Croat: 'I, Gojko Gagro, father of the deceased Marinko, wish that all that is left of my son be used for peace and against war.' The campaign again impressed some judges in the ad world, specifically the Art Directors clubs of New York and Tokyo, which gave Benetton new awards. But it also provoked two human-rights groups in Germany to seek legal action against the company's exploitation of the Bosnian tragedy.[19] A poll sponsored by *Der Spiegel* discovered that more than eight out of ten Germans found the Benetton ads 'distasteful.'[20] Later a group of German retailers claimed that Toscani's advertising had dramatically reduced sales, so they sought release from their contracts with Benetton, though in the end the courts ruled in the company's favour.[21] In certain circles the slogan had become 'United Horrors of Benetton.'[22]

The angry or upsetting images continued into 1995. A new campaign for the company's SportSystem Division employed, for example, twin images of German and American athletes, the first giving the Nazi salute and the second a black-power salute at the Olympics: Toscani added the question, 'DO YOU PLAY RACE?'[23] But Benetton had already begun to change its tactics. In 1991 the company launched its global magazine, *Colors*, where it could mix sensational photos and new fashions in a medium that did not cause the same upset. A certain playfulness returned to the main campaigns as early as 1993 when Luciano Benetton appeared nude in ads, though discreetly covered by the words 'I WANT MY CLOTHES BACK,' to promote the collection of clothing for people in need. That campaign had been organized with the assistance of the Red Cross and other relief agencies. Increasingly, Benetton sought to work with non-profits, whether SOS Racisme or AIDS agencies or a peace group like War Child, a strategy which gave credibility to its advertising and blunted criticism. Perhaps most important, its advertising had become less confrontational and more positive. The image of a wooden spoon against a white background worked to promote (along with the international Food and Agriculture Organization whose logo also appeared) the World Food Summit in Rome, in November 1996. A year later came a witty product ad for the company's Undercolors: the AIDS red ribbon was strategically placed against white underwear worn by a white male and a black woman. In the spring of 1998, Benetton allied with the United Nations Organization of Italy to celebrate the fiftieth anniversary of the Universal Declaration of Human Rights by running ads and posters throughout much of the affluent world, featuring the bright and beautiful faces of youth. Had events come full circle?

In early 1996, the story of one of Toscani's failures came to light: he had tried unsuccessfully to get Subcommandante Marcos, the masked face and public voice of Mexico's Zapatista insurgents, to agree to allow a team to photograph him and his associates for Benetton's purposes. A letter laid out what the admaker claimed was the history and purpose of the Benetton project: [24]

For a long time United Colors of Benetton has chosen to use a large part of its advertising budget to address the most dramatic problems of this century: AIDS, war, racism, intolerance. It's a way to create a different dialogue with the 'consumers,' who for us are first of all 'men and women.' We have always chosen to photograph 'true persons' – not models – in the places where they actually live. In this way, we have highlighted the beauty of the Chinese, of the Turks, of the inhabitants of a little Italian village, and, recently, of the Palestinians of Gaza.

Today, we address ourselves to you because we sense that you know that communications can be a form of struggle. We ask you to give us an opportunity to photograph you with the men, women, and children of your group, the Zapatista National Liberation Army. We would like to give you a chance to show the beauty of the faces of those who struggle in the name of an idea. We believe that an ideal brightens the eyes and lights up the faces of those who fight to realize it. We do not believe in the beauty myths propagated by consumerism. For this reason, we ask you to receive us among your people and to give us the opportunity to find another way of making your lives and your history known.

Benetton put on airs, of defiance and of superiority. Toscani and the company constantly proclaimed their special virtue in a corrupted world. They went to great pains to distinguish what Benetton was doing from ordinary advertising. 'I'm offended by traditional advertising,' Toscani had declared,[25] because it specialized in the fake. 'Agencies are very cautious, creating bland and boring advertising,' asserted John Poerink, advertising manager for Benetton North America.[26] Ad agencies 'don't want to know what's going on in the world. They create a false reality and want people to believe in it. We show reality and we're criticized for it.'[27] Corporations had a responsibility to take a stand in ways which provoked people to think and discuss matters of importance. So Toscani's photographs were labelled part of a communications policy, presented as a kind of public service.

Benetton was also selling, of course, and what it sold was a public attitude or pose. That pose demanded confrontation, in itself deemed a virtue. '"A message which doesn't stir controversy," says Oliviero Toscani, "is bland, mediocre. Perhaps it's calculated precisely not to give trouble."'[28] Toscani's propaganda had a decidedly heterodox quality. The ads sneered at tradition and convention, challenged taboos, mocked authority. 'Lots of people need to be shocked to understand.'[29] The old was unwanted. 'We are after youthful rather than young people who have a lively sense of questioning, who accept new ideas and who are constantly questioning social taboos and social mores.'[30] The aim was to identify the virtuous and to celebrate a special kind of community, a new global tribe of youthful rebels amenable to the corporate vision of the socially conscious Benetton.[31] The obligation level was kept very low. What these people did, how these people voted was, ultimately, less important than their very being – and their awareness of the issues. So Benetton communications were not really 'catalysts,' at least not in the normal sense, since they were not intended to motivate a particular public behaviour. The overarching admonition?: Think Right. Wearing Benetton became a badge that signified progressive attitudes.

Benetton had set out to brand itself. The company wanted to become a celebrity in the world of capitalism – and Toscani wished to be the artistic maestro of this cultural triumph. Benetton relished the limelight, welcoming the awards and the controversy because both meant loads of free publicity. The excitement generated by a photograph of a newborn child complete with blood and umbilical cord reportedly filled Luciano Benetton with glee: 'It strengthens the product, the whole world is talking about us.'[32] Such statements could easily be taken by critics as evidence of the company's hidden agenda. But the agenda was not really hidden. The whole purpose, admitted a Benetton document, was 'to create a long-term, homogeneous, international image which focuses on the ethos of the product, i.e.: the infinite variety and use of colours and the fact that the Benetton label is accessible and affordable to everyone.'[33] The company saw itself as 'a concerned, socially-active, cutting edge and global fashion apparel company' which manufactured both 'a progressive approach' and 'colourful sportswear.'[34] Altruism and self-interest were inextricably linked. Benetton's communications were a most ingenious way of realizing that consistent aim of corporate advertising: to establish the sponsor as a public good.

The project was extraordinarily successful. According to the company's own figures, sales rose roughly a half again in five years, from 2,069 billion lire in 1990 to 2,940 billion lire in 1995.[35] A Reuters report of March 1997 found that Benetton was loaded with so much cash that it could eliminate its debts and still build up its bank account.[36] Of course, the increase in sales might be explained by many different factors. But what was most impressive was the claim that the Benetton name ranked 'among the five best-recognized trademarks of the world.'[37] That had resulted from the excitement and the publicity generated by Benetton's propaganda.

Perhaps the single most significant legacy of Toscani's enterprise was the booming of shock advertising as a technique of selling private goods. All the controversy attracted opportunists, especially in the clothing business. Just what did Esprit, a clothing firm, mean when it ran an American ad featuring a fed-up young black woman and the command, 'End racism and the killing of my people in the street,' wondered the London *Times* (29 September 1991). Buy an outfit and save a life? In the mid-1990s Superga shoes, an Italian firm, linked its brand to the spirit of rebellion when it ran a TV commercial (entitled *The Challenge*) that featured police violence at an animal rights demonstration. Kadu, a small Australian manufacturer, won an award in 1994 for a gross image of a pair of shorts, still perfect, in the remains of a shark's stomach.[38] One might hold Benetton responsible for the wide variety of shocking images that have grown more and more frequent in consumer advertising in the 1990s. However, few of these examples share the justification of artistry and innovation which belonged to Toscani's creations.

2 Cause Marketing

By the mid-1990s the Benetton project could be depicted as just the most spectacular example of a more general phenomenon called cause or cause-related marketing (CRM). 'Cause Related Marketing is a commercial activity by which a company with an image, product or service to market builds a relationship with a cause or a number of causes for mutual benefit,' enthused one British advocate. 'It is nothing more than enlightened self-interest. When Cause Related Marketing works well, everyone wins; the company, the charity or cause and the customer.'[39] The imperatives of commerce, however, were supposed to be in the ascendant: 'Cause-related marketing is a strategy for selling, not for making charitable donations.'[40] The money came out of the marketing budget.[41] CRM represented an attempt by a company to appropriate the moral strength of propaganda in order to advance a commercial agenda.

The resulting amalgam of advertising, public relations, and special promotions has become one of the fads of the 1990s, first in the United States and then in other affluent zones. One estimate put American spending on CRM at $600 million in 1996, not a great deal compared to other kinds of marketing, perhaps, but double the amount of three years earlier.[42] A British survey of corporate executives in 450 corporations found that over 90 per cent did 'some level of Cause Related Marketing spending' (averaging £275,000), and over half the chief executives admitted that CRM was 'important to the overall aims of their company.'[43]

Cause marketing had a long history, albeit under different names. Corporations had long desired to win a reputation for social responsibility. Seagram had run ads urging the wisdom of moderation on drinkers since the end of Prohibition in the United States. Esso had sponsored a popular 'energy conservation' campaign on German television in the mid-1970s.[44] One American survey of 'eleemosynary promotions' in 1974 noted that Sara Lee and Seven-Up worked with the Jerry Lewis Muscular Dystrophy Telethon, Colgate assisted Boy and Girl Scouts (the 'Help Young America' campaign), Campbell Soup sponsored 'Labels for Education' (elementary schools returned labels from cans of soup or beans in return for audiovisual and sports equipment), and so on. All of these good works were touted in ads.[45] But the credit for remaking (and naming) cause marketing was bestowed upon a former vice-president of American Express, Jerry Welsh. It was AMEX which successfully applied the techniques of cause marketing outside the domain of charities. In 1983 the company went national with ads for a Statue of Liberty campaign: AMEX contributed a penny a charge, and a dollar per new card or vacation sold, to the effort to restore the famous lady to her previous glory. In three hectic months the number of new cardholders increased 45 per cent, card use went up 28 per cent, and the campaign generated $1.7 million for the patriotic cause.[46] That campaign was later criticized because it was so short-lived, producing a sales spike but not a long-term brand loyalty. Even so, the lesson remained that CRM could generate spectacular results.

The hyper-competition of the 1990s drove marketing managers to investigate the virtues of cause marketing. CRM might deliver that crucial 'value-added differentiator' (in marketing-speak) which would help a product stand out in the clutter of advertising.[47] The persistent, obsessive reconnaissance of consumer attitudes had detected an increasing willingness to reward companies that contributed to solving social ills. Consumers found a good deal of price and quality parity among competing products, so they were 'feeling free to indulge their consciences every time they open their pocketbooks.'[48] Specifically, an estimated two-thirds of American consumers in one 1999 report indicated a willingness to switch brands or retailers on the basis of a moral assessment of a company's commitment to a cause, other things being equal. One-third in a 1998 report claimed that they frequently used such a judgment when making a purchase. And the most affluent buyers were also the most receptive to this line of reasoning. Even if these figures were inflated – what people said did not always match what they did – the fact remained that a well-executed strategy of cause marketing could stem brand defections, win new custom, and build consumer loyalty. The emotional bond might become so deep that customers would turn into '"apostles" – people who will go out and tell their friends about a brand they really like.'[49] The boom in cause marketing subjected consumers to an increasing variety of messages that sold public and private goods, or relabelled the private as public. These ads derived at least part of their force from the presence of something different or unexpected, however trivial, such as an endorsement or an insignia of some advocacy organization, in the normal mix of ingredients which made up any ad.

There were very different ways to do cause marketing. Companies might go it alone – that is, simply announce their commitment to a cause. The commercial *Roundeye* (U.K.) was a very clever critique of racism – but the ad ended with a strange query, 'WHAT'S STOPPING YOU BUYING A CAR FROM KOREA?'[50] The sponsor was Hyundai. This kind of advertising seemed too self-serving to earn much credibility. Such practices invited a media exposé. Corporations were wise to seek a partner, a non-profit or a government body whose presence would enhance the believability of the advertising. In 1991 Shoppers Drug Mart, a large drugstore chain in Canada, contributed about $1 million to advertise Fair Play, a public-private partnership, to eliminate violence, drugs, and cheating from sports.[51] Over a period of five years, the Coors beer company spent roughly $40 million working with a number of non-profits, including the National Volunteer Literacy Campaign and Service, Employment, Redevelopment (SER)–Jobs for Progress, to assist the cause of literacy in the United States.[52]

The key was to find the right issue – ideally, in the jargon of marketing, to 'own' the issue. A few companies, such as Britain's Body Shop (cosmetics) and America's Ben and Jerry's (ice cream), contributed funds to a variety of different causes and non-profits, thereby identifying themselves (*à la* Benetton) as progressive. In 1988 Reebok committed itself to human rights: that led to work with rock stars (including Bruce Springsteen and Sting) to raise funds for Amnesty International. But many firms looked for causes which suited the nature of their business pursuits: Stay in School (McDonald's, 1988), HomeAid (Building Industry Association of Southern California, 1989), Avon's Breast Cancer Awareness Crusade (TV campaign, 1993), the pro-sport PLAY (Nike, 1994), healthy eating (Kellogg's and Health Canada, 1995). Avon cosmetics, for example, went to considerable effort to find the right cause, meaning one that would 'resonate' with its sales force and its customers. Its research identified the issue of breast cancer and set off a whirlwind of activity, if we are to believe Avon's own account of events.[53] The company joined with a collection of organizations, including the National Alliance of Breast Cancer Organizations and the Centers for Disease Control, to educate women, especially low-income and minority women, about the perils of breast cancer. The company's sales force distributed forty-eight million brochures. A 1993 television campaign moved thousands to phone a 1-800 number for more information. In 1994 English- and Spanish-language versions of 'The Breast Cancer Test,' a PBS special underwritten by Avon, spread the word about the National Cancer Institute's information services. By 1996 Avon representatives had raised $16.5 million for community-based programs by selling pink-ribbon pins and pens. Avon could not claim to 'own' the breast-cancer issue (which attracted a variety of other sponsors in the mid-1990s), but Avon certainly had the predominant share.

Avon's director of public affairs was clearly pleased with the results of the crusade.[54] There could be difficulties for the corporate partner, however. In 1987 Fleischmann's (purveyors of various food products, including margarine) had to pull out of a partnership with the American Academy of Family Physicians to wage war on heart disease. The campaign would have warned the public that smoking, along with a poor diet, was a cause of heart disease. Fleischmann's was a division of RJR Nabisco, so a tobacco company would have endorsed one of the charges of the anti-smoking lobby. In 1991 Fuji upset advocates of the mentally disabled with a British television campaign that actually sought to dishonor bigotry of all kinds. Fuji had used the moral appeal to dress up the promotion of its own film. It had worked with interested parties, including Mencap, before the campaign ran. But the public response was sufficient to compel Mencap to demand the withdrawal of the ads. A co-branding agreement in 1997 between the American Medical Association (AMA) and the Sunbeam corporation was especially disastrous. Sunbeam was marketing a new line of Health at Home appliances, such as thermometers and heating pads. The agreement meant substantial royalties for the AMA. A 'firestorm' of criticism compelled the AMA to seek an escape from the agreement, which led Sunbeam to threaten a lawsuit.[55]

The breakdown of the AMA/Sunbeam deal was evidence that the other partner might also suffer disappointment. Witness the case of the National Cancer Institute (NCI). The NCI had worked well with Kellogg's in the mid-1980s: tracking studies indicated that Kellogg's ads had increased consumption of high-fibre cereals (and not just the company's product) as well as spreading the NCI message about a proper diet. In 1987, the Campbell Soup Company approached the organization with a similar proposal to assist the company's anti-cancer claims for its bean and pea soups. Even though there was no formal agreement, Campbell's advertising explicitly referenced the NCI recommendations. The NCI objected because the high sodium content of the product made it a less-than-optimal source of fibre. But all it could do was to take its name out of the ads and refer the matter to the Federal Trade Commission (which did not act on the issue).[56]

Cause marketing represented an alliance between two quantities once deemed opposites, commerce and conscience. The practice strengthened the emerging links between the non-profit and the business sectors. Its currency reflected the changing attitudes among the public. 'Baby Boomers want to apply their social consciences when they buy,' mused one Canadian marketer.[57] Conscience had been commodified: people wished to invest in a cause when they bought their hamburgers, a bra, a trip, the new car, and so on. One of the American surveys mentioned earlier found that levels of public scepticism about CRM had fallen dramatically, from 58 per cent in 1993 (people who thought CRM was just a 'show') to a mere 21 per cent three years later. More people were coming to expect large corporations to help, and especially to help local causes, because government funding was in decline. On the other hand, the focus of public attention was not constant: the interest in crime, education, poverty, and the environment had gone up, whereas the worry about drug abuse and homelessness had waned.[58] So cause marketing could easily reflect the flavour of the season, the actual causes being subject to the same fads and fashions that afflicted any other commodity. After all, corporations were moved first by what might capture the public fancy, not by what might be an urgent social need. That was left to philanthropy.

3 Parody and Subversion

The Benetton project had dealt in fun as well as shock. And not only by presenting its own poster boy: the obscured picture of a nude Luciano Benetton. The company had joined in a publicity stunt that put a giant condom on the obelisk in the Place de la Concorde in Paris to support AIDS awareness. In 1996 Toscani authored *Horses*, the image of a black stallion mounting a white mare, supposedly to tout the virtues of authenticity.[59] This playfulness harked back to a tradition of the carnivalesque which had been part of advertising since its beginnings in the early nineteenth century.[60] The carnivalesque was in some ways oppositional: admakers satirized, and occasionally subverted, by using words and images that mocked convention or upset authority. Humour and irony might be part of the mix. But most telling was parody, where the artist worked off an actual model to produce something which criticized.

One form of parody spoofed propaganda. The whole idea was to heighten the distinction of a brand, usually to position it as signifying rebellion against the officially sanctioned morality. So in 1993 Diesel, an Italian firm, gave its jeans a burst of notoriety by running magazine ads which encouraged the use of guns ('teaching kids to kill helps them deal directly with reality') and heavy smoking ('Why stop at bronchitis when a faster heartbeat and a shorter life are just around the corner?').[61] One of its TV ads (*Stay Up with Rubber,* 1992), styled on a government safety message, had a beautiful woman divert male drivers, who promptly crashed, in order to steal the inner tubes of their tires to make a rubber float for the family pool.[62] The ads certainly brought the hitherto little-known firm recognition (one magazine dropped the gun ad and apologized to readers). In 1994 Perrier, famous for its bizarre advertising, ran a print ad in which the shock image was a gun, loaded with Perrier bottle caps, pointed directly at the reader. The slogan delivered the ironic charge (translated), 'If only man were satisfied with the violence of a Perrier.' Other images in the French campaign showed a dummy riddled with Perrier caps and the chalked outline of a bottle as a corpse. Perrier proclaimed itself a 'source déclarée d'intérêt publique!' Yet another jeans maker, Pepe in 1995, targeted Euro-youth with a mock PSA (*How to Talk to Your Teenager*): while the voice-over offered up clichés, the screen shows a boy stealing his parents' Mercedes-Benz, which he and his friends later trash. The final maxim: 'Take the long view. Don't treat minor mishaps as major catastrophes.' In the spring of 1998, R.J. Reynolds Tobacco produced reformulated ads for its Camel brand that spoofed anti-smoking claims: the ads warned 'Viewer discretion advised' and contained such ominous claims as 'may contain pop mythology' or 'subliminal imagery.' The whole point, admitted a company spokesperson, was to 'position the brand as offbeat and entertaining.'[63]

One of the most elaborate applications of this form of parody had occurred the year before. A $40-million campaign, eventually called 'TV Is Good,' hyped ABC's new fall shows for 1997 by lampooning the

Vince   *Larry*

Figure 19: Scenes from *Post Crash*

process of advertising as well as the product being sold. Viewers were told that watching TV might be bad for the body or the mind but never for the soul. 'TV. What would you watch without it?' 'Eight hours a day, that's all we ask.' 'Don't worry, you've got billions of brain cells.' 'TV is like muscle, if you don't use it you lose it.' According to the ad agency, TBWA Chiat/Day, the purpose was to set ABC apart – 'to develop an attitude for ABC.'[64] The novel campaign certainly got noticed, and perhaps gave ABC an edgier personality, though it did not really increase ABC's ratings (which may well have been the fault of the programs, of course).

All this was fun and games, very much a part of the strategy of irony which was so common in advertising circles during the nineties. The tone was more serious when advocates employed parody. The aesthetics of suffering had become the prevalent style of civic advocacy, outside of corporate advertising and some government messages. But humour, albeit black humour, had always been part of the repertoire of this propaganda. One of the most effective examples was the Crash Test Dummy campaign about the trials and tribulations of Vince and Larry, mounted by the Department of Transport in the United States. In *Post Crash* (1985), while Vince and Larry are talking – and here is the source of the macabre humour – they pull bits of the car from their bodies, reorganize what is still attached, reattach arms, and so on: in short, order themselves for the renewal of their labours. The spot suggested damage – wrenched heads, severed limbs, metal driven into the body – yet distanced the viewer from these horrors. That was the whole point: the creatives felt that people could not imagine themselves as the 'crushed corpses' they had seen in earlier ads. It worked, or at least it appealed: Vince and Larry lasted for years, well into the nineties.[65]

The tone was much more bitter when radicals of whatever kind tried to subvert the official order, a tactic called 'culture jamming' whose target was a consumer advertising that was branded as both immoral and untrue. All kinds of actions might count here. One sporadically popular move was the creative alteration of billboards, adding graffiti or spray paint, or, more often, simply defacing the ads: in the early 1990s, for example, some African-American leaders in New York and Chicago attacked liquor and cigarette billboards that targeted black populations. Gran Fury, part of the militant wing of the AIDS support community, ran a Benetton parody on buses in New York and San Francisco in 1989, showing kissing couples of mixed races, two of whom were gay. The headline read, 'Kissing Doesn't Kill: Greed and Indifference Do.' From the mid-1980s onwards, a group of female artists in New York known as the Guerrilla Girls (they wore gorilla masks in public) and styled as 'The Conscience of the Art World' waged war against sexism and racism using, among other means, a series of posters that attacked the powers that be. One of the most famous took the Metropolitan Museum (1989) to task: 'Do women have to be naked to get into the Met. Museum? Less than 5 per cent of the artists in the Modern Art sections are women, but 85 per cent of the nudes are female.' What really caught the eye, and got the ad banned, was the image, based on Ingres's *Grande Odalisque*, of a naked woman wearing a gorilla head and holding in her hand what looked more like a penis than a fan.[66] Later efforts in the 1990s attacked tokenism, Newt Gingrich and the Republicans, and even O.J. Simpson.

The most prolific source of 'subvertising' and 'uncommercials' was a Vancouver-based group called the Media Foundation, better known as Adbusters after their magazine of the same name. The foundation was spun off in 1989 from the green movement, specifically, the anti-forestry campaigns in British Columbia; but now the target was the mental environment. Its leaders, Kalle Lasn and Bill Schmalz, sought airtime for spots against the forestry industry and eventually against television (the Tubehead ads), consumption ('Buy Nothing Day'), advertising, the automobile industry, even the discipline of economics. The foundation also sponsored a host of clever spoofs of famous campaigns for Marlboro and Camel cigarettes, Absolut vodka, Calvin Klein, American Express, and so on. One of their ads put a milk moustache on the serial killer and cannibal Jeffrey Dahmer, playing off a famous American campaign for milk; another, entitled 'Obsession,' had a semi-nude young man look down his underpants, labelled 'Calvin Kline,' presumably staring at his manhood.

The problem was how to deliver these parodies to a broad audience. Understandably, Kalle Lasn championed the old notion that television should be a forum, open to all forms of advocacy.[67] The foundation could publish examples in *Adbusters*, sell videos of the uncommercials, and set up a Web site where the interested browser might download material. But it had serious difficulties getting its messages into the mainstream. It could hardly hope for free coverage. Space and time were always costly, even if the media had been willing to sell a platform. One report had an ABC spokesman argue that airing the 'Say no to television' spot 'would be tantamount to shooting the industry in the foot.'[68] Not surprisingly, the most subversive propaganda appeared only on the fringes of society: posters on the street, a late-night TV slot, maybe part of a newspaper or TV story, in little magazines and university classrooms, on a few Web sites, and sometimes in art galleries. Otherwise, it was lost in the profusion of other messages that bombarded the population daily.

The technology of advocacy advertising might be available to anyone with the will and the skill; but the ability to use that technology effectively depended on much more, both money and power. The game was obviously skewed towards the big organizations, the government and its agencies, and the corporations. 'Culture jamming' could remain only a marginal phenomenon, an interesting diversion, but hardly a tool of significant resistance.

The SWF-TV attack on violent programming was an extreme expression of a priority shared by most campaigns of truth, namely the promotion of public anxiety. The rationale for the aesthetics of suffering so apparent in health advocacy or charity ads was its ability to shock, to make people worry about themselves, their families, and their world. One sure way to mobilize potential donors was to scare or anger them. 'There are two kinds of money,' mused Grover Norquist, president of Americans for Tax Reform. 'There's sophisticated giving and there's emotional giving where you get $50 checks from people who say, "Oh my goodness, aren't things terrible!"'[1] Such approaches made these forms of propaganda one of the technologies shaping an emerging risk society – touted by the theorist Ulrich Beck, among others, as the next stage of modernity.[2]

The troubles of contemporary science and technology have brought the risk society into recent prominence: we live in dangerous times when a variety of global catastrophes seem all too possible. Yet the origins of the risk society lie in the story of actuarial science and the insurance industry, where the concept, the calculus, and the management of risk were first developed.[3] A risk, such as smoking, is a construct. It may well refer to a particular peril, such as lung cancer. But it is a danger that has been subjected to some rational process of analysis that makes it general and predictable. A risk can exist only within the context fashioned by an expert body of knowledge that is owned by a particular institution. For a risk has been defined, understood, calculated, and dramatized by some agency (or more often agencies) which will deploy the risk to advance an agenda or generate a profit. The agency offers the public assurances and guarantees, perhaps a promise to reduce the risk or to compensate for the risk, providing a degree of security. The public, consequently, lives in a world of uncertainty where each person must constantly calculate the risk of acting – or not acting. 'The panic about mad cow disease,' noted one caustic critic, 'took off in a society which has become preoccupied with collective fears of impending doom and with individual anxieties about threats to health, security and safety.'[4] As a result, risk theory, or at least this elaboration, becomes part of the theoretical universe built by Foucault: the construction of risks becomes a consequence of those 'apparatuses of security' that he argued were the 'essential technical means' of governmentality.[5]

Propaganda serves not just to alert the public but to dramatize risk, whether the 'bad' in question is smoking or overeating or famine or racism or television. It is addressed to each and to the many, to the individual sinner and to a target population. Civic advocacy publicizes the order, the classifications, the predictions, the remedies produced by a range of professionals and managers. Indeed, this activity signifies their political importance – and their will to manage – in the competitive marketplace of signs. It also propagates, along with much else, the perception that we live in unsafe times, surrounded by all kinds of threats and perils, requiring constant efforts by ourselves and experts to reduce the level of harm.

Consider the anti-AIDS crusade that exploded onto the public scene in the mid-1980s. The disease was novel, apparently incurable, expensive to alleviate, and eventually fatal. Its spread was linked to particular patterns of sexual behaviour, especially homosexual practices and heterosexual promiscuity, both of which were still under a moral cloud in much of the world. The fear was that AIDS would ravage whole populations unless people could be convinced to practice 'safe sex' – or to forego 'illicit' sex. The perceived threat placed a heavy burden on propaganda: 'Public education is the only vaccine we have,' argued Britain's health secretary.[6] Reasoning like that could readily be used to justify hard-hitting scare ads, such as those initially commonplace in Britain, Australia, and the United States. These efforts took on the appearance of a state-orchestrated panic, which, as one activist warned, fostered 'ADS' (meaning acquired dread of sex).[7] The British campaign, for example, was attacked because it associated sex and death, provoked fear and guilt, even affirmed the stigma against gays, cast as the initial carriers of the new plague.[8] In fact, the overt purpose was not so much to change behaviour – 'that a television spot cannot change,' noted one ad man – but to 'create awareness' and 'draw attention' to the new risk so that people would be compelled to seek more information from health authorities.[9]

The scare ad persists: one 1997 ad shown in Slovakia depicted the slow disappearance of youthful couples – they vanished into the air – at some macabre dance.[10] But long before then the propaganda had become less frightening and more concrete in North America and western Europe. For authorities settled on using condoms as the solution to halt the spread of AIDS. In *The Visit* (U.S.A. 1989), a grandfather talks of the virtues of condoms, before asking his thirtysomething grandson whether he can bring a few when next he comes to the retirement home. The Health Education Authority used a weathered senior in *Geronimo* (U.K.,

1991) to explain to youngsters how bad things had been in his day when the condom really was 'a rubber.' 'If Mr. Brewster put up with Geronimo you can use a condom.' A take-off called *Advice* (Canada, 1992) borrowed Hitchcock's visual style to evoke life in fifties suburbia where a mother's final warning to her departing child was, of course, 'Don't forget your rubbers.' Was the risk of AIDS now so domesticated that it could become an object of black humour?

This focus was a boon to condom manufacturers, not only because it fostered a spurt in business but also because the panic opened up channels of advertising, such as the American TV networks, that had previously been closed to their products: hence the comment from an unnamed executive: 'AIDS is a condom marketer's dream.'[11] Risk produced profit. It also produced controversy. Selling condoms upset some moral conservatives because it seemed to sell sex as well. Late in 1997, Durex, the world's largest condom manufacturer, launched its 'Truth for Youth' campaign in the United States: this cause-marketing effort preached the virtues of 'comprehensive sexuality education' (including information on contraceptives) instead of 'abstinence-only education' (which was to be funded under the Welfare Reform Act). The company allied with an assortment of agencies, including Planned Parenthood, prepared a press kit, and recruited the celebrity Jane Fonda to ensure media notice – its agency would claim '197 million media impressions' a year later. The goal was to promote 'the full truth,' or, rather, to convey 'a message of social responsibility' and 'create brand awareness for Durex.'[12] In fact the international crusades represented a victory of medical and administrative officials as well as entrepreneurs over more traditional moral authorities, especially the Catholic and fundamentalist churches in the United States. Once upon a time, the condom was associated with promiscuity, the illicit, the taboo. Now it was linked to health and happiness: the National Center for AIDS Prevention in Belarus ran an ad in 1998 that simply showed a blue condom imprinted with the image of a beating heart – the prescription, translated, read 'LOVE LIFE.'[13]

The campaigns of truth, in short, were always more than a technology of risk. Most were not just a vehicle for that negative logic which lies at the heart of the risk society. They were part of the discourse of advertising. They provoked desire as well as fear. They dealt in solutions as well as problems. They offered comfort as well as anxiety – recall Whoopi Goldberg's fatuous suggestion that volunteers could dispel all the ills of American life. They pushed commodities, albeit public goods, as well as warned of social risks. Even SWF-TV was selling an alternative to the horror of violent television. The campaigns of truth, like civic advertising in general, boasted a positive logic which was grounded in a world of goods. Perhaps these campaigns should be counted a transitional form, a part of the 'dying' industrial society as well as the 'emerging' risk society.

PART IV: PROGRESS AND ITS ILLS

*RICOEUR: UTOPIA/DYSTOPIA

The Utopian way of life provides not only the happiest basis for a civilized community, but also one which, in all human probability, will last forever. They've eliminated the root-causes of ambition, political conflict, and everything like that.

Hythlodaeus in Thomas More's *Utopia*

Arthur Herman has coined the term 'declinism' to refer to a species of deep pessimism that represents the West as horribly flawed, in a state of severe decay, usually on the edge of catastrophe. That radical doubt he finds pervasive nowadays and in the recent past. 'We live in an era in which pessimism has become the norm, rather than the exception.'[1] Perhaps so, especially in circles frequented by the best educated. Herman cites a considerable range of thinkers, profound or otherwise, who believe things are getting worse, and getting worse rapidly.[2] But what Herman does not consider is the persistence of an opposite tradition of devout optimism, a counter-school, especially popular outside academe, which celebrates a West that is now global as the pattern of the future. The grand old idea, and myth, of progress has its adherents still, and their views are extremely well represented in the marketplace of signs. Utopia is nigh?

'Utopia' and 'utopian' are terms that resist easy definition. According to Frank Manuel, one of the leading historians of the utopian tradition, 'utopia' has developed a double meaning, both 'an ideal longed-for' and 'a crackpot scheme.'[3] While the cautious *Encylopaedia Britannica* might declare utopia 'a visionary commonwealth,' Freud dismissed utopian schemes as 'lullabies of heaven.' A more sympathetic critic of utopia, George Kateb, offered a different twist, calling utopia 'the negation of a negation,' 'the absence of radical evil.'[4] What seemed crucial was the ability of utopia 'to transcend the ubiquitous, seemingly unassailable present':[5] Northrop Frye thought utopia 'an imaginative vision of the *telos* or end at which social life aims,' and Crane Brinton argued, 'Utopias deal basically with ideas about human potentialities.'[6] Personally, I favour a generous definition, coined by Jan Relf, to encompass the enormous range of possible expressions: 'utopia is an image of desire, rooted in present dissatisfaction.'[7]

Yet the concept of utopia remains vague and unformed in such proclamations, which raises the question, What is not utopian? This vagueness is one reason why such an accomplished scholar of the phenomenon as

Krishan Kumar has suggested that only the special breed of novels of social analysis and criticism pioneered by Thomas More can properly be considered the vehicle of utopia.[8] The difficulty here is that such a dictum narrows the field of play much too severely. The Manuels, among others, rightly talk about a utopian propensity or impulse that encompasses not just More but Marx, novels as well as blueprints, fiction and speculation.[9]

The great strength of Paul Ricoeur's approach is that he managed to satisfy the need for rigour as well as the need for breadth. He did so by carrying forward the project Karl Mannheim initiated many years ago, namely, investigating the dialectic between ideology and utopia. A master of hermeneutics, perhaps best known as a literary theorist, Ricoeur brought to political philosophy a sensibility and expertise that was unusual. He saw the contrasting purposes of ideology and utopia as typical of the double-sided structure of the cultural imagination. Their dialectic was the political expression of a more fundamental distinction between pictures, things that preserve, and fictions, things that explore.

His *Lectures* considered first what a range of thinkers (including Marx, Weber, Althusser, and Habermas) had to say about ideology, and then what a much smaller group (Mannheim and two nineteenth-century utopians, Saint-Simon and Fourier) contributed to the understanding of utopia.[10] The contrast demonstrated how important ideology and utopia were to the fabric of everyday life, or, to be more precise, how they helped to constitute 'the symbolic structure of social life' (8). Ideology, he theorized, was variously 'distortion, legitimation, and identification' (310). Utopia also operated on three levels: sometimes as fantasy and escape, a form of delusion; sometimes as an alternative, a challenge, a reaction to what exists; and sometimes as an innovator, exploring the possible, a source of extreme novelty. 'A utopia is not only a dream but a dream that wants to be realized. It directs itself toward reality; it shatters reality' (289).

Although he never addressed the issue, or the man, in these *Lectures*, Ricoeur's formulation offered a way out of the box Foucault's theory of power/knowledge had created for humanity. 'At a time when everything is blocked by systems which have failed but which cannot be beaten – this is my pessimistic appreciation of our time – utopia is our resource,' he mused. 'It may be an escape, but it is also the arm of critique' (300). Ricoeur emphasized that 'the problem of authority' was central to the study of utopia (and ideology as well): 'What is ultimately at stake in utopia is not so much consumption, family, or religion but the use of power in all these institutions' (17). The unmatched virtue of utopian thinking was its ability to create a space, an exteriorized nowhere, 'to work as one of the most formidable contestations of what is' (16). The result was that a person could stand outside the existing relations of power, question them, and imagine others.[11] Indeed, Ricoeur's formulation made plausible that utopian dream of the public sphere which Habermas had earlier explored.

There are flaws in Ricoeur's schema. His understanding of ideology is open to question, not least because it seems to deny the possibility of a revolutionary ideology. Even he admitted that utopia could play roles his schema assigned to ideology. He recognized, for example, the way the utopian element in human thought also contributed to identity: 'What we call ourselves is also what we expect and yet what we are not' (311). In practice, and that means in analysis as well as in history, it is difficult to justify so stark a distinction between ideology and utopia. Consider the case of William Morris's *News from Nowhere* (1890), one of the major utopian novels of the nineteenth century. His personal vision of the blessed countryside in a future England was imbued with ideas drawn from agrarian myth and socialist doctrine – in a word, ideology. Any utopia will bear the imprint of ideology. That was recognized by Karl Mannheim, who started this enterprise. 'The utopias of ascendant classes are often, to a large extent, permeated with ideological elements.'[12] Mannheim's comment, furthermore, points to the fact that élites of various sorts may project their own visions of a perfected future, something which Ricoeur's schema does not allow. For this reason, I have treated Ricoeur as a guide, regarding his *Lectures* as a source of insight and structure rather than dogma. In particular, I have largely dispensed with his theory of ideology, focusing attention instead upon the phenomenon of utopian rhetoric and imagery.

Utopia is ideal, desire, and critique. That ideal is concrete; or, rather, it is expressed in ways that give it a specificity, at best making the ideal appear both unique and bold, an aesthetic triumph. It bears a signature: 'Utopias are assumed by their authors,' claimed Ricoeur, 'whereas ideologies are denied by theirs' (2). Morris's countryside was not authentic – the sheer goodness of this future England strained credulity – but that vision was compelling and, as such, could easily become an object of desire. A desire for the workers' paradise conditioned the imaginations of millions of socialists and Communists in the first half of the twentieth century – the revolutionary promise of utopia might well carry more weight than the arguments of any doctrine. That desire also presumed rejection. *News from Nowhere* rested on a vigorous no: it was directed against both the capitalist rule of Morris's England and the mechanistic utopia propagated by another socialist, the American Edward Bellamy in *Looking Backward* (1888). Morris offered a critique of the actual present and of a possible future, a duality which is often apparent in visions of utopia. Indeed, one expert, Melvin Lasky, has talked about the 'double metaphor,' the hope and the despair, embedded in 'the utopian longing.'[13]

That doublet is also apparent in utopia's dark twin, the anti- or counter-utopia, more commonly known as the dystopia. It was the semiotician A.-J. Greimas who made abundantly clear how the presence of any value in language must invariably produce its negation.[14] Thomas More's *Utopia* came out in 1516; the first dystopia, Bishop Hall's *Mundus Alter et Idem*, in 1605. The most famous dystopia of them all, George Orwell's *Nineteen Eighty-Four* (1949), was a warning against present and future totalitarianism, particularly against Stalin's Russia. But if dystopia is critique, it is also spectre and fear. The spectre is equally specific, and in Orwell's case the future England even more compelling – or rather repellent – than Morris's vision. The emotion generated is not desire but fear: readers are expected to change their ways to make this prophecy untrue. (Orwell instructed readers: 'Don't let it happen. It depends on you.')[15] Still, dystopias are the shadows of utopia, bleak and pessimistic fictions which none the less embody utopian dreams of a better life that may still be possible.

The visions of a Morris or an Orwell we count as personal. But not just personal. They grew out of a 'political unconscious,' to borrow the pleasing term of Fredric Jameson,[16] a common symbolic storehouse where reside a host of recurring images, ideas, prejudices – and both dreams and nightmares. The individual artist or author will draw inspiration and sustenance from this storehouse. Thus the utopia, and also its shadow, may well be singular, a unique performance, but that performance must express some wider yearnings. Otherwise how could it play, as Ricoeur suggests, 'a *constitutive* role in helping us to *rethink* the nature of our social life?' (16).

One of the first popular or collective utopias has come down to us from a medieval poem as the Land of Cockaigne.[17] This was a land of peace and plenty, free from strife and work, where food, drink, and sex were abundant – a utopia for heterosexual males, in particular. Here were rivers of wine, already roasted geese eager to be eaten, spiced birds that fly into the mouth, and so on. Cockaigne was the paradise of the body, a sensual place, a land of perpetual carnival. It stood in stark contrast to the drudgery, routine, and scarcity that shaped the daily lives of many ordinary folk, then and later (outside of holidays and festivals). No wonder the dream of gluttony would reoccur in many different forms with the passage of time.[18] That nowhere of Cockaigne was realized, albeit in a partial and ambiguous fashion, by the victory of the consumer society in postwar America. Even before, and certainly throughout the twentieth century, it has been evident behind the rhetoric and art of consumer advertising.

But that utopian element is usually hidden deep within the performance. On the surface, consumer advertising fulfils the role of ideology in the social mainstream. Consider again Ricoeur's distinction between ideology and utopia: ideology can spread distortion, legitimate power, and preserve identity. The ordinary kind of advertising that stuffs newspapers and floods television screens focuses on satisfying present needs. A lot of the hype for cosmetics or cleansers – in fact, for all sorts of private goods and services – contains a heavy dose of distortion, as people are well aware.[19] Aside from its effectiveness as a tool of marketing, such advertising does serve to legitimate the culture of consumption and the prevailing capitalist order, an ongoing source of outrage for radicals during the late twentieth century. One way in which consumer advertising achieves that aim is by offering consumers the building blocks of identity: brand images, markers of status, emblems of lifestyles, out of which the affluent can construct or bolster a self-image. The Marlboro Man, one of the most famous campaigns of the half-century, worked by affirming and propagating a macho imagery of manhood that proved appealing not just to males but to many females as well (Marlboro became a kind of power smoke).[20] The beautiful lies of consumer advertising fashion castles in the air, but these are illusions of an attainable good life – attainable, at least, by some people in the affluent world. Only in places of misery and poverty can these lies serve both a utopian and a revolutionary purpose.[21]

By contrast, 'selling utopia' expresses one of the cultural roles of contemporary propaganda. Although this is hardly the obvious purpose of civic advocacy, it is one of its accidental effects. The nature of the game required that civic ads embody a yearning for a better world. That is an excellent way to reach out to the public. Rarely can the sponsors promise people the kind of tangible reward that comes with purchasing a brand and its image. They seek to educate people's minds, maybe to raid their pocketbooks, and often to alter their behaviour, each a far more difficult task than shaping their choices as consumers. So sponsors strive to connect their messages to the broader utopian impulse or propensity of the public: to imply, sometimes to show, how their purpose will remedy a wrong, avoid some evil, confirm a value, and so on. They try, in a phrase, 'to impassionate society' (borrowing here from the language of Saint-Simon via Ricoeur) in order to 'move and motivate it' (296). Embedded within civic advocacy is that 'inner dialectic of utopia, its rational and emotional sides' (287). Appeals draw upon an eclectic variety of desires: for plenty, community, potency, order, freedom, and sometimes peace and equality. Increasingly, many advocates have evoked dystopia, images of catastrophe and horror, to strike fear into the hearts of viewers. What, after all, are those constructs the postmodern city and the Third World? Although rarely does a single performance represent anything approaching a full picture of the ideal life, or of hell on earth, collectively propaganda has built compelling images of societies good and bad.

This property is most evident in two contrasting genres of propaganda, corporate advertising, what is often called its 'image' campaigns, and green advertising, mounted on behalf of the environment and animal rights. By the late 1970s, these genres coexisted in the marketplace of signs, though they rarely intersected, then or later. These opposites articulated very different views of a future transformed, and so fashioned contradictory perspectives on both the past and the present. Each used utopian imagery and utopian hopes, and could be a vehicle for a variety of utopian projects. But neither was the pure form of utopia extolled by Ricoeur: ideology always tainted the visions of this propaganda. The latter variety fitted better Ricoeur's schema: the label 'green' connoted a wide range of different groups that constituted a social movement, outside the circles of authority, which worshipped at the altar of 'Nature' rather than 'Mammon.' Its enemy, however, did not fit Ricoeur's schema well: corporate advertising was and remains the voice of capitalism as utopia, and capitalism has become the dominant 'ism' of the age as well as the description of a particular concentration of power. Once again, the site of any debate was in the minds of citizens, in their responses to the stimuli provided by the ads and other sources of information. No matter: the coexistence of the corporate and the green directed attention to what might be called the politics of utopia. Together these two streams of propaganda raised the issue of legitimacy, the rationale for the civilization and for the dominance of the West, thus fulfilling a role that Ricoeur assigned purely (and wrongly, as it turns out) to the project of ideology.

8

Technopia and Other Corporate Dreams

'Let's Make Things Better.' So announced Philips, the transnational electronics giant, in a new global ad campaign launched in September 1995. The company explained how the theme and slogan were a far better representation of its purposes than the more obvious brag, 'We make better things.'[1] In fact, the statement was pathetic: bland, vague, and hackneyed. No wonder it fostered an initial flurry of boring ads which featured a smiling employee saying trite things to magazine readers. More interesting than Philips's lack of inspiration was its commitment of time and funds to this kind of image campaign. Here it followed an American lead. The company's action conformed to a pattern of behaviour that had first attracted big enterprises in the United States: they endeavoured to position themselves as friends or benefactors or innovators – in short, as public goods in their own right. Out of this practice emerged a renewed explanation of the virtues of capitalism, including a much-hyped redefinition of utopia.

1 One Corporate Nightmare

That bright vision had a shadow, though. There was one very dark portrait of the future, a warning of where America should not go. It arose out of the far different genre of corporate advocacy; indeed, it was one last expression of that burst of attack propaganda, financed by big business and directed against big government, which had elicited so much discussion in the previous decade.

This time the sponsor was W.R. Grace and Company, a sizable conglomerate, that had already earned a name for itself in earlier advocacy campaigns over tax policy.[2] In 1982, U.S. president Reagan appointed

J. Peter Grace, the company's head, to chair a commission on government cost control. Thereafter, he became a crusader against government
waste, in particular the mounting deficit. He set up Citizens Against
Waste to build grassroots support and to lobby Congress to implement
the commission's budget-cutting recommendations. In 1985, W.R. Grace
allocated a reported $2.3 million to make and air a commercial entitled
Baby, which won some fourteen awards and generated (or so the company claimed) 118,000 phone calls.[3]

That success led to a second effort in 1986 to show Americans what
would happen if Congress did not mend its ways. This ominous sixty-
second message was crafted by the ad agency Lowe, Marschalk, at a
reported cost of around $300,000. The agency hired the celebrated
movie director Ridley Scott (and commercial director: he had previously
done *1984*, the famous Apple Macintosh commercial), who chose to
shoot the commercial in an abandoned church in London, England,
because the setting suggested 'devastation.' For the purpose was to drive
home the message that unchecked deficits were a threat to American
potency.[4]

Deficit Trials, 2017 A.D.: We are dropped into the midst of a sci-fi drama. (One
report noted how the setting, 'a dark and crumbling meeting hall,' was reminiscent of a scene from George Orwell's *Nineteen Eighty-Four*.)[5] The opening shot
reveals the inside of a vast structure, light streaming through tall windows to
display pillars, a dirty floor, a standing figure, and – roughly in the middle of the
screen – a peculiar cylindrical object, topped off with a translucent bubble that
glows blue. Then appears the first clue: 'THE DEFICIT TRIALS, 2017 A.D..' A
plethora of other signs – the incessant roar of the wind, discordant music, bits of
rubble, sickly coughs, a general dinginess, stoic and staring figures, the greyed-
out tone of the commercial itself – would serve to convey a mood of despair.
Here is a snapshot of a dismal future where exhaustion reigns, where decline and
decay have replaced prosperity and progress. The energy has run out of America.

The object in the centre is the defendant's box. There, imprisoned, stands a
tired old man. He is on trial for his sins against the future: he represents the
America of the mid-1980s, that time of excess and indulgence. 'I've already told
you,' the elder says wearily: 'it was all going to work out somehow. There was even
talk of an amendment, but no one was willing to make sacrifices.' The prosecutor
is a young man, really a teenager, dressed in revolutionary garb – the American
Revolution of long ago, that is. High above his head hangs a huge golden eagle,
yet another symbol of the American way. But it is the young man's face which is
so striking: smooth, handsome, aristocratic, even arrogant. His gaze and his

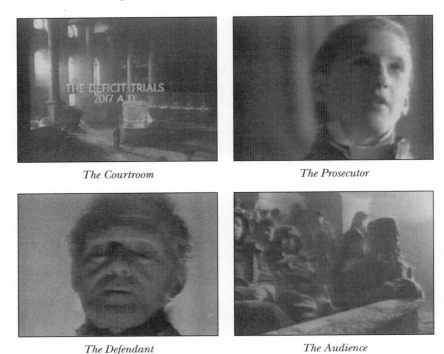

The Courtroom   *The Prosecutor*

The Defendant   *The Audience*

Figure 20: Scenes from *The Deficit Trials, 2017 A.D.*

voice accuse. He represents the anger of this future, an America despoiled by a
spendthrift present. 'I'm afraid the numbers speak for themselves. By 1986, for
example, national debt had reached TWO TRILLION DOLLARS.' He speaks
directly to a blurred audience of young people, dressed in rags, huddled against
the cold, who watch passively – they constitute the victimized future. 'Didn't that
frighten you?' he asks the defendant, almost gently. The face of the defendant
fills with guilt as he recognizes how his generation betrayed their own children.
'Are you ever going to forgive us?' he pleads. Certainly the prosecutor won't: he
looks without mercy at the fool on trial.

   Meanwhile, the crucial message is delivered by a sober, male announcer, the
unseen voice of authority. He admits he cannot say what the spiralling national
debt might do to America. No matter: the pictures have already displayed that
truth. Now, against a background of young victims, he adds: 'But we know this
much. You can change the future. *You have to.*' The answer lies in our souls:
exercise self-restraint, stop the waste, control the madness of government spend-

ing. Then, superimposed on the screen, comes the final sponsor identification, the source of that voice of authority:

GRACE
One step ahead
of a changing world.

W.R. Grace & Co.

Deficit Trials never did get on network television. TV executives were disturbed because the commercial took what appeared to be a controversial stand on a matter of public debate.[6] The decision provoked a First Amendment fight in which spokespeople for W.R. Grace railed against this unwarranted censorship of opinion. Eventually, the ad ran on CNN, many member stations of the Association of Independent Television Stations, and some of ABC's 'owned and operated' stations. A print version appeared in the *Wall Street Journal*, the *Washington Post*, and the *Washington Times*, presumably to reach business and political leaders. The Grace company soon departed from the public sphere, reportedly because it was losing money. But the company had left behind one of the most intriguing forecasts of a dystopia in the annals of recent American propaganda. Whatever its effects, it was a singular expression of a right-wing paranoia about the debt and the deficit which would shortly prevail throughout the affluent world.

2 Technopia: The Ultimate Good

The retreat of W.R. Grace was not unusual. Other crusaders, such as Kaiser Aluminum or United Technologies, had also closed down their advocacy projects. Even Mobil Oil had cut back. All this, so one report claimed, because in the Reagan years corporate advocacy was no longer as necessary as it had been in the days of Presidents Ford and Carter.[7] Instead, large enterprises put more money into building their corporate images, though nowhere near the sums spent on selling product.[8] And the mania spread to other lands: one report in Britain's *Financial Guardian* (15 October 1986) pointed to image campaigns by British Petroleum, Shell, British Rail, British Telecom, and so on. The result was the construction of a much brighter vision of the future. *2012* (BC Tel, Canada, 1993), for instance, displayed a host of busy people going about their business in a future Vancouver, forever using mobile phones to connect with the Internet, record, fax, chat, and shop. 'Imagine,' intoned the unseen announcer.[9]

We are in the presence here of what I call 'technopia,' the corporate version of a technological utopia.[10] This brand of utopia was a modern archetype that had emerged in the 1880s in the United States, where the panacea of technology was highlighted in a series of works – largely forgotten now, except for Edward Bellamy's *Looking Backward* (1888) – that continued well into the twentieth century. Their chronicler has emphasized how technological utopianism was usually mainstream, less about revolt than about going faster, and down a road already chosen.[11] Perhaps its most famous literary expression was in Britain where H.G. Wells published *A Modern Utopia* (1905), about a global future shaped by science. Wells made clear that his and, by extension, any technological utopia was a dynamic entity, where change and innovation would be a constant fact of life (and thus quite unlike many earlier versions of utopia).[12] The archetype found further expression in the dreams of skyscraper cities popular with some architects during the 1920s and in the efforts of designers who put together that most famous of World's Fairs, New York's 'World of Tomorrow' of 1939–40.[13] In his account of the event, David Gelernter found that venues such as General Motors' Futurama or the Democracity, the two favourites of fairgoers, were really designs for a promised land which would, in so many respects, be realized by 1970.[14] If so, it was an ever-changing world brought by corporations that were wedded to advancing technology. For that World's Fair marked the corporate takeover of the dream – the visions of a technological utopia were sponsored by companies such as General Motors, RCA, Chrysler, Westinghouse, and General Electric which had poured money into popular exhibits.[15] It was also always possible later for an outsider to explore a future shaped by science, though the weight of educated opinion would swing more and more to those critical of technology.[16] It was also always possible to find other vehicles that enthused about the future and science, such as *Popular Mechanics*. But the true believers, and the most active proselytizers, were undeniably the corporations and their admakers.

In 1944, around the time corporate America had possessed the dream of a technological utopia, Max Horkheimer and Theodor Adorno, refugees, philosophers, and key figures in what became known as the Frankfurt School of Critical Theory, published a piece of polemic entitled *Dialectic of Enlightenment* which became something of an underground classic and was eventually popularized in the 1960s and 1970s by a new generation of social critics. Their diatribe assigned to the Enlightenment a special project, 'the disenchantment of the world; the dissolution of myths and the substitution of knowledge for fancy.'[17] Everything was now forced to submit to a calculus of rationality and the tools of technology. The very success of that endeavour had apparently produced a host of ills, from alienation to the subjugation of women to totalitarianism. One of the few remaining instruments of dissent was art. ('The work of art still has something in common with enchantment: it posits its own, self-enclosed area, which is withdrawn from the context of profane existence, and in which special laws apply.')[18] But what Horkheimer and Adorno could not foresee was how the postmodern champions would work to re-enchant the world with their own brand of mystery – how, in short, they sought to colonize the popular imagination with new myths, with their own art.[19] Corporate propaganda set out to transform the prosaic into the poetic, the familiar into the exciting, to make technology magical, a project that was part of a more general process of re-enchantment which, ironically, sought to counteract the way science had produced a regulated, predictable, even humdrum world. Here the corporate advocate allied with novelists and artists and, even more, with the makers of popular culture. This form of civic advocacy hoped to create a sense of wonder by means of what was really a kind of mystification.

Technopia is not just a fiction, to use Ricoeur's terminology; it is a virtual fiction, meaning that it has no concrete existence in any one artifact. There is no master text which spells out its properties, nor an ur-text which laid its foundations. Rather, technopia is assembled out of the disparate projects of particular sponsors, each bent on pushing its own agenda and its own merit, mostly (but not exclusively) active in communications and other realms of high tech. Or, rather, the presence of technopia is indicated by a number of recurring markers found in assorted image campaigns, and occasionally product campaigns as well, although the whole ensemble is not apparent in any one performance.

a) The Idea of Progress

Hawking (British Telecom, 1993): Saatchi and Saatchi designed this long sermon (just over two minutes) on the merits of talking for their telecommunications client. They used as the storyteller that icon of popular science Stephen Hawking, a man crippled by nature but liberated by his will, his intelligence, and above all by a science that enabled him to overcome his disabilities to achieve fame and success. The soundtrack is a majestic classical piece that suggests solemnity.

The visuals are a mix of very different shots: the gigantic head of an ancient Greek statue, a monkey climbing up branches, a fresco, a Mayan pyramid, a Greek theatre, and scenes of battlefield devastation. Throughout we are shown clips of Hawking's face, sometimes his wheelchair, once his hands grasping a control device. At the end we see a shot of a gigantic dish antenna with BT and its logo clearly visible.

What ties this disparate collection together is Hawking's explanation. We had escaped the fate of the animals when we discovered the ability to talk. That had proved the source of our greatest achievements. When we failed to talk, then we suffered (on screen the scenes of war). 'Our greatest hopes could become reality in the future,' says Hawking, repeating a commonplace of utopian prophecy. 'With the technology at our disposal [British Telecom's dish is on screen], the possibilities are unbounded. All we need to do is make sure we keep talking.' Just in case the message wasn't sufficiently clear, the admakers superimposed over the distant shot of the dish the claim, 'BT is helping to keep the world talking.'[20]

Here was the march of progress retold: how humanity had overcome nature, unleashed its potential, and realized more and more of its hopes. IBM in Japan offered a different take, reworking the theme of evolution to show how its new computer had origins in the remote era before the dinosaurs. Apple Computer in the United States had a young miner muse about the way sophisticated technology could liberate the human spirit and dispel gloom.[21] But all would agree that there was no end to this story of triumph. Technopia was an evolving project, not a culmination so much as a work always in, and of, progress. The vision was emphatically, compulsively optimistic. It equated material and moral progress; or, rather, it cited the facts of technological innovation as proof of social improvement, the advance of civilization itself.

The endeavour created a sense of time 'filled by the presence of the now.' This phrase, borrowed from the work of Walter Benjamin, suggests how the fiction of technopia has mixed past, present, and future, at least since the onset of the twentieth century, into a single zone of time.[22] How ironic that Benjamin developed that notion as part of a critique of the very idea of progress, a critique in which he celebrated the special moments of revolution. The point is, however, that in their propaganda corporations had appropriated and tamed the rhetoric of revolution, turning it to their own purposes. Their time was not 'empty' or 'homogeneous,' as Benjamin had charged against the champions of progress in his day, but rather full of legendary moments when some triumph of technology was born.

Baseball (General Electric, U.S.A., 1981): This ad told how General Electric brought light to the game of baseball by creating night baseball in 1924. The re-enactment is a form of self-congratulation: the ad pushes forward the unknown, unremembered heroes, the company's engineers (they are named, and labelled 'pioneers') who are the human face of the corporation. The action is centred on the display of the happy moment when the lights go on. The announcer and the pictures build to this moment, which leads to an extended treatment of the act of turning on the lights, to the amazement of the spectators. Finally, there is a joyous dénouement showing happy players and spectators, then and 'now.' For the story suddenly flashes to the present, to pictures of an arena full of ecstatic, cheering fans watching a game in the immediate present. Thus the ad positions General Electric as a leader in the history of American progress. It does so by highlighting a little-known, even trivial event, which none the less has become important to the leisure pursuits of so many Americans. And, in the process, it joins together Americans of a past generation with the present in the celebration of a revolutionary event. Here was an example of that effort to re-enchant the world.[23]

General Electric had 'distilled' a triumph of technopia past. IBM celebrated technopia now in *Italian Farmers* (1996). A grandfather, his eyes cast toward the sky, exclaims, 'You know ... it's a great time to be alive.' Why? Because he has just completed a doctorate that depended on researching, via the Internet, the digitized library (IBM did it) of the University of Indiana! And *Vision, Future Space Station* (1996) offered images of an elegant future designed around Malaysia Airlines: a huge but gracious airport, a sky in which gigantic cylinders rise upward, and an appealing if bizarre supercraft reminiscent of two joined scimitars. 'Imagine,' commands the voice-over, 'the future for an airline that already flies more passengers than any other from Southeast Asia.' That command, if not the word 'imagine,' reoccurs time and again in this propaganda. Readers and viewers are told to enjoy the programmed daydream, to place themselves within the blessed realm of technopia. So Singapore Airlines had a boy dream, in *Imagine* (1996), about the extraordinary pleasures of flying (including viewing the sci-fi classic *Metropolis*) in its Megatop. Technopia is a state, a condition of being wherever the good life depends upon technology, no matter what the era.[24]

b) Illusions of Mastery

Horkheimer and Adorno found the guiding principle of the Enlightenment in a ruthless desire to dominate nature, and not just the land, the seas, and the animals but what was natural in humanity as well. The will to power which these critics found so sinister was honoured in the imagery of corporate propaganda.

The fascination with huge structures apparent in *Vision* (the ad of Malaysia Airlines) was a symptom of one portrayal of technopia.

Scotford (Shell Canada, 1984): The purpose of this ad was to demonstrate how Shell Canada had benefited the Canadian economy by building a gigantic petrochemical factory in Alberta. The strong, male voice-over, the didactic script, and the strident music were designed to construct awe. Yet what was so striking were the visual presentations of this so-called 'technology of the future': distance shots of huge, metallic towers that command the horizon; a close-up of flickering screens and a wide-angle shot of control devices; a circling shot upward that turns the silver towers into looming sentinels of science; moving pans of a plant that is extremely ordered and clean. The people in the ad exist to serve: anonymous, white-coated technicians walk down a circular staircase; a group of five uniformed workers, in blue garb and yellow safety helmets, march underneath giant girders; other workers clamber around the towers to perform some ritual necessary to the machines. Here is a place that has been totally manufactured by the amazing force of technology. The mood is almost religious.[25]

Much the same kind of mood was present in two efforts by Britain's Electricity Council, *Power Station* (1980) and *Environment* (1987), which unveiled pictures of massive technoscapes that demand our respect – or is it worship? Likewise, ITT's *Growing Cities* (1996) showed American eyes how a city burst forth: the camera moved above small buildings and farm lands to reveal the sight of one block of buildings after another suddenly appearing – and these buildings glisten and shine as if alive. The purpose? To hype ITT's System 12, which boasted the capacity to handle an ever-expanding telephone traffic. This version of technopia was masculine in gender, expressing in its obsession with size, height, structures, ordered views, and panoramas a male fantasy of dominion, a desire to control and shape. The natural – mountains, rivers, plains – has submitted to the dictates of humanity.[26]

But this is hardly the only illusion. Corporate propaganda often gave a postmodern twist to technopia, displaying a public place geared to private pursuits, commonly personal pleasure. What fascinated here were all the helpful machines which enhanced users' lives.

'You Will ...' campaign (AT & T, U.S.A., 1993): *Book, Movie,* and *Toll* were the initial

Figure 21: Two Magazine Ads from the AT & T Campaign

trio of commercials designed by N.W. Ayer for an ongoing AT & T campaign which, a year later, was estimated (*Advertising Age*, 9 May 1994) to have cost between $15 and $20 million, involving radio and magazines as well as TV, and designed to lay claim to the near future.

In fact, the trio actually comprised one extended ad made up of nine vignettes (one repeated twice) that showed, briefly, assorted people using new technologies to realize some purpose. Always featured were the marvels themselves: a computer screen, a new type of automated teller machine, a videophone, a tiny fax machine. The male voice-over told the story in the form of a series of questions.

Have you ever borrowed a book ... from thousands of miles away ... crossed the country ... without stopping for directions ... or sent someone a fax ... from the beach?
Have you ever watched the movie you wanted to ... the minute you wanted to ... learned special things ... from far away places ... or tucked your baby in ... from a phone booth?
Have you ever paid a toll ... without slowing down ... bought concert tickets ... from a cash machine ... or tucked your baby in ... from a phone booth?

Each spot ended with the promise, 'You Will,' plus the claim, 'And the company that'll bring it to you? AT & T.' Running in the background was a happy melody which, towards the conclusion, added voices singing 'oooh' and 'aaah,' signs that the viewer should be in awe of what AT & T had in store for lucky Americans.[27]

The campaign was about convenience, speed, efficiency, simplicity, and efficacy: it promised that you would be able to work, play, or whatever, much more easily in times to come. Each of the innovations, however trivial, defeated time and space, thus increasing the personal control an individual could exercise over his or her environment. None of the people were shown in awe of their enhanced capacity; rather, they treated the innovations as appliances that did something useful. They had become 'natural,' expected. We, the viewers, were expected to supply the awe. Of course, each action and, by implication, one's life in this near future, was organized around the marvels of a technology that was brought courtesy of a corporation. Here the 'lifeworld,' to borrow from the vocabulary of Jürgen Habermas, has become wholly dependent on the miracles of machinery.

There were all sorts of variations on this motif. So TelecomASIA (*Daddy*, Thailand, 1993) had a father at the airport telling his daughter a bedtime story by videophone. Nynex (1996) showed how its video wall at Ellis Island (once an immigrant reception centre) engaged children in the stories of their people's histories. Ameritech's 'Test Town' campaign (1996) added a dose of humour, indeed, so much so that its commercials offered up what seemed to be 'technology for dummies.' Very ordinary folk in a barber shop (learning how to cut hair), a diner (with personal videophones, beepers, smart cards), an icehouse (ordering food), just driving around (using voice technology) tested the virtues of an assortment of devices – 'Because if technology doesn't work for people, it doesn't work.' Allegheny Hospital (1996) backed its 'New Age of Healthcare' campaign with a mix of Gregorian chants and New Age music, presumably to excite a sense of awe among the viewers looking at pictures of a range of medical machinery.[28]

But it was left to that giant of the information age, IBM, to sponsor one of the most compelling portrayals of technopia in a mid-1990s campaign entitled 'Solutions for a Small Planet.' The flock of television commercials hoped to persuade American viewers that IBM technology offered solutions to all manner of different problems in all parts of the world. The result was to give a special global spin to the now-familiar saga of the age of the computer. Each commercial (fifteen were listed on the IBM

Web site early in 1997)[29] focused on a different part of the world and touted a different product or service:

Italian Farmers: Digital Library	*Hungarian Organ Grinder*: 365 Thinkpad
South African Kids: KidRiffs (music program)	*Fashion Models*: Data Mining (Italy)
	Upper Tonga: COMDEX 95
Brazilian Rain Forest: OS/2 Warp Connect	*Japanese Surgeons*: Aptiva
Moroccan Guys: Openness	*Thai River*: Consulting
Monks: Lotus Notes (Tibet)	*Chinese Opera*: Housecall (computer repair)
French Guys: Optical Storage	*Prague Nuns*: OS/2
Greek Fishermen: Global Network	*Tango*: Voice Recognition (Argentina)

The focus was on the conversation of a few people, not necessarily ordinary but certainly far removed from the laboratory where the technology was created. These could be businessmen (*Moroccan Guys*), two senior citizens (*French Guys*), children (*South African Kids*), a taxi driver (*Thai River* – a water taxi, that is). The conversation was in the native tongue of the participants, so this was translated on screen into English for the benefit of Americans. Action and dialogue were always spiced with a bit of humour. For example, the merits of operating systems are discussed by two nuns (*Prague Nuns*), one of whom is disturbed by her beeper. *Fashion Models* was even more bizarre: where else but in the admakers' universe would two Swedish supermodels performing on a runway in Milan be found discussing the merits of IBM's data mining as a way of generating new business ideas? But the weirdest scenario (*Monks*) had a bunch of Tibetan monks on a mountain top pondering via telepathy the extraordinary potential of work groups communing happily throughout the universe – now there was a 'cosmic' brand of 'spiritual harmony.' Once again, the spiel contained that invitation to dream, 'Just imagine ...' We were asked to imagine how the particular technology or service could release the creativity of the unscientific masses. Here high tech was humanized.[30]

Only two of the spots dealt with religion, though *Prague Nuns* was probably the most famous in the series. But these ads highlighted one of the key motifs of the campaign, namely, the harmonious union of the traditional and the technological. That was part of a much grander, and fundamentally utopian, dream of reconciling opposites: IBM promised to bridge the gap between the powerful and the friendly (*Japanese Surgeons*), the artistic and the scientific (*Italian Farmers*), the big and the little (*Greek Fishermen*). The dream of harmony was uppermost in one final commercial in this series.

Something Magical ... (1996): The spot opens on a shot of a wise, old, congenial African male, a kind of traditional sage, who speaks the words of enchantment – 'Something magical ... is happening to our planet.' Then a collection of people, male and female, old and young, from around the world, speak directly to us about the new age of connectivity. Once more their speech is translated into on-screen text:

> 'It's growing smaller.'
> 'Everyday the global network of computers ...
> '... weaves us more tightly together'
> 'Join us.'
> 'Wander through a distant library.'
> 'Turn your corner store into a mini multinational.'
> 'Curious?'
> 'IBM can get you there.'
> 'Just plug in ...'
> 'and the world is yours.'

That last comment is delivered again by the sage. The next image shows a globe with the IBM Web address, and that is followed by the campaign signature:

IBM
Solutions for a small planet

Here we have the personalizing of the illusion of mastery: each of us is told that all we need is the will to use the new technology to achieve some sort of greatness. And we are left with a vision of a world where all is connected, thanks to the wondrous technology of computers.

c) Houses of Invention

What filled this corporate propaganda – in dramatic contrast to *Deficit Trials* – were the signs of potency. Viewers might be bombarded with a fast-paced succession of images to signify energy and motion. *A Day in the Life* (Sydney County Council, 1984) flashed so many pictures of activities that only the collage could register, and that collage preached satisfaction with, even adoration of, the life force of electricity that enabled everything else to happen. One of the most unusual sets of symbols and metaphors, however, was put together for a French bank.[31]

Life Cycle (Banque Nationale de Paris [BNP], France, 1994): This surreal spot opens on a uniformed cyclist who cannot get his wheels to turn properly. He gets off the bike. That suddenly releases the powerful, urgent sounds of *Carmina Burana*. He adds oil, labelled BNP, to his gears. The gears move swiftly, setting off a chain reaction on what is now revealed as a strange contraption attached to the bike. A kettle finally releases a burst of steam which the cyclist allows out the window to roam over a dull, featureless plane where only the house of magic stands. The steam rises to impregnate a huge bank of roiling clouds and rain immediately falls to the ground. So fertilized, huge buildings full of lights emerge from the plain to constitute a new megalopolis. 'Oiling the wheels of industry is the job of Banque Nationale de Paris.'

The brag was a variation on a very common theme. The saga of technopia positioned the corporation as the source of progress. That conceit had some historical foundation. Horkheimer and Adorno had labelled Francis Bacon, the champion of science, the new Lucifer of the Age of Enlightenment.[32] Rightly so, because Bacon had penned one utopia, *The New Atlantis* (1629), where rationality reigned supreme, in which the dominant force was a gigantic research centre, 'the very eye of the kingdom,' known as Salomon's House. The ambitions of its elders were limitless: 'The end of our foundation is the knowledge of causes, and secret motions of things; and the enlarging of the bounds of human empire, to the effecting of all things possible.'[33] That example and that mission aptly suited the self-image corporations manufactured in their own world of propaganda.

Consider some of these, mostly American, boasts. General Electric: 'We bring better things to life' (*Tribute*, U.S.A., 1993). Du Pont: 'Better things for better living' (*Wedding*, U.S.A., 1988).[34] Unicom: 'We Don't Predict the Future. We Create It' (1996). Lockheed Martin: 'We are the architects of tomorrow's technology' (*Mission Success*, 1996) – part of a long description of its extraordinary presence in space, aviation, defence, energy, 'civil government' (security), information systems, and other such industries.[35] 'Be there first' was the self-proclaimed motto of United Technologies (1996), which tagged 'the global economy' 'an arena' 'where technology advances at warp speed.'[36] 'The 21st century is going to be truly amazing': that prediction by Toshiba Japan concluded a spot (*Voice Recognition*, 1990) which explored the future of voice technology and computers. [37] Corporate propaganda was a never-ending source of cliché.

How could admakers get any public to listen to such rhetoric? They might, of course, use startling images to impress an audience: a giant hand that lifted buildings; a shot of Toronto's CN Tower, purportedly a symbol of Canadian pride; firefighters smashing through flames that could not consume their protective clothing; the launching of a rocket and then its satellite over Japan.[38] But the most clever pieces of propaganda fashioned an ensemble of rhetoric and images around some particular motif. Each of these performances managed to make concrete, even to personalize, that message of technological supremacy.

Mirror, Mirror (Northern Telecom, Canada, 1987):[39] The commercial revolves around metaphors of sight: the mirror, looks, illusions, perceptions. It draws upon an old favourite, the fairy tale of Snow White and the Seven Dwarfs, where the mirror on the wall identifies the fairest of them all. 'Appearances can be deceiving,' argues a dapper, impeccably dressed man, who stands smartly and smugly just to one side of his image in the mirror. That allows him to go on to assert, though never to explain, how complicated the technology of the telephone is, and how Northern Telecom is unmatched in this realm. His pose, his words, his dress, all suggest arrogance and authority. Often he looks directly at us, so as to enhance his credibility. Then he does something amazing: he puts his hands into the mirror – the mirror is made not of glass but of some viscous fluid which ripples and streams. He has turned science into magic. 'Telecommunications? Don't be fooled by illusions.' 'Northern Telecom: there's more to us than meets the eye.' Here the corporation has become a wizard that does marvellous and mysterious things.

Bullet Proof (Pilkington, U.K., 1986):[40] The action juxtaposes the storyteller, a substantial older male in a blue suit, and his potential slayer, a younger man, looking a bit Germanic, who assembles a rifle before our eyes. The most dramatic moment comes when the assassin shoots ... and fails, because his victim stands behind an unseen shield of bullet-proof glass. For Pilkington is a maker of glass, and not just any maker but 'the world's leading glass company.' This commercial drew upon a motif of decline, used earlier by oil corporations such as British Petroleum (the 'Britain at Its Best' campaign) to tout their excellence.[41] 'There aren't many things today in which Britain leads the world,' the storyteller told viewers. 'Our motorcycle industry is almost vanished, and our shipbuilding industry is not what it used to be.' Not so in the realm of glass manufacture, though. Which, of course, enhances the stature of Pilkington as the upholder of British prestige in a post-imperial present. The spot neatly positions the corporation as both patriot and pioneer, a strategy not unusual in the annals of corporate advertising.

Sarah (Eli Lilly, U.S.A., 1996):[42] Here is a much softer claim: gentle music, a pastoral setting, a blonde girl running through the field, an old-fashioned farm house, a daughter snuggling up to her dad, kids at play – it all evokes that utopia of America past which has played a crucial role in the political propaganda of the 1990s. Yet that motif is married to the thesis of technopia: 'knowledge is powerful medicine,' the ad will conclude. Initially, the camera focuses on the girl, Sarah, while the voice-over tells us what she doesn't and can't be expected to know – about how Eli Lilly has developed the medicine (note not the 'drug,' a tarnished word) to control her diabetes and continues to search for better means of combating illness. Soon Sarah has to share the screen's attention with pictures of devoted women and men, meant as evidence that the company has given authority to women, who are shown working for the good of all. Eli Lilly is 'leading the search for better, more affordable treatments, preventions, and cures, so Sarah and the rest of us can all lead healthier, more active lives.' Eli Lilly, public benefactor: that claim blends with a much wider range of corporate advertising which represents companies as the friends of consumers, citizens, and humanity.[43]

d) Dark Shadows

Lurking within these visions of technopia were dystopian denials. The very effort to fashion vivid pictures and compelling stories contained the seeds of negation. For this imagery might easily evoke an alternative reading reflecting the differing experiences and outlooks present in the public sphere. *Scotford*'s celebrations of monumentality, for instance, could easily awaken a sense of horror at the cold, sterile world in store for humanity. The abundance of gadgetry in 'You Will ...' might conjure up images of a hectic, artificial world saturated with the trivia of an unrestrained technology. An untitled ad by Lockheed Martin lovingly displayed a sleek weapon of destruction, the F22, ruling the skies – 'the twenty-first century begins today' – an image evocative of the ongoing threat of the American war machine.[44] It was possible, in short, to subvert these performances by highlighting the contradictions and ambiguities and absences that were so much a part of their vision.

The Last Passenger (Philips Nederland, 1989):[45] This *tour de force* (two and a half minutes long) is a reconstruction of the capture of an international drug financier at the Lausanne airport in Switzerland. It employs the familiar action-adventure format of so much television drama. Most striking are its highly sophisticated graphics and its production values, far better than those of most dramas: *The Last Passenger* uses a host of very quick cuts, stop-action shots, jerky motion, weird camera angles, overlays, blends, and computer images to create an air of frenzy. That mood is enhanced by the soundtrack and the short, sharp bursts of dialogue. The performance focuses on the successful effort of an unidentified official, call him Mr Police, to discover who the man was and what crime might justify his arrest. We are treated to pictures of Mr Police thinking and acting, the criminal moving through the airport, and the actions of superfast machinery. Mr Police is able to command a massive array of communications and computer systems, built by Philips, of course, to generate answers. A voice-over tells us at the end that the villain was captured and later extradited to the United States, where he was tried and found guilty.

Here was a celebration of the surveillance society. The apparatus of men and machines constituted a technology of power which operated to discover the identity of a man who had entered a public place. That airport had become Foucault's Panopticon, though the quarry never recognized that he was under such close scrutiny. The police apparatus could call into play a wide variety of other people and expertise – most especially through its video cameras, telephones, and computers. Indeed, the airport seemed riddled with video cameras. Mr Police drew information from databases at home in Switzerland and around the world. The point was that high technology had created a powerful brand of surveillance which could focus the police gaze upon any individual. It had enhanced the power of society to protect itself – or, more properly to police everyone. There was, it seemed to say, no escape.

There is no telling how many of the people who viewed *The Last Passenger* gave it such a sinister reading – presumably not those judges who assigned this an award in the 1990 competition at Cannes. But its vividness, its implacability, could evoke one shadow of technopia, a transparent society where authority could always get its man.

3 Arcadian Idylls

'This bird sanctuary is an example of something our company has always believed: that man and nature can live and work together.' That assertion came in a Canadian commercial of 1973. *Bird Sanctuary* looked much like a nature documentary, complete with gentle music, the sounds of birds, and inspiring shots of trumpeter swans in flight. The sanctuary had been built thanks to the efforts of one far-sighted company. And the company? MacMillan Bloedel, one of the major producers of lumber –

and of the devastation of the landscape – in British Columbia.[46] The purpose of the campaign (there were two other commercials) was clearly to counter a widespread image of MacMillan Bloedel as anti-nature. It demonstrated how some corporations attempted to appropriate another branch of the utopian tradition, the dream of Arcadia, to meet the threat of environmentalist criticism.

Happy Valley (Shell, U.K., 1981):[47] One of the more memorable efforts, later referred to as the 'invisible pipeline' spot,[48] tells how Shell restored a Welsh valley to its pristine state of natural beauty – after driving a pipeline through it. The voice-over phrases the story in the form of an 'if/then' query:

> If we told you that a certain oil company wanted to push a pipeline through this lovely Welsh valley, a pipeline which would stretch for seventy-eight miles across the countryside, which would cut a swath thirty yards wide, which would mean digging seven feet down into the earth, sending bulldozers into the Snowdonia National Park, you would probably, quite rightly, feel very alarmed.

All the while the screen is full of close-ups of animals, many more than a visitor might see outside the zoo: birds, a frog, a rabbit, a red fox, either a wild boar or a porcupine (the image was unclear), cows, and more birds. The point is that the natural paradise so beautifully laid before our eyes is actually the valley *after* Shell has worked its will. The images evoke feelings of awe, pleasure, and beauty. But what is particularly stricking is the gendered subtext. The company is masculine, thrusting, instrumental, dominant, planning a pipeline that threatens a rape of the countryside. The valley is feminine, beautiful, delicate, passive, saved from rape by the company itself. Here is a portrayal of the way nature's plenty can be preserved by a corporation. 'Can we develop the industry we need, without destroying our countryside?' The answer is obvious: 'You can be sure of Shell.'[49] We are witness to a world of harmony, where nature and business can live in peace as allies rather than foes.

The motif of reconciliation – the happy union of supposed opposites – is played and replayed in this species of propaganda. Perhaps that is why there is such a forced quality to corporate 'green.' Britain's Imperial Chemical Industries explained that its technology had transformed an African river into a public good: *River* (1991) showed how central the plentiful supply of now clean, pure water was to the lives of villagers. [50] That kind of conceit seemed especially pleasing to chemical companies.

In 1997, Mississippi Chemical, a maker of fertilizers, told television watchers, and Web browsers, 'We feed the soil. We make things grow.' (Ironically, the opening of the commercial evokes a horror story, since superimposed on pictures of fertile land is a moving something that, we are told, is 'alive,' 'breathes,' 'thirsts,' 'Its hunger is constant' – meaning soil!) Here was Nature Improved: put another way, the propaganda converted Arcadia into a province of technopia.

There were other, less presumptuous tropes. In 1993, Southern California Edison, an American utility, ran a trio of ads (*Light, Stand-Up*, and *Plans*) in which wise souls explained ways of achieving energy efficiency that both help the environment and improve profits. That same year Anheuser-Busch (most famous as the maker of Budweiser beer) positioned itself as the guardian of nature: *Nature* mixed superb photography of wilderness and animals with an explanation of the laudatory practices of the corporation. Sometimes a similar impulse fostered cause-related marketing. The Nature Conservancy expressed its pleasure over a three-year arrangement with S.C. Johnson, involving 'wildlife-themed coupon promotions' for its wax products, that had generated $350,000 and much new exposure for the non-profit organization since 1995.[51] In July 1998, American Forests listed on its Web site a series of corporations, large and small, which had partnered a Global ReLeaf project that promised 'to plant 20 million trees to green our cities, towns and forests': the list included Eddie Bauer (outdoor clothing), Briggs and Stratton (lawnmowers), Sterling Vineyards (wines), the Switzerland Cheese Association, Texaco, Interstate Power, even Aramis cologne from Tommy Hilfiger. Here was Nature Served, where business appeared to admit the priority of the environment.[52]

But by far the most common ploy was to work an association, often unstated, between the environment and the corporation. Consider one especially clever effort by Young and Rubicam. In *Invitation* (U.K., 1986), a rapidly moving camera supplied panoramic shots of a beach and water, birds in flight, mountains, farmhouses in a tamed countryside, rugged terrain, and, eventually, a clean, orderly industrial complex. Classical music accentuated the mood of peace and harmony. The admaker used a voice-over to emphasize the economic importance of the plant, and to deliver a message about visiting one of the most maligned of the engines of modernity, Sellafield, a nuclear-fuel reprocessing plant in Cumbria. It was part of a multimillion pound campaign of British Nuclear Fuels (BNFL) to sway public opinion, after a series of alarms, and in a fashion that did not seem like advocacy (for the Independent Broadcasting

Authority had rejected an earlier script).[53] While nothing was actually said, the ad tried to establish an image of Sellafield in the warm embrace of a pristine landscape. Call this Nature Deluded or, rather, a utopia where the modern, the wild, and the pastoral are one.

4 The Corporate 'Claim'

An early report on the impact of the BNFL campaign was hardly auspicious: the first set of ads produced only a slight improvement in the image of Sellafield.[54] The task of 'selling nukes' was never easy, even in France where the nuclear industry enjoyed considerable public support. A four-year marketing effort begun in the late 1980s by Atomic Energy of Canada purportedly 'made almost no discernible difference in public opinion.'[55] Indeed, any image campaign, and not just for so controversial an industry as nuclear power, had to overcome a fund of public cynicism about its purposes. It suffered the normal discount the public gave to advertising, perhaps a greater discount because so much of image advertising celebrated its sponsors.[56] Procter and Gamble stumbled badly in its launch of Ariel Ultra, a new washing powder, which was promoted as more green than its rivals. That encouraged *Today* to run a front-page story which claimed that the new brand had been 'tested on animals.'[57] Indeed, the whole genre of green marketing was tarnished by the doubtful or incomplete claims made in the early 1990s. According to one survey, mentioned in the British marketing magazine *Campaign* (17 December 1993), nearly eight out of ten people interviewed agreed with the charge that 'Companies look after their image ... to mask their unacceptable activities.' But cynicism could melt: an ITT campaign begun in the United States early in 1974, for example, was credited within a year of establishing the company's reputation as 'a leader in technology' among three-quarters of respondents.[58] Firms persevered because a good reputation could pay off in sales or in safety, meaning that the sponsor might avoid some unwelcome political attention.

Ricoeur's theorizing explains the wider significance of this image advertising. Ricoeur borrowed the concepts of 'claim' and 'belief' from Max Weber, a German sociologist of the late nineteenth and early twentieth centuries who had pondered deeply about the issue of legitimacy.[59] These concepts offer a more subtle formulation of the ways and means of managing opinion than Gramsci's much more comprehensive notion of hegemony. Ricoeur argued that authority must cultivate legitimacy, must put forward specific evidence of its virtue, to ensure order, stability, and power. Interest, habit, and tradition are not sufficient to maintain a structure of domination. What allowed the claim 'to be accepted, assumed, or taken for granted' by the citizenry was something else. The necessary something lay in the realm of culture, and Ricoeur argued that ideology filled 'this credibility gap' between claim and belief.

Perhaps so. But I presume that a much less coherent collection of generalized hopes, fears, ideas, and assumptions than any ideology provides could and did play the same role. This collection, too, operated in the realm of the cultural imagination. And the intriguing fact remains that much of the corporate claim took the form not of rational discourse, let alone an explanation of ideology, but of utopian dreaming, using an assortment of pictures and rhetoric to condition the popular imagination. The claim was the cumulative result of individual intentions: together, big business had developed what Ricoeur called a fiction, a saga of technopia which allowed these private powers to claim public status. That fiction presented an ideal and expressed a desire, though it replaced critique with celebration. This was an abbreviated utopia, then.

The saga had enormous appeal. It suited the mood of the times. Look at the statistics. A six-year survey of opinion in Canada during the 1980s discovered that what were defined as high-tech industries consistently won the 'trust' of Canadians far more than any others. The ratings for this star reached a high of forty, and never fell below twenty, whereas banks fell to zero, oil was twice around minus twenty, and chemicals dropped to an abysmal minus thirty.[60] The ratings were all the more striking because Canadians worried a lot about the motives and principles of captains of industry, though perhaps not as much as their American cousins.[61] Look at the popular culture. High-tech entrepreneurs like Steve Jobs of Apple and later, to an ever greater extent, Bill Gates of Microsoft became popular American heroes – Gates's speeches and writings in the mid-1990s purveyed his own kind of technological utopianism. Among the most successful brands of entertainment were science-fiction dramas such as *Star Trek* (the original TV series, the movies, and the successor TV shows), *Close Encounters of the Third Kind*, and the *Star Wars* series.

Everywhere, the corporate claim, sometimes by firms outside the realm of technology, reflected, exploited, and accentuated the glamour of high tech. Technopia offered a counter to the emerging risk society. The saga emphasized the optimistic side of modernity, the constructive force of that ongoing capitalist revolution which had persistently reshaped the 'lifeworld.' Here reigned order, efficiency, and satisfaction as well as change. Technopia was a place where risk was banished, where technology was a boon to humanity (and nature), and where people could enjoy a never-ending supply of marvellous new gadgets. No other competitor for public favour, and certainly not big labour, which had its own image problems,[62] could match the renewed positioning of business as a public good, an engine of progress.

9

Green Nightmares:
Humanity versus Nature

Barsebäck (*Ekstrabladet*, Denmark, 1986): We see billowing white clouds against a light-blue background, hear the sounds of a harsh wind. The clouds part to reveal a gruesome picture: a skeleton of the famous Little Mermaid that sits atop a rock in the harbour of Copenhagen. It's a foretelling of doom. A sombre male voice has already begun to explain:

> In 1975 the Swedish state opened Barsebäck atomic power station. Barsebäck was the world's most dangerous nuclear power station, located only twenty kilometres from the centre of the Danish capital of Copenhagen. The people of Copenhagen, living in the dangerous radioactive zone, had been fighting and demonstrating for years for the closure of Barsebäck ... before ... the catastrophe ... happens.

As he concludes, the image changes to show that catastrophe. A glow spreads out on the horizon. The white clouds next to the mermaid turn yellow. An organ plays grim music. A yellow-and-white blaze spreads across the screen. Rolling text identifies the sponsor as *Ekstrabladet*, a Copenhagen newspaper. We hear first a whirring sound and then a long sizzle. Now everything has turned a sinister white. That ends this apocalypse.

Exit technopia. Exit the Land of Cockaigne, as well. This is an example, albeit one of the more extreme versions, of a genre of civic advocacy I call 'green nightmares.' Here is a very different realm, where technology threatens the survival of humanity. Risks abound. 'Progress' is a sinister word that signifies not improvement but its reverse. The obsession with private goods fosters social risks: masses of garbage, devastating explosions, air and water pollution, ozone depletion, toxicity, cruelty to animals, and species extinctions. Standing against the tide are the greens, the champions of the environment and the animals. Especially in the late

1980s, their propaganda portrayed a scary world of crisis, loss, fear, peril, and horror. The purpose of this advocacy was to disturb, to shock, to repel, in order to preserve an embattled nature against the advances of technology and consumption.

1 The Dystopian Mood

'America exists today in a post-utopian twilight,' claimed David Gelernter, and suggested that it had done so since roughly 1970.[1] That was an exaggeration: witness the cult of technopia. Even so, the questioning of the 1960s did bring a rebirth of declinism. One indicator was the way pessimism came to inflect science fiction which, at one level, is a popularization of utopian fiction.[2] The older tradition of technological optimism certainly persisted, as did the fascination with 'bug-eyed-monsters,' space flights, and heroic individuals. But a new group of authors – among them Anthony Burgess, Brian Aldiss, Harry Harrison, D.F. Jones, Philip K. Dick, R.A. Lafferty, and Norman Spinrad – won fame by writing stories with a social twist that explored emerging fears of catastrophe.[3] John Brunner, a British writer, actually came to specialize in dystopia. His *The Sheep Look Up* ends memorably when a character in Ireland can smell America burning! Apparently, the only way to save the world was to 'exterminate the two hundred million most extravagant and wasteful of our species.'[4]

That comment highlighted one of the chief themes of this fiction: the sins of excess. Excess could take many forms, of course: supermachines, overconsumption, video spectacles, and so on. Some authors filled their stories with the marvels of technology, such as Dick's androids or Lafferty's mechanical killers, but these signs of a false progress offered humanity no comfort. D.F. Jones's master computer actually decided to take over, revealing the consequences of hubris – the computer's creator became its prisoner. Harry Harrison's America of 1999 was the direct result of too many people (344 million citizens) trying to consume too much of the world's resources. The population grew so large on the Earth of Brian Aldiss that its awesome hunger ravaged the sea and the land to produce a chemically saturated food that sickened people. A similar lack of restraint produced the extreme wealth of Golden Astrobe (a new America) in R.A. Lafferty's story of 'Mankind's third chance,' a chance that was again failing because material abundance could not satisfy the spiritual needs of humanity. Philip K. Dick's survivors of a nuclear holocaust pursued alienated lives in a synthetic environment where people dialled up their moods, consumed huge quantities of television, and yearned to own real (not artificial) animals. The extraordinary power of TV or its successors kept re-occurring in these tales. One major character in John Brunner's *The Jagged Orbit* was a 'spoolpigeon,' who used his television show to reveal the deceit of the high and mighty; similarly, the hero of Norman Spinrad's *Bug Jack Barron* was the host of a TV call-in show of such popularity that he could challenge – meaning expose – the power of the one man who rules America. In short, the settings these authors fashioned were in one way or another counter-times and counter-worlds to the perverted utopia that America had become (and to the future it was creating for the world).

A similar kind of critique was part of the newly emerging green crusade. Or, rather, that crusade drew upon this same rhetoric and mood. Consider some early classics of the movement. Rachel Carson's *Silent Spring* (1962) probed the threat to humanity posed by the widespread use of pesticides. Paul Ehrlich's *The Population Bomb* (1968) predicted the horror of mass starvations in the Third World during the next decade. The Club of Rome's *Limits to Growth* (1972) presented evidence of a future global catastrophe on a host of fronts, a doom that grew directly out of the technological mastery of the West.[5] Peter Singer's *Animal Liberation* (1975), widely considered the Bible of the animal-rights movement, was a nasty exposé of 'the tyranny of human over nonhuman animals.'[6] One exception to all this gloom and doom was Ernest Callenbach's *Ecotopia* (1975), subtitled 'the novel of your future,' which explored the merits of a green haven, born in 1999 as a result of an earlier secession of America's Northwest. Of course, this portrayal worked in part by positioning America, proper, as ugly, backward, and unnatural – the ex-American reporter who narrates the story decides to stay in paradise. The spectre of dystopia was embedded in the founding texts of the green movement.

2 The Practice of Shocking

The headline 'Global Warming Ads Wrong, Say Scientists' topped a *Sunday Times* (10 November 1991) report about the 'doom-mongering' evident in propaganda sponsored by the British government. Critics had assailed two newspaper ads that tried to scare the population by linking the greenhouse effect to a major storm (labelled a 'hurricane') in 1987. Even Collett, Dickenson and Pearce, the ad agency responsible for the campaign, admitted that the evidence for a connection was 'flimsy.' The pictures of the storm had been chosen because they were so 'vivid and memorable.' According to the account manager, 'Inevitably, advertising picks on dramatic images and simplifies things in order to get people's attention.'

That was certainly true of green ads. Publicity was the lifeblood of a movement initially well outside the main corridors of authority. Its champions constantly performed on the public stage: releasing reports, holding press conferences, and organizing confrontations and stunts, all to capture the eye of the media and so win the attention of the public. Civic advocacy was only one tool, and was usually at the disposal of only the larger organizations and, later, sympathetic government agencies. But it was the most visible, and most widely distributed, of the vehicles of persuasion available, excepting the sporadic 'free' publicity provided by television and the press. Sponsors were always on the lookout for a 'potent symbol.' That was the phrase used by a campaign director of the Royal Society for the Prevention of Cruelty to Animals, who justified the publication of a nasty picture of 'a dead pony hanging from a meat hook,' even though the pony had actually been slain in a legal and humane fashion.[7] Creating the image – that was all important. 'A PSA shouldn't have to be preachy ... A poignant image is more powerful,' mused Nick Boxer, the executive producer for a series on protecting the planet. 'After more than twenty years, we still remember the public service announcement from the 1970's depicting a Native American man canoeing down a polluted river with a tear in his eye.'[8] He was referring to *Chief Iron Eyes Cody*.

Using this approach, green advocates, or their admakers, fashioned some of the most graphic and disturbing propaganda in the annals of advocacy advertising. Purposes varied. Lynx, a British anti-fur organization, set out to cause revulsion when it sponsored *Insects* (1987), in which viewers were treated to close-ups of flies and maggots feeding on the flesh attached to the inside of coats in a swank furrier.[9] Greenpeace tried to frighten in a spot against genetically engineered products, primarily soybean-based: the commercial was full of sinister signs – a roulette wheel (signifying the gamble), ominous music, close-ups of glowing cells (signifying radiation), a baby's cry (the vulnerable), plus the constant repetition of an 'X' (signifying denial, danger) – to move people to reject the dangerous, unwanted novelty.[10] The Department of Water and Power in Los Angeles plagiarized the style of the slasher movie in *Scream* (1991), part of a paid campaign to encourage water conservation – we are the predatory camera, the victim is a woman enjoying a shower, and the action takes us down the hall, through the bathroom, and into her private space. But what happens is that the bill gets delivered, hence the shriek: you waste, you pay.[11] Serious or mock, green advertising sometimes became a species of attack propaganda.

Not surprisingly, there were always efforts to censor the most radical of these ads. Politicians and business executives in the United States, for example, took issue with the claim made in a Sierra Club PSA that 'America's being paved over.' Thereafter, the network demanded documentation to support claims in PSAs of all sorts. In 1986, Britain's Independent Broadcasting Authority refused a Greenpeace ad that compared the Sellafield nuclear power plant to the infamous Soviet disaster site of Chernobyl. At the same time, efforts by the Campaign for Nuclear Disarmament were confined to posters, the press, and the cinema because of a rule against what was called 'political' advertising. A bit later, in Canada, the CBC refused to sell time to students who were fighting a proposed Slowpoke nuclear reactor at the University of Saskatchewan, even though the Canadian Nuclear Association was on the air promoting the virtues of nuclear energy. When in 1991 the Des Moines *Register* had the temerity to publish an anti-meat ad (the ad drew an analogy between the killing of animals for food and the Jeffrey Dahmer serial murders), cattle interests removed $1 million worth of advertising from the Iowa paper. Other newspapers in the Midwest and Southwest simply turned down pro-vegetarian ads.[12] The necessity to win media approval not only acted as a constraint; it prevented some messages from getting through to the public at all. Certain kinds of campaigns – for example, 'meat stinks' or 'meat is murder,' were kept on the margins, at least until the mid-1990s. Yet this censorship was only further evidence that green advocacy could strike at the core values of the social (and corporate) mainstream.

3 The Ravaged Planet

In the eyes of critics, sometimes in the words of its own leaders, the grand target of green advocacy was no less than the civilization of the First World. Rarely did green propaganda attack 'modernity' head on, at least outside the advertising of a radical fringe. Instead, the ads focused on more specific problems, such as pollution. Yet there were a few recurring narratives that hinted at the subtext of opposition and alienation.

a) Violation

Rede Globo, billed as Brazil's largest television network, employed one of these narratives when it sought to protect an endangered landscape. Why would a network be so concerned? Perhaps to combat outside pressures. The Amazon rain forest had been widely celebrated throughout the First World as one of the last bastions of a wild nature and therefore a treasure sacred to the green cause. Yet that rain forest was a contested place, its ecosystems and its creatures constantly threatened by progress. Little wonder that the Brazilian authorities were harshly criticized by foreign organizations for their commitment to the priorities of growth. Rede Globo merely gave the green critique a local flavour.

Indian (Rede Globo, Save the Rainforest, Brazil, 1989): An aboriginal boy represents the rain forest. At first we hear some Indian flute music along with the sounds of birds and water. The image of the boy fills the screen: he is shown face on, with a thick mat of hair covering the top of his head and flowing down behind his ears onto his shoulders and thence to his chest. We see him passive, apprehensive, and eventually unhappy. No wonder: his hair is machined off by a heavy-duty electric razor, to the sound of a chainsaw – and the twittering of birds. At the end he is almost bald. Finally comes the command, 'Preserve the Amazon forest.' The screen freezes. We hear the falling of a huge tree.

Indian depicted a kind of rape, the plenty of an untouched land despoiled, ravaged by the advance of progress. The admaker presumed the Romance of Nature, that nature was a thing of beauty and value, without ever stating such a transcendental notion. The ad proposed no solution, offered no hope. Rather, it accused. Something precious was being lost. *Rain Forest Burn*, a later ad (1991), made a similar grand but ultimately hollow appeal. Here we were treated to the burning of an array of green-tinted matches that constituted a part of the Brazilian flag. What message did the boldly named Brazilian Ecological Movement wish to convey: 'Green covers the greatest area of the Brazilian flag. It's necessary to preserve it, before it's too late.'[13]

There were other contested regions around the earth, of course, and these, too, were occasions for mourning. Consider the pollution of coastal waters by oil spills: ordinary people looked on in dumb sadness at the corruption of the common sea, the terrible sludge left by the wrecking of a tanker (*S.O.S. Bretagne*, Croix Rouge Française, 1977). Consider the plight of all too many beaches: a disembodied voice lamented the trashing of such places of beauty, and all because of the thoughtlessness of humanity (*Contrapunto*, Ministerio de Obras Publicas y Urbanismo, Spain, 1984). Such ads, often poignant, dwelt on the themes of violation and betrayal. They amounted to a moral judgment, a plea to humanity to mend its ways.[14]

b) Excess

The Friends of the Earth (FOE) used a related narrative to reflect on the very different site of the city. Born in the United States in 1969, FOE had soon spread out into the wider world, where it claimed more than fifty separate national organizations by the mid-1990s. The American parent registered an early and continuing mission as 'a principal steward' of the air and the water.[15] Witness this recruitment ad aimed at the people of Hong Kong, a population not known for its interest in green issues.

Dirty TV Screen (Friends of the Earth, Hong Kong, 1992): The simple ad worked off the common fear of dirt, here positioned as a hidden poison, a menace to health. It is a collection of different panels, five with text, presented in one continuous sequence. The panels are supposed to represent a television screen, in itself a symbol of modernity. A soundtrack full of the noise of driving and the honking of horns locates them in the context of the big city. The message is straightforward:

JUST HOW DIRTY IS THE AIR YOU'RE BREATHING?
TRY THIS SIMPLE TEST.
MOISTEN A TISSUE AND WIPE IT ACROSS YOUR TV SCREEN.
[That action produces a cleaned swipe against a dirty background.]
SHAME YOU CAN'T DO THE SAME THING WITH YOUR LUNGS.
JOIN THE FIGHT AGAINST POLLUTION/JOIN FRIENDS OF THE EARTH.

Here was a brief tale of decay. It suggested just how badly we had treated our living spaces. It drew upon memories, real or ersatz, of fresh air, open spaces, a pure nature. And it represented the big city as a ruined place that required salvation.[16] There were more dramatic expressions of this story of decay. In the same year, the Hong Kong government tried to shock residents to stop pollution. One television commercial featured a fish that oozed 'slime and filth,' while the other depicted garbage that actually attacked the people who had tossed it aside.[17] Dead fish served as the motif in *Nouvelle Cuisine*, a piece of dark satire sponsored by Greenpeace in Spain. Thus, the picture of two large fish surrounded by garbage was labelled 'Dover sole with dressing.' 'Keep adding these ingredients and we won't be able to eat fish at all.'[18] A second Greenpeace effort, *Schutzschild* (1989), warned West Germany about the menace of ozone depletion. Two medieval knights in armour, one with a sword and the other with a shield, perform a metaphorical battle: in their struggle, the blows of the sword shatter the life-preserving shield which protects the earth from dangerous radiation.[19]

Such propaganda sought to demonstrate how the degradation of the environment imperilled humanity itself. The Romance of Nature was replaced by the Test of Utility. All the dirt we threw into the water and the air and onto the land was steadily increasing the risk that we, too, would become the victims of an ecological disaster. A similar fate was in store if we continued to deplete our resources. A succession of water utilities during the 1980s warned their publics about the perils of extravagance. Singapore's utility board told citizens how 'millions of litres' were wasted daily, and in a land without rivers, springs, or lakes. One authority in South Australia used that symbol of greed, the pig, in this case a toy half full, to depict how the water supply was a resource that had to be used wisely. New York City's Department of Environmental Protection dried out a big apple (another name for the city) in an effort to slow down consumption.[20]

The assault on both decay and waste was also about excess, one of the defining features of daily life in the affluent world. It was this theme that the Environmental Defense Fund (EDF) played up in its recycling campaigns. Their ads spoke to the ongoing, if low level, moral distress which afflicted many well-off North Americans who could never suffer abundance too easily. The EDF had emerged in 1967 out of the efforts of a collection of conservationists exercised by the use of the pesticide DDT to spray marshes on Long Island. A victory in the courts led the group to launch other legal actions until the banning of DDT in the United States in 1972. That campaign produced further battles – against leaded gasoline, and so on. By the late 1980s the EDF had rehyped that old problem of trash.

Wasteland (EDF, U.S.A., 1987): Trash was now a threat to America's very future, or so it would seem. The spot opens on the clean, wholesome, white face of a young teen, a blonde girl, singing her heart out in what we soon realize is a choir. We are shown other faces, other races, girls and boys, all singing 'America the Beautiful.' What better way to symbolize hope and patriotism? But then an ill wind blows, and we see six kids, dressed in red robes, surrounded by a wasteland of trash, rocks, a dead tree, a golden hazed sky. Voice-over: 'America is burying itself in over half a million tons of trash every twenty-four hours. If you're not recycling you're throwing it all away.' A later and more famous spot called *Earth* actually shows a blue-and-white globe which is then grabbed by two hands, crumpled, and dropped: the planet itself has become garbage.[21]

c) The Web of Life

The sceptre of an ecological collapse was given a special twist by the WWF, known both as the World Wide Fund for Nature and the World

Wildlife Fund (in Canada and the United States). Another of the new champions of conservation, started in 1961 by British activists but based in Switzerland, three decades later the WWF claimed the largest international membership of any of the groups at roughly five million supporters across five continents. Indeed, it boasted investing 'over US$1,165 million in more than 11,000 projects in 130 countries' since 1985. All the projects supposedly played a part 'in the campaign to stop the accelerating degradation of Earth's natural environment, and to help its human inhabitants live in greater harmony with nature.'[22] Hence its efforts to save the rhinoceros, and, more broadly, every endangered species, whether flora or fauna.

Web of Life (World Wildlife Fund, U.S.A., 1996): 'A fatal metaphor of man's disregard for co-existence on planet Earth,' or so claimed the anonymous writer who described this spot once featured on the Ogilvy and Mather Web site. In fact, the ad was much more. A man armed with a chainsaw marches boldly through the sand, his steps accentuated by a drumbeat, until he reaches a series of huge placards, planted in that sand, each sporting a picture and a title. He starts his saw with a swift pull and viciously assaults the first sign, marked 'Rhino.' That soon tumbles onto its neighbour, 'Tree,' which starts a domino effect, knocking down one placard after another. The voice-over explains: 'The rhino ... he's just one species. But if he goes, he could take a few things with him.' Indeed 'he' does, for the placards are arranged in a circle, ending with 'Medicine' and 'Oxygen' – and behind the last is the man himself, representative of a thoughtless humankind. The culprit looks up, startled then horrified, as the final placard falls, presumably crushing him. Then the camera swiftly moves out and up to reveal a circle of fallen signs, placed across North Africa, the Mediterranean, southern Europe, and the Near East. The command?: 'PRESERVE THE WEB OF LIFE.' The final screen lists the sponsor's name, complete with its famous Panda logo and a 1–800 number.

Viewers or, more properly in this case, browsers, had just received a simple lesson in ecology, one of the fundamental creeds of green science. *Web of Life* celebrated diversity and difference. More important, it revealed, better yet constructed, an ecological truth: the connectedness of all living things. Nothing should be lost. Everything was precious. Humanity was not something separate, something superior, whose technology allowed it to do as it wished to nature. Rather, humanity was part of a common and vast ecosystem that, once destroyed, would bring down the arrogant species which believed itself supreme.

Such lessons had become banal, especially in America. Indeed, the WWF had been waging a propaganda war against species extinctions in many countries at least since 1980.[23] But it hardly acted alone. The U.S. Forest Service showed Americans (*Imploding House*, 1986) how a forest fire could swiftly wreak havoc and eventually strike back at people, symbolized by the burning of a home.[24] MTV, that madcap source of hectic music videos, lent its style and weight to this narrative of connectedness in its 'Save Earth Now' campaign of 1990: for example, *Running Water* shows, very swiftly, how brushing the teeth puts demands on water resources that can well affect the supply of food.[25] Late in 1996 the Earth Communications Office (ECO), something of a Hollywood front that specialized in ecological PSAs destined for cinema viewing, heavily promoted its new *Neighbors*, which promised to focus on 'how the health of our oceans and of the creatures which live in the oceans is critical to our own health.'[26] The web of life was a narrative that could bear endless repetition.

d) The Bleak Future

Greenpeace offered two visions of the dystopia that might await a humanity which refused to listen. Greenpeace is the most celebrated of the organizations that make up what is sometimes called 'big environment.' It emerged in Vancouver in 1971 out of a protest against the testing of nuclear weapons by the American government off Amchitka Island in Alaska. It won worldwide fame a year later when it produced films showing French commandos beating a Greenpeace official in another anti-nuclear protest and soon became notorious for an assortment of stunts and confrontations, designed to save whales, stop atomic tests, and, ultimately, 'create a green and peaceful world,' albeit in its own radical image. Along the way, the media-savvy organization, soon centred in Europe rather than America, sponsored some of the most striking pieces of propaganda in the green repertoire.[27]

Meltdown, also known as *Nuclear Cemetery* (Greenpeace, U.K., 1987): This minidrama depicts the burial of one 'Adam Smith,' here a child aged seven, the victim of nuclear pollution, who lived, purportedly, between 1982 and 1989. The name 'Adam Smith' represented a sort of joke, a reference to the founding theorist of a now-triumphant market economy. But that is the only piece of humour in this otherwise dark premonition of a coming catastrophe.

The setting is very bleak: bare hills, an absence of vegetation, a dirt road, a guardpost, and the grave site. The music is sombre, the colours dull. There is no voice-over, nor is one needed. The drama leaves the impression of a routine, suggesting how ordinary this has become, a mood which makes the presentation all the more tragic. We are shown the drive to the cemetery; a meeting at the guardhouse, where a soldier, who has watched the arrival on his video screens, raises the barrier; the participants are dressed in radiation suits, which suggests a general death. We see the solemn march to the burial plot, the careful place-ment of the lead casket, the sad embrace of the mother and father, a flower thrown into the grave, of course a mother's tear. While two people shovel dirt onto the casket, the camera slowly pulls back to reveal an enormous array of burial sites (each marked with the nuclear symbol). Finally, the screen goes black and we are asked whether nuclear energy is worth it.

That commercial sought to evoke the terror of radiation. It drew upon the memories of Three Mile Island, even more of Chernobyl, plus a host of science-fiction dramas. Its potency lay in the way it offered a compel-ling fiction of what could happen if the world did not mend its ways. Risk had been made tangible.[28]

Air Supply (Greenpeace, Canada, 1990): Here Greenpeace revealed a future in which a public good, the air we breathe, had become a scarce, private good. This is everyday life in the near future. Everything is hazy, as if some mist or dust covers the outside. The women and men shown walking (and the shots are in slow motion) wear oxygen masks and carry oxygen containers. One man, a derelict, first seen hacking out his lungs, begs for assistance. A woman gives money which allows him to purchase, briefly, a shot of oxygen from a strange contraption. The clean-air machine has a slot for coins, a panel called Hygiene Control, and its sides are made of some translucent substance, through which can be seen the fuzzy outline of a cluster of leaves, as of some superplant that produces pure, life-giving air. But we see no more of this marvel. The camera briefly focuses upon a frog gulping for air. Then back to the derelict, now upset and frustrated because the clean air is cut off. The commercial ends with the slogan and the sponsor identification superimposed on the screen. The last sound is of someone struggling to breathe.

Clean air had become a commodity, for sale, in this sad future, made such by the carelessness of the present generation. It opened as a puzzle – we do not initially have sufficient information to determine exactly what the pictures mean. What made the performance so clever was that it

The Walkers

The Derelict

The Air Machine

Figure 22: Scenes from *Air Supply*

represented something ordinary, the walk to (perhaps from) work – in which there was a beggar. But the significance of the scene was transformed because what the man required was the means to breathe – the demand had gone beyond food and drink. The whole scene was tainted: this was a future transformed by a subtraction, clean air, and an addition, pollution. Once again, the excesses of modernity had devastated life.[29]

Such fine, bold performances as these were rare. The U.S. Forest Service sponsored one equivalent, much earlier than Greenpeace, called *Oxygen Mask*. A grandpa and his granddaughter tramp through a desolate wilderness as he explains what things were like before the burning of all the trees. At the end they both wear oxygen masks.[30] The theme of ecological collapse, or rather of nature's revenge, however, was much more widespread. Indeed the narrative of collapse was the culmination of other arguments, implicit in the stories of violation, degradation, depletion, and connection. Together they constitute another collective or virtual fiction, this (in part) an answer to technopia. Except here it is a vision of dystopia, of an Arcadia defiled by the agency of humanity and the instruments of progress.

4 The Oppressed Kingdom

That was not the only dystopia common in green circles. The other, which might be called 'Arcadia perverted,' was built upon the moral outrage of animal rights. Past visions of Arcadia presumed the harmony of human and non-human animals.[31] But today, it was claimed, people dispose of animals in cruel and sadistic ways, to suit their vanity, their stomachs, or their whims. The animal kingdom is seen as oppressed, enslaved to a voracious and immoral tyrant.

Hunter (International Fund for Animal Welfare [IFAW], Canada, 1974): 'Where does your candidate stand on the killing of baby seals? Demand an answer.' That message concluded a startling political ad directed against the baby seal hunt in Newfoundland. What had gone before were scenes of the callous 'harvesting' of a baby seal on an ice flow, presumably somewhere off Canada's eastern seacoast. The first image we see is of this unfortunate seal – a small, white, fluffy oval, looking both adorable and sad – held in place by the boot of a hunter. He slams his large truncheon down: blood splatters the head of the seal. In the background we hear the sounds of an animal screaming. The hunter looks over the horizon at a helicopter. He prepares to cut open and skin the seal. Except it isn't dead: it twists and turns in pain. So, disgruntled, he raises his truncheon to finish off the job – and that's when the camera freezes.[32]

Hunter was an expression of the first major international campaign to expose humanity's brutal treatment of animals. The ad carried the issue into the enemy's camp, attempting to sway the opinions of a Canadian electorate. For, initially, the campaign was centred in Europe, and especially Britain. Brian Davis had founded the IFAW in 1968, after pictures of the killing of seals appeared in a British newspaper. Greenpeace joined the campaign in 1976. A variety of European celebrities lent their presence to the cause. In 1983, Europe banned the import of products using the victim's fur, two years later a Canadian commission concluded that public opinion would never condone the seal-pup hunt, and in 1988 the Canadian government banned the killing of baby (though not adult) seals.

Hunter played only a bit part in this drama. Its task was to reposition fur. The spot lay at the beginning of an effort to construct evil, to manufacture a public bad. What the ad focused on, consequently, was the process rather than the product: the viewer was shown just how nasty was the hunt that produced the glamorous fur coat. The propaganda emphasized that the raw material of fashion was a living creature, indeed a cuddly *baby*. There was speculation that the very shape of the seal evoked feelings of warmth, of empathy. The appeal was visceral – people were supposed to flinch when the hunter smashed the head of the hapless victim. The effort was to extend the sphere of moral concern to encompass something that was so vulnerable and so innocent. Thereby *Hunter* forecast two of the themes which would prevail in the animal-rights propaganda thereafter.

a) The Slaughter of the Innocents

We witness a never-ending series of tragedies in this collage of ads. First we see the animals in their proper settings: the majesty of the elephant, the grace of the dolphin, a cute hare skiing in the snow, an inquisitive wolf, a playful weasel. This is how it should be. But now humanity enters the picture. Their sign is the gun, the knife, the trap, weapons used in a war against the animals. Perhaps we see the fishing net that snares the dolphin or the leg trap that awaits the unwary mink. We are even shown just how many bullets are required to wipe out the remaining black rhinos of Tanzania. Thence, inevitably, the camera moves in on the slaughter of the innocents. Hunters kill elephants for their ivory. The elephant will be virtually extinct in ten years, we are told. Fishers destroy dolphins caught in nets meant for tuna – no less than 250,000 a year: 'And that's how we know they scream like us.' The big cats which once roamed Florida freely have been replaced by the 'fat cats' who build condos – here the problem is overdevelopment. Another horror is driven home when suddenly the trapper hunts people wearing fur coats and bludgeons a group of women who play out the role of baby seals. We watch as some pets drive an Italian man to a garbage-strewn site where he is abandoned to his fate. Can you sympathize now? Finally, the screen is full of scenes of pain, blood, and death. There is a lynx trying to pull its leg free from the trap. Here is a picture of a dog being put down at an animal compound. See that pile of dead elephants? Hear the dolphins scream? For we who buy the fur or the ivory, we who eat the tuna, we who discard pets, we are the villains of this horror story.[33]

b) The Brutalization of Humanity

The brutality of the hunter is often marked on the body of the villain. Hunters slouch around like subhuman beasts. A beautiful woman wear-

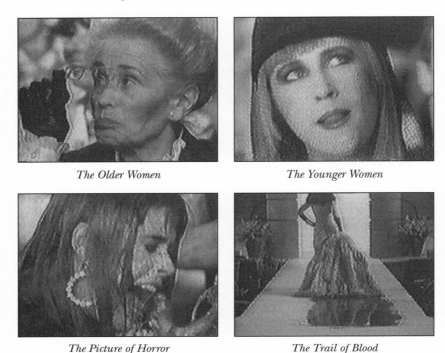

The Older Women   *The Younger Women*

The Picture of Horror   *The Trail of Blood*

Figure 23: Scenes from *Dumb Animals*

ing white fur becomes a monster, blood dripping from her fangs: she feeds on the misery of the innocent. The upscale types in a fur salon are equated with the flies and maggots that flourish in the decaying flesh of dead animals. A smart gentleman, caught up in the fox hunt, turns into a demented boy, madly riding a wooden horse. The pain people visit on animals returns to haunt the perpetrators in the ethical universe of animal rights.[34]

The theme of transformation was best expressed, again, by Greenpeace. Its moral fable, made by Yellowhammer, at a cost of £186,000, won the Grand Prix at New York's International Advertising Festival.[35] The commercial worked the contrast between pleasure and revulsion, glamour and horror, in an especially deft way.

Dumb Animals (Greenpeace then Lynx, U.K., 1985):[36] We are at a fashion show surrounded by precious people and eager paparazzi. Beautiful young models

wearing exquisite fur coats sashay down the runway. We watch, marvel, judge –
and around us people clap and hoot, cameras flash, and the excitement rises. An
older woman stares intently at the luxury through square-rimmed glasses; a
young soulmate licks her lips as if to taste the sensation. Watchers and perform-
ers blow kisses at each other. Oh, what a marvellous occasion! Then the mood
changes. One of the models swings her coat, and a red speck smears on the
cheek of a blonde woman. Blood pours down onto the runway from a twirling fur
coat. The applause turns to horror. Yet the models continue to pose and swirl.
Spectators' faces are soon drenched with blood. They howl in anguish. Finally,
the last model walks away, dragging her fur behind, and leaving a trail of blood.
On screen comes the message:

> It takes up to 40 dumb animals
> to make a fur coat.
> But only one to wear it.
> Greenpeace

The viewer could read a lot into this piece of criticism: the shallowness
of the world of fashion; the artifice behind the face of glamour; the evils
of consumption; the nastiness of human beings. But *Dumb Animals* sought,
above all, to dishonor, to establish that acquiring the skins of animals was
fundamentally a moral transgression, a sin against nature. Commercials
like this worked to convince people to stop buying and wearing furs –
real furs, any way, since the *faux* fur industry soon experienced a new
popularity.

5 Saving Nature

The publicity and propaganda and scares of the green offensive did have
an effect, at least in western Europe and North America. The results were
apparent in many different ways, some significant, some trivial. During
the 1970s an estimated $50 million in money and/or donated time and
services kept alive the name and image of Smokey the Bear – nearly all of
the respondents (98 per cent) recognized this American icon in one
1976 survey (which, admittedly, used a form of aided recall).[37] The
worldwide use of images of 'harpooned whales and blood-spattered
corpses of seal pups' turned Greenpeace into 'a cash-flush eco-lobby with
an $11 million budget by 1982.'[38] In Britain, an RSPCA campaign to
reinstate dog licensing ('When the Government killed the dog license
they left us to kill the dogs') excited sufficient public support to increase

membership and funds as well as to embarrass the government.[39] The combination of imaginative advertising and mandatory water rationing in Los Angeles worked a change in the morning habits of some residents: they started taking noticeably shorter showers.[40]

On a broader scale, the environmental lobby had reshaped public opinion. Consider the case of Canada, sometimes a target of green propaganda. In a book devoted to charting the changing opinions of Canadians in the 1980s,[41] Allan Gregg and Michael Posner termed one of their chapters 'Turning Green.' There they published one statistic after another to show that people were worrying, and worrying in larger numbers, about water and air pollution, chemical pesticides, ozone depletion, oil spills, acid rain, the greenhouse effect, and so on – in a phrase, about Nature's Revenge. Indeed, a rival polling firm discovered that in July 1989 Canadians registered the environment as the single most pressing issue on the public agenda. This priority did not last, of course: the environment fell to second place in July 1990, down to a tie for third place a year later, and thereafter persisted among the chaos of other issues at the bottom of the pyramid of concerns.[42] But the conviction that action was necessary did continue: a 1996 poll found that over three-quarters of respondents wanted 'stricter environmental laws.'[43] Saving nature had become one of those fortunate causes that enjoyed widespread, though hardly uncontested, support among the public.[44]

That fostered a different kind of propaganda, what the American group ECO referred to as 'positive reinforcement,' which explained how viewers' efforts were making, or could make, a difference. One of its most celebrated efforts was a PSA entitled *The Power of One* (1993), purportedly displayed on 15,000 movie screens. The commercial was a pastiche of scenes drawn from the news showing people who had demonstrated how an individual could change the world, including Gandhi at prayer and Mother Teresa at work, the person who blocked the tank in Tiananmen Square, a little black girl escorted into a segregated school, and rainforest inhabitants stopping the bulldozers of developers. The pictures were backed by a piece of original music, African in style, that served to inspire, to evoke a sense of awe. A later effort, *Neighbors* (1996), ended with the message, 'You Have the Power,' and called on people to phone 1–800–POWER to hear more inspiring messages. The Captain Planet Foundation fostered a campaign that told kids 'The Power Is Yours.' Australia's Planet Ark, another upbeat organization, had the movie star Pierce Brosnan explain how public pressure had moved Congress to save the dolphins once (in 1990) and assert that people could do it again (in 1996).[45]

Planet Ark sponsored a whole host of environmental messages, each boasting a celebrity, including Dustin Hoffman, Jeff Goldboom, and Paul and Linda McCartney. The readiness of celebrities to endorse green causes suggests just how popular they had become (though when the country singer k.d. lang fronted for an anti-meat commercial she infuriated people in her home town, located in Alberta's ranching country). Inspiring messages were never enough, of course. Planet Ark sought to show how people could do their bit for the environment. Its stars urged us to use less water or lukewarm water when washing (Bob Geldof), water your garden early in the morning (Corbin Bernsen), fix leaking taps (Dustin Hoffman), or even 'go veggie' (Linda McCartney). MTV's nature spots commanded viewers to 'use a rag' (to save the forests) and 'use a mug' (to stop ozone depletion), which an unkind observer might think merely trivialized the problem. The Evergreen Foundation urged Canadians to plant a tree to make the cities more livable. A Japanese power company used comic performances to get people to turn off lights and close the refrigerator door, to save energy. California's Fish and Game Department hoped taxpayers would contribute a little something extra via their tax forms to protect endangered species. There was even an effort to popularize a particular mark, a 'Green Seal,' that could identify the correct, environmentally friendly brand for concerned shoppers. All sorts of agencies played the 'how-to' game, offering some sort of technique to redeem nature. In a way, the propaganda commodified nature, offering people the chance to purchase a social product that would bring the personal satisfaction of doing something saintly, if not necessarily something that would realize the promised global salvation. Here was a different form of privatization.

Saving nature had been made into a routine, even mundane practice. That coincided with the emergence of a new media frame, at least in North America, which focused on the troubles, even the decline, of big environment. The *New York Times* (1 January 1995) portrayed a movement that in the 1980s had binged on too many causes, too much money, and too many members and was now suffering a general recession. It cited an academic report, by a business-cum-economic organization, that chastised the major organizations for using 'fear and apocalyptic prophecies,' a strategy which had purportedly fostered a counter-movement. *Time* (24 April 1995) counted up the troubles of a 'battered U.S. green movement,' plagued by a Republican Congress and a corporate-engineered assault on such treasures as the Clean Water Act. The claimed chumminess with corporate America, especially corporate donors, of the

Sierra Club, the Environmental Defense Fund, the Wilderness Society, and others, was a source of furious criticism from Earth First!, a radical green faction.[46] *Time* International (10 June 1996) spoke of the re-fashioning of Greenpeace, where a new corporate style of management had taken command and the leaders seemed prepared to work with big business and big government. The Toronto *Globe and Mail* (2 October 1997) carried a story explaining 'Why Greenpeace Faltered' in its effort to save what was called the 'Great Bear Rain Forest' in British Columbia. One reason given was a falling off in international concern, which also reflected a new sense of malaise over lack of progress. A large part of the problem, at least according to Earth First!, was 'the vision thing': the green movement had lost its critical edge when it went mainstream.

6 Apocalyptic Dreams

In fact, however, the spectre of global destruction that had energized the green crusade in the past generation had not disappeared. It persisted in the official art of big environment – its propaganda. Consider a WWF campaign running on Eurosport, a satellite channel in Europe, during the summer of 1994. The four fifteen-second spots were animated, in itself a sign that the propaganda was light rather than frenzied or hor-rific. Each ad featured an adult, sometimes a few adults, who represented both past and present humanity, and a boy, the stand-in for future generations. The adult(s) variously filled the planet with factories and the oceans with waste, cut down all the trees, and turned the Earth into a garbage can. What happened then? Pollution covered the globe and suffocated the adult; water turned to dirty sludge; the earth dried out and crumbled; and, finally, the planet became a bomb that exploded, covering adult and child with trash. In every case, the boy was not pleased, since he and his friends would suffer the ills of this unrestrained progress. Here was *comique-noir*, green style. The WWF campaign em-ployed the ironic strategy so common in the advertising of the nineties. Yet this was still a green nightmare: the form had changed, but the message of disaster remained the same.

The triumphalism of corporate advertising spoke to one side of the postmodern sensibility; the doom and gloom of its green rival spoke to another. Commentators have detected a taste for 'playful despair,' espe-cially among intellectuals but evident as well in the popular culture. 'Fear of apocalypse – of that merging of clarity and oblivion – itself merges with fascination and desire for such a definitive, and perhaps even ecstatic, catastrophe.'[47] Sometimes people like to flagellate themselves, or their world, with thoughts of decay, decline, and collapse. Roughly a quarter of Americans, according to one *Time*/CNN poll, believed that 'the end-times' would start around the year 2000. Another 31 per cent thought that the coming of an apocalypse was 'possible.'[48] The most fruitful source of apocalyptic thinking, of course, has always been religion, and most recently its fundamentalist variety. [49] But what Arthur Herman has termed a pervasive 'eco-pessimism' has done much in recent decades to popularize apocalyptic imagery and rhetoric.[50] Severe droughts or unusual storms, the mass deaths of frogs, the retreat of glaciers, these and other calamities become signs of an impending collapse, and so an agent of anguish. Environmentalism and animal rights activism are much more than just affectation. But they are also that, a fashionable pose which the affluent may indulge to satisfy a desire for a moment of moral despair. Green propaganda has done its bit to sustain that indulgence.

PART V: HYPERREALITIES

*BAUDRILLARD AND COMPANY:
SPECTACLE, IMAGE, SIMULACRUM

Our society is one not of spectacle but of surveillance ... We are much less Greeks than we believe. We are neither in the amphitheatre, nor on the stage, but in the panoptic machine ...
Michel Foucault, 1975[1]

Foucault was wrong. Not completely wrong, because 'the panoptic machine' certainly did work to discipline the individual, but wrong about spectacle, a power which has waxed greatly in the twentieth century. Understanding why and how requires a quick tour through both theory and history.

Discipline and Punish opened with a gripping discussion of premodern publicity, including 'the spectacle of the scaffold' (32)[2] where punishment was enacted on the body of the criminal to reaffirm the authority of the sovereign. This account was a gruesome exploration of the ways in which, as Jürgen Habermas argued, lordship represented its publicness in the Middle Ages.[3] The trouble with this spectacle, Foucault claimed, was its inadequacy – public torture and execution were intermittent, inefficient, and often ineffective: they could incite the spectators to an unplanned violence, turning lesson into carnival, perhaps converting the criminal into a popular hero. That was why authority had looked increasingly to other means to affirm and produce relations of power. Foucault treated spectacle as *passé*, characteristic of 'antiquity,' where multitudes occasionally observed a few men or objects, and surveillance as modern, 'the exact reverse of spectacle' (216), for now a few souls constantly watched over the multitudes.

What he failed to recognize was that spectacle had undergone a process of transformation to fit the new requirements of discipline. Later, one of Foucault's followers tried to employ his theory of power (mixed with a dash of Gramsci) to remedy the neglect of spectacle.[4] In *The Birth of the Museum*, Tony Bennett explored the development of an 'exhibitionary complex,' mostly during the nineteenth century, in which the 'technologies of surveillance' were linked with 'new forms of spectacle' to produce a novel mode of domination (61). The Great Exhibition of 1851 at the Crystal Palace in London seemed to mark the maturing of the techniques of display that would be practised thereafter. Bennett found the exhibitionary complex embodied in the later organization of museums, world's fairs, and amusement parks, where sights were constructed by authority to impress and thus discipline the crowds. So the museum became a way of arranging 'things and peoples' (95) as well as reforming 'public manners' (99), a place where people could observe themselves as an ordered body, and, indeed, 'the primary instrument of civil education' (102) in the bourgeois democracies.

But I wonder: the mundane significance of this apparatus, especially the museum, could hardly be so substantial, simply because going to the museum was not a daily event. The industrialization of spectacle owed much more to that image explosion brought about in what Walter Benjamin long ago called 'the Age of Mechanical Reproduction,' moving from photographs in the 1840s, to movies in the 1890s, talkies in the 1930s, and eventually television in the 1950s – though television occurred well after Benjamin's seminal article (1936).[5] Each of these innovations spread the presence of 'manufactured sights'[6] – a good workable definition of images – farther across and deeper into society. The plethora of images, moreover, marked a radical break with the tradition of art, or so Benjamin argued. While the reproduced image lost some properties, notably its special 'aura' (221) and its 'cult value'[7] (224), that artifact acquired a new cultural force through its enhanced 'exhibition value' (225). In particular, as art escaped the world of ritual it began 'to be based on another practise – politics' (224). Benjamin was especially excited by the potential of film to involve and engage the populace, and to enrich 'our field of perception' (235), a capacity which suggested its revolutionary potential. But he also feared the way authority could exploit the new technology. 'The logical result of Fascism is the introduction of aesthetics into political life' (241). Through it – and here Benjamin seems to have had in mind Germany as well as Italy – the élite could divert and control the populace.

In fact, however, the 'aestheticization of politics,' or rather of some political events, had been apparent well before the twentieth century: consider, for example, the Roman triumphs, the extravagance of the baroque palace, or the jubilees of Queen Victoria.[8] The more virulent forms of spectacle had emerged, initially, out of Bolshevism, a phenomenon about which Benjamin, as a Marxist, had a blind spot. What was novel was the scale and persistence of persuasion. The Russian Revolution of 1917 brought the birth of an entity Peter Kenez has called the first propaganda state.[9] The grand ideology of Communism gave the Bolshevik leaders the confidence that utopia was possible. During the 1920s they set out to transform the nature of humanity and society, to 'create the New Socialist Man,' by means of a total and permanent brand of propaganda. The task of political education affected virtually every mode of public communication that was allowed to exist in the fledgling state: school texts, theatre, painting, cinema, posters, books, newspapers, and radio. One of the most innovative, if short-lived, vehicles (common during 1918–20, the period of the civil war) were the *agitka*, short films between five and thirty minutes long that strove to drive home a simple revolutionary message to the uneducated. Much more famous were the works of the film director Sergei Eisenstein, whose propaganda became an internationally acclaimed art: his *Battleship Potemkin*, for instance, was a celebration of revolution, a story of violence and heroism that showed how the oppressed masses finally rose up in righteous anger to exact revenge against their tyrannical and cowardly masters. Although the Bolsheviks could never realize their ambitions, the perpetual agitation and the constant mobilization left a mark: propaganda established a political idiom and an appropriate behaviour which embodied the slogans and the presumptions of the Soviet order.

The next propaganda states were Fascist Italy in the 1920s and Nazi Germany in the 1930s, as Benjamin had suggested. Indeed, the first regime to realize the full potential of the industrialized spectacle was the Third Reich. At its core, Hitler's Germany was 'spectacular, gripping theater,' according to Modris Eksteins:[10]

> Early on, to arouse a sense of belonging, of 'community,' the party began to emphasize the importance, above everything else, of ritual and propaganda – the flags, the insignia, the uniforms, the pageantry, the standard greetings, the declarations of loyalty, and the endless repetition of slogans. Nazism was a cult. The appeal was strictly to emotion. The assault was on the senses, primarily visual and aural. The spoken word took precedence over the written. Drama, music, dance, and later radio and film were accorded more importance than literature. Nazism was grand spectacle, from beginning to end.

Adolf Hitler had been mightily impressed by the wartime propaganda campaigns of the Allies. Consequently, he backed the efforts of that master propagandist Joseph Goebbels to re-educate the German population according to the dictates and dreams of National Socialism. Goebbels was especially adept at the use of mass rallies to concoct or present images of unity and strength. In addition, he swiftly established his control over the new media of radio and the cinema. One of the great rallies (the national party meeting in Nuremberg in 1934) was preserved in Leni Riefenstahl's *Triumph of the Will*, which became another example of film propaganda that attained the stature of world-famous art. Here, too, utopian, as well as dystopian, visions played an important part in the new iconography of the state: the ideals of '*das Volk*' (the people) and '*Herrenvolk*' (the master race), the celebration of the Führer myth, as well as the fears of racial inferiority and the Jewish peril, all were presented via cinema, photographs, paintings, posters, and illustrations. These presentations fitted into an even wider structure of organizations, national celebrations, and ritual behaviour that linked action and symbol. David Welch has argued persuasively that Nazi propaganda was remarkably effective in ensuring at least passive support: it worked to the degree that it reflected and reinforced attitudes that were widely held among the people.[11]

The lessons of this success were far fewer than contemporaries imagined, however. The Soviet Union and Nazi Germany prohibited any autonomous public sphere, so propaganda could reign largely unchallenged by counter-images or arguments. That was hardly the case in the formal democracies. Moreover, the postwar centres of the emerging empire of images were not in Europe but in North America, more properly in New York and Hollywood. This was where the modernized version of spectacle seemed so commonplace. In 1962 Daniel Boorstin popularized this notion in a bestseller entitled *The Image*, a cry of alarm that become a classic of the sixties.[12] Boorstin feared an approaching triumph of 'illusion.' 'The American citizen ... lives in a world where fantasy is more real than reality, where the image has more dignity than its original' (37). Illusion might doom the republic: 'Our national politics has become a competition for images or between images, rather than between ideals' (249). He called upon his readers to shake loose from their addiction to images and rediscover 'reality,' though he could not make clear just what this reality was. More imaginative was his take on American history: he highlighted 'the fantastic pace' since the late nineteenth century of 'the Graphic Revolution,' the 'ability to make, preserve, transmit, and disseminate precise images – images of print, of men and landscapes and events, of the voices of men and mobs' (13). This ability had fostered a new way to communicate, particularly a new visual mode of communication, via symbol and stereotype, that proved far more appealing than either the spoken or the written word, the traditional vehicles of rationality. '"When the gods wish to punish us," Oscar Wilde might have said, "they make us believe our own advertising"' (239). It was exactly this phenomenon that the enormously influential

Pop Art movement embodied and celebrated in the 1960s:[13] the look of the commodity and the celebrity, a mass culture of entertainment and abundance that had become a popular culture of consumption and carnival. America was already well set on a course that would make its show-business products its number two export (behind military equipment) by the 1990s.[14]

It was left to yet another French theorist to proclaim the final triumph of the image, however. Indeed Foucault's observations about spectacle were directed in part against a one-time intellectual rival, the heterodox Marxist Guy Debord, who had been the master force in the Situationist International, a movement that reached the height of its influence during the chaotic days of May 1968.[15] The year before, Debord had brought out *The Society of the Spectacle*, a bizarre call to arms which boldly announced that spectacle in its many forms, whether news or propaganda, advertising or entertainment, had prevailed over all other forms of power.[16] 'All that once was directly lived has become mere representation,' he proclaimed (12). This hardly pleased Debord, since he regarded the new order as the final result of capitalist domination. By spectacle he meant not just 'a collection of images' but 'a social relationship between people that is mediated by images,' a visual structure that was 'both the outcome and the goal of the dominant mode of production' (12, 13). That marked the triumph of the commodity: 'commodities are now *all* that there is to see; the world we see is the world of the commodity' (29). In such passages, Debord seemed to believe that the crucial phenomenon was an advertising run rampant, which consumed *every* other mode of expression. In any case, he held, people's ability to resist this visual tyranny was negligible, unless they were aided by the wisdom of a revolutionary vanguard. His book served more to demonize than to analyse: 'The spectacle is the self-portrait of power in the age of power's totalitarian rule over the conditions of existence' (19). Such declarations harked back to the happier days of Marxist intransigence, even though Debord's thesis offered a foretaste of the postmodern fascination with an image-saturated culture.

Debord's star waned swiftly in the 1970s. Not so his ideas.[17] They lived on, albeit in a perverse fashion, in the work of Jean Baudrillard, who became the postmodern guru of the 1980s, when the fame of his essays, notably 'The Precession of Simulacra,' spread deep into the realms of art and academe in the United States.[18] Like so many other theorists of his generation, Baudrillard had emerged out of a Marxist background, though his early work drew upon semiotics and focused on the new cultural environment constructed by mass communications. After the mid-1970s, Baudrillard broke with Marxism, indeed with any interventionist strategy, to elaborate a dogma of simulacra and hyperreality which embraced aspects of Debord's polemic. This new Baudrillard loved hyperbole. What was dying in the postmodern era, Baudrillard argued, were 'all referentials' (2), whether ideologies, oppositions, or truths – in short, *'the real itself'* (1). What had replaced the classic sign was the simulacrum, a wholly autonomous image that claimed 'no relation to any reality whatsoever' (6). The aggressive, unrestrained image was murderous, bringing an end to both Foucault's 'panoptic system' (29) and Debord's 'society of the spectacle' (30) – indeed, to power as history knew it. Elsewhere, Baudrillard suggested that Foucault's 'theory of discipline' was itself 'passé.'[19] 'Power floats like money, like language, like theory' (24). Baudrillard talked instead of 'simulation,' 'implosion,' 'deterrence,' situations in which what appears is, surfaces command depths, and humanity exists in a constantly re-created world of flux. The apocalypse had already happened – but there was no revelation because there were no secrets.[20]

All of which was the result of the surge of information, an excess of signs, the prevalence of electronic codes at the close of the twentieth century which had overstimulated – more properly, overwhelmed – the culture. The argument was reminiscent of the claims of Marshall McLuhan, whose name did figure occasionally in Baudrillard's texts. And like McLuhan, Baudrillard sometimes emphasized the significance of advertising, which became not just a master discourse but an imperial one as well. For advertising could absorb, translate, and simplify all sorts of content.[21] It had, in short, imposed its form everywhere, on the political and the social. 'Today, all things ... are condemned to publicity, to making themselves believable, to being seen and promoted ...' he once wrote. 'An evil genius of advertising' had penetrated 'the very heart of our entire universe of signs,' its 'ingenious scriptwriter' then 'pulled the world into a phantasmagoria, and we are all its spellbound victims.'[22] Witness 'the vicissitudes of propaganda':[23]

> The whole scope of advertising and propaganda comes from the October Revolution and the market crash of 1929. Both languages of the masses, issuing from the mass production of ideas, or commodities, their registers, separate at first, progressively converge. Propaganda becomes the marketing and merchandising of idea-forces, of political men and parties with their 'trademark image.' Propaganda approaches advertising as it would

the vehicular model of the only great and veritable idea-force of this competing society: the commodity and the mark. This convergence defines a society – ours – in which there is no longer any difference between the economic and the political, because the same language reigns in both, from one end to the other; a society therefore where the political economy, literally speaking, is finally fully realized.

Baudrillard had a point, as did Debord before him. Even if Baudrillard was excessive, outlandish, certainly reductionist, his insights could be compelling. Image, spectacle, simulacrum, call it what you will, was precisely the contemporary form of power, a visual presence become so commonplace that it was both the symptom and a cause of the postmodern moment.

10

When Politics Becomes Advertising:
The American Scene

In November 1996, by one measure, the United States dropped out of the list of mass democracies. The incumbent president, Bill Clinton, had won easily over the Republican challenger, Bob Dole. But the real landslide was the non-vote against the two contestants: less than half of the voting-age population cast a ballot for president.[1] In off years voter turnout was even worse: less than 40 per cent of the same population brought about the 'Republican revolution' of 1994 that transformed the partisan complexion of the Congress. Such dismal totals take us back to Jürgen Hàbermas, who counted the level of participation in the public sphere as a crucial sign of democracy. The American democracy, at least for the moment, amounts to one of Baudrillard's sorcerous images – 'it masks the *absence* of a profound reality' – on its way to becoming a simulacrum.[2]

The fall from grace was only the most remarkable aspect of the contest. There were other shocks, all related. The campaign commenced in the late summer of 1995, more than a year before the actual voting, when Clinton set out to reinvigorate his cause using targeted advertising, making this the longest presidential race in recent American history. The campaign was also the most expensive ever run, costing more than half a billion dollars for the presidency alone, never mind the many other battles for congressional seats. And much of the money raised from business, granted by government, and drawn from personal coffers (for the contest attracted the super-rich) was spent on a blizzard of political advertising, which at times turned politics, even in the news media, into little more than a projection of propaganda. Some $400 million was spent by all candidates, presidential and congressional, on television alone, according to the Television Bureau of Advertising.[3] In short,

Americans were subjected to the most prolonged, expensive, and intensive marketing efforts ever mounted to determine their political choices.
How ironic that these efforts served to disenchant as well as to energize,
and thus promoted the massive indifference or animosity of most of the
electorate. The presidential race of 1996, so full of excess, may serve as a
kind of prism through which to view both recent American experience
and the wider phenomenon of politics as advertising.[4]

1 Making Leaders

Never Afraid to Lead (Pat Buchanan, 1996): His pugnacious face stares out from
the screen, his firm mouth lectures us, the import of the words emphasized by
gesture – a repeated, sharp jab of his head to his right – and by the camera – it
moves in slowly to end on a close-up of this representation of character. Here is
Pat Buchanan, sometime broadcast columnist, usually a rogue Republican, but
now a presidential hopeful, as he concludes his biographical spot.

Throughout the first part a trumpet plays a fast-paced military tune, evoking
the impression of a herald announcing the arrival of the new monarch. The spot
opens with shots of Nixon and Reagan, followed by the explosion of the *Challenger*, marines moving into shore, some meeting of high-ranking heads of state.
Why? To accompany Buchanan's claim that 'Through triumph and tragedy, war
and peace, I served the two most important presidents of our time.' That asserts
Buchanan's expertise, and announces his stand as an unregenerate fan of the
tarnished hero Nixon, a stand uncommon among Republicans seeking high
office. The point was that these presidents (more pictures of the dynamic duo,
this time with a youthful Buchanan present) were not 'men of compromise, and
neither am I.' He has proven this in 1992 by successfully challenging ('because I
thought he was wrong') the incumbent, George Bush, in the New Hampshire
primary. This statement leads into the focus on Buchanan alone, situated in a
study decorated in conservative colours, books on one side, a window on the
other: 'The convictions I learned from my parents – Work, Family, Faith, Character – have served me well. I've never been afraid to speak my mind; I will never be
afraid to lead you.'

Here was a classic example of that assertion of self so common in
presidential campaigns. At one level Buchanan was addressing what has
been called 'the character issue,' which since Nixon (and because of
Nixon?) has been a hardy perennial in every election. Americans do not
place much trust in politicians: a voter may exempt some person, provi-
sionally, from the general doubt, but the distrust will linger, always a

corrosive, able to produce a swift discounting of any candidate's claim. According to a British source in 1992, 'one recent survey in the U.S. suggested people were more committed to their brand of cat litter than to their favourite politician ...'[5] Indeed, throughout much of the 1990s only around a fifth of respondents to a Gallup poll admitted that they had a 'great deal' or 'quite a lot' of confidence in Congress. The presidency at least ranked higher, trusted by between one-third and one-half of respondents.[6]

Dick Lugar, another Republican aspirant, had raised the problem in *Trustworthy*, where he declared his belief that 'public trust is fundamental in the presidency,' but found no better way of encouraging trust than to show himself in military and political service. Other candidates offered testimonials from people in whom voters might place more faith: sometimes the truthteller was an ordinary person (such as 'Fred Taylor, Iowa Voter' in Lugar's *Doing the Right Thing*), or a man known for his integrity (James Brady, the unintended victim of an attempt on Reagan's life, in Bill Clinton's *Seconds*), or even an intimate (which explains the appearance of Elizabeth Dole, a very appealing personality in her own right, who claimed in *From the Heart*, late in the campaign, that her husband really would do what he promised to do – cut taxes!). All these claims were a necessary but pathetic ritual of the election spectacle, since they could never wholly dispel the miasma of doubt. A poll released just before the 1996 election found a substantial 'trust deficit': many more participants gave the federal government a negative than a positive rating (though they were less negative about the two main contenders for the presidency).[7]

One way out was to fashion a compelling persona in which people could invest some belief, whatever their distaste for politicians as a species. Buchanan's efforts to present himself as a populist mocked and derided by élites (as he did, for instance, in an ad called *Montana*) sounded convincing because he was usually at odds with everyone else, including his own party. Bob Dole tried that stunt early in the primaries, appearing in *One of Us* amid a gaggle of farmers in Russell, Kansas, his home town, musing about how great it would be if they could talk agricultural policy in the White House. That effort to pose as just 'ordinary folks' (complete with a testimonial saying that he was a homeboy) was quite a stretch, given the fact that Dole had been in federal politics for decades. But the most outlandish simulation was to deploy the super-rich maverick Ross Perot, the entrepreneur *extraordinaire*, as an outsider, locked out of the presidential debates (see *NAFTA Debate*) by Clinton and

Dole because corporate money ordered it. Purportedly, 'the eleven big companies that fund the debate commission' (on screen roll such titles as AT & T, Dow Chemical, and Ford) had 'pumped millions into forcing NAFTA through Congress,' the trade deal Perot had vociferously opposed. 'He'll end the corruption and influence-peddling in Washington, and *return power to the people*.' Note the transformation of that famous slogan of the 1960s.

Democrats in earlier years, when the party did not boast an incumbent president, slipped more easily into the garb of the outsider. In 1988, for example, in *We Need Him,* Jesse Jackson, an African-American leader-cum-celebrity seeking the nomination for president, used a testimonial from a white farmer who explained how Jesse had stood up to the bankers to prevent foreclosure on the mortgage of the man's farm. The style was first employed by Jimmy Carter in 1976. *Lawyers,* one of his primary ads, positioned Carter, dressed casually and shown at work in his fields, as a businessman and farmer, somebody who had worked with his hands, not a lawyer (though he allowed that his oldest son was a lawyer), unlike his rivals who were running for Congress. 'It's time to have a non-lawyer in the White House for a change ...' he declared. Another of his spots had the candidate meeting ordinary people in ordinary settings, such as the labour hall and the street, while Carter described how he had begun with virtually nothing – 'I didn't have any political organization, not much money, nobody knew who I was.' Of course, the next series of images showed people cheering the candidate, visual proof that he headed a people's movement. 'To special interest groups I owe nothing; to the people I owe everything.' That boast came, in reality, from a wealthy entrepreneur who had been planning to win the presidency for at least four years.[8] The strategy might be termed 'populist lite': the attempt to channel resentments against insiders, experts, and the privileged, while never evoking the spectre of class.

There were other saleable personae. *Never Afraid to Lead,* for example, cast Buchanan as a tough, macho leader, not one to forget his principles. In 1988, a fast-talking, rough Al Gore looked the same in an untitled spot, drawn from an actual debate held in Dallas, where he first ripped into rival Democrat Dick Gephardt and then concluded with a ringing declaration of the need for firmness. 'And the next president of the United States has to be someone the American people can believe will stay with his convictions and, if pressure comes ... you gotta be willing to stand your ground and be consistent.' One of the most impressive presentations of vigour and rigour, however, was *Iran,* made for Senator Howard

Baker, a Republican candidate in the primaries of 1980. The spot opened with an intense Baker proclaiming: 'America must resolve that she's not going to be pushed around.' The admakers used actual footage of a public meeting where Baker shouted down a shaggy-looking, dark-skinned, youthful heckler (a 'foreigner' in short) by boldly announcing his determination to save the lives of the fifty Americans held by the revolutionary government of Iran – complete with shots of a cheering crowd of white Americans. Here indeed was a man no one would dare to push around. The stance evoked classic notions of masculinity. What was apparently at stake here was gender – in each case the candidate was proclaiming his devotion to a tradition of manliness where you talked straight and acted tough. He was saying, figuratively, that he was the better man for the job.

Yet the most compelling persona was that of the redeemer,[9] for reasons that will become clear when I discuss the role of utopia in election propaganda. In both 1992 and 1996, Ross Perot sought to play this role. A whole series of ads in 1996 tried to make Bob Dole into a conservative messiah: a patriot wounded in war (*Hero*), a devout American whose experiences had given him 'a strong moral compass' (*The Story*), and who shared with other citizens a belief in 'basic values like honesty and decency and responsibility and self-reliance' (*Proud*). His first 'conservative agenda' promised lower taxes, less government, workfare not welfare, a war on Hollywood immorality, and so on, policies he claimed would fashion a national renewal, though in the end this did not produce much movement in his standing in the polls. No more successful was a challenger of twelve years before, Gary Hart, who enjoyed a brief spurt of fame in the race for the Democratic nomination of 1984. 'My candidacy,' he claimed, 'was for those who still dream dreams, who will stand together once more to build an American future.' What completed this ad were scenes from the sixties of racial troubles and the Vietnam War plus a close-up of the candidate's youthful face, placed in a window against a geometric background that conveyed the impression of high tech, the forward-looking spokesman for a baby-boom generation come into its own. But it was not easy to get elected by suggesting you could undo the past.

Ironically, the team which originated this persona also worked for a failing candidate, President Gerald Ford, in 1976. In the primary race against Ronald Reagan and the later race against Jimmy Carter, Ford's team touted the incumbent as the man who had saved America from foreign wars, turmoil in the streets, inflation, doubt, and assorted other ills. They filled ads with pictures of happy people and cheering fans, a bouncy campaign song, and sickly lyrics such as 'I'm feelin' good about America.' In 1980 the dictates of marketing required that Reagan's persona as saviour be softened to ensure that he would neither offend nor frighten. His handlers discovered that his 'major negative' was a reputation as a warmonger. 'After he was advised to alter key phrases in his speeches such as "peace posture" instead of "defense posture" and to avoid the term "arms race," stressing instead the need to re-establish the "margin of safety," his image gradually moved closer to that of the "ideal president" who would "stand up to the Russians," attaining peace through strength.'[10] Sixteen years later, the Clinton team had an easier time presenting their man as the saviour of America. In one ad after another the incumbent appeared busy in his office, often at his desk, or out meeting ordinary Americans, always active, always engaged, seeking to forestall a rapacious Congress and fashion a bright future. Indeed, *Opportunities* celebrated the turnaround in the economy since 1992 – 'We make more autos than Japan!' – and explained how the president was 'building a bridge to the twenty-first century.' The announcer drew the obvious conclusion: 'The President [equals] ... growth and opportunity.'

Opportunities was reminiscent of a far more impressive collection of ads mounted to gain Ronald Reagan his second term in 1984. His admakers offered viewers a parade of inspiring images and encouraging words. 'Imagine Norman Rockwell as art director. The Reagan spots are absolutely first-rate, so good they're scary,' enthused a writer in *Advertising Age* (28 May 1984). 'The eight glowing commercials – four 60s and their 30-second versions – are at once patriotic, soothing and optimistic.' One effort stood out.

Morning in America: This lullaby ranks with *Daisy* and the later Willie Horton ads as among the most famous spots in the annals of political advertising. Except that, unlike the others, *Morning in America* was unmitigatedly positive – even the announcer spoke in dulcet tones, and the background music was gentle and sweet.

Video	Text
A fishing boat pulls into the docks.	It's morning again in America.
Busy people on a city street. Rancher and his cattle.	Today, more men and women will go to work than ever before in our country's history.

| A stationwagon pulls up in front of a traditional house. Bride and family embrace. | With interest rates and inflation down, more people are buying new homes. And our new families can have confidence in the future. |
| A flag-raising ceremony. Two worshipful boys watch. The American flag flies. | America today is prouder, and stronger, and better. Why would we want to return to where we were, less than four short years ago? |

The final screen said 'PRESIDENT REAGAN,' and showed a small picture of the incumbent attached by golden tassels to an American flag. Here was a patriotic and poetic equation that linked a happy America, the proud Stars and Stripes, and a fatherly president in a warm embrace.

How fitting. As an ex-actor, Ronald Reagan suited a politics where simulation was deemed especially valid. 'Reality is the effect of the sign,' Baudrillard once mused. 'The system of reference is only the result of the power of the sign itself.'[11] *Morning in America* was a superb promotional sign which worked to create its object as a leader who could appeal in this case to virtually every voter who could swallow the notion of a national revival. Such propaganda sought to undermine the demands of class or ideology or section by manufacturing claims to a charismatic authority. It embodied a fascination with style over substance; or, rather, it transformed style into substance, celebrating surfaces and denying depths (to repeat a postmodern chant).

Whether the propaganda persuaded enough voters or not, one result was to give politicians an extraordinary presence in the daily lives of Americans. Consider this anecdote. 'During one of my political campaigns in Florida, I was marching in a parade and shaking hands with spectators,' wrote Bob Graham, sometime governor of Florida and later a senator from that state. 'As I approached a man with a little boy perched on his shoulders, the child looked down and said excitedly: "Daddy! Daddy! There's the man who lives in our TV!"'[12] That recognition was what millions of dollars worth of television ads could buy, in 1986 anyway.

2 A Tide of Negativity

At the height of the Republican primary season, early in 1996, the character and tone of the campaign itself became a matter of heated debate. 'It is, of course, very postmodern. There are no real events anymore, just the image of events,' exclaimed William Kristol, a conservative activist. 'Years ago, genuine photographs of campaign events were transformed into photo ops. Now I suppose one could say the campaign itself is being transformed into a "campaign op."'[13] Even in December of the previous year, Lamar Alexander had run against mudslinging (see *Merry Christmas*), later what he called mudballs (see *Mudballs*), that is, the style of his opponents. During the New Hampshire primary, the publishing magnate Steve Forbes labelled rival Phil Gramm a 'Washington politician' – now there was a sneer – who had worked with Dole to engineer a massive tax increase (see *Gramm*). Dole soon denounced Forbes because he had unleashed a barrage of attack ads to shake the position of the front-runner. Of course, Dole's team responded to the threat with *Forbes*, where this champion of a flat tax was tagged with the negative 'Untested Leadership, Risky Ideas.' Eventually Forbes, who spent an estimated $30 million in his campaign, mostly on advertising, admitted that his aggressive strategy had been a mistake, especially in Iowa, where Republican voters took umbrage at his attacks.[14]

Going negative had been a common strategy ever since 1988, when George Bush's team managed to take control of the election campaign by launching a furious assault on the views and actions of Michael Dukakis.[15] A New Jersey focus group in May supplied the Bush people with the evidence that crime was an especially potent issue.[16] During the summer, the story goes, Vice-president George Bush was told that he was far down in the polls, a fact sufficient to persuade him that the campaign must go negative. The Bush team ran a series of attack ads that slammed Dukakis's, record as Governor of Massachusetts, citing his tax increases, his policies on defence and the environment, but above all his approach to crime.

Weekend Passes (National Security Political Action Committee [NSPAC]) and *Revolving Door* (Bush/Quayle Campaign): These two spots, the first sponsored by a conservative attack group[17] and the second by the Bush campaign, constituted a part of the 'Willie Horton' ads which were received by the media and the public as a single assault that sought to smear Dukakis with the label 'soft on crime.'

Weekend Passes is a relatively simple ad which uses a series of stills, each in a separate window, superimposed text, and a voice-over to explain the dangers of Dukakis's views. His policy of weekend passes let out such criminals as Willie

Figure 24: Scenes from the 'Willie Horton' Ads

Horton, featured in a particularly ugly shot, an African-American who escaped to kidnap and assault a couple. Two other NSPAC ads in the series highlight the white victims of Horton. These spots seemed an attempt to mobilize not only fear but racism as well.

The Bush ad is a much slicker affair. It never actually refers to Horton by name. The action is set outside, in a prison, showing the prisoners walking through a metal gate. The ad uses the metaphor of the revolving door to suggest how criminals have escaped. The visuals are jerky, slowed. In the background plays a harsh music, soon joined by the sound of marching feet. Together these signs produce a sinister effect, suggesting menace. The final scene of an armed man standing ready atop a building 'signals' how Bush would stand on guard against efforts to free such criminals. The voice-over explains the rest:

> As Governor he vetoed mandatory sentences for drug dealers, he vetoed the death penalty, his revolving-door prison policy gave weekend furloughs to first-degree murderers not eligible for parole. While out, many committed other crimes like kidnapping and rape, and many are still at large. Now Michael Dukakis says he wants to do for America what he has done for Massachusetts. America can't afford that risk.

The Dukakis team never effectively responded to the assault. That was disastrous. Not only were these spots played over and over again (the first ad received much more 'free' than 'paid' coverage because it captured the attention of television journalists),[18] they were also reinforced by print and radio ads, referenced in speeches by Bush, excerpted and replayed in news programs, and even buttressed by press conferences given by Horton's victims. So the ads wove what Kathleen Hall Jamieson has called 'a coherent narrative' that identified Dukakis as a failure, a liberal – in a word, a risk.[19] The rise of Bush in the polls merely confirmed the impression that Dukakis was doomed. Three years later Jamieson carried out a test of voters' recollections of the election, only to find that Michael Dukakis and Willie Horton were now 'twinned' in the public memory. Yet the irony was that this permanent association was purely the consequence of propaganda. However compelling, what the Horton narrative asserted about Dukakis was a nasty fiction – once more, spectacle and simulation had triumphed.

The example of 'Willie Horton' was only one agent of the tide of negativity in 1996. The other was 'Harry and Louise,' a peculiar couple of worried, middle-aged yuppies who made the political life of Bill and Hillary Clinton very miserable indeed. The decay and then the disappearance of the Fairness Doctrine in the late 1980s had opened up television to all manner of advocacy, whether to forward or to forestall such things as the Star Wars initiative, the Contra cause in Nicaragua, Supreme Court nominations, the practice of abortion, and so on. But what made issue advertising suddenly a powerful weapon was the battle over the Clinton Health Initiative in 1993–4.

The polls suggested a lot of support for the idea of a government health plan in September 1993, when the White House announced its Health Security Act to Congress. Enter the Health Insurance Association of America (HIAA), 'the trade association for small- and mid-size insurance companies,' encompassing 'roughly a third of the nation's 180 million health insurance policy holders.'[20] The HIAA had formed part of a coalition that defeated a 1992 health-reform proposition in California, where television commercials, made by Goddard Claussen/First Tuesday, were part of the anti-reform strategy. In September 1993 the HIAA launched what became a multimillion-dollar television campaign, using the same agency, to foster public doubt about the wisdom of the Health Security Act.

The 'Harry and Louise' campaign (HIAA, 1993–4): The campaign began with Harry and Louise at home criticizing the details of the Clinton proposal. Here is the transcript of one such minidrama:[21]

HARRY: This says Congress is moving ahead on health care reform.
LOUISE: If they can just cover everyone.
HARRY: But they're talking price controls.
LOUISE: Right. Government-imposed spending limits for every region of the country.
HARRY: So if our plan runs out of money ...
LOUISE: Rationing, the way I read it. You know, long waits for health care, and some services not even available.
HARRY: Government-controlled health care. Huh. Congress can do better than that.
LOUISE: They will if we send them that message.

In a commercial right at the end of the series, Louise has moved out of the home into the office, where we find her chatting with a co-worker, a well-dressed black woman:[22]

CO-WORKER: Louise ...
LOUISE: Mmm ...
CO-WORKER: Know anything about this tax on health benefits?
LOUISE: Congress may load on a bunch of new taxes for their health-care plan, *including* a tax on plans they think are too expensive.
CO-WORKER: Too expensive?
LOUISE: You know, the quality we like, the doctors we want, plans like ours.

The Well-Informed Louise   *The Concerned Co-Worker*

Figure 25: 'Harry and Louise': Scenes from the Office Chat Ad

CO-WORKER: Wait a minute, I thought health care reform was supposed to save us money?
LOUISE: Don't count on it.
CO-WORKER: Well, this isn't the reform we want.
LOUISE: We need to send Congress that message.

Note the elements: well-off people – that is, people able to afford plans or covered at work; the ordinary settings, at home or in the office, to suggest how commonplace this talk might be; the expressions of worry, highlighting one aspect of the proposals, making that a risk, to emphasize the attack on what people already enjoy; and the distrust, sometimes explicit, of government as a tool of health reform. In short the 'Harry and Louise' ads targeted the haves, the people with money and health care, who were identified as the losers should government health care ever be implemented. And it enacted, or rather 'distilled,' their fears about new taxes and bothersome regulations.

'Harry and Louise' was a 'catalyst.' The HIAA barrage grabbed control of the debate. Partly that was because the White House never responded effectively (shades of the Dukakis error of 1988). Its marketing efforts were pathetic, especially in the first few crucial months.[23] Not that vigorous counter-advertising would necessarily have neutralized 'Harry and Louise.' The fact is that journalists were moved by the ads: they were struck by the novelty of the campaign – nothing quite like this had ever occurred in Washington – and by the quality of the assault. Reporters found it easy to cover what 'Harry and Louise' were saying, to use them as a means of exploring a very complex issue and proposal, so they incorporated the campaign messages and images into their own stories, which gave the assault greater reach and added clout.[24] When Democrats lashed out against the ads (Hillary Clinton even mentioned them in one speech), this, too, enhanced the news interest of the campaign. Six months after the unveiling of the Health Security Act, the polls indicated that support had fallen eighteen points, and that fully 46 per cent of the respondents now opposed the White House plan. 'Harry and Louise' mobilized the fears of a middle-class public that government health care, or at least the Clinton brand, posed a threat to their well-being.

Other groups jumped into the fray, of course, some adopting a much harsher tone than 'Harry and Louise.' Even Clinton was moved to comment: 'Many of you still have doubts about reform, and I sure can understand why. I see the same TV ads you do. Never in the history of the republic has so much money been spent to defeat an idea.' The irony was that his comment itself appeared in a television ad, paid for by the Democratic National Committee.[25] It was too little, too late. Health-care reform died one year after the initiative began.

The combined legacy of 'Willie Horton' and 'Harry and Louise' scripted the negative tone of the Clinton/Dole contest in 1996. The two party committees plus assorted allies, such as the AFL-CIO in the case of Clinton, launched issue ads – which did not count towards the limits on candidate expenditures – to berate opponents over a balanced budget, medicare, welfare, abortion, and on and on. The opposing tickets sponsored straight negative ads, direct response replies (neither side wanted to replay the Dukakis error), and a new style of comparative ads where a negative front-end was contrasted with a positive finish. The Clinton campaign constantly attempted to attach Bob Dole to Newt Gingrich, the unpopular speaker of the House of Representatives, by running black-and-white clips of the two men apparently conspiring against the common good. The Dole campaign highlighted the contradictory statements and actions of Clinton in his previous four years of office.

Both approaches caused a lot of comment in the press. 'Political advertising has never been an exemplar of truth, justice or what used to be called the American Way, but in recent years it has turned even more nasty and brutish,' mused *US News Online* (19 February 1996). 'A decade ago, negative ads were rare; today, half the political advertisements on television attack a candidate's opponent rather than emphasize his or her own strengths.' But the fuss about attack ads, in 1996 and earlier, reflected one of the paradoxes of America's political culture. People said they did not like negative advertising. But, done properly, such advertising worked because these ads mobilized the mood of anti-politics, the sense of mistrust that gripped so much of the electorate. In the 1984 race for the Democratic nomination for president, Walter Mondale's campaign manager used focus groups to discover that voters had doubts about Gary Hart's ability to handle a foreign crisis; that finding lay behind the infamous *Red Telephone*, which questioned Hart's competence, an ad the campaign kept running through the California primary because it proved so effective.[26] The fact was that both the voters and the media listened to attack ads – indeed, some might actually be included in newscasts, thus acquiring added credibility. Studies indicated that even when TV news organized critical ad-watches, the very replay could extend the effects of the negatives.[27] Besides, attack ads could set the news agenda, even the news vocabulary, which turned journalists into unwitting accomplices of the consultants. 'They move poll numbers faster than any other technique,' noted one analyst,[28] and he spoke the common wisdom of the political consultants who now determined the tenor of campaigns. 'Voters will tell you in focus groups that they don't like negative ads, but they retain the information so much better than the positive ones,' Roger Stone, a partner in a firm of Republican consultants, informed *Advertising Age* (10 November 1986). 'The point is: People like dirty laundry. Why do tabloids sell?'

3 The Troubled Utopia

Many ads, positive as well as negative, drew sustenance from a compelling vision of America as a realized utopia – and its reverse, a utopia unravelling. 'Utopia has been achieved here and anti-utopia is being achieved ...' argued Baudrillard in his bizarre travel book *America*.[29] The double vision excited sponsors and admakers because it evoked both desire and fear, the two triggers of advertising as psychology.

The utopia of a Traditional America was focused on a legendary past, a land of small towns, happy families, and smiling people, where reigned the virtues of self-reliance, hard work, patriotism, love, faith, honesty, and the like. This kind of nostalgic imagery would seem most appropriate to a Republican:

Proud (Bob Dole, 1996): The overt purpose of this early ad was to fix the message that Dole was 'a man every American would be proud to call President,' unlike the tarnished Clinton. But consider instead some of the images that the admakers employed to represent a vision of the ideal, and idyllic, life:

1 The happy fisherman: a dad, we presume, teaching his boys to fish, in some bright pastoral setting. Here is a portrayal of togetherness.

2 The family attending church: An image of happy Christians that evokes the feeling of a small town, where community and faith are living realities. In short, another image of togetherness, though seemingly located in some past paradise.

3 Saluting the flag: A white woman and a black man honour the American flag, a celebration of the military but with a modern face. This signifies both obedience and patriotism.

Each of these images speaks about 'what made America great,' to use Dole's words.

But the Democrats had learned to deploy the same kind of pictures:

Families First (Democratic Party, 1996): 'Remember our hopes when we were young?' asks the announcer. 'Those are hopes we still believe in.' The purpose is to explain, in very homely terms, just what the Democrats want – among the many virtues are security, neighbourhood, opportunity, and responsibility, but above all, 'families first.' This message is cleverly presented through a series of home movies, complete with soft music, showing grandparents, bright babies, and kids playing, while the voice-over explains the traditions of the party. Here is the Democratic answer to the cry of family values, made famous by Christian activists and Republican right-wingers in earlier campaigns.

The prominence of children's faces throughout *Families First* points to what became a fetish of Democratic advertising in 1996: the happy child. It seemed that the Clinton campaign set out to brand that type of kid. *Protects Our Children* showed picture after picture of solemn or bewildered children while the voice-over talked about Republican cuts, but ended on the image of a smiling, blond boy after describing the marvels of Clinton's balanced-budget plan. *Counting* located the President in a setting full of healthy, happy babies and loving mothers, while again a voice-over, this time female, proclaimed how his policies ensured the future of these children. The implicit point? The Democratic child represented the projection of America Past 'into the twenty-first century,' to borrow the rhetoric of the ads. The President's plan, a talisman waved constantly at the mean Republicans, would ensure the preservation of what made the American Way such a source of contentment. That was a brilliant piece of positioning: a Harris poll taken in the spring of 1997 found that Americans were most satisfied, above the 90 per cent ranking, with their family, marriage, home, and 'life overall.'

What almost two-thirds did not feel good about were 'the morals and values of Americans in general.'[30] That fact suggested the reverse of the utopian dream, the fear that things were coming apart. Again, much interest focused on children. The Republicans played on this theme more often than the Democrats, especially in negative ads about illegal immigration and drugs, where the specific agents of decline could be clearly identified. Dole's *Threat* was an intriguing example of plagiarism. The opener was stolen from that most famous of attack ads, the Democrats' *Daisy* of more than thirty years before. Once more, the little girl plucked away at her daisy, except that, where once 'the biggest threat' was nuclear war, now 'the threat is drugs,' as the female voice-over explained. More particularly, the threat was to teenagers, so the Republicans offered images of hurt teens to counter the Democrats' happy children. What followed were a series of pictures of drug users and drug use, with a voice-over explaining how Clinton and his people had weakened the war against drugs. A second ad in the series made reference to Clinton's jocular response on MTV to the question about whether he would inhale the smoke of marijuana had he the chance to do it over again: 'Sure, if I could; I tried before' (see *School,* apparently one of the largest ad buys of the Dole campaign). And yet a third, one of the last commercials, released on 23 October, actually found a teenage pot smoker, shown lying supine on a bed, who cited President Clinton's behaviour as a rationale for her actions (see *Nicole*). 'Remember, our children have to live with the President we give them.'

Clinton and the Democrats exploited the same kinds of fears by focusing on different evils, especially crime, teenage smoking, and domestic abuse. Teenage smoking now carried the sign of death as well as sin: one in three teens who started puffing would die of tobacco-related illness, claimed *First Time,* and Dole opposed the President's ban on cigarette ads aimed at children. The issues of crime and violence, however, allowed the Democrats to deliver the most frightening of all the images of menace, disorder, and anguish. *Tough on Crime I* mixed still pictures of victims and moving images of the loading of an assault rifle. *Victims* used scenes of damaged women as the visual prop to support praise of Clinton's plan to halt domestic abuse. *Tough on Crime II* gave viewers blurred pictures of the agents of evil apprehended because Clinton had waged war on crime.

These twin themes of utopia achieved and utopia undone were well worn by 1996. Indeed, their expressions in the Clinton/Dole contest were relatively mild by comparison with those of earlier contests. Twenty years before, the happy-times messages of the Ford campaign had reflected the perception of one admaker that 'the winner will be the man who most closely portrays the traditional values that America is yearning for ...'[31] In 1984, according to a commentator, 'Mondale's commercials painted images of nuclear holocaust, starvation, and poverty while Reagan's showed sunsets, a parade of flags, a bride, picturesque landscapes, and pretty faces.'[32] Both sides in the 1988 contest played variations on the motif of an ecological disaster, the Bush team offering up images of a heavily polluted Boston Harbour, the legacy of Dukakis's tenure as governor, and the Democrats a sci-fi drama in which Republican environmental policies had prevailed, making beaches unsafe and forcing schools to close in some unhappy future. [33]

Like all forms of advertising, this election propaganda was carefully designed to reflect the prejudices of the populace. If both the utopia and its shadow were simulations, fictions, they were and are usable fictions sufficiently evocative to be constantly re-enacted in the presidential races. These narratives, sometimes smug, sometimes shrill were also an instrument which shaped opinion and gave specific expression to prejudices. At one level, then, this propaganda amounted to a form of common, if not necessarily popular, art.

4 Political Psychoses

What that art described, and confirmed, was the emergence since the 1960s, and especially since Watergate, of a highly disturbed political culture. Consider the findings of one of the many surveys of American opinion (the very profusion of such surveys in the 1990s suggests just how much confusion and concern the topic provokes). The '1996 Survey of American Political Culture' was the result of a combined effort by the Gallup Organization and the Post-Modernity Project, an academic group situated at the University of Virginia.[34] The survey's findings rested on personal interviews with 'a nationally representative sample' of more than 2,000 adults, carried out in the spring of 1996 – that is, during the campaign but well short of its finish.

The most important finding repeated, if in different terms, a commonplace of polling, namely, the discovery of a deep commitment to what the authors called the 'American creed' that ran counter to a deep cynicism about American practice. In overwhelming numbers, people supported the democratic rhetoric that justified the United States. But most were also pessimistic, a good number exceptionally pessimistic, about the state of the nation; roughly half were willing to agree that America was in decline.

1 Majorities, some very substantial, thought the governing élites, notably the politicians, incompetent, wasteful, arrogant, and self-interested, though they also concluded that these élites were 'well-meaning' and 'patriotic.'
2 Most people, especially at the lower end of the social scale, felt dis-empowered, lacking any say in government. Eight out of ten conclud-ed that politics was more 'theater or entertainment' than something serious.
3 Those designated the 'Christian Right' were the most pessimistic, convinced that someone had stolen their utopia. They were firm believers in the narrative of a moral collapse in America.
4 The 'most worried, upset, and angry' were not the poor, who actually showed less antagonism to government than other groups, but the haves – that is, the white, educated middle class. The authors put their anxiety down to a fear of a coming 'insignificance,' because of cultural change, as well as the 'ineptitude' and 'machinations' of the élite.
5 The more privileged Americans, well-off professionals and managers and entrepreneurs, evidenced the least traditional and the most lib-eral views, suggesting a sort of ideological divorce from much of the rest of the populace
6 Roughly one-fifth to one-quarter of those surveyed fell into the rebel camp which believed that government, and the élites in general, were engaged in a conspiracy against the people. The authors noted how assiduously these folk practised politics – they were more likely to vote, to discuss politics, and to write letters.

Whatever else such findings signify, they do suggest a country rife with political psychoses – using the terminology as metaphor rather than as a clinical diagnosis. Manic depression: the paradox of a community com-mitted to the American ideal but hostile to its perceived reality. Hysteria: the excitement of the anxious haves, whose convulsions in the congres-sional elections of 1994 supposedly produced the Republican revolution. Paranoia: the widespread belief among a substantial minority that politicians, officials, and experts are engaged in plots against the people. Above all, the findings suggest schizophrenia: a populace that is fragmented, insecure, deluded, disconnected, and unable to fashion a coherent understanding of politics. Indeed, schizophrenia, as a 'linguistic disorder,' seems to be the social disease of choice in postmodern times.[35] The cultural critic Fredric Jameson proclaimed that affliction (which he also saw as 'euphoria') to be a consequence of 'the breakdown of the signifying chain,' a breakdown which left in its wake 'a rubble of distinct and unrelated signifiers' that cannot offer a vision of coherence or identity.[36] But the political condition of rampant psychoses may have as much to do with the sheer excess of rhetoric and simulacra which has bombarded the public in the past two decades.

The surge of marketing, positive as well as negative, offers spectacle, sometimes entertaining theatre, but does not compel compliance. Political propaganda has increasingly become a kind of noise that people may watch but that only some will attend to. This may explain the steady increase in non-voting: it is not evidence of paralysis, or even of alienation in the classic sense, but rather of disdain, a resistance through evasion of all the demands to believe and speak and perform which the political élite makes of voters. 'The present argument of the system is to maximize speech, to maximize the production of meaning, of participation,' Baudrillard reasoned. 'And so the strategic resistance is that of the refusal of meaning and the refusal of speech ... It is the actual strategy of the masses.'[37] Baudrillard's declarations about the contemporary strategy of resistance has not convinced critics.[38] But the American case suggests that this brand of disobedience may well suit a time and a place when citizens are subjected to so much direction by authority. People will evade that direction, whether in the realm of politics or morality or behaviour, by their absence, by not listening, by being passive. Increased propaganda, beyond a certain point, will provoke neither compliance nor argument but a collective turn-off, a psychic blindness and deafness that resist efforts to sell any and all public goods.

Conclusion: Postmodern Democracy

Your Body (Prochoice, U.S.A., 1989): On a poster is the image of a woman's face, perhaps in her late twenties or early thirties; certainly, she is attractive. She looks us in the eye. The photograph has been cropped, cutting off the top of her hair. Most startling is the exact division of her face into positive and negative halves. That makes her look not just eerie but unfinished. Superimposed on the face is the slogan 'Your body' (at the top) 'is a' (just above the middle) 'battleground' (near the bottom), in white block letters on a red card. Above the 'positive' eye, in the same format but smaller, are two more lines of text: 'March on Washington / Sunday, April 9, 1989'; and above the 'negative' lip, three lines: 'Support Legal Abortion / Birth Control / and Women's Rights.' Right at the bottom is the call to arms: women and men must join for a march because the Bush administration hopes the Supreme Court will overturn the famous *Roe v. Wade* decision (the legal basis of abortion rights in the United States) in a case that would shortly commence.

The poster was by Barbara Kruger, a radical, a feminist, a film critic, and an artist already well known for her unusual presentations of social and political dissent. The next year that image would appear in an art book entitled *Love for Sale*, published by Abrams, further evidence of Kruger's stature. During the 1980s and 1990s she has had exhibitions throughout the United States, in western Europe, and in Australia and New Zealand. Kruger was trained in the graphic arts and worked, in the 1970s, at Condé Nast Publications. One source of her inspiration was feminism. Another was French theory, the books of Foucault, Barthes, Kristeva, and Baudrillard, in particular, and most especially their views on power. Her work has taken on sexism, racism, war, capitalism, consumption, the state – all the usual villains in the radical universe. An Australian exhibition in 1996, for example, attacked bigotry in its various forms: the hatred of difference, of the ugly, of other religions, of demanding women, and so on.[1] Once again, Kruger used image fragments and pointed slogans ('Hate like us') to convey her political message.

Her use of such material is what makes her work so interesting. Kruger has imaginatively perverted ad designs and sayings to shape a form of attack propaganda. She often takes pictures from other sources, usually anonymous. She uses such techniques as cropping, enlarging, collage, and overprinting to construct this material into compelling images that evoke stereotypes. But her work attempts to subvert these stereotypes, to frustrate their ability to hail and to influence. Sometimes the images themselves are grotesque, too large or too harsh, occasionally twisted, a style of excess which suggests a taste for the carnivalesque. More often she uses words as ironic slogans or questions that ground the image in a critical frame of reference. And she employs pronouns – 'we' and 'us' and 'our,' 'you' and 'your,' 'I' and 'me' – to incorporate the spectator into the contradictory performance. The resulting collage of signs, always busy, sometimes difficult, draws on utopian notions of equality, freedom, or a common humanity to make an impact. At her best, Kruger delivers ideology critique in a visual form.

Your body ... is a warning and a condemnation, a cry to resist the way authority controls the person of the woman. Kruger's art seeks to awaken people from a troubled slumber: 'Propped up and ultra-relaxed, we teeter on the cusp of narcolepsy and believe everything and nothing.' We are not the masters of our own fate. 'Polling has become the measure of us; the way we are made to count or not,' she has claimed. 'And to those who understand how pictures and words shape consensus, we are unmoving targets to be turned on and off by the relentless seductions of remote control.' [2] Her nightmare of a soft fascism – not at all uncommon these days – grows out of the ways in which a new technology of power has organized the democracies of the late twentieth century.

1 Habermas Revisited

Jürgen Habermas returned to the discussion of his seminal work, *The Structural Transformation of the Public Sphere*, in a lengthy article, 'Further Reflections on the Public Sphere,' published in the early 1990s.[3] There he modified his theoretical approach, though he did not alter his basic thrust. His was still a 'discourse-centered concept of democracy' (FR, 448): the key remained the prevailing forms of communicative action.

He advanced once more the ideal of a single 'political public sphere' (FR, 446) in which ordinary people would engage in rational debate about common issues, and do so as equal and impartial participants who could transcend self-interest and their initial preferences. He favoured 'a public sphere that is not geared toward decision making but toward discovery and problem resolution and that in this sense is *nonorganized*' (FR, 451). He had integrated the ideal of the political public sphere with his 'two-tiered concept of society as lifeworld and as system' that had first emerged in the philosophical work he wrote after *The Structural Transformation.* The public sphere was part of the lifeworld. System meant the market economy and the state apparatus. So the goal of the moment was 'to erect a democratic dam against the colonializing *encroachment* of system imperatives on areas of the lifeworld' (FR, 444).

Habermas did not believe that either the classic public sphere, whether labelled bourgeois or liberal, could be resurrected. The historical and the material situations had changed much too dramatically to allow something so bizarre. *The Structural Transformation* had held out the faint hope of a rebirth of reasoned argument and critical publicity in an 'intraorganizational public sphere' (*STPS*, 248). A 1973 essay, 'The Public Sphere,' argued that the new basis for democracy must rest upon 'a rationalization of the exercise of social and political power under the mutual control of rival organizations committed to publicness in their internal structure as well as in their dealings with the state and with one another' (TPS, 404). In 'Further Reflections,' however, he touted a pre-existing source of 'opinion-forming associations' (FR, 454) that might produce a public communication to counter the manipulations of 'media power' (FR, 437). The practice of debate depended upon the 'institutional core of a civil society,' that is, 'voluntary unions outside the realm of the state and the economy,' from churches and sports clubs, 'groups of concerned citizens,' and 'grass-roots petitioning drives,' to political parties and trade unions (FR, 453–4). Also, he now believed that education and the like had enhanced the ability of 'a pluralistic, internally much differentiated mass public' (FR, 438) to resist or refashion the messages of authority. Habermas had reintroduced an element of struggle into the routines of the contemporary public sphere. Although he recognized problems, especially administrative outreach and the deployment of media power, he was less pessimistic about the prospects for a move towards a radical democracy, buoyed up by the recent revolutions in eastern Europe. In a way, Habermas's lament had mellowed with time.

The practices of rational debate and critical publicity have persisted throughout the affluent West, especially on the margins. From the late 1960s onwards, oppositional or counter-publics, some committed to human rights, feminism, or ecological goals and others to a right-wing agenda expressing neo-liberal dreams or a conservative morality, demonstrated the ability to fashion their own internal networks of argument as well as to condition the agenda of media discussion and to mobilize the public. But even more evidence underlined the fact that both practices have increasingly become residual in the centre, in the mainstream, especially on the national level of the formal democracies, where they appear as tattered survivors of a liberal constitutional state whose lingering decline Habermas had so ably chronicled in *The Structural Transformation*. It was precisely through the advance of civic advocacy that the ways of the market (and these surely are 'system imperatives') had colonized the public sphere and, by extension, its home, the civil society, in postmodern times. As Nancy Fraser put it, the classic public sphere was 'a theater for debating and deliberating rather than buying and selling.'[4] Less and less was that so in recent times – for 'market relations' now conditioned 'discursive relations.' Some of those very elements of the civil society, the non-profits (Habermas's 'groups of concerned citizens') as well as the parties and the occupational associations, routinely used the media to organize the political public sphere. What emerged was indeed a new kind of public sphere, where one of the prominent discourses and some of the prevailing routines generated a democracy hardly congenial to the utopian visions of a Habermas. Instead, the polity embodied many of the sins that so troubled him when he wrote *The Structural Transformation*.

2 Unequal Access

Fundamental to the ideal public sphere was the free communication of ideas by each and by all. 'Access to the public sphere is open in principle to all citizens,' Habermas theorized (TPS, 398). Instead, however, the postmodern public sphere was filled with ever-increasing doses of promotion manufactured by a relatively small circle of interests. In the spring of 1990, the journal of the Gannett Center for Media Studies was devoted to the issue of publicity, defined as a sort of masked promotion, neither advertising nor journalism.[5] One of the authors, the historian Christopher Lasch, repeated the surprising statistic that an estimated 40 per cent of all the news in American newspapers had its origin in press releases. The journalist Randall Rothenberg noted how video news releases had become common as news fodder for local television stations around the country in search of cheap programming. A Washington correspondent, Anne Groer, reported that she had received 228 pieces of publicity in five short days, the largest amount on the environment because Earth Day was approaching. Charles Salmon, a professor of communications, described how public-interest groups worked the news system, using what has come to be called 'media advocacy' to ensure the coverage of their concerns: the Natural Resources Defense Council, for example, had managed to secure all kinds of exposure on TV (*60 Minutes, MacNeil/Lehrer*) and in the press (*New York Times, Washington Post, Los Angeles Times*) for its scare over 'alar-contaminated apples.' Its campaign was an excellent example of risk creation. The marketplace of signs is full of self-interested 'claims,' to use the vocabulary of Ricoeur, which seek to attract notice and cultivate support so as to justify present or future authority.

One grand source of propaganda was and remains the state and its many agencies. The exercise of state authority in the classic public sphere had been subordinated 'to the requirement of democratic publicness' (TPS, 399). But a phenomenon of the times has been the expanding scope of governance or, rather, the collapse of so much that was once private into the public sphere, out of which the interventionist state waxed strong – for a while. During the 1970s and 1980s the Canadian state was a world leader in the use of civic advertising to make its citizens aware of the public import of their private actions; it ranked at the top of the list of ad spenders in the country. In 1971 Health Canada, for example, started Participaction to cajole a lazy public into becoming fit. Over the next twenty-five years this agency managed to raise some $28 million, mostly from corporate sources, to supplement its $16 million of tax monies.[6] Government agencies, provincial as well as federal, used communications to fight drugs and smoking, to end domestic violence, to rehabilitate the image of disabled persons, even to sell the country. And, on occasion, to unsell the country: the separatist Parti Québécois, which controlled the Quebec government in the late 1970s, increased its spending on communications from $124 million (1977) to $157 million (1980), largely to promote its notion of 'sovereignty-association' for an independent Quebec.[7] These were signs pointing towards an administered society run by a nanny state.

That was not to be. More recently, a second phenomenon has been the partial retreat of the state. The process has often been interpreted as the withering away of the public sector. But at another level it has meant a privatization of direction. The innovator in this regard was the United

States, partly because the welfare state never made such inroads there as elsewhere, and partly because the effort to restrict the state's reach first occurred there. The Americans built necessary ensembles of different interests, assembling money and expertise and passion in agencies that exercised public power. The story of the National Crime Prevention Council and the McGruff advertising campaigns illustrates how state agencies, business, and non-profits could coalesce behind specific projects.[8] Consider McGruff's parents: the initiative came in 1977 from representatives of the Federal Bureau of Investigation, the Department of Justice, police associations, the AFL-CIO, and the Advertising Council, plus one crucial individual, the businessman Carl M. Loeb, Jr, who provided both funds and leadership for what became the National Citizens' Crime Prevention Campaign. Out of this project came the National Crime Prevention Council, associated with an umbrella grouping of non-profits, government bodies, and law-enforcement agencies called the Crime Prevention Coalition of America. The council worked with police, government agencies (perhaps the closest link was with the Department of Justice), schools, and community groups to create or assist programs that would energize local action against crime. In 1987 it sought corporate associates to realize specific tasks: among its partners were Radio Shack, Allstate Insurance, ADT Security Systems, and Master Lock. By the mid-1990s the council was funded by government, business, foundations, and individuals. Its board of directors included a raft of people designated 'civil leaders,' lawyers, business people, educators, policemen, even politicians – and a representative from the Ad Council.

Communications were central to the project: the council boasted that it 'disseminates information on effective prevention practices to thousands of individuals and organizations every year; and publishes materials that reach millions, young and old.' Right from the beginning, Loeb and his associates sought to combat the unfortunate perception that 'you can't do anything about crime.' The most visible program remained making propaganda. The council always worked with one volunteer agency, Saatchi and Saatchi, which created a changing series of campaigns tailored to suit the expanding initiatives. Ads to celebrate the activists, to frighten the vulnerable, and to commiserate over the victims, all in one way or another drew upon notions of fairness and justice already embedded in the cultural imagination to generate that necessary element of 'belief' (to use, again, Ricoeur's terminology).[9]

The National Crime Prevention Council counted as one component in a wider apparatus that had as its target the population, or rather the law-abiding citizenry, and as its mission the protection of life and property, the security of this citizenry. It was accredited by governments, and by all levels of government, but it drew its authority from the representation of an assortment of interests and the alliance with even more. It was élitist, playing a leadership role, and constructing the citizenry as subjects who required guidance. It employed expertise, analyses, calculations, all sorts of procedures to identify the risk and then to manage the problem of crime. One of these procedures was a constant but tailored propaganda disseminated through the most important of the media, television. In sum, the council was an excellent example of those mechanisms of governmentality which Foucault argued had become the dominant forces in contemporary life.

A third phenomenon has been the escalating importance of issue or advocacy advertising in national politics. That technology of persuasion pioneered by corporations was soon appropriated by governments. During the late 1980s, for example, the Thatcher regime used advertising to sell such policies as privatization.[10] But again the most important agents became a new series of non-public authorities. One of the most spectacular interventions in Canada's political history occurred during the 1988 federal election when business interests spent directly an estimated $19 million to sell the Free Trade Agreement to the electorate via an assortment of promotional vehicles.[11] During the 1990s, pro-life/anti-abortion associations mounted one of the longest TV campaigns on record in an effort to alter American attitudes – and laws. In the 1996 U.S. election, the champions of handgun control, nuclear energy, pro-life and pro-choice positions, seniors, tax reform, the American flag, the Sierra Club, the Teamsters, the AFL-CIO, all and more broadcast issue ads to condition the national debate.

Action is infectious: the more agents employ advocacy, the more their opponents feel the need to match such efforts. In 1987, for example, the liberal People for the American Way adopted tactics made infamous by conservatives – including direct mail, grassroots lobbying, and negative ads – to vilify Supreme Court nominee Robert Bork, who was represented as a threat to freedom.[12] To a degree, the new order required organizations to recognize the import of publicity and polling, or else their ability to exercise power would suffer, a situation that the Labour party in Britain came to recognize after the mid-1980s. Ironically, by the late 1990s a very savvy Tony Blair, the Labour prime minister, was being accused of trying to 'rebrand Britain' as 'Cool Britannia' in an effort to construct a new sense of national identity.[13] Having money made civic advocacy far easier – for corporations and for a Steve Forbes, of course, which is one reason why the right so often had an advantage. In Canada, for example, the well-financed National Citizens' Coalition, founded in the mid-1970s, earned notoriety by running newspaper ads and funding posters against big government, overtaxation, and left or liberal villains, including the unions. In the absence of such resources, agents required alternative means, particularly moral weight (organizations such as Mothers Against Drunk Driving) or expert status (groups like the American Medical Association), to establish a presence. Even so, some American advocates hoped for a return to the days of the Fairness Doctrine: the National Abortion Rights League called for its 'reinstatement' in 1994 so that stations would air their counter-ad to the pro-life/anti-abortion campaign of the DeMoss Foundation.[14] The notion of television as an open forum, by now a cliché, persisted in the world of politics and energized some groups such as Adbusters and culture jammers generally, though there was little prospect that their hopes would be realized. Extremists and outcasts, labelled as such by the media, were often censored, their images kept hidden and their voices silenced. North American television does not sell time to the drug lords, no matter how much money they command. The gatekeeper role of the media in particular ensures that propaganda is mostly a tool of what Habermas called, with some disdain, 'authorized opinions' (*STPS*, 245).

Here, around the issue of access, the postmodern variant of democracy breaks most violently with the ideal in two different ways. First, the principle of 'universal accessibility' acted 'as the precondition that guaranteed the truth of a discourse and counter-discourse bound to the laws of logic' (*STPS*, 219). By contrast, propaganda emphasized both hierarchy and exclusion, establishing that a very few voices would be far more significant than the rest. The near total exclusion of the whole pro-drug position, for example, played 'a *constitutive* role' (FR, 425) in the debate over drugs. Second, the strict separation of society and state ensured the autonomy of the public sphere as a mediating institution. But civic advocacy was a common practice that mingled public and private authorities, that acted as one agent (among several) of 'the integration of state and society' (FR, 436), in which the state spread its authority over private behaviour while competing interests programmed the state's bureaucracy. The result was such hybrid projects as the wars on crime or smoking or AIDS. Postmodern democracy might also be discourse-centred, but its nature seemed to fit better Foucault's notions of relations of power than Habermas's dreams of communicative action.

3 Staging Debate

The public sphere was the great manufactory of public opinion. What Habermas meant by this opinion was the collection of 'critical reflections of a public competent to form its own judgements' (*STPS*, 90). People's views had to be subjected to the discipline of reasoned argument before they could serve as the foundation of democracy. But recall Koupal's dictum: 'Never debate.' That admonition was a bit hyperbolic. Instead, civic advocates set out to organize debate, meaning to still some clamour, to restrict or script expression, to rebut an opponent, perhaps to provoke discussion. In the summer of 1998, for instance, conservatives' sponsorship of newspaper ads highlighting 'reformed' homosexuals produced a counter-propaganda, one ad showing 'smiling Republican parents and their lesbian daughter' (*New York Times*, 2 August 1998). That hardly amounted to a classic debate, but it certainly did constitute a competition.

Marketing was, among other things, a technology of managing opinions. Marketing encompasses the two modes of visual power: polling constitutes surveillance, just as advertising becomes spectacle. The use of opinion surveys and focus groups, of tracking studies and the like, are ways to discover what moves the public, how to tailor an advertising campaign, and whether the campaign has had the desired effects. According to Dick Morris, a paid political consultant, he masterminded such a marketing initiative in the fall of 1995 to resell the Clinton presidency to the American public.[15] The idea was to build momentum before the campaign actually began, momentum which could then be protected or enhanced during the following year. Morris's team carried out extensive polling prior to advertising, 'to measure public reaction to each element of the president's legislative program and to that of the Republicans.' They then fashioned different versions of ads, which were tested at malls across the nation. Similar kinds of tests were run on Republican ads attacking Clinton. 'The key is to advertise your positions only if the public agrees with them.' The resulting advertising focused particularly on policies or, rather, on the products that Clinton had designed and the obstacles the Republicans had mounted. Political ads and issue ads, positive ads and negative ads were combined in novel hybrids meant to provide specifics. Morris's agents bought time from local affiliates rather than the networks, not just to place the campaign where advertising seemed most likely to be effective, but also to avoid the critical attention of the national media. All of this effort cost very large sums of money – and Morris noted in his memoirs how bitterly the President complained about the pressure to raise funds. But the constant barrage worked, or so Morris believed: the repetition convinced sufficient voters in enough states by the end of 1995 to give Clinton the necessary momentum.

The pro-Clinton campaign had a lot going for it: consistency, longevity, lots of volume, even a near monopoly, at least in the realm of propaganda, though hardly of news. So, too, did California's anti-smoking effort in 1990–1 (minus the monopoly, because of the presence of tobacco advertising), which was also deemed an effective brand of persuasion. The mix of factors was as close to a recipe for success as existed, though in fact nothing could actually guarantee a sponsor what was desired. If initially the assault on AIDS was so widespread that it helped, along with the scary messages of the news media, to foster a panic in Britain and America, in time the ads suffered 'wear out' – their impact waned because people stopped taking notice. The phenomenon of wear out, of course, was a commonplace of agency lore because it was the bane of consumer marketing generally.

Still, a few ads or campaigns became 'catalysts' for thought and action which energized all sorts of people and left marks in the collective memory of the public sphere. These spectacles have attained the status of art, credited with making the ordinary extraordinary. The fame of *Daisy* (1964) persisted because it demonstrated that just one ad could excite the passions of all sorts of people. Britain's 'Clunk, Click' (seat-belts) and Canada's Participaction (fitness) campaigns in the 1970s both generated the required actions and were remembered, though the actual effects were not long-lasting. *Chief Iron Eyes Cody* managed to exploit the sense of guilt many Americans apparently felt about the way they had treated the land, enough so that the memory of this critique persisted for years afterwards in public discussions. The single most famous image of the Partnership for a Drug-Free America (PDFA) assault on drugs appeared early on when *Fried Egg* (1986) popularized the notion that drugs cooked your brains. A tall, weathered man, reminiscent of a veteran coach, broke an egg into a hot pan and shoved the result into our faces – 'This is your brain on drugs.' How the egg sizzled when it hit that pan. The sound and the pictures together worked a special magic: the presentation seemed such a fitting analogy because it embodied notions of the way drugs could instantly devastate – giving a concrete expression to a widespread fear. The ad's impact rested much more on emotion than on reason, though it might also have provoked discussion and even changed behav-

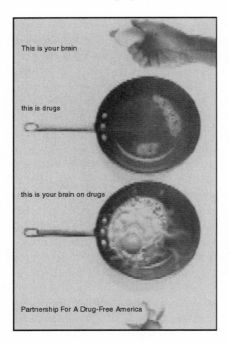

Figure 26: *Fried Egg*. Here is a print version of the famous commercial which summarizes the argument, such as it is. In that commercial, the main character is a weathered, tough-talking male, reminiscent of a seasoned coach, who explains the analogy quickly and easily.

iour. So memorable was the commercial that it was remade in 1998 when the Clinton administration and the PDFA launched their renewed assault using paid PSAs, planned as a $400-million campaign, half public and half private, 'the largest government merchandising effort in history,' according to Frank Rich in the *New York Times* (15 July 1998).

Rich's comment highlights how the news media may play a crucial part in the career of any one piece of propaganda. The civic ad has become, at some level, a provocation meant to capture the attention of journalists (which is why Morris's stealth strategy in 1995 was so unusual). It operates in that place both celebrated and denigrated by Baudrillard, the media-saturated environment in which television in particular but also radio and print dispense a barrage of images, impressions, and commentary about the world around us. What the media notice they also affect:

the significance, sometimes the meanings, of the ad alter. At times, that notice is unfavourable, as with Rich, who thought the new anti-drug effort an expensive waste of time. In 1995, the National Rifle Association (NRA) ran into a firestorm of criticism (and ex-President Bush resigned from its ranks) when it referred to federal agents as 'jackbooted thugs' in a fund-raising letter and ran an ad attacking the Bureau of Alcohol, Tobacco, and Firearms, an initiative taken just after the 19 April bombing of a federal building in Oklahoma City. More often, the media spotlight enhances the impact of propaganda. That occurs especially in the realm of Habermas's 'political public sphere.' The potency of the Willie Horton commercials (1988) depended upon the willingness of TV and print to air the charges in a variety of different ways, thus giving them greater exposure and credibility. But the multiplier effect has also occurred in the wider public sphere. That effect worked in favour of Phil Sokolof, a millionaire activist who used newspaper ads during 1988 in his 'Poisoning of America' series against such corporations as Quaker Oats, Procter and Gamble, General Foods, and Nabisco, attacking them for using 'chloresterol-rich tropical oils' in the preparation of packaged foods: the consequent media coverage generated sufficient notice to convince most companies to change their evil ways, though it required another effort to bring Nabisco to surrender.[16]

The reverse works as well. Civic advocacy shapes debate in the media. Mobil Oil recognized that when it took up corporate advocacy in the 1970s. So, too, did the various animal-rights groups who used publicity to win media attention in order to stop the slaughter of whales and baby seals. During the 1990s, the media in North America have treated advocacy advertising as a major item in the news. In Canada, the ongoing propaganda war between the right-wing provincial government and its unionist foes was a running story in the Ontario media during the late 1990s. U.S. journalists routinely watch and discuss election advertising, especially in presidential years, testing claims and counter-claims, delivering judgments, and assessing effects. The 'Harry and Louise' campaign had such an effect on the whole medicare debate because it persuaded journalists to cast a critical eye upon specific aspects of the Clinton Health Initiative. Even a single spot may start all sorts of comment: for example, the airing of *Oblivious* (1994) in Ontario, featuring scenes of men hitting women, provoked commentary on radio and in print about whether such a graphic ad was actually a form of male bashing. At the end of the Canadian federal election in 1997, the Reform party sparked heated discussion in the media and elsewhere about whether a Quebec resident had held the top office in Canada too often by raising the question in one of their ads. Propaganda can set the agenda (determine what issues are of importance), prime discussion (determine what criteria are used to assess a person or issue), excite controversy (where news outlets take different stands), or generate support (where the media elaborate its message). Whatever its impact, the result is productive – of comment, argument, and discourse.

4 The Moral Gaze

Advertising as propaganda has colonized the public sphere with styles of rhetoric and imagery, a way of perceiving problems and solutions, derived from the operations of the marketplace. That might be counted part of the successful effort to commodify just about everything in the late twentieth century, including politics and leisure, art and learning, even dissent – a commodification that is by now a familiar motif of postmodern commentary.[17] The so-called mass democracies are fast becoming market democracies in political as well as economic terms; or, to be more exact, they are marketplaces of democracy. But signifying yet another triumph for the commodity is not the end of the story. For civic advertising has also worked to subject its products, both public goods and social risks, to a moral logic, a calculus of right and wrong. That has proved the most effective way to package the sell, because a moral logic reaches across boundaries of class, gender, race, and belief. Issues, politicians, ideas, policies, and behaviours are all transformed into moral commodities. The results have been so promising that the practice of moralizing has begun to condition the selling of private goods as well.

Habermas laid special emphasis on the moral dimension of rational discourse and the moral core of practical questions. There was, and here he specifically agreed with other philosophers, a 'moral point of view' (FR, 447) that should ground both reason and argument so that debate produced fair and universal results. The way moral judgment worked out in the practice of the contemporary public sphere, however, was hardly ideal. The calculus of right and wrong was eventually built into the structure of the propaganda. The process of honouring and dishonouring – and sometimes both are apparent in one commercial – is at the core of the whole phenomenon. Consider two examples from South America.

The '*Sí*' campaign in Chile's referendum battle (1988), which sought to perpetuate the *status quo*, tried to energize support for the regime of Augusto Pinochet using the spectres of decline, violence, and decay. A

lively classical composition played in the background as an ironic coun-
terpoint to one scene after another of violence and destruction: street
youth, a burning car, a looted office, rock throwing, red flags, lots of
guns. Presumably these were pictures of the civil strife that Chile had
suffered before Pinochet seized power. Near the end a red tide (blood?,
Communism?) leaked down the screen to mark the close of the display of
violence. Then a voice-over told viewers why they must vote the right way.
The intent was obvious: say yes if you want to avoid a return to those days
of evil.[18] Mobilizing fear, building a moral panic, was not only an American disease.

Nor were American politicians the only leaders to employ the motif of
the redeemer. During the early 1990s an Argentine ad (*Don't Stop History*)
for the governing Justicialism Party positioned its candidate, Carlos
Menem, as the tool of progress. The ad employed a rapid-fire sequence
of pictures covering the country's history, backed up by vigorous classical
music. There were images of all sorts: work, play, war, political events,
even tragedy, including the sinking of an Argentine battleship in a war
with Britain over possession of the Falkland Islands. The ad ended with a
series of shots of a smiling, energetic Menem, soon shown with Bush,
Gorbachev, and Pope John Paul II. The camera froze on a profile of
Menem's face, looking up (to God, to the future, who knows?) – accompanied by the slogan 'NO DETENGAMOS LA HISTORIA' ('LET US
NOT STOP HISTORY'). The spot left the impression that Menem had
ensured Argentina's return to the path of progress, that he was building
a state which would (or had already?) – taken its place among the nations
of the world.[19]

Jackson Lears has called consumer ads 'fables of abundance.'[20] By
contrast, civic ads are fables of vice and virtue, or more simply sermons,
though authored by a very different kind of clergy. The typical ad
concludes by ascribing virtue to its sponsor and prescribing the appropriate conduct, which normally translates into buying, figuratively rather
than literally, a particular politician, object, sacrifice, or behaviour – in
other words, an actual or a virtual product. Or sometimes the ad sells *not*
buying that product. For example, in the pro-life/anti-abortion campaigns of the nineties, advocates strove to occupy the moral plane, to
label opponents evil as well as to celebrate their own righteousness. One
sponsor, the DeMoss Foundation, first represented adoption as a moral
alternative by highlighting the loving parents to be ('Life. What a Beautiful Choice') and later positioned abortion as murder by using the ultra-
sound image of an embryo ('Anywhere in the country I can be aborted

right now').[21] The ads put out a few years later by the Child Protection Fund in its war against partial-birth abortions were even more poignant, emphasizing how cruel, how gruesome was that method of killing the unwanted 'baby.'[22]

What lingered in people's minds was the moral charge of an ad. A major effect of anti-smoking campaigns, noted one Canadian advocate, had been to convert 'happy smokers into guilty smokers.'[23] The waves of anti-drug ads in the early 1970s and again in the late 1980s apparently convinced increasing numbers of youth that doing drugs was wrong, though that did not always translate into obedience. A focus-group test of the American army's famous 'Be All You Can Be' campaign revealed that actual soldiers were generally not impressed, feeling that the ads promised what experience never delivered. But there was one exception: an ad called *We Were There* celebrated the traditions and the sacrifices of the ordinary soldier – an honouring which they deemed both appealing and realistic.[24]

The ability to dishonour constituted the most significant tool at the disposal of the advocate; not surprisingly, then, its exercise provoked outrage. In 1990, Neighbor to Neighbor, a left advocacy group, ran an ad on WHDH-TV in Boston as part of its campaign against the corporate supporters of the regime in El Salvador. The ad was ugly: an image of blood seeping from an overturned coffee mug while TV star Ed Asner urged a boycott of Folgers – all because the brand included coffee beans from El Salvador and so apparently helped support the civil war. 'What it brews is misery and death.' The owner of the Folgers brand, Procter and Gamble, was understandably furious at this 'defamatory and destructive' attack. The company responded by withdrawing all its ad business, estimated at $1 million a year, from the offending station, hardly a suitable 'advertising environment.' *Advertising Age* reported that no other station took the commercial (purportedly twenty-eight other stations had wisely turned down the ad). The boycott failed to catch fire. [25]

When the moral gaze fell on the misconduct of lesser mortals – the smoker, the addict, sometimes men in general, sometimes black youth, the tax evader, the non-voter, or the woman who wears fur – those targeted usually could not retaliate so effectively. Gays were often upset by campaigns, especially in the late 1980s, which seemed to blame homosexuals for the new plague of AIDS. Smokers phoned health offices to express their resentment over the bluntness of California's new assault on smoking in 1990. The Gasoline Dealers' Association in Halifax was angered by an anti-drug message in 1991 which represented the local gas attendant as a drug dealer. African-American leaders in Chicago in 1992 spoke out against a campaign which stigmatized gangs as worse enemies of black America than the Ku Klux Klan and neo-Nazis – the ad was modified, but only slightly. One person misread an Ontario ad (1991) attacking drinking and driving as urging punishment of offenders by electrocution; others thought the young man pictured in the ad was contemplating suicide. In either case, the admakers were pleased because such responses demonstrated that the ad was working.[26]

One of the problems with humour was that it might, unintentionally, dishonour its sponsor or the cause. *The Last Supper* was a Canadian commercial made for the Roman Catholic Share Life campaign in Ontario. It was supposed to create more young donors through a parody of Leonardo da Vinci's famous painting. Jesus and his disciples are disturbed by a phone call:

ACTOR 1: Who was it?
ACTOR 2: Oh, it was just some charity. Why do they always call during dinner?
ANNOUNCER: Imagine if even the most devout among us forgot the true meaning of Christian charity. Please, give to Share Life and help those in need.

The ad did not run. Whatever its appeal to youth, focus groups revealed that core donors – older Catholics, in short – might find this ironic treatment of something holy too bold and so unpleasant.[27]

The effort to dishonour could, in fact, provoke a dangerous backlash. That was apparent in the case of Canada in the federal election of 1993. Late in the campaign, a desperate Conservative party, then in power but clearly about to be beaten, sponsored an attack ad that featured an ugly photograph of the face of the Opposition leader, Jean Chrétien, whose mouth sagged because of a childhood illness. The claim, 'I would be embarrassed to have him as a prime minister,' strengthened the impression that the ad hoped to exploit an apparent deformity. That was the way the news media treated the ad, and its interpretation fostered an immediate 10 per cent drop in support for the Conservatives in public-opinion polls, even after the ad was withdrawn and the then prime minister, Kim Campbell, apologized. The fiasco contributed to a general débâcle in which the party lost so many seats it was reduced to minor party status in the House of Commons.[28]

There is one detailed study of the structural import of attack propaganda. In 1995 Stephen Ansolabehere and Shanto Iyengar published *Going Negative*, which showed, as their subtitle states, *How Advertisements*

Shrink and Polarize the Electorate.[29] The authors used a variety of controlled experiments to assess the effects of political commercials on audiences. They also monitored contests at the local, state, and national levels in California during the early 1990s. People did pay attention and did learn from advertising, sometimes much more than from any other media source, they concluded. But negative campaigns disenchanted the un-committed and the independents; that is, they constructed non-voters who came to see the whole process as corrupt. 'In our experiments the effect of seeing a negative as opposed to a positive advertisement is to drop intentions to vote by nearly 5 percentage points' (112). Turnout rates were noticeably higher in Senate races (1992) where positive cam-paigns were waged, so much so that, without the dark effects of negative ads, an estimated additional 7.6 million people would have cast a vote for a candidate (109). The demobilization of the uncommitted and the independents, of course, enhanced the significance of partisans (al-though some of these also dropped away in intensely negative contests), an effect which, over time, emphasized the extremes in the political spectrum. Indeed, one other major effect of advertising, both positive and negative, was to reinforce the loyalty of most partisans, to convince them of the virtue of a party, its platform, and its candidates. Attack ads were particularly effective among Republican and conservative voters because they especially disliked government (92). The authors had traced the way political advertising was transforming the American polity into a marketplace, wherein parties and candidates merchandise various moral commodities to please the inclinations of persistent consumers.

Let me return to one acclaimed comment of Walter Benjamin: 'The logical result of Fascism is the introduction of aesthetics into political life.'[30] The obverse of this much-quoted assertion has not been recog-nized, however: that the thrust of the aesthetic into the public sphere fosters a brand of despotism, at least when despotism is defined in terms of style rather than ideology. Habermas likewise linked spectacle and authoritarianism. Civic advocates have, as it were, 'practised Gramsci.' They have sought to construct what amounts to a moral hegemony in the public sphere, to ensure that their conceptions of good and evil, right and wrong become the official norms, if not common sense.

5 'Refeudalization'

The evocative term 'refeudalization' figured prominently in *The Struc-tural Transformation* (though it did not appear in 'Further Reflections') where it signified the unhappy reversion to the autocratic style of rule prevailing in medieval Europe. To a degree, Habermas found an 'affinity' between 'modern publicity' and 'feudal publicity' (*STPS*, 200), since both sought to represent authority, and to enhance the reputation or prestige of that authority, before a largely passive public. The underlying purpose of 'staged or manipulated publicity' (*STPS*, 232) was to assemble a sort of sham public sphere in which people might acclaim some already-decided public policy. The 'liberal fictions' (*STPS*, 211) of public debate and public opinion were required to legitimize the exercise of authority in formal democracies.

Crucial to democracy in a marketized sphere is not so much rational discourse as rational choice. In fact, the issue has become whether many citizens will make any choice whatsoever. Eastern Europe's revolutions of 1989–90 caused a certain amount of soul-searching in the West. Observers argued that people in the Communist states had gone out into the streets to resist an armed authority in order to win democracy. By contrast, the civil society in various affluent countries, especially in the United States, was in a sad state of repair (and that concern even surfaced in the occasional ad) because of the deepening indifference of so much of the public.[31] Mass involvement in traditional organizations such as labour unions, parent-teacher associations, and political parties had fallen off dramatically. 'Surveys show sharp declines in many measures of collective political participation, including attending a rally or speech (off 36 per cent between 1973 and 1993), attending a meeting on town or school affairs (off 39 per cent), or working for a political party (off 56 per cent).'[32] The popular culture offered far more pleasures, and demanded far less, than the political culture.

All the propaganda of the past decades has had two long-term, if contradictory, effects on the public: it has worked to manufacture both militancy and indifference, and both effects are grounded in an aesthetic response to the individual ads and to the discourse. The barrage of ads increased the commitment of the nearly and the already convinced, strengthening their resolve and their righteousness, a development noted by Ansolabehere and Iyengar in the realm of American politics. That has been part of a wider phenomenon, namely the rise of a non-profit sector which used the mails, the telephone, and the media to organize its membership. These partisans were and are moved to action, not to discovery, and rarely to dialogue. Propaganda intensifies what Habermas called 'generalized particularisms,' an ugly but telling phrase that denotes 'the privileged assertion of local and group-specific interests' (FR,

451). At the same time, the rising volume of promotional noise became less a 'catalyst' than a turn-off for increasing numbers of people already bombarded by the other communications of the mass media. These citizens have adopted, in effect, that strategy *à la* Baudrillard of evasion and silence, some leaving the public sphere altogether. The ad yells, 'You can make a difference.' But many listeners discount such claims, and others do not care. Witness compassion fatigue or backsliding (the return of smoking and unsafe sex) or non-voting. Even in Canada, where traditionally turnout has been much higher than in the United States (at the 80 per cent level in the early 1960s), participation has fallen off in the 1990s, reaching around two-thirds in the 1997 election. At the bottom end of society, especially among the young, people are being demobilized – or are rarely awakened. In the United States, for example, low-income voters are much less likely (the ratio is 1 to 2) to participate than high-income voters.[33] Propaganda and marketing foster a divided public sphere, composed of small clusters of activists and engaged souls – together, a citizen class – and a larger collection of usually passive or indifferent consumers. That situation, of course, may well be closer to the historical norm of public life in regimes of representative government, democratic or otherwise, than the ideal posited by Habermas.[34]

'It is not by chance that advertising, after having, for a long time, carried an implicit ultimatum of an economic kind, fundamentally saying and repeating incessantly, "I buy, I consume, I take pleasure,"' reasoned Jean Baudrillard, 'today repeats in other forms, "I vote, I participate, I am present, I am concerned" – mirror of a paradoxical mockery, mirror of the indifference of all *public* signification.'[35] However, the success of marketing as philosophy and apparatus has not turned the public sphere into a total sham. In some ways, advocacy advertising has seemed a necessary response to the depoliticization encouraged by popular culture. But this soft power of persuasion has undeniably corrupted the practices of democracy. Perhaps a medical analogy will help here: civic advocacy constitutes a kind of virus which debilitates the body politic. If the public sphere has retained its discursive character, propaganda now shapes and suppresses debate. The sphere remains a site for the production of a public opinion that is given concrete form by surveys and polls which, to a degree, actually fashion the opinion through the process of asking certain questions (and not asking others). Because of an excess of goods and risks competing for attention, the sphere continues to be a contested arena; however, much of the excess is manufactured by people and institutions with money, moral clout, or other forms of power. The mass media play out a double role here, both as the vehicle of competitive spectacles and as the source of news, a different kind of discourse, though again a monologue and now contaminated by the ubiquity of publicity. Popular participation is restricted, usually being limited to the response people as consumers and spectators have to the commodities and sights on offer. Illusion more than substance, manipulation but some resistance, both indifference and militancy, are all part of the complex environment fostered by propaganda and its associates. Postmodern democracy, in short, does have something of a 'refeudalized' quality.

One final thought. The Op-Ed column in the Sunday *New York Times* (26 July 1998) dealt with the political meaning of 'cured' or 'reformed' homosexuals. More interesting than the text, however, was the accompanying image, another piece of moral critique from Barbara Kruger. The image displayed the anguished face of a woman in a fractured mirror: 'You are not yourself.' The work spoke not just to the issue at hand, but to the ongoing plight of democracy at the end of the twentieth century.

Notes

Abbreviations

Most of the commercials cited in the text are parts of particular collections, especially awards tapes. That is why so many of the commercials, whatever their origin, are translated into English, which was deemed the common world language of advertising. Listed below are the abbreviations used to refer to these collections. In the case of awards, I have attached a date, which is usually a year after the commercial was first aired.

- Ad Council. The special Advertising Council exhibit, part of the collection of the Museum of Television and Radio in New York City.
- Bessies. Canadian television advertising awards.
- BEST. *Advertising Age*'s television advertising awards.
- BTAA. British Television Advertising Awards.
- Cannes. International television and cinema advertising awards.
- Clios. American, and occasionally international, television advertising awards.
- IBA. International Broadcasting Awards, based in the United States.
- IS. International Showcase, a special collection of international commercials, attached to the Bessies.
- Lürzers. A European-based service which releases special tapes of commercials during the course of a year.
- NMPFTV. The National Museum of Photography, Film and Television, based in Bradford, U.K.
- Y&R. The Young and Rubicam Collection, held by the Museum of Television and Radio.

- Since so many references are to articles in *Advertising Age*, I often use the abbreviation *AA* to refer to this magazine.

Introduction: Advertising as Propaganda

1 Ted Wood, 'U.S. TV addicted to drug commercials,' *Marketing*, 30 April 1990, 20.
2 The notion of public goods is derived from the discipline of economics. See Richard Cornes and Todd Sandler, *The Theory of Externalities, Public Goods, and Club Goods* (Cambridge: Cambridge University Press 1986). One application of this notion to political action can be found in Dennis Chong's *Collective Action and the Civil Rights Movement* (Chicago: University of Chicago Press 1991). I found especially helpful one source that was available on the World Wide Web in March 1997: Roger A. McCain, ch. 13: 'Government and Efficiency: Public Goods and Externality,' *Essential Principles of Economics: A Hypermedia Text*, First Revised Draft (*http://william.king.www.drexel.edu/top/prin/txt/EcoToC.html*).
3 Cited in Leo Bogart, *Commercial Culture: The Media System and the Public Interest* (New York: Oxford University Press 1995), 87.
4 Frances Kelly, 'Baring All to Battle AIDS,' *Marketing*, 1 June 1992, 30.
5 Zygmunt Bauman, 'A Sociological Theory of Postmodernity,' in his *Intimations of Postmodernity* (London: Routledge 1992), 198–9, although the whole paragraph draws upon the ideas in this essay. The comment on risk, however, is derived from Ulrich Beck's *Risk Society: Towards a New Modernity* (London: Sage 1992).
6 'Largely,' but not completely unrecognized. See, for instance, Kevin Robins, Frank Webster, and Michael Pickering, 'Propaganda, Information and Social Control,' in Jeremy Hawthorn, ed., *Propaganda, Persuasion and Polemic* (London: Edward Arnold 1987), 1–17. There, the authors talk broadly about the need to recognize 'an ever more extensive information apparatus – propaganda, censorship, advertising, public relations, surveillance, etc. – through which opinion management has become not only authoritarian, but also routine and normative' (16).
7 Consequently, Anthony Pratkanis and Elliot Aronson in *Age of Propaganda: The Everyday Use and Abuse of Persuasion* (New York: W.H. Freeman 1991) simply admit that they employ the term 'to refer to the mass persuasion techniques that have come to characterize our post-industrial society' (9). Even more general is the operative definition of propaganda as 'the propagation of ideas and actions' (12) used in James E. Combs and Don Nimmo, *The New Propaganda: The Dictatorship of Palaver in Contemporary Politics* (New

York: Longman 1993).

8 Consider these definitions: 'The deliberate attempt by the few to influence the attitudes and behaviour of the many by the manipulation of symbolic communication,' Terence H. Qualter, *Opinion Control in the Democracies* (London: Macmillan 1985), 124; 'Propaganda is the deliberate and systematic attempt to shape perceptions, manipulate cognitions, and direct behavior to achieve a response that furthers the desired intent of the propagandist,' Garth S. Jowett and Victoria O'Donnell, *Propaganda and Persuasion* (Newbury Park: Sage 1986), 16; 'By propaganda, then, I mean the deliberate attempt to persuade people to think and behave in a desired way,' Philip M. Taylor, *Munitions of the Mind: A History of Propaganda from the Ancient World to the Present Era* (Manchester: Manchester University Press 1995), 6.

9 Hence this definition of propaganda: 'The intentional control, manipulation and communication of information and imagery in order to achieve certain political objectives,' Tim O'Sullivan, John Hartley, Danny Saunders, Martin Montgomery, and John Fiske, *Key Concepts in Communication and Cultural Studies* (London: Routledge 1994), 246–7.

10 That is, to 'good citizens,' broadly defined. The model person acts appropriately at home, at work, and in public; he or she performs those duties and behaves in ways to ensure his or her own social (and so moral) health. Thus, the initial address may be to the individual as man or woman, neighbour, or friend.

11 See Noam Chomsky, *Necessary Illusions: Thought Control in Democratic Societies* (Montreal: CBC Enterprises 1989), 10–12, and Michael Schudson, *The Power of News* (Cambridge: Harvard University Press 1995), 4. The other difficulty with Chomsky's account revolves around the issue of intention: the act must be deliberate if it is to count as propaganda. Thus, even a reader sympathetic to Chomsky should decide whether the bias of the news media is systemic or sponsored. And it is very, very difficult to prove intention. Of course, to the sympathetic reader the decision may not be all that important: the media are either the dupes or stooges of corporate and state authority in Chomsky's America.

12 First identified by David L. Altheide and John M. Johnson in *Bureaucratic Propaganda* (Boston: Allyn and Bacon 1980). In a slightly different vein, there is the more recent and popular book by Cynthia Crossen, *Tainted Truth: The Manipulation of Fact in America* (New York: Touchstone Books 1996).

13 My comments on the purposes of museums result from a reading of Tony Bennett, *The Birth of the Museum: History, Theory, Politics* (London: Routledge 1995).

14 See Stephen Ansolabehere and Shanto Iyengar, *Going Negative: How Political Advertisements Shrink and Polarize the Electorate* (New York: Free Press 1995), on the effects of attack ads. The Ketchum message was available on its Web site, 10 November 1995, at *http://www.ketchum.com/advertising/great/ don'tbg.gif.*

15 Clara Grove, 'Ad World Reels in Indonesia,' *Advertising Age International*, 13 April 1998, 1.

16 Jean Baudrillard, 'The Masses: The Implosion of the Social in the Media,' in *Selected Writings*, ed. Mark Poster (Stanford: Stanford University Press 1988), 209–10.

17 See Gillian Cohen, 'Schemata,' in Michael W. Eysenck, ed., *The Blackwell Dictionary of Cognitive Psychology* (Oxford: Blackwell 1994), 316.

18 See the reference to some research on this issue in Margaret Matlin, *Cognition*, 3rd ed. (Philadelphia: Harcourt Brace 1994), 245–6.

19 See, for example, the excellent articles by William J. McGuire: 'Attitudes and Attitude Change,' in Gardner Lindzey and Elliot Aronson, eds, *Handbook of Social Psychology*, vol. 2: Special Fields and Applications (New York: Random House 1985), 233–346; and 'Theoretical Foundations of Campaigns,' in Ronald E. Rice and Charles K. Aitkin, eds, *Public Communication Campaigns*, 2nd ed. (Newbury Park: Sage 1989), 43–65.

20 See Richard E. Petty and John T. Cacioppo, 'Central and Peripheral Routes to Persuasion: Application to Advertising,' in Larry Percy and Arch Woodside, eds, *Advertising and Consumer Psychology* (Lexington, Mass.: D.C. Heath, Lexington Books 1983), 3–23; and John T. Cacioppo and Richard E. Petty, 'Central and Peripheral Routes to Persuasion: The Role of Message Repetition,' in Linda F. Alwitt and Andrew A. Mitchell, eds, *Psychological Processes and Advertising Effects: Theory, Research, and Applications* (Hillsdale, N.J.: Lawrence Erlbaum 1985), 91–111.

21 The term is used by Pratkanis and Aronson, *Age of Propaganda*, 31.

22 See for example the studies in Stuart J. Agres, Julie A. Edell, and Tony M. Dubitsky, eds, *Emotion in Advertising: Theoretical and Practical Explorations* (New York: Quorum Books 1990).

23 Ann Marie Seward Barry, *Visual Intelligence: Perception, Image, and Manipulation in Visual Communication* (Albany: State University of New York Press 1997), 17–19.

24 Which, of course, has been a staple of scare books about advertising. See, for example, Vance Packard's classic *The Hidden Persuaders* (New York: Pocket Books 1958).

25 Mihaly Csikszentmihalyi and Rick Robinson, *The Art of Seeing: An Interpretation of the Aesthetic Encounter* (Malibu, Calif.: J. Paul Getty Trust 1990), 18.

26 The campaign is discussed in Daniel Slocum Hinerfeld, 'How Political Ads Subtract,' *Washington Monthly* 22 (May 1990): 13–16.

27 Celia K. Lehrman, 'PSAs for Criminals,' *Public Relations Journal* (May 1986): 11.

28 Discussed in Kathy Myers, *Understains: The Sense and Seduction of Advertising* (London: Comedia 1986), 109–18. She claimed that this campaign marked a major shift in the attitude of the British left towards the acceptance of advertising as a necessary tool of politics.

29 *Globe and Mail* (Toronto), 2 April 1997, A5. The Tories, or Progressive Conservatives, were one of the opposition parties. Their strategy did not work; the existing Liberal government returned to power in the election.

30 Joy Rosen, 'Playing the Primary Chords,' *Harper's Magazine* (March 1992): 24, 26. This was an abbreviated version of Rosen's 'The Return of the Expressed,' which appeared in the February issue of the *Boston Review*.

31 Andrew Wernick, *Promotional Culture: Advertising, Ideology and Symbolic Expression* (Newbury Park: Sage 1991), 184.

32 What I mean by 'discursive formation' is simply a specific fragment of a wider discourse, in this case the discourse of advertising, which is about selling. The term comes from Michel Foucault, *The Archeology of Knowledge*, trans. A.M. Sheridan Smith (New York: Pantheon Books 1972), esp. 31–9.

*Habermas's Lament

1 Jürgen Habermas, *The Structural Transformation of the Public Sphere: An Inquiry into a Category of Bourgeois Society*, trans. Thomas Burger with Frederick Lawrence (Cambridge, Mass.: MIT Press 1991), 203.

2 Jürgen Habermas, 'Concluding Remarks,' in Craig Calhoun, ed., *Habermas and the Public Sphere* (Cambridge, Mass.: MIT Press 1992), 469. The Frankfurt School, a variant of Marxism, was especially critical of mass culture and its effects. See Martin Jay, *The Dialectical Imagination: A History of the Frankfurt School and the Institute of Social Research, 1923–1950* (Berkeley: University of California Press 1973).

3 The book was published in English only in 1989 by the MIT Press. All references in parentheses in the text are to this edition.

4 Detlef Horster, *Habermas: An Introduction* (Philadelphia, Pa.: Pennbridge Books 1992), 5.

5 See the essays by philosophers, historians, and media scholars in the already cited *Habermas and the Public Sphere*, for example. The field of media studies has been especially affected: see the essays in Peter Dahlgren and

Colin Sparks, eds, *Communication and Citizenship: Journalism and the Public Sphere* (London: Routledge 1991).

6 Even simpler is a later definition: 'The bourgeois public sphere can be understood as the sphere of private persons assembled to form a public.' Cited in Jürgen Habermas, 'The Public Sphere,' a 1973 essay reprinted in Chandra Mukerji and Michael Schudson, eds, *Rethinking Popular Culture: Contemporary Perspectives in Cultural Studies* (Berkeley: University of California Press 1991), 401.

7 Cited in Richard Kilminster and Ian Varcoe, 'Sociology, Postmodernity and Exile: An Interview with Zygmunt Bauman,' in Zygmunt Bauman, *Intimations of Postmodernity* (London: Routledge 1992), 217. Bauman then goes on to reject Habermas because he became enmeshed in 'a straightforward positivistic re-hashing of Parsons,' another sociologist and system-builder. It may be worth noting, of course, that Habermas has also emphasized his continued belief in the modern/ist project, while Bauman is very postmodern.

8 Even sympathetic historians have taken issue with the details and the broad outlines of the story Habermas told in his initial account: see, in particular, the essays by M. Schudson and G. Eley in *Habermas and the Public Sphere*. See also Nancy Fraser's 'What's Critical about Critical Theory? The Case of Habermas and Gender,' in *Unruly Practices: Power, Discourse and Gender in Contemporary Social Theory* (Minneapolis: University of Minnesota Press 1989), 113–43, where she argues that Habermas has often been blind to the import of gender.

9 Entitled *Propagandes* in French. That book swiftly found its way into English (New York: Alfred A. Knopf 1965), probably because Ellul was already known as the author of *The Technological Society*.

10 Ibid., 75.

11 For example: 'propaganda builds monolithic individuals. It eliminates inner conflicts, tensions, self-criticism, self-doubt. And in this fashion it also builds a one-dimensional being without depth or range of possibilities.' Ibid., 165.

12 Ibid., 121.

13 The phrase is taken from Peter Kenez, *The Birth of the Propaganda State: Soviet Methods of Mass Mobilization, 1917–1929* (Cambridge: Cambridge University Press 1985).

14 See, for example, the work of Arthur Marwick, *The Sixties: Cultural Revolution in Britain, France, Italy, and the United States, c. 1958–c. 1974* (Oxford and New York: Oxford University Press 1998), esp. 291–3. Marwick sees Marcuse as one of the most accomplished mystifiers in that decade of agitation.

15 Herbert Marcuse, *One-Dimensional Man: Studies in the Ideology of Advanced Industrial Society*, 2nd ed. (Boston: Beacon Press 1991), 86–95, the extended quotation from 86.

16 See Max Horkheimer and Theodor Adorno, *Dialectic of Enlightenment*, trans. John Cumming (New York: Continuum Publishing Company 1995), esp. 'The Culture Industry: Enlightenment as Mass Deception' (120–67). The book was originally published in 1944.

17 Chapter 13, entitled 'The Mass Society' in C. Wright Mills, *The Power Elite* (New York: Oxford University Press 1956), 298–324.

18 Ibid., 310.

19 There is an interesting survey of this set of attitudes in Bernard Rosenberg and David Manning White, eds, *Mass Culture: The Popular Arts in America* (New York: Free Press 1957). See especially the article by Rosenberg, titled simply 'Mass Culture in America.'

1 The Imperialism of the Market: The United States, 1940–1970

1 Cited in George Will, 'The Other Guy Started It,' *AA*, 18 January 1988, 66.

2 The 1970 edition was published in the New American Library as a paperback, and it is this edition I have used to discuss Galbraith's arguments. The original edition was published in 1958.

3 Ibid., xii.

4 Eric Hobsbawm, *Age of Extremes: The Short Twentieth Century, 1914–1991* (London: Abacus 1994), 257–86. Hobsbawm points out that the boom was even more emphatic in western Europe because of its recovery from the desperate years of the war. He also claims, countering Galbraith, that 'between the 1940s and the 1970s nobody listened to such Old Believers' in the market (271).

5 Ibid., 275.

6 Cited in O.J. Firestone, *Broadcasting Advertising in Canada: Past and Future Growth* (Ottawa: University of Ottawa Press 1966), 32.

7 David Potter, *People of Plenty* (Chicago: University of Chicago Press 1954).

8 Galbraith, *Affluent Society*, 203–4.

9 Useful accounts of early-twentieth-century campaigns can be found in Roland Marchand, 'The Fitful Career of Advocacy Advertising: Political Protection, Client Cultivation, and Corporate Morale,' *California Management Review* 29, no. 2 (Winter 1987): 128–56; Stephen Vaughn, *Holding Fast the Inner Lines: Democracy, Nationalism, and the Committee on Public Information* (Chapel Hill: University of North Carolina Press 1980); George A. Flanagan, *Modern Institutional Advertising* (New York: McGraw-Hill 1967); and Richard

S. Tedlow, *Keeping the Corporate Image: Public Relations and Business, 1900–1950* (Greenwich, Conn.: JAI Press 1979). The story of public relations in the early twentieth century has been told by Stuart Ewen in *PR! A Social History of Spin* (New York: Basic Books 1996). The most substantial study of the activities of big business is Roland Marchand's magnificent work *Creating the Corporate Soul: The Rise of Public Relations and Corporate Imagery in American Big Business* (Berkeley: University of California Press 1998).

10 This story is based on Frank Fox's *Madison Avenue Goes to War: The Strange Military Career of American Advertising, 1941–45* (Provo: Brigham Young University 1975).

11 Cited in Marchand, *Creating the Corporate Soul*, 320. The U.S. government had declared in May 1942 that it would allow the deduction of advertising costs before the calculation of profits, and that at a time when 'an excess profits tax of 90 percent was in effect.'

12 There are many sources for this figure, though it is no more than a guess. The Ad Council itself says 'an average of $300 million a year in media advertising' during World War II (4) and '$1 billion in advertising' (8). The source is an exhibition catalogue: 'A Retrospective of Advertising Council Campaigns: A Half Century of Public Service' (New York: Museum of Television and Radio, 1991).

13 The postwar course of the Ad Council is admirably discussed in Robert Griffith's 'The Selling of America: The Advertising Council and American Politics, 1942–1960,' *Business History Review* 57 (Autumn 1983): 388–412.

14 'Cartons for Worthy Causes,' *Sales Management* 80 (21 March 1951): 106–7.

15 These grand claims are cited in Flanagan, *Modern Institutional Advertising*, 194.

16 The estimate came about in a simple fashion: in 1942, before Smokey, 30 million acres went up in smoke; but in 1958 only one-tenth as much was burned. 'Smokey: A Symbol Saves $1 Billion,' *Printer's Ink* 267 (8 May 1959): 71.

17 The dull slogan of the campaign read 'Peace Begins with the United Nations – and the United Nations Begins with You.' The campaign is discussed in Charles K. Atkin, 'Mass Media Information Campaign Effectiveness,' in Ronald E. Rice and William J. Paisley, eds, *Public Communication Campaigns* (Beverly Hills, Calif.: Sage 1981), 268; and Everett M. Rogers and J. Douglas Storey, 'Communication Campaigns,' in Charles R. Berger and Steven H. Chaffee, eds, *Handbook of Communication Science* (Newbury Park, Calif.: Sage 1987), 827.

18 Paul Lazarsfeld and Robert Merton, 'Mass Communication, Popular Taste and Organized Social Action,' in Bernard Rosenberg and David Manning

White, eds, *Mass Culture: The Popular Arts in America* (New York: Free Press 1957), 469–73. The article was first published in 1948 in Lyman Bryson, *The Communication of Ideas.*

19 William F. Whyte, *Is Anybody Listening?* (New York: Simon and Schuster 1952), 7.

20 Griffith, 'Selling of America,' 408.

21 Marchand, 'Fitful Career,' 149–50.

22 Discussed in Flanagan, *Modern Institutional Advertising,* 23–8.

23 See Whyte's *Is Anybody Listening?*

24 Marchand has argued that this psychic effect was significant: 'A few people were listening very intently and with great satisfaction to advocacy ads. Of uncertain efficacy in other respects, they provided their sponsors the significant and undeniable satisfactions of enhancing their self-esteem and winning the respect of their peers' ('Fitful Career,' 151).

25 Cited in Edwin Diamond and Stephen Bates, *The Spot: The Rise of Political Advertising on Television,* 3rd ed. (Cambridge, Mass.: MIT Press 1992), 36.

26 The advertising of this campaign has received a lot of attention. Diamond and Bates (ibid.) offer a chapter devoted to 1952 (44–63). There is also a chapter in David Halberstam, *The Fifties* (New York: Villard Books 1993), 224–42. Phillip Niffenegger uses the term 'positioning' in 'Strategies for Success from the Political Marketers,' *Journal of Consumer Marketing* 6, no. 1 (Winter 1989): 46–7.

27 Lynda Lee Kaid and Anne Johnston, 'Negative versus Positive Television Advertising in U.S. Presidential Campaigns, 1960–1988,' *Journal of Communication* 41, no. 3 (Summer 1991): 53–64.

28 That is the reason one expert has given this election low marks in her assessment of contests where candidates actually dealt with what was significant. See Kathleen Hall Jamieson, *Dirty Politics: Deception, Distraction, and Democracy* (New York: Oxford University Press 1992), 245–9.

29 Diamond and Bates, *The Spot,* 123.

30 Ibid., 125. These authors claim that the ad ran on a CBS evening movie program. Jamieson, by contrast, quotes (*Dirty Politics,* 137) a Johnson aide who claimed it was an NBC movie. That quotation also notes how the other two networks ran the ad free on later news shows.

31 Diamond and Bates, *The Spot,* 128.

32 Thomas Frank has argued of *Daisy:* 'Its stark division of the world into flower-child and technocratic death-count couldn't have caught the mood of the nation more accurately or more presciently.' See his *The Conquest of Cool: Business Culture, Counterculture, and the Rise of Hip Consumerism* (Chicago: University of Chicago Press 1997), 72–3.

33 Laura Bird, 'The Guru and the Activist,' *Adweek's Marketing Week* 32 17 (June 1991): 23.

34 Diamond and Bates, *The Spot,* 147–76.

35 'Government Role Advocated in Political News and Ads,' *Editor and Publisher,* 28 December 1968, 9.

36 'The bill's most important provision restricts the amount that a candidate can spend on broadcasting to 7 cents for each vote cast for candidates for the same office in the previous election or $20,000, whichever figure is highest.' 'Buying Time,' *Economist,* 22 August 1970, 37.

37 'Future of Bill Limiting Political TV Spending in Doubt after Veto,' *AA,* 19 October 1970, 85.

38 *John F. Kennedy* is part of the Ad Council collection.

39 *Beach,* Y&R.

40 *Politics,* Ad Council.

41 'Ad Council Aims Four Campaigns at Improvement of Urban Conditions,' *AA,* 8 July 1968, 3.

42 *No Children* was made for the National Alliance of Businessmen and forms part of an Ad Council Retrospective entitled 'A Half Century of Public Service,' held by the MTR. *Slumlord* was made by Young and Rubicam and forms part of the 'Y&R and Broadcasting' exhibition of radio and television advertising, also held by MTR.

43 'Urban Coalition Uses TV Drive to Promote Racial Harmony,' *AA,* 29 December 1969. My copy of *Love* came from the NMPFTV in England. A radio commercial of 1968, entitled *Dr. Martin Luther King, Jr.,* targeting blacks, also promoted harmony and specifically condemned burning and looting. This too is part of the Ad Council Retrospective.

44 *Controversy Advertising: How Advertisers Present Points of View in Public Affairs,* sponsored by the International Advertising Association (New York: Hastings House 1977), 108–9.

45 See the stories in *AA,* 10 and 24 June, 22 and 29 July.

46 See Mitchell Hall, 'Unsell the War: Vietnam and Antiwar Advertising,' *Historian* 68 (09-01-1995): 69 as listed at the Web site of the Electric Library. The campaign continued into 1972, under the auspices of Clergy and Laymen Concerned, which Hall identifies as 'the nation's largest religiously oriented antiwar organization.' The actual ad is in International Advertising Association, *Controversy Advertising,* 111.

47 See, for example, Milan D. Meeske, 'Editorial Advertising and the First Amendment,' *Journal of Broadcasting* 17, no. 4 (Fall 1973): 417–8 or International Advertising Association, *Controversy Advertising,* 44–6

48 'Population Explosion Worries Foote Group; Ads in Dailies Tell of World

Starvation,' *AA*, 22 January 1968, 2. Another headline was equally startling: 'By the time 1968 is over, more than 3,500,000 people will die from starvation, most of them children. Happy New Year.'

49 It may well be, though, that the fact of these counter-ads was more dramatic than their message. The few examples I've seen were all very general admonitions to quit smoking or to get others to butt out.

50 Cited in David Paletz, Roberta Pearson, and Donald Willis, *Politics in Public Service Advertising on Television* (New York: Praeger 1977), 109–10. The book is a superb account of the whole field of PSAs in the 'seventies, based upon interviews, analysis of commercials, and a wide variety of research studies.

51 See Stanley Cohen, 'Counter Ad Battle Continues; Nets Reject Consumer Spots,' *AA*, 1 May 1972, and 'Stern Concern Offers Counter Ads to Print Media,' *AA*, 8 May 1972. The potential impact of the anti-Bayer spot was assessed in James Lull, 'Counter Advertising: Persuasibility of the Anti-Bayer TV Spot,' *Journal of Broadcasting* 18, no. 3 (Summer 1974): 353–60. Some of the spots, however, did appear on individual stations: 'Stern Counterads Find First Taker,' *Broadcasting*, 24 July 1972.

52 There is a detailed discussion of the whole referendum, complete with examples of the ads, in S. Prakash Sethi, *Advocacy Advertising and Large Corporations* (Lexington, Mass.: D.C. Heath 1977), 179–234. Sethi's book was a pioneering account of the wave of corporate advocacy in the 1970s.

53 G.D. Wiebe, in 'Merchandising Commodities and Citizenship on Television,' *Public Opinion Quarterly* 15 (Winter 1951–2): 679–91.

54 Cited in Nancy Gabler, 'The Art of Making a Politician Sexy,' *Marketing/Communications* (November 1970): 28. In this article, Bob Goodman claimed that he had set out to make Spiro Agnew sexy in the 1966 gubernatorial campaign.

55 Cited in Halberstam, *The Fifties*, 230.

56 A Kennedy Backer, 'GOP Ignored Ad Men – and Lost,' *Printer's Ink*, 2 December 1960, 43. The GOP stands for the Grand Old Party, or the Republicans.

57 Cited in 'Political Ads: They Win Some, They Lose Some,' *Broadcasting* 17 March 1980, 70.

58 Michael Posner, 'Repositioning the Right Honorable,' *Canadian Business* (May 1992): 40.

59 Cited in Bruce Newman and Jagdish Sheth, 'The "Gender Gap" in Voter Attitudes and Behavior: Some Advertising Implications,' *Journal of Advertising* 13, no. 3 (1984): 4.

60 David Ogilvy, *Confessions of an Advertising Man* (New York: Dell 1963), 197.

*Gramsci: Hegemony

1 R. Miliband, *Capitalist Democracy in Britain* (Oxford: Oxford University Press 1982), 76, cited in Paul Ransome, *Antonio Gramsci: A New Introduction* (New York: Harvester Wheatsheaf 1992), 132

2 The term 'hegemony' came from the revolutionary discourse of Russia. Gramsci had used it during his years as a party activist, although he did not develop his unique theory until after his imprisonment. See Carl Boggs, *The Two Revolutions: Antonio Gramsci and the Dilemmas of Western Marxism* (Boston: South End Press 1984), 159.

3 The editors of one set of selections have emphasized how the *Notebooks* constitute an 'open text': 'Unfinished by their author, the texts are open to us because there is no point at which they could, or can, be closed.' That makes them sound almost postmodern. Could this attribute also explain their popularity since 1970? See the introduction to Antonio Gramsci, *Selections from Cultural Writings* (hereafter *SCW*), ed. David Forgacs and Geoffrey Nowell-Smith, trans. William Boelhower (Cambridge, Mass.: Harvard University Press 1985), 9–11.

4 See Antonio Gramsci, *Further Selections from the Prison Notebooks* (hereafter *FSPN*), trans. and ed. Derek Boothman (Minneapolis: University of Minnesota Press 1995), respectively 39, 80 and 82, 357 or 394, 233, 123 and 345, 247, and 207 or 232.

5 *FSPN*, 332 and 357.

6 See, for example, Antonio Gramsci, *The Modern Prince and Other Writings* (New York: International Publishers 1957), 137–88.

7 Raymond Williams, 'Hegemony,' *Keywords: A Vocabulary of Culture and Society* (London: Fontana 1983), 145.

8 Raymond Williams, 'Base and Superstructure in Marxist Cultural Theory,' in Chandra Mukerji and Michael Schudson, eds, *Rethinking Popular Culture: Contemporary Perspectives in Cultural Studies* (Berkeley: University of California Press 1991), 412.

9 Thus this definition of hegemony: 'A concept developed by Gramsci in the 1930s and taken up in cultural studies, where it refers principally to the ability in certain historical periods of the dominant classes to exercise social and cultural leadership, and by these means – rather than by direct coercion of subordinate classes – to maintain their power over the economic, political and cultural direction of the nation.' Tim O'Sullivan, John Hartley, Danny Saunders, Martin Montgomery, and John Fiske, 'Hegemony,' *Key Concepts in Communication and Cultural Studies*, 2nd ed. (London: Routledge 1994), 133.

10 Raymond Williams, *Marxism and Literature* (Oxford: Oxford University Press 1977), 112.

11 Used in Ibid., 110.

12 Here John Fiske employed hegemony theory, mixed with a dash of Michel Foucault, to explain the submission and resistance of the body to assorted stimuli. John Fiske, *Power Plays, Power Works* (London: Verso 1993), 254–7. There appears this suggestive comment: 'Affect can be emancipatory only in its relation with this repressive complex of hegemony and imperializing power: peeing in the pants is not in itself liberatory, but in certain social relations it can be. The body (or, in this case, bladder) outside of a field structured by hegemony and power could never behave in this way.'

13 Stuart Hall, Chas Critcher, Tony Jefferson, John Clarke, and Brian Roberts, *Policing the Crisis: Mugging, the State, and Law and Order* (London: Macmillan 1978). The authors use hegemony theory to explain the emergence of crisis and the actions of authority in Britain during the late 1960s and the mid-1970s.

14 The addition of the term 'public sphere' to the definition of hegemony is not without precedent. Gramsci's own 'civil society' at times takes on the character of a public sphere, standing in opposition to the state. See Benedetto Fontana, *Hegemony & Power: On the Relation between Gramsci and Machiavelli* (Minneapolis: University of Minnesota Press 1993), 142–6.

15 Even though such a comment rests on the recent study of discourse, it is worth noting that Gramsci paid much attention to the politics of language, especially to issues of grammar and innovation. See *SCW*, 164–88.

16 This comment is derived from an argument by Roger Chartier on people's response to mass culture. 'Belief and disbelief go together, and the acceptance of the truth in what one reads or hears does not diminish the fundamental doubts retained about this presumed authenticity.' Roger Chartier, 'Texts, Printing, Reading,' in Lynn Hunt, ed., *The New Cultural History* (Berkeley: University of California Press 1989), 172.

17 See the comments of Terry Eagleton on the 'dynamic' nature of hegemony in *Ideology: An Introduction* (London: Verso 1991), 115.

18 The phrase 'ideological sentinels' comes from Ralph Miliband, *The State in Capitalist Society* (London: Weidenfeld and Nicolson 1969), 190. Miliband was concerned with the issue of legitimation.

19 Michel Foucault, 'Powers and Strategies,' in *Power/Knowledge: Selected Interviews and Other Writings 1972–1977*, ed. Colin Gordon (New York: Pantheon 1980), 142.

20 Thus Gramsci wrote of the escalation of an intellectual struggle 'until the

point is reached where one of them, or at least one combination of them, tends to predominate, to impose itself, to propagate itself throughout the whole social sphere, causing, in addition to singleness of economic and political purpose, an intellectual and moral unity as well, placing all questions around which the struggle rages not on a corporative, but a "universal" plane and creating in this way the hegemony of a fundamental social group over a number of subordinate groups.' *The Modern Prince*, 170.

21 T.J. Jackson Lears, 'The Concept of Cultural Hegemony: Problems and Possibilities,' *American Historical Review* 90, no. 3 (June 1985): 574.

22 *FSPN*, 157.

23 Gramsci, *The Modern Prince*, 183.

24 Williams was thinking of the key agencies, such as the schools, rather than the key means, such as propaganda. Williams, 'Base and Superstructure,' 414.

2 Restoring Order: Nixon's America, Etcetera

1 Paul Messaris, *Visual Literacy: Image, Mind, and Reality* (Boulder, Col.: Westview Press 1994), 106–12.

2 *Order in the United States*, my title by the way, appeared in an ABC News Documentary, 'Lights, Cameras, Politics,' 1980. My thanks to George Kerr for supplying me with this copy.

3 Peter Carroll, *It Seemed Like Nothing Happened: The Tragedy and Promise of America in the 1970s* (New York: Holt, Rinehart and Winston 1982), 5.

4 Discussed in Edwin Diamond and Stephen Bates, *The Spot: The Rise of Political Advertising on Television*, 3rd ed. (Cambridge, Mass.: MIT Press 1992), 139–41.

5 Edward Jay Epstein, *Agency of Fear: Opiates and Political Power in America*, rev. ed. (London: Verso 1990), 38.

6 Quoted in Diamond and Bates, *The Spot*, 196.

7 Quoted in Carroll, *It Seemed Like Nothing Happened*, 88.

8 I am not suggesting that Nixon won simply because of the ideology of order, whether in its domestic or its global expressions. McGovern had proven himself a political incompetent with his mishandling of the Thomas Eagleton affair. Eagleton, the Democrats' vice-presidential nominee, was forced out of the race because of news of his history of mental difficulties. There were other reasons than Nixon's propaganda to reject McGovern.

9 My understanding of the phenomenon of moral panics is derived from Philip Jenkins, *Intimate Enemies: Moral Panics in Contemporary Great Britain*

(New York: Aldine de Gruyter 1992), where he deals with media-created panics of the 1980s.

10 See Michel Foucault, *Discipline and Punish: The Birth of the Prison* (New York: Vintage Books 1979), 271–85, where he talks about the political virtues of delinquency.

11 The sensitizing of the media and the release of figures is discussed in Epstein, *Agency of Fear*, 165–77. Epstein argues that the drug war was really an attempt by Nixon and his team to concentrate power in the White House, to work a kind of *coup d'état* in America.

12 Grey Advertising was so overcome by its sense of mission that it offered all its anti-drug material free to the United Nations to mount a global campaign of salvation. 'Grey Asks United Nations' Support in Globally Expanding Anti-Drug Abuse Drive,' *AA*, 5 October 1970.

13 'Valenstein Plan Helps Students to Learn of Drug Ills,' *AA*, 7 December 1970.

14 See the summary of research findings in Nancy Signorielli, *Mass Media Images and Impact on Health: A Sourcebook* (Westport, Conn.: Greenwood Press 1993), 120.

15 Newspaper and transit ads carried the headline, 'The Biggest Drug Problem in America Is Right in Your Glass There, Kiddo.' John Revett, 'Blue Cross Group Ad Calls Alcohol Main Drug Problem,' *AA*, 12 July 1971, 25.

16 'Illinois Ads Aim to Deglamorize Dope,' *AA*, 10 August 1970, 40.

17 Helping youth help itself was a favourite theme of the project. A New York campaign targeted the eight-to-sixteen-year-olds, both those who were clean and those who had experimented with drugs. It, too, presumed that a youth culture was victimizing the vulnerable. According to spokesperson Mark Strook of Young and Rubicam, 'Our purpose is to give them ammunition and the moral support to hold out.' '"Don't Join the Living Dead" Is Theme of Y&R Drug Ads,' *AA*, 17 April 1972, 72.

18 Consider, for instance, these comments from Paul Ricoeur's *The Symbolism of Evil*, trans. Emerson Buchanan (Boston: Beacon Press 1969): (1) 'What do we think of when with Pettazzoni we define defilement as "an act that involves an evil, an impurity, a fluid, a mysterious and harmful something that acts dynamically – that is to say, magically"?' (25); (2) 'Punishment falls on man in the guise of misfortune and transforms all possible sufferings, all diseases, all death, all failure into a sign of defilement' (27).

19 *Dragnet* was an enormously popular cop series on television in the 1950s and 1960s in which Jack Webb played the leading character, Sgt Joe Friday. Presumably, the hope was that his persona as the instrument of law and order would enhance the credibility of the spot.

20 *Ten Little Indians* is part of the 1972 Cannes collection of award-winning spots. It was one of the civic ads that formed part of the White House-inspired campaign.

21 Indeed, this is an example of an even more extreme variation of othering known as 'abjection,' where what was once part of us is cast out as loathsome to become a source of continuing threat. See Julia Kristeva, *Powers of Horror: An Essay on Abjection*, trans. Leon S. Roudiez (New York: Columbia University Press 1982).

22 He was, of course, excepting the ads of his own agency. '"Don't Join the Living Dead" Is Theme of Y&R Drug Ads,' *AA*, 17 April 1972, 72.

23 See the summary in Charles K. Atkin, 'Mass Media Information Campaign Effectiveness,' in Ronald E. Rice and William J. Paisley, eds, *Public Communication Campaigns* (Beverley Hills, Calif.: Sage 1981), 269.

24 Epstein, *Agency of Fear*, 172.

25 'Polls indicate that in the mid-sixties "major companies" and "big business leaders" enjoyed the confidence of 50 to 60 percent of the American people. That dropped to around 30 percent in 1974 when Watergate, recession, and the energy crisis brought public disillusionment with virtually every institution.' Herbert Waltzer, 'Corporate Advocacy Advertising and Political Influence,' *Public Relations Review* 14 (Spring 1988): 41.

26 'A recent study conducted for the federal government of public attitudes toward the American economic system showed that 56 percent of Americans want more government regulation, while only 35 percent want less. The study found that a great majority of Americans expressed negative attitudes toward the free enterprise system.' S. Prakash Sethi, *Advocacy Advertising and Large Corporations* (Lexington, Mass.: D.C. Heath 1977), 3.

27 The phrase 'accusatory journalism' was coined by Herbert Schmertz of Mobil Oil: cited in *Controversy Advertising: How Advertisers Present Points of View in Public Affairs*, sponsored by the International Advertising Association (New York: Hastings House 1977), 21.

28 O'Toole was then president of Foote, Cone and Belding. He is quoted in International Advertising Association, *Controversy Advertising*, 17.

29 Cited in International Advertising Association, *Controversy Advertising*, 67.

30 Cited in S. Prakash Sethi and Cecilia M. Falbe, *Business and Society: Dimensions of Conflict and Cooperation* (Lexington, Mass.: D.C. Heath 1987), 555. This figure may well be exaggerated, however, since the data were notoriously unreliable.

31 See the brief description of the Mobil vehicles and messages in Bernard Rubin, 'Advocacy, Big Business, and Mass Media,' in his *Big Business and the Mass Media* (Lexington, Mass.: D.C. Heath 1977), 34–5.

32 I base that observation on a reading of a number of advertorials appearing in the *New York Times* in the fall of 1970 and early in 1978, as well as the findings of Gerri Smith and Robert Heath, who analysed eighties ads in 'Moral Appeals in Mobil Oil's Op-Ed Campaign,' *Public Relations Review* 16, no. 4 (Winter 1990): 48–54.

33 These illustrated sheiks sometimes occupied the top half of an ad, although more often they appeared as a small signature at the bottom of the ad.

34 The AEP campaign is discussed at length by Sethi, and he includes all thirty-six of the ads – see his *Advocacy Advertising*, 115–78. Sethi also has a long analysis (complete with some ads) of the aggressive campaign waged by Bethlehem Steel from 1976 to 1979: see *Up against the Corporate Wall: Modern Corporations and Social Issues of the Eighties* (New Jersey: Prentice-Hall 1982), 162–205.

35 This paragraph is based wholly on the chapter in Sethi's *Advocacy Advertising* (179–234), which explores the contest at length. Massive advertising did not always work, however: in Maine in 1976 a referendum was won by the advocates of returnable bottles, even though the opposition spent heavily. See Rubin, 'Advocacy,' 10.

36 A series of interviews with senior management conducted by the research team for the International Advertising Association's *Controversy Advertising* (58) concluded that there were four reasons for the bias towards newspapers: a desire for 'long verbal clarifications,' the preference for a 'dignified environment,' the hope that the ad would take on 'the appearance of news,' and a discomfort with 'vivid illustrations.'

37 In ads entitled *U.S. Coal Reserves* and *Dinosaur*, respectively, both 1975 vintage. The former played around with a map of the world, one that represented the relative holdings of oil and coal, which showed a swollen United States and a tiny Arabia when the deposits of coal were represented. Chevron's ad was an animated history lesson of oil, from the dinosaur to you, in which a voice-over offered this bit of drivel: 'No, we're plumb out of dinosaurs, pterodactyls, and the like, and it doesn't look like they're coming back. So don't waste. The next time you jump in your car, remember some prehistoric creature gave his or her all for that tank of gas. So go easy, and America's energy will go a lot further.'

38 David Paletz, Roberta Pearson, and Donald Willis, *Politics in Public Service Advertising on Television* (New York: Praeger 1977), 17.

39 John Revett, 'Business Sees No Ill Effects from Ford Anti-inflation Plan,' *AA*, 21 October 1974.

40 'WIN Themes Abound as Admen Heed Ford's Plea,' *AA*, 18 November 1974.

41 Cited in Paletz et al., *Politics in Public Service Advertising*, 16.
42 'Ad Council Campaign to Stress Productivity,' *AA*, 6 August 1973, 2.
43 Witness this finding: 'Across all groups, the study states, Americans typically consider government intervention as the way to correct what they don't like in the economy. For every three respondents who think there isn't enough government regulation there are about two who complain of over-regulation. The study cites an "ambivalence" toward big business among respondents. Economies of production scale are appreciated by 45%, and big industries' job creation is lauded by 30%. Yet "big business" is adjudged to have monopolistic tendencies [40%], excessive political power, especially over taxes [19%], and power to dictate prices [17%].' Bob Donath, 'Ad Council Sets Economics Ads,' *AA*, 4 August 1975, 39.
44 Cited in Paletz et al., *Politics in Public Service Advertising*, 1. The initial suggestion had been made by Howard J. Morgens, of Procter and Gamble, in a speech to the Ad Council in 1973. 'Mr. Morgens urged that the council and business "do whatever we can to make sure that this miraculous business system of ours is not gradually crippled by a public and a Congress who do not understand it. We can do this only by educating the public about how this system works," said Mr. Morgens.' John Revett, 'Congressman Rips U.S. Funding,' *AA*, 4 August 1975, 39.
45 'Ad Council Sees Record "Economic System" Effort,' *AA*, 14 June 1976.
46 See these reports: 'Counter-unit to Confront Ad Council Push on Economics,' *AA*, 19 January 1976; 'Another Group Out with Economic Education Ads,' *AA*, 27 September 1976; 'Economics Ads Get NBC Green Light,' *AA*, 2 August 1976.
47 Karen Fox and Bobby Calder, 'The Right Kind of Business Advocacy,' *Business Horizons* 28 (January–February 1985): 9.
48 Less than ten years later, however, yet another productivity campaign was underway in the United States. See 'Fifteen Associations Join Council's Productivity Push,' *Association Management* 36 (August 1984): 19–20.
49 Cited in International Advertising Association, *Controversy Advertising*, 50. I should add that some corporate advocates were equally uninterested in debate: a spokesperson admitted that Bethlehem Steel 'usually (almost always) ignore our opponent's arguments.' Cited in Sethi, *Up against the Corporate Wall*, 163.
50 Cited in Paletz et al., *Politics in Public Service Advertising*, 53.
51 See Todd Gitlin, *The Whole World Is Watching: Mass Media in the Making and Unmaking of the New Left* (Berkeley: University of California Press 1980). As Gitlin points out, however, the public significance of the New Left was also in some sense the creation of the news media.

52 Roger Hickey, Public Media Center's Washington director. Cited in 'Another Group out with Economic Education Ads,' *AA*, 27 September 1976, 6.

53 John Revett, 'FEA Blasts Ad Council, C&W for Turning Down Anti-oil Ads,' *AA*, 16 June 1975, 1, 85.

54 The National Association of Broadcasters actually took out ads in the *Washington Post* and *Star News*, on 23 January 1973: 'If everyone who disagrees with a television commercial were given free time to put on his own "counter commercial," then television's towers would turn into modern-day Towers of Babel, transmitting countless claims and counter-claims to bewildered viewers at home. The result: chaos. The television system we have today would disintegrate.' Cited in Paletz et al., *Politics in Public Service Advertising*, 51. And this comment: 'Each such advocacy announcement would automatically set the stage for an opposing point of view or counter claim,' wrote Ad Council Washington vice-president Lewis Shollenberger. 'In turn, the opposing "point of view" would encourage a rejoinder, a "counter-counter claim," and so on ad infinitum, releasing a veritable tower of Babel from a myriad of interested parties ...' Cited in 'FCC Warned Re Ad Council Ad Time Limits,' *AA*, 2 August 1976, 43.

55 Louis L. Jaffe, 'The Editorial Responsibility of the Broadcaster: Reflections on Fairness and Access,' *Harvard Law Review* 85, no 4 (February 1972): 779.

56 Discussed in Steven J. Simmons, *The Fairness Doctrine and the Media* (Berkeley: University of California Press 1978), 102–45.

57 There was one partial exception, however: the FCC did allow a complaint by the United People of Dayton, Ohio, against United Way PSAs, on grounds that suggested that the United Way was controversial because of its corporate connections and funding policies. Noted in Paletz et al., *Politics in Public Service Advertising*, 106.

58 As a result the offending station, WNBC, did broadcast some anti-pollution messages.

59 Cited in Milan D, Meeske, 'Editorial Advertising and the First Amendment,' *Journal of Broadcasting*, 17, no. 4 (Fall 1973): 422.

60 'The print and broadcast ads were cited for alleged misleading claims about energy crisis causes and environmental effects of corporate activities.' 'FTC Won't Act Against Energy, Corporate Ads,' *AA*, 5 May 1975, 6. A few years later, a consistent foe of Big Oil, Senator James Abourezk (South Dakota), used his position on the Senate Judiciary Subcommittee on Administrative Practice and Procedure to get samples of corporate advocacy from oil companies and their agencies, as well as to investigate what actions, if any, federal agencies were taking to police this kind of speech. See Richard

Gordon, 'Senate Panel Subpoenas Oil Companies' Image Ad Data,' *AA*, 3 April 1978.

61 Richard Gordon, 'Corporate Ads Get High Court Boost,' *AA*, 1 May 1978. The decision and its consequences have been critically assessed in Herbert Schiller's *Culture Inc.: The Corporate Takeover of Public Expression* (New York: Oxford 1989), 46–65.

62 Seymour Martin Lipset and William Schneider, *The Confidence Gap: Business, Labor, and Government in the Public Mind*, rev. ed. (Baltimore: Johns Hopkins University Press 1987). First published in 1983.

63 Paul Ricoeur, *The Symbolism of Evil* (Boston: Beacon Press 1969), 43.

3 Governing Affluence: The First World in the Seventies

1 *Searching* won an International Broadcasting Award in 1976, though under the title 'Fire Prevention,' and is part of the IBA collection for that year.

2 The Conference Board of Canada sponsored the conference, held in Toronto in November 1981, and an edited version of the proceedings was published under the title *Advocacy Advertising: Propaganda or Democratic Right*, ed. Duncan McDowell (A Report from the Public Affairs Research Division of the Conference Board of Canada, May 1982).

3 These campaigns have been defined as 'purposive attempts to inform, persuade, or motivate behavior changes in a relatively well-defined and large audience, generally for noncommercial benefits to the individuals and/or society, typically within a given time period, by means of organized communication activities involving mass media and often complemented by interpersonal support ...' Ronald Rice and Charles Atkin, eds, *Public Communication Campaigns* 2nd ed. (Newbury Park, Calif.: Sage 1989), 7.

4 Lawrence Wallack, 'Mass Communication and Health Promotion: A Critical Perspective,' in Rice and Atkin, eds, *Public Communication Campaigns*, 354.

5 Cited in Philip Kotler and Eduardo Roberto, *Social Marketing: Strategies for Changing Public Behavior* (New York: Macmillan 1989), 222.

6 This 'revolution' has been discussed at length in Thomas Frank, *The Conquest of Cool: Business Culture, Counterculture, and the Rise of Hip Consumerism* (Chicago: University of Chicago Press 1997).

7 *Pistol*, Drug Abuse Information, U.S.A., NMPFTV, 1971; *Life Jacket*, Workmen's Compensation Board of British Columbia, Canada, Bessies 1973; *Human Bomb*, National Heart Foundation, Australia, Cannes 1977; *The Difference*, Central Office of Information, U.K., Cannes 1978.

8 See, for example, this international mix of downbeat images: *S.O.S. Bretagne* (water pollution), Croix Rouge Française, Cannes 1978; *The Hangover*, Alco-

hol Information, Finland, IBA 1973; *Nothing, Closer Look* (child disability), U.S.A., IBA 1977; *Broken Bottles,* Seat Belt Campaign, U.K., NMPFTV 1974; *Schoolroom,* United Negro College Fund, U.S.A., Ad Council 1975.

9 It is worth noting, however, that British parties had employed ad agencies well before the late 1970s. For example, Barry Day, a British admaker who volunteered his services for the Tories in 1970, had been much impressed by the *Daisy* commercial and tried to use American techniques to promote the Conservative party of the day. See Ivan Fallon, *The Brothers: The Rise and Rise of Saatchi and Saatchi* (London: Hutchinson 1988), 152.

10 See Anthony Thorncroft, 'Conservatives Anything But in Ads,' *AA,* 21 August 1978, 65, and Camille Elebash, 'The Americanization of British Political Communications,' *Journal of Advertising* 13, no. 3 (1984): 53. The charge was made that the unemployed were actors or Saatchi and Saatchi employees. According to Fallon, they were in fact Young Conservatives from South Hendon. *The Brothers,* 159.

11 'U.S. Strategists Vie for Venezuelan Vote,' *Advertising Age International,* 13 November 1978, 125, 135.

12 Here are the sources of the commercials: *Cookie Monster, V.D. Is for Everybody, Get off Your Rocker, Faces* – Clios 1976; *Drinking Bird* – Bessies 1976; *Aging Man, Walkies, The Surprise, How Could I Tell You, Who's Master* – Cannes (respectively 1978, 1978, 1981, 1981, 1982); and *The Hang Over* – IBA 1976.

13 Bernard Rubin, 'Advocacy, Big Business, and Mass Media,' in his *Big Business and the Mass Media* (Lexington, Mass.: D.C. Heath 1977), 48.

14 International Advertising Association, *Controversy Advertising* (New York: Hastings House 1977), 26.

15 Ibid., 29.

16 Cited in Phil Ryan, 'Miniature Mila and Flying Geese: Government Advertising and Canadian Democracy,' in Susan Philips, ed., *How Ottawa Spends, 1995–96* (Ottawa: Carleton University Press 1995), 266.

17 Cited in Edward Said, *The World, the Text, and the Critic* (Cambridge, Mass.: Harvard University Press 1983), 173. The Trilateral Commission was an international organization of important people – businessmen, politicians, lawyers – constituted in 1973 by David Rockefeller of the Chase Manhattan bank. See Peter Carroll, *It Seemed Like Nothing Happened: The Tragedy and Promise of America in the 1970s* (New York: Holt, Rinehart and Winston 1982), 134.

18 American and Canadian statistics from Patrick Boyer, 'Government Advertising: Some Wheat, Too Much Chaff,' *Business Quarterly* 47 (December 1982): 35–6. British statistics from Torin Douglas, 'The High Price of a Low Profile,' *The Times* (London), 11 December 1984. Thereafter, government

advertising declined, estimated at about £20 million in 1979–80 – see Tony
Dawe and Sheila Gunn, 'Government Gives Away £4 Billion in Three
Weeks,' *The Times* (London), 6 March 1992.

19 Cited in Phil Ryan, 'Miniature Mila and Flying Geese,' 266–7.

20 Ibid., 267.

21 This now conventional wisdom was evident in the comments of such Liberals as Jean-Jacques Blais, Jim Fleming, and Gerald Regan, all in 1981. See,
respectively, Mark Smyka, 'Feds Now Convinced of Ad Power,' *Marketing*,
11 May 1981; 'Gov't. Not Guilty of Using Advocacy Ads to Sway the Public,
Fleming,' *Marketing*, 13 July 1981; and Regan's speech in McDowell, ed.,
Advocacy Advertising, 37–42.

22 'Gov't. Not Guilty of Using Advocacy Ads to Sway the Public, Fleming.'

23 'If Governments in the affluent 1960s dealt with economic and social problems by throwing money at them through various ad hoc programs, today,
as those same governments approach insolvency, the programs are being
scrapped (in the name of restraint) and money is instead thrown to the ad
agencies to convince us that the problems do not exist, or at least are about
to disappear. By the fall of 1982, the Federal Liberal ads told us: "Energy
self-sufficiency? It is this close." Translation: our recent energy "crisis" is
virtually over. Phew!' Boyer, 'Government Advertising,' 34.

24 Francis Phillips, 'Ad Critics Have Go at Ottawa,' *Financial Post*, 15 May 1982,
16.

25 Those unfamiliar with poststructuralist and postmodernist terminology may
wonder about the use of words such as 'reading' and 'text' to refer to the
practices of interpretation or to a television commercial. The terminology
betrays the origins of these approaches in literary and linguistic theory.
This devotion to literary metaphors can become inappropriate to an understanding of audiovisual phenomena. However, I will conform to the usages
common in this interpretive discourse.

26 Mark Poster, *The Mode of Information: Poststructuralism and Social Context*
(Chicago: University of Chicago Press 1990), esp. ch. 2, 'Baudrillard and
TV Ads,' 43–68.

27 I have used extensively the excellent list of concepts and definitions in Irena
Makaryk, ed., *Encyclopedia of Contemporary Literary Theory: Approaches, Scholars,
Terms* (Toronto: University of Toronto Press 1993), hereafter *ECLT*, as a
guide to postmodern critique. I have supplemented this source with a set of
definitions provided in Tim O'Sullivan, John Hartley, Danny Saunders,
Martin Montgomery, and John Fiske, *Key Concepts in Communication and
Cultural Studies* (London: Routledge 1994), hereafter *KCCCS*.

28 Douglas Kellner, 'Marxist Criticism,' *ECLT*, 98. This discussion also reflects

Terry Eagleton's discussion of 'ideological strategies' in *Ideology: An Introduction* (London: Verso 1991), 45–61.

29 Priscilla Walton, 'Totalization,' *ECLT*, 646. See also Fredric Jameson, *The Political Unconscious: Narrative as a Socially Symbolic Act* (Ithaca, N.Y.: Cornell University Press 1981), 26–8 and 50–7.

30 Cannes 1978.

31 Sheldon Zitner, 'Universals,' *ECLT*, 649, and Gordon Slethaug, 'Centre/decentre,' *ECLT*, 518–20.

32 David Paletz, Roberta Pearson, and Donald Willis, *Politics in Public Service Advertising on Television* (New York: Praeger 1977), 79.

33 Clios 1976.

34 Nathalie Cooke, 'Closure/dis-closure,' *ECLT*, 522–4. See also John Hartley, 'Closure,' *KCCCS*, 42–3.

35 Barbara Godard, 'Intertextuality,' *ECLT*, 568–71.

36 Venice International Awards 1972.

37 See these *ECLT* entries: John Thurston, 'Louis Althusser,' 230–1; Ross King, 'Interpellation,' 566–7; and John Thurston, 'Ideological State Apparatuses,' 558. There is a more critical appraisal in John Hartley's 'Interpellation,' *KCCCS*, 155–6.

38 Herbert Marcuse, *One-Dimensional Man: Studies in the Ideology of Advanced Industrial Society*, 2nd ed. (Boston: Beacon Press 1991), 92. Marcuse was particularly interested in 'you' and 'your.'

39 *Max*, NMPFTV; *Carol*, Cannes 1973.

40 The ad won the Gold Bessie in 1973.

41 Cannes 1979.

42 *Confrontation*, Ad Council; *Good Housekeeping* and *Uncle Joe*, NMPFTV; Exxon campaign, Clios 1976; *Brand Labels (Tiger)*, IBA 1980.

43 Danny Saunders, 'Frame,' *KCCCS*, 122–3.

44 *Grandpa's Oil Lamp*, *Swimming Pool*, *Dolls*, Cannes 1978, 1979; *Spoon*, Bessies 1976.

45 Danny Saunders, 'Displacement,' *KCCCS*, 95–6.

46 *Sewing Machine*, *National Drinking Game*, *Two Georges*, Cannes 1972, 1973, 1978; *Jim Ryun*, *Merry-Go-Round*, Ad Council.

47 The discussion of the nature of the KAB in the 1970s is derived from information in Paletz et al., *Politics in Public Service Advertising*, 17–18.

48 An early KAB effort certainly tried to remind Americans of that fact. It introduces a saccharine character called Susan Spotless who instructs her father, in the shadow of the Statue of Liberty, to pick up his litter. 'Every litter bit hurts,' apparently. The hope was that Susan Spotless would match Smokey Bear in popularity. She didn't. Ad Council 1962.

49 See *Don't Pass on Responsibility* (1982), a moral drama from Japan's Advertising Council. A discarded can is kicked around and around a public coach, until an attractive pair of female legs gets up, walks over, kicks the object, which is then picked up by a hand and placed in the garbage. All this action provides the opportunity for the voice-over to cajole people to recognize their responsibility to get rid of trash.

50 An animated spot called *Garbage* (the Gold Bessie 1969), sponsored by Ontario's Department of Highways, shows a cad who chucks his garbage out of the car while driving. But authority has the last word: along comes a truck and buries him, his car, and his driveway under a ton of trash. A succession of people toss out their litter in a later British ad (*My One Little Wrapper*, NMPFTV 1973) – a woman in a car, a child on a city street, a boy throwing a bottle into a stream, a father flinging a can into a bush – all declaring, 'My one little wrapper can't do any harm.' But it does: the camera suddenly shows a sea of litter and then moves out to reveal a city street that has been completely trashed. Litterbugs are denounced as a 'selfish minority.'

51 See *The Gleaners* (1979): This Japanese effort opens on Jean François Millet's painting *The Gleaners* (1857). The camera narrows its focus until it reveals a pop can under the hand of one of the figures. Then the action switches to a classy living-room where the can flies into a trash container. The slogan (translated): 'Your Town. Beautiful Town.' Cannes 1980.

52 The ad forms part of the Ad Council collection, and it was also available on the Web at *www.ktb.org/psa.htm*, the site of the Texas branch of the KAB, in March 1999. Chief Iron Eyes Cody retained his fame as a naturalist. He died in January 1999.

53 Cited in *The Waste Stream Journal* (Spring 1998), available on the Web site of the Georgia Department of Community Affairs, in March 1999. Cody's image had been used in a new PSA from Keep Texas Beautiful.

54 Ibid.

55 'A tidal wave of federal advertising inundated Québec in the days preceding the referendum. Ads urged Québec drinkers to say "Non, merci." [A 'non' vote in the referendum meant 'oui' to Canada.] Ads reminded Québec tourists that the Rocky Mountains provided 'so much to stay for.' During one hour of a widely viewed tennis championship on CFTM, a private French-language station in Montréal, federal ads appeared nine times: at 2:04, the Department of Energy, Mines and Resources; at 2:08, Customs; at 2:15, an ad urging people to buy Canadian; at 2:17, the Department of Regional Economic Expansion; at 2:37, Health and Welfare; at 2:41, Energy, Mines and Resources (again); at 2:51, Public Works; at 2:53,

Energy, Mines and Resources (yet a third time); at 2:58, a tourism ad.'
Morris Wolfe, 'The Case against Advocacy Advertising,' *Saturday Night*
(December 1980, 17).

56 The saccharine ad is preserved by the NMPFTV.

57 The case is discussed in Kotler and Roberto, *Social Marketing*, 102.

58 Cannes 1978.

59 Cannes 1979.

60 *Amnesty International* (Cannes 1977). The words of the announcer are telling: 'All over the world, one million people are imprisoned on account of
their political or religious convictions. Amnesty International fights for the
rights of these people, for decent human conditions in prisons, for the
abolition of torture and maltreatment, and above all for the release of these
prisoners. To date Amnesty International has helped more than 8,000
people to gain their freedom.' [Sounds of gunfire, Sound of a dog barking.]
'Help us to help all victims of gross injustice.' 'Amnesty International for
human rights.'

61 Eagleton, *Ideology*, 5–6.

*Foucault: Discipline

1 In fact, that is a comparatively modest claim. Witness this comment by Alan
Ryan in a review of three books about Foucault's life: 'When Michel
Foucault died in June 1984, he was the most famous intellectual figure in
the world.' 'Foucault's Life and Hard Times,' *New York Review of Books*,
8 April 1993, 12. Similarly, a contemporary, Gilles Deleuze, was no less
unstinting: 'Foucault's thought seems to me one of the greatest of modern
philosophies.' Cited in Didier Eribon, *Michel Foucault*, trans. Betsy Wing
(Cambridge, Mass.: Harvard University Press 1991), 4.

2 One list counted nearly 300 publications authored by Foucault, many of
which had been translated into English. James Bernauer and Thomas
Keenan, 'The Works of Michel Foucault 1954–1984,' in James Bernauer
and David Rasmussen, eds, *The Final Foucault* (Cambridge, Mass.: MIT Press
1994), 119–58.

3 There is a very interesting attempt to apply this Foucauldian apparatus to
the analysis of one climactic event in history: see Keith Michael Baker, 'A
Foucauldian French Revolution?' in Jan Goldstein, ed., *Foucault and the
Writing of History* (Oxford: Basil Blackwell 1994), 187–205.

4 'I am far from being a theoretician of power.' 'I am not developing a theory
of power.' 'Critical Theory / Intellectual History,' in Michel Foucault,
Politics Philosophy Culture: Interviews and Other Writings, 1977–1984, ed. Law-

rence D. Kritzman; trans. Alan Sheridan et al. (New York: Routledge 1990), 39. But Foucault loved to play coy when it came to his own achievements or purposes. Critics have simply presumed that his explorations do constitute a distinct theory of power. See, for example, Axel Honneth, *The Critique of Power: Reflective Stages in a Critical Social Theory*, trans. Kenneth Baynes (Cambridge, Mass.: MIT Press 1991) and the essays in Michael Kelly, ed., *Critique and Power: Recasting the Foucault/Habermas Debate* (Cambridge, Mass.: MIT Press 1994).

5 Michel Foucault, 'Truth and Power,' in *Power/Knowledge: Selected Interviews and Other Writings, 1972–1977*, ed. Colin Gordon (New York: Pantheon Books 1980), 119.

6 Michel Foucault, 'Power and Strategies,' in *Power/Knowledge*, 142.

7 The Vintage Books edition appeared in February 1979, trans. Alan Sheridan and published in New York by Random House (Penguin Books had published an earlier English edition in Great Britain). But the translated title could not capture the emphasis on the visible embodied in the French original *Surveiller et Punir*, which was published by Editions Gallimard in Paris in 1975.

8 This argument had been prefigured in 'The Birth of the Asylum,' a chapter in Foucault's first major work, *Madness and Civilization: A History of Insanity in the Age of Reason*, trans. Richard Howard (New York: Vintage Books 1988), 241–78.

9 Michel Foucault, 'Two Lectures,' in *Power/Knowledge*, 105.

10 Suggested by Laura Engelstein, 'Combined Underdevelopment: Discipline and the Law in Imperial and Soviet Russia,' in Goldstein, ed., *Foucault and the Writing of History*, 220.

11 Cited in Roger Chartier, 'The Chimera of the Origin: Archaeology, Cultural History, and the French Revolution,' in Goldstein, ed., *Foucault and the Writing of History*, 182.

12 Michel Foucault, *Discipline and Punish: The Birth of the Prison* (New York: Vintage Books 1979), 183.

13 Ibid., 211 and 304.

14 Once again the translation of the title was not exact: it had been originally published in 1976 as *La volenté de savoir*.

15 Michel Foucault, *The History of Sexuality. Volume I: An Introduction*, trans. Robert Hurley (New York: Vintage Books 1990), 139–45.

16 Cited in Colin Gordon, 'Government Rationality: An Introduction,' in Graham Burchell, Colin Gordon, and Peter Miller, eds, *The Foucault Effect: Studies in Governmentality* (Chicago: University of Chicago Press 1991), 1.

17 In 1979 Foucault delivered the Tanner Lectures on Human Values at

Stanford University. The title was 'Omnes et Singulatim: Towards a Criticism of Political Reason.' These have been reproduced as 'Politics and Reason' in *Politics Philosophy Culture*, 57–85.

18 Michel Foucault, 'Governmentality,' in *The Foucault Effect*, 102. See Peter Miller and Nikolas Rose, 'Governing Economic Life,' in Mike Gane and Jerry Johnson, eds, *Foucault's New Domains* (London: Routledge 1993), 75–103, for an extended application of Foucault's approach to the British experience in the late twentieth century.

19 Foucault, 'Truth and Power,' 131.

20 Ibid., 132.

21 On the global expansion of this sector, see Lester M. Salamon, 'The Rise of the Nonprofit Sector,' *Foreign Affairs* 73, no. 4: (July/August 1994): 109–22.

22 See, for example, Lawrence Wallack, 'Improving Health Promotion: Media Advocacy and Social Marketing Approaches,' in Charles Atkin and Lawrence Wallack, eds, *Mass Communication and Public Health: Complexities and Conflicts* (Newbury Park, Calif.: Sage 1990), 147–63.

23 Cited in Lenore Skenazy, 'Ads with a Special Payoff,' *AA*, 26 June 1989.

24 Van Wallach, 'Matters of Survival,' *AA*, 9 November 1988.

25 Michael Aymong, vice-president corporate affairs of General Mills, then involved with the Concerned Children's Advertisers in Canada. Cited in Jim McElgunn, 'Ad Industry Helps Fight War on Drugs,' *Marketing's Creativity* (24 September 1990).

26 See 'Broadcasters Take Offensive with Drug, Alcohol PSA Campaign,' *Broadcasting*, 29 October 1984; 'PSAs against Drunk Driving Provided by NAB,' *Broadcasting*, 10 December 1984; 'TV Stations Mount Strong Campaigns against Overdrinking,' *Television/Radio Age*, 27 May 1985; and 'Beer-Wine Strategy Moves to Counterads,' *Broadcasting*, 27 May 1985.

27 Which is a play on a phrase that crops up in Foucault's work about politics or power as war by other means, itself a reversal of Clausewitz's assertion about war. See, for example, *Discipline and Punish*, 168; 'Two Lectures,' 90; or 'Truth and Power,' 123.

28 Foucault, *Discipline and Punish*, 170.

29 'A body is docile that may be subjected, used, transformed, and improved.' Ibid., 136.

4 Healthy Bodies, or the New Paranoia

1 Two items for the record. First, I am no longer a cigarette smoker, nor do I have shares in any tobacco firm. Second, I am fully aware of the fact that the tobacco companies have sponsored their own junk science to counter

the hysteria of the anti-smoking crusade. Indeed, that is the point: a further indication of how marketing has infected public discourse.

2 Ann Pederson, Michel O'Neill, and Irving Rootman, *Health Promotion in Canada: Provincial, National and International Perspectives* (Toronto: W.B. Saunders Canada 1994). A claim that health promotion represents a 'postmodern' challenge or style of knowledge occurs in the summary article by the three editors, 'Beyond Lalonde: Two Decades of Canadian Health Promotion,' 382 and 385.

3 Nancy Signorielli, *Mass Media Images and Impact on Health: A Sourcebook* (Westport, Conn.: Greenwood Press 1993), ix.

4 Deborah Cohen, 'Promoting the Health of the Nation,' *New Scientist* (13 May 1989): 50–5.

5 See, for example, Ron Labonté, 'Death of Program, Birth of Metaphor: The Development of Health Promotion in Canada,' in Pederson, O'Neill, and Rootman, eds, *Health Promotion in Canada*, 72–90; Lawrence Wallack, 'Mass Communication and Health Promotion: A Critical Perspective,' in Ronald E. Rice and Charles K. Atkin, eds; *Public Communication Campaigns*, 2nd ed. (Newbury Park, Calif.: Sage 1989), 353–67; and Lawrence Wallack, 'Improving Health Promotion: Media Advocacy and Social Marketing Approaches,' in Charles Atkin and Lawrence Wallack, eds; *Mass Communication and Public Health: Complexities and Conflicts* (Newbury Park, Calif.: Sage 1990), 147–63.

6 Lalonde Report cited in Labonté, 'Death of Program,' 75; the American government cited in Cohen, 'Promoting the Health,' 51.

7 Michel O'Neill and Ann Pederson, 'Two Analytical Paths for Understanding Canadian Developments in Health Promotion,' in Pederson, O'Neill, and Rootman, eds, *Health Promotion in Canada*, 50.

8 In America it was not only the anti-drug and the anti-AIDS campaigns which took on the status of wars. In January 1989 the American Medical Association proudly announced its 'Campaign against Cholesterol,' which it labelled a 'war on one of America's leading killers' that could justify efforts to 'blitz the public and physicians with ads, brochures, TV programming, and a cholesterol reduction book.' Cited in Philip Kotler and Eduardo L. Roberto, *Social Marketing: Strategies for Changing Public Behavior* (New York: Macmillan 1989), 4.

9 The Health Promotion Directorate had been established in 1977, supposedly the first of its kind. In 1987–8 the unit's budget was nearly tripled, at a time when other government agencies faced austerity, because it had to mount social-marketing projects to combat drugs, impaired driving, and AIDS. See Lavada Pinder, 'The Federal Role in Health Promotion: The Art

of the Possible,' in Pederson, O'Neill, and Rootman, eds, *Health Promotion in Canada*, 100. Pinder had been director general (1987–92) of the directorate.

10 That description appears in a published paper by Eric Young, the director of Manifest Communications Inc., a business which engaged in social marketing. The paper was part of a Health Canada collection entitled *Social Marketing in Health Promotion* (January 1994).

11 The French versions were, respectively, 'Fumer, c'est fini' and 'Drogues, pas besoin.' The following description of these campaigns is based on two self-publications, Health and Welfare Canada, *Making a Difference: The Impact of the Health Promotion Directorate's Social Marketing Campaigns (1987–1991)* and Health Canada, *Making a Difference II: The Impact of the Health Promotion Directorate's Social Marketing Campaigns 1991–1992*. It should be noted that these were not the only campaigns of the directorate. It was also involved in an assault on impaired driving, though that had been merged with the anti-drug campaign in 1992, and a campaign on diet and exercise.

12 An earlier anti-smoking campaign, called 'Freedom Gained,' also employed the soft sell: see Rob Wilson, 'Anti-smoking Ads Try a Soft-sell Approach,' *Marketing* (21 June 1982).

13 This is based on a planning document, entitled *Social Marketing Campaign to Support the Tobacco Demand Reduction Strategy*, prepared for Health Canada by McKim Communications Ltd, Winnipeg, 15 November 1994. The campaign did run in the media in 1995, but the plans for an ongoing, massive effort were eventually undone by the priority of deficit fighting.

14 Cited in Lawrence Wallack, 'Mass Media Campaigns: The Odds against Finding Behavior Change,' *Health Education Quarterly* 8, no. 3 (Fall 1981): 232. Johnson was referring specifically to the selling of over-the-counter drugs.

15 One American study found that after doctors and dentists, television was the chief source of health information. Cited in Lawrence Wallack, eds, 'Mass Media and Health Promotion: Promise, Problem, and Challenge,' in Atkin and Wallack, eds, *Mass Communication and Public Health*, 43. See also Wallack, 'Mass Communication and Health Promotion: A Critical Perspective,' in Rice and Atkin, eds, *Public Communication Campaigns*, 362–3.

16 Rina Alcalay and Shahnaz Taplin, 'Community Health Campaigns: From Theory to Action,' in Rice and Atkin, eds, *Public Communication Campaigns*, 115. The ad won the overall campaign the attention of newspapers.

17 See Nancy Signorielli, 'Television and Health: Images and Impact,' in Atkin and Wallack, eds, *Mass Communication and Public Health*, 96–113, and Nancy Signorielli, *Mass Media Images and Impact on Health*.

18 'An effective PSA is more likely to intrude upon individuals' perceptual barriers than a lengthy article in a magazine or an entire broadcast program devoted to health-related issues.' Alan J. Bush and Gregory W. Boller, 'Rethinking the Role of Television Advertising during Health Crises: A Rhetorical Analysis of the Federal AIDS Campaigns,' *Journal of Advertising* 20, no. 1 (1991): 30.

19 To be precise, 43.5 per cent – David Paletz, Roberta Pearson, and Donald Willis, *Politics in Public Service Advertising on Television* (New York: Praeger 1977), 69.

20 Cited in Richard K. Manoff, *Social Marketing: New Imperative for Public Health* (New York: Praeger 1985), 7.

21 'Birth Control Film Banned by IBA,' *The Times*, 11 May 1983. The struggle over the use of words like 'contraceptive' and 'condom' was even more heated in America: 'Birth Control PSAs,' *Television/Radio Age*, 11 November 1985, 73; 'OB/GYNs Overcome Media Opposition to Public Information Campaign,' *Association Management* 38 (January 1986): 14; 'Censors "Do It" to Teen Pregnancy Spots but PSAs Finally Get on Network TV,' *Television/ Radio Age*, 11 July 1988, 20.

22 Joe Mandese, 'PSAs: Too Many Issues, Not Enough Time,' *AdWeek's Marketing Week*, 18 May 1987, 52 and 56.

23 So one survey found that, on ABC, prime time PSA time fell from an hourly average of twenty-two seconds in May 1992 to three seconds in May 1996. Apparently, the drop-off occurred when broadcasters were no longer required to report the amount of time given to PSAs at licence-renewal time. See reports in *AA*, 17 March 1997, 8; and 12 May 1997, 3 and 87.

24 For a lengthy discussion of British efforts to alter the bad reputation of condoms, see Paul Jobing, 'Keeping Mrs. Dawson Busy: Safe Sex, Gender and Pleasure in Condom Advertising since 1970,' in Mica Nava, Andrew Blake, Iain MacRury, and Barry Richards, eds, *Buy This Book: Studies in Advertising and Consumption* (London: Routledge 1997), 157–77.

25 Cited in Cecilia Reed, 'Partners for Life,' *AA*, 9 November 1988, 122.

26 Re Ketchum: David Kalish, 'When the Subject Is Sex,' *Marketing and Media Decisions* 21 (October 1986): 32; re Ontario: James Pollock, 'AIDS Ads Come out of the Closet,' *Marketing*, 16 March 1992; re France: *Globe and Mail* (Toronto), 10 August 1994.

27 *Dos Pechos*, Cannes 1994 and *Stay*, NMPFTV 1988.

28 'Tough Messages Hit Drunk Drivers Worldwide,' *AA*, 15 August 1983.

29 'In sum, a fear appeal is most effective when (1) it *scares* the hell out of people, (2) it offers a *specific recommendation* for overcoming the fear-arousing

threat, (3) the recommended action is perceived as effective for reducing the threat, and (4) the message recipient believes that he or she *can* perform the recommended action.' Anthony Pratkanis and Elliot Aronson, *Age of Propaganda: The Everyday Use and Abuse of Persuasion* (New York: W.H. Freeman 1991), 165.

30 Health Canada, *Social Marketing in Health Promotion*, 105.

31 IS 1995.

32 See Leslie Papp, 'Emotional Ads Target Carnage on Roads,' *Toronto Star*, 21 June 1994.

33 *Honeymoon*, Cannes 1973; *Use Your Seat Belt*, Cannes 1985; *The Evil Effects of Drinking*, Cannes 1990.

34 *Prevention*, Cannes 1988; *Tracing*, NMPFTV; *Car* and *Roof*, both for the National Institute of Drug Abuse and the Department of Health and Human Services, Ad Council; *Love*, Cannes 1988.

35 The two *Truth* ads from Cannes 1995.

36 Clios 1996.

37 IBA 1985.

38 The Vogt comment is from William F. Gloede, 'Antismoking Ads Ill-conceived?' *AA*, 17 December 1984.

39 Noted in Brian R. Flay and Dee Burton, 'Effective Mass Communication Strategies for Health Campaigns,' in Atkin and Wallack, eds, *Mass Communication and Public Health*, 133.

40 IS 1993.

41 *Baby*, Cannes 1986; *Dave*, BTAA 1996; *The Dive*, Cannes 1994; *Marionette*, Cannes 1986.

42 IS 1989.

43 'Anti-AIDS Ads Have Youths Saying Yes to Condoms,' *Marketing*, 24/31 December 1990.

44 Michael S. LaTour and Robert E. Pitts, 'Using Fear Appeals in Advertising for AIDS Prevention in the College-Age Population,' *Journal of Health Care Marketing* 9, no. 3 (September 1989): 10.

45 *Quick Time*, Bessies 1994; *One Is No One*, Cannes 1987; *Faces*, Cannes 1988; *Control* and *Dummy*, NMPFTV.

46 Cited in Martin Davidson, *The Consumerist Manifesto: Advertising in Postmodern Times* (London: Routledge 1992), 155–60.

47 IS 1988.

48 Ad Council 1988 and 1987.

49 The Centers for Disease Control in the United States sponsored *Parents/ Kids* (1992), in which a smoking father is shown playing with his boy. What changes the meaning of this happy scene is a sudden cut to a different

screen: 'CHILDREN EXPOSED TO SECONDHAND SMOKE HAVE NICOTINE IN THEIR URINE.' BEST 1993.

50 Cited in J.P. Pierce et al., *Tobacco Use in California: An Evaluation of the To-bacco Control Program, 1989–93* (La Jolla, Calif.: University of California, San Diego 1994), 20.

51 This quotation from the script of the ad is cited in Bob Garfield, 'AdReviews,' *AA*, 16 April 1990.

52 The controversy was highlighted in the *Los Angeles Times*, 14 October 1994, and covered on the Mother Jones Web site, which also contained a replica of what it referred to as the suppressed PSA.

53 Also in 1996, Massachusetts ran *Que Sera, Sera*, which opened with pictures of happy, healthy teens but ended with these and others smoking, as well as a few more shots of an aged victim of cancer. 'One in three children who start smoking will die from it. It doesn't have to be.' That same year MTV carried a PSA for the American Cancer Society in which a group of industry types audition a young woman for the 'part' of smoking, to replace those smokers who have died. Two years later, a Florida campaign (ironically, funded by tobacco money under an agreement with the state) caused a lot of noise when it represented teen voices speaking out against all the other vehicles of the tobacco plague, ad agencies, movies, media, distributors. 'Attention movie industry: We're your best customers. So why are you trying to kill us?' (Ira Teinowitz and Jeffery Zbar, 'Tobacco Marketers Charge Fla. Ads Violate Pact,' *AA*, 20 April 1998, 3 and 49.)

54 See Health Canada, *Making a Difference II*, 42.

55 Dilip Subramanian, 'Campaign Turns Spotlight on Drunks' Image,' *Marketing*, 2 March 1992.

56 Janet Meyers, 'Learning to Deploy a Strategic Weapon,' *AA*, 9 November 1988.

57 Gail Chiasson, 'Participaction Calls on the Inactive,' *Marketing*, 9 July 1990.

58 Scott Hume, 'Lubow's Fire Ads Give Spark That Saves Lives,' *AA*, 30 September 1985. The campaign was made for the National Fire Protection Association. 'One press clipping quotes a boy as saying he did "just what I saw Dick Van Dyke doing in the tv commercial" when he crawled out of his burning apartment.'

59 Thomas A. Hedrick, Jr, 'Pro Bono Anti-drug Ad Campaign Is Working,' *AA*, 25 June 1990.

60 Christopher S. Wren, 'Phantom Numbers Haunt the War on Drugs,' *New York Times*, 20 April 1997.

61 Donald F. Roberts and Nathan Maccoby, 'Effects of Mass Communication,'

in Gardner Lindzey and Elliot Aronson, *Handbook of Social Psychology*, (New York: Random House 1985), 567–9; William J. McGuire, 'Attitudes and Attitude Change,' in ibid., 279; Cohen, 'Promoting the Health of the Nation,' 53; Manoff, *Social Marketing*, 233.

62 Alfred McAlister, Amelie G. Ramirez, Christine Galavotti, and J. Gallion Kipling, 'Anti-smoking Campaigns: Progress in the Application of Social Learning Theory,' in Rice and Atkin, eds, *Public Communication Campaigns*, 295.

63 The decline in deaths was roughly 50 per cent, in serious injuries, 40 per cent. These data from a report by Anne Randall, 'Reduction in Drink Driving in Victoria,' available online in December 1998 at *http://raru.adelaide.edu.au/T95/paper/s14p5.html.*

64 Peirce et al., *Tobacco Use in California*, 63–80.

65 Leon S. Robertson, 'The Great Seat Belt Campaign Flop,' *Journal of Communication* 26 (Autumn 1976): 41–5.

66 Barry Day, 'Testing Ads about AIDS,' *AA*, 5 October 1987.

67 James E. Grunig and Daniel E. Ipes, 'The Anatomy of a Campaign against Drunk Driving,' *Public Relations Review* 9 (Summer 1983): 36–52.

68 See Lisa Priest, 'Smoking Increase First in 30 Years,' *Toronto Star*, 21 June 1994; Timothy O'Keefe, 'The Anti-Smoking Commercials: A Study of Television's Impact on Behavior,' *Public Opinion Quarterly* 35, no. 2 (1971): 242–8; Wallack, 'Mass Media Campaigns,' 228; and Kotler and Roberto, *Social Marketing*, 106.

69 On the issues of drugs, AIDS, and teenage pregnancy see Alan J. Bush and Gregory W. Boller, 'Rethinking the Role of Television Advertising during Health Crises: A Rhetorical Analysis of the Federal AIDS Campaigns,' *Journal of Advertising* 20, no. 1 (1991): 28–37; Kim Cleland, 'Anti-drug Effort Relies on Positive Themes,' *AA*, 7 February 1994; and Jesse Green, 'Flirting with Suicide,' *New York Times Magazine*, 15 September 1996. The quotations and the statistics are from Green.

70 Terry Eagleton has reflected, critically, on all this 'body talk' in his *The Illusions of Postmodernism* (Oxford: Blackwell 1996), 69–75.

71 *Family*, NMPFTV 1986; *Don't Die ...*, Cannes 1987.

72 The award was a BEST, given out by *Advertising Age*. See the issue of 26 May 1997, supp., 5, for a description.

73 Brian Massumi in his edited book *The Politics of Everyday Fear* (Minneapolis: University of Minnesota Press 1993), viii.

74 Other similar instances would include the tampering with Jaffa oranges from Israel, which exercised western Europe in 1978, and with Tylenol capsules in the United States in 1982. The Chilean grape affair became the

subject of a case before the American courts: see the report on *Fisher Bros. Sales, Inc. v. The United States of America*, which was available on the World Wide Web from the Villanova Center for Information Law and Policy (in July 1997 at *http://www.law.vill.edu/Fed-Ct/Circuit/3d/opinions/ 94a0947p.htm*). That affair and the two others were the subject of a paper on 'Consumer Terrorism' which was listed on the Web by DragNetCo.UK (in July 1997 at *http://www.multiplex.co.uk/dragnetco/conter.html*).

75 The emergence of the issue of 'medical marijuana' at the end of the 1990s in California, much to the anger of anti-drug authorities at the federal level, has threatened this silence. See Michael Pollan, 'Living with Medical Marijuana,' *New York Times Magazine*, 20 July 1997.

5 Charitable Souls: The Practice of Altruism

1 The information for this paragraph comes from a wide variety of materials, all of which were available on the World Wide Web in the summer of 1997. Britain: the Charity Commission (*http://www.charity-commission.gov.uk/ ccfacts.htm*) and the Charities Aid Foundation (*http://www.charitynet.org/*); Canada: Revenue Canada (*http://www.rc.gc.ca*) and Statistics Canada (*http:// www.statcan.ca/*); and the United States: The Digest of Educational Statistics 1996 (*http://www.ed.gov/NCES/pubs/d96/D96TO29.html*).

2 SCF statistics cited in Angela Penrose and John Seaman, 'The Save the Children Fund and Nutrition for Refugees,' in Peter Willetts, ed., *'The Conscience of the World': The Influence of Non-Governmental Organizations in the U.N. System* (Washington: The Brookings Institution 1996), 245; Oxfam statistics from its Web site at *http://www.oneworld.org/oxfam/*.

3 The assorted quotations are taken from the Web sites of the various organizations. City Harvest was a New York agency which collected surplus food from business for distribution to the poor. CAFOD stood for Catholic Fund for Overseas Development.

4 See, for example, Steven Smith and Michael Lipsky, *Nonprofits for Hire: The Welfare State in the Age of Contracting* (Cambridge, Mass.: Harvard University Press 1993). Much of this funding goes to small, local agencies.

5 Michael Maren, *The Road to Hell: The Ravaging Effects of Foreign Aid and International Charity* (New York: Free Press 1997), 7, 62–3.

6 Reported in the *Globe and Mail* (Toronto), 21 July 1997.

7 Information available on the America's Charities Web site, 28 December 1995.

8 Information available on the Charge against Hunger Web site, 1 March 1996. The project ended in 1997.

9 The phrase appears in Ramesh Mishra, *The Welfare State in Capitalist Society* (Toronto: University of Toronto Press 1990), 108.

10 See Smith and Lipsky, *Nonprofits for Hire*, 171–87.

11 See Michael Longford, 'NGOs and the Rights of the Child,' in Willetts, ed., *'The Conscience of the World,'* 214–40.

12 The phrase appears in a March 1987 document of *On Air Off Air* that was available from the Independent Television Association Film Library. The smaller charities had opposed the change because they feared they would be further disadvantaged in the new competition.

13 Bessies 1988.

14 Lürzers Collection 1990. The comparison is made obvious by pictures of other retired folk enjoying themselves in Florida.

15 See Jamie Talan, 'Getting a Message of Help Across,' *AA*, 2 August 1982.

16 NMPFTV 1992.

17 Maren, *The Road to Hell*, 139–61, contains a lengthy discussion and critique of this product.

18 From material on the Oxfam Web site, November 1995 (see n2 above).

19 Available on the Web at *http://www.netvideo.com/tv0/outreach/literacy.mov* in May 1996.

20 Debbie Seaman, 'Cutting the Red Tape for a Good Cause,' *Adweek's Marketing Week*, 30 March 1987.

21 Cited in Van Wallach, 'Matters of Survival,' *AA*, 9 November 1988, 120.

22 *Ken Livingston* and *Concentration Camp*, Cannes 1990, and *Toilet*, IS 1990.

23 Cited in Talan, 'Getting a Message of Help Across.'

24 Patricia Potts, 'Collecting your Conscience Money?' *Guardian*, 28 September 1983.

25 Bessies 1991.

26 Larry Hollon, 'Selling Human Misery,' *The Christian Century* 100 (26 October 1983): 968.

27 Consider these examples. An aged veteran is constantly haunted by the sounds and images of war, evoked by the noises of the city (*Veteran*, The Poppy Appeal, U.K., 1991). A boy suffering schizophrenia and his family despair because there is no answer (*Richard*, Ontario Friends of Schizophrenics, Canada, 1992). Homeless New Yorkers sing out how much they would like to be a part of their great city (*New York, New York*, Coalition for the Homeless, U.S.A., 1992). A teenager (*'I#*?'*, Second Harvest, Canada, 1994) talks to us about our lack of interest: 'If I said the word "fuck," it would probably bother you. If I told you I was hungry, it probably wouldn't. Fuck, I'm hungry.' *Veteran*, IS 1992; *Richard*, Bessies 1993; *New York, New York*, Cannes 1993; *'I#*?'*, Bessies 1995.

28 Cannes 1986.
29 Drought: *Water Gun* (Netherlands, Global Village, 1993) tells us that you do not play with water in Zimbabwe, 'because you need every drop to stay alive.' War: *Children's Drawings* (Netherlands, Red Cross, 1987) shows children traumatized by scenes of conflict and violence in Asia: 'Will these children ever draw flowers, birds, or butterflies again?' Violation: *Eviction Notice* (CARE Canada, 1990) drives home the reality of dispossession by simulating a Canadian family – like 'sixteen million people in the Third World' last year – forced from their home by soldiers. Deprivation: *Embryo* (U.K., Christian Aid Week, 1991) contrasts various shots of a contented foetus with these words of wisdom: 'For millions of people in the Third World, these will be the best months of their lives. Later on, there is little nourishment, less shelter, and no comfort. We're working to give everyone a chance of a real life, because we believe in life before death. Do you?' *Water Gun*, IS 1994; *Children's Drawings*, IBA 1988; *Eviction Notice*, Bessies 1991; *Embryo*, Lürzers 1991.
30 IBA 1993.
31 IS 1994.
32 *Etiopia*, Cannes 1985; *Put Their Fears to Rest*, Bessies 1991; *Gift*, IS 1994.
33 *Metamorphosis*, Cannes 1985.
34 The United Way commercials, in IBA 1991 and Bessies 1992; Salvation Army campaign, Bessies 1995.
35 IS 1995.
36 'The advertisement showed an iced cake. A white hand cut a small slice but took the rest of the cake. Then a black child's hand took the slice. During that sequence a voice announced: "Did you know that our third of the world's population ... enjoys almost four-fifths of the world's income?"' *The Times* (London), 25 September 1976.
37 Cited in *Focus on Images*, a piece of text available on the Web site of Save the Children in Britain on 19 November 1995.
38 *Pumps*, BEST 1992; New Zealand series, Lürzers 1991; *Walk*, Bessies 1985.
39 Respectively, IBA 1988 and Bessies 1992.
40 Cannes 1986.
41 This untitled gem was available at the Web site of an advertising agency, DahlinSmithWhite, in March 1996. The reference then was *http:// www.dsw.com/ movies/special.mov*.
42 Cannes 1985.
43 Melinda Wittstock and Michael Dynes, 'Honest Images Beat Donor Fatigue,' *The Times* (London), 11 March 1991, 7.
44 *Love Story*, Cannes 1988; *Unforgettable Visit*, Lürzers 1991; *Billy*, IBA 1994; *Puzzle*, Cannes 1981; *Break the Cycle*, NMPFTV 1990.

6 Administered Minds, or Shaming the Citizenry

1 Cannes 1989.
2 See Ruth Benedict's *The Chrysanthemum and the Sword: Patterns of Japanese Culture* (New York: World Publishing 1972), first published in 1946, esp. pages 222–7, for an account based on this dichotomy of guilt and shame cultures. That dichotomy was elaborated and criticized by Milton B. Singer in his 'Shame Cultures and Guilt Cultures,' in Gerhart Piers and Milton B. Singer, *Shame and Guilt: A Psychoanalytic and a Cultural Study* (New York: W.W. Norton 1972), first published in 1953, 57–100. Erving Goffman's seminal book *Stigma: Notes on the Management of Spoiled Identity* (Englewood Cliffs, N.J.: Prentice-Hall 1963) focused not on shame *per se* but on identity. Some more recent explorations are Michael Lewis, *Shame: The Exposed Self* (New York: Free Press 1992), where shame is a global attribute while guilt is specific; Mario Jacoby, *Shame and the Origins of Self-Esteem* (London: Routledge 1994), where shame means a self that is devalued, whether by oneself or by others; and Donald Capps, *The Depleted Self: Sin in a Narcissistic Age* (Minneapolis: Fortress Press 1993), where shame becomes 'the experience of a self-deficiency' (72), which is very close to the old definition of guilt.
3 Noted in Lawrence Wallack, Lori Dorfman, David Jernigan, and Makani Themba, *Media Advocacy and Public Health: Power for Prevention* (Newbury Park, Calif.: Sage 1993), 116. The authors also note that Schwartz was a champion of shaming.
4 And with the same lack of result: Lord Young, the man held responsible for the boom, argued, 'I just think that means that at long last governments have grown up and begun to realize that marketing pays. We should be going out there and explaining what we do and getting our message home to people.' Louis Heaton, 'When Does Information Become Propaganda,' *The Listener*, 10 March 1988.
5 Respectively, IBA 1993 and Cannes 1993.
6 The centre was so proud of its effort that it offered these ads, going back to the mid-1970s, on its Web site in 1997.
7 *Breezes*, 1996. Particularly explicit were a series of claims made in *Rebecca*, 1989: 'If you'd like to give your house some minor tweaks, fix up eensy teensy leaks, run a shop that's all your own, buy yourself a cozy home, *steer away from crummy deals, protect your car from roof to wheels*, trim your tummy thighs and hips, *go on safe exotic trips, stay away from hacks and quacks*, blow away those sneeze attacks, teach your kids the ABCs, how to write and how to read, *get rid of little pests that bug you*, ones that crawl or buzz above you, *ban the junk food in your diet, know what's inside before you buy it*, bank on stocks

and count on bonds, *stay away from market cons*, then you'll want this free and helpful book ...' (italics added).

8 Respectively, *X-Ray*, the U.S. Environmental Protection Agency, 1988 (Ad Council 1989); *Cowboys*, Australia's Ministry of Police, 1989 (IS 1990); *Don't Let Your Kids Go to Sleep in the Dark*, ABC Canada, 1989 (Bessies 1990); *Warning Chorus*, Tokyo's Metropolitan Government, 1992 (IBA 1993); *Tom Selleck*, California, 1992 (made available on one of the state government's Web sites, May 1996, then at *http://wwwdwr.water.ca.gov/dir-Gr_Services/*).

9 Consider *Swimming Pool*, U.K., Manpower Services Commission, 1978 (Cannes 1979); *Help*, Community of Madrid, 1986 (Cannes 1987); *The Circle*, France, Ministry of Labour (Cannes 1982); *Bridge*, Belgium, Ministry of Employment, 1987 (IS 1988).

10 Ontario story in *Marketing*, 25 November 1991, and Peruvian story in *AA*, 18 January 1992.

11 The Deciding Vote Inc. built an impressive feminist minidrama, called *Empowerment* (IBA 1993), around this ploy. The commercial showed a young, attractive mother who found it impossible to get male bureaucrats in a hospital to act swiftly upon her pleas to assist her baby. The announcer told women they could be heard, they could change things, they could protect health care, they could make a difference, if they voted. That positioned voting as a form of power, a public good that could work its magic only when the frustrated and the alienated decided to use it.

12 Respectively, National Association of Secretaries of State (IBA 1991); International Association of Clerks, Recorders, Election Officials, and Treasurers (IS 1993) and IS (1992).

13 Witness this comment from Stephen Lambright, a vice-president and group executive: 'We're not doing this to satisfy our critics. We're doing this because we are committed to an effective solution, not a quick fix like ad bans or counteradvertising.' 'The don't drink ad is not a message that will do any good.' Cited in *Broadcasting*, 18 March 1985, 34.

14 *Card Game*, Cannes 1981; *Crashing Glasses*, Cannes 1984; *Michael*, Bessies 1985; *Mike*, Ad Council 1990.

15 *Scream Bloody Murder*, Ad Council *circa* 1970; *Impaired Driving*, Bessies 1973; *Caught*, Attorney General, Bessies 1984; *The Party's Over*, California Broadcasters Association, Cannes 1985.

16 Michael Dynes, 'Safety on Roads a Matter of Social Conscience,' *The Times* (London), 5 December 1990.

17 *Eyes*, NMPFTV 1992; *The Girlfriend*, IS 1992; *Kids*, Bessies 1995; *Kathy*, IS 1992; *Fireman*, IBA 1988; *Drink-Drive*, from a brewer Holsten Pils, Cannes 1996.

18 Some of the better Mormon efforts won awards: *Think Again*, IBA 1980; *Bryan*, IBA 1982; *The More I See You*, Cannes 1986; and *High Chair*, Bessies 1994.

19 *Animals*, Cannes 1991; unnamed ad in NMPFTV 1989; *Chaplin*, Cannes 1991.

20 The reference here is to a hodgepodge of commercials: *For the Soldiers*, U.S. Army, IBA 1994; *The Great Defenders*, California Department of Veterans' Affairs, undated, on a state government Web site in May 1996; *Mangy Dog*, Returned Serviceman's League, IS 1992; *Noble Breed*, Ontario Ministry of Agriculture, Bessies 1993; *Walk Tall Miner*, South Africa Chamber of Mines, IBA 1991; *Cardiac Arrest*, U.S.A., National Commission on Nursing Implementation Project, Ad Council 1990; *If the Press Didn't Tell Us*, U.S.A., Society of Professional Journalists, Ad Council 1987.

21 A carpenter and a steelworker in two spots (U.S.A, 1985) who give their time to help people. In a slightly different vein was *Julie* (Canada, Act Foundation, 1990) who used cardiopulmonary resuscitation (CPR) to save her father.

22 *Candles*, Ad Council 1991.

23 *Whoopi Goldberg*, Ad Council 1987.

24 Consider *The Wall* (Bessies 1991): It used scenes of the dismantling of the Berlin Wall, and the celebrations, along with a suitably buoyant tune – trumpet music. Then the voice-over asks, 'While the rest of the world is tearing down walls, why do some Canadians want to build them?'

25 Stan Sutter, 'Politicians Set to Sell Canadians on Constitution,' *Marketing*, 7 September 1992.

26 Cited in Hugh Winsor, 'Bidding to Quicken Patriotic Heartbeat,' *Marketing*, 28 May 1992.

27 This thought was occasioned by the work of one of my ex-graduate students, Dr Elsbeth Heaman, who once argued that Confederation had fashioned a promotional commodity for the advertising of the advantages of Ontario, Quebec, and so on.

28 Cannes 1982.

29 Cannes 1983.

30 See, for example, the following pieces in *AA*: 'A Call to Admen: Help Stop Riots,' 4 May 1992; 'Ad Council Targets Racism in Wake of L.A. Riots,' 11 May 1992; 'Ueberroth Names Holt to "Rebuild L.A." effort' and 'From King to T-Shirts,' 18 May 1992.

31 Kathleen Barnes, 'S. Africa Media, Agencies Join to Push Peace,' *AA International*, 18 January 1993.

32 IBA 1994.

33 Alvin Wasserman, then vice-president and creative director, McKim Advertising, Vancouver. Cited in Jim McElgunn, 'Broadcasters Up the Ante,' *Marketing*, 20 August 1990. But there was evidence, according to government sources, that such upbeat ads pleased at least a part of the citizenry: in 1991 the Department of Citizenship and Multiculturalism claimed it was happy with the response to its bus and subway posters that featured a bicycle built for all sorts of riders and the slogan 'Together We're Better! / Ensemble on ira loin!' Sandra Porteous, 'Bike Ad Earns Canadians' Favor,' *Marketing*, 29 July 1991.
34 Clios 1996.
35 Cannes 1982.
36 First ad, IBA 1988. The second ad won a Clio in 1996. The comment from Antoni Shelton, executive director of the alliance, cited in *Toronto Star*, 6 June 1995.
37 Cannes 1990.
38 *Nobody Is Better*, IBA 1994; *Brains*, Cannes 1996; *Anti-Discrimination*, Cannes 1992.
39 Rivera was then a television celebrity noted for his sensational journalism. He spoke out here on behalf of the Working Organization for Retarded Children and Adults – as well as on local television stations. The PSA was available on his own Web site in December 1996.
40 Bessies 1989. Part of an ongoing campaign by the Ontario Office of Disabled Persons to turn around the prevailing stereotypes attached to mental disorders.
41 Cannes 1984. From the Ministry of Labour.
42 This statement is based respectively on *Friends*, Alberta Human Rights Commission, Bessies 1984; *Handicapped*, Consejo Publicitario Argentino, Cannes 1985, and *Disability Awareness*, Fundación ONCE, Spain, 1995; *Babies*, Trades Union Council, U.K., Cannes 1987; *Bashing* and *Innocent*, PFLAG (Parents, Families, and Friends of Lesbians and Gays), U.S.A, 1997. The two PFLAG commercials were relative newcomers to the genre of attack propaganda, and I have no idea whether they received much air time. In 1994, Ontario television stations refused PSAs from the Coalition for Lesbian and Gay Rights in Ontario in support of the drive for marital rights for same-sex couples (*Toronto Star*, 4 January 1994). The suspicion of homosexuality was still so widespread in North America that homophobia could not be easily labelled a prejudice on television. The two ads were available on PFLAG's Web site in January 1997.
43 In 'Two Lectures' Foucault referred to these as 'a whole set of knowledges that have been disqualified as inadequate to their task or insufficiently

elaborated: naive knowledges, located low down on the hierarchy, beneath the required level of cognition or scientificity.' *Power/Knowledge: Selected Interviews and Other Writings 1972–1977*, ed. Colin Gordon (New York: Pantheon Books 1980), 82.

44 These figures are the estimated number and rate of offences known to police. Violent crime is defined as murder, forcible rape, robbery, and aggravated assault. See Kathleen Maguire, Ann L. Pastore, and Timothy J. Flanagan, eds, *Sourcebook of Criminal Justice Statistics 1992*, U.S. Department of Justice, Bureau of Justice Statistics (Washington, D.C.: USGPO 1993).

45 For example, surveys carried out by the Roper Center for Public Opinion Research, in 1974, 1982, and 1991, revealed that consistently six out of every ten women and 'Black/Other' admitted they feared to walk at night in close-by neighbourhoods. Ibid., 190–1.

46 Ad Council 1979. The collection has a lot of McGruff ads.

47 Cited in James A. Files, 'Study Shows That Public Information Campaigns Work,' *Public Relations Journal* 40 (January 1984): 8–9. See also Garrett J. O'Keefe and Kathleen Reid, 'The McGruff Crime Prevention Campaign,' in Ronald E. Rice and Charles K. Atkin, eds, *Public Communication Campaigns*, 2nd ed. (Newbury Park, Calif.: Sage 1989), 210–12.

48 These statistics are from the executive summary of a special report by the Bureau of Justice Assistance which was made available at the Web site of the National Crime Prevention Council in the spring of 1997, then *http:// www.ncpc.org/*.

49 *There's Nothing Cool about Violence*, National Association of Television Program Executives (NATPE), 1996.

50 *Excuses*, Cannes 1992. See, as well, *Punch and Judy*, Australian Hospital Benefits, Cannes 1981 (the horror of children); *Static*, Parents Anonymous, U.S.A, Cannes 1989 (the angry mother); *Boxer*, NSPCC, U.K., NMPFTV 1989 (the brutal father); *Barbara Bush*, National Committee for Prevention of Child Abuse, U.S.A., Ad Council 1990 (the problem family).

51 'In Quebec, more than 200,000 women are victims of domestic violence.' Quebec Social Services, Cannes 1988.

52 BTTA 1996.

53 On the ESPN Web site, December 1996.

54 *Date*, Bessies 1993, and *Oblivious*, 1994. The latter caused some upset because of its apparent anti-male emphasis. I was on a radio panel to discuss the ad, which is how it came into my possession.

55 *Between the Lines*, Women's Aid, IS 1995.

56 'For example, although evidence indicates that as many as 95 percent of domestic violence perpetrators are male, focus groups have demonstrated

consistently that both women and men strongly resist framing men as the enemy, wanting instead to see them as part of the solution. Campaigns that encourage men to hold other men accountable for their violence are therefore likely to be successful, and those that indiscriminately blame all men for the problem are not.' Marissa E. Ghez, 'Communications and Public Education: Effective Tools to Promote a Cultural Change on Domestic Violence,' rev. ed. of a paper delivered to Violence Against Women, Strategic Planning Meeting, National Institute of Justice, Washington, D.C., 31 March 1995, made available on the World Wide Web, on 16 May 1996, at *http://www.ecovote.org/fund/difference/nij.html.*

57 *Taste and Decency,* Lürzers 1992.

58 *Toronto Star,* 20 April 1994. Earlier, however, an advocacy group had warned in *One Week* (1993) that there was far more violence displayed on television than was evident on the streets. *One Week* was a very simple commercial. Black screen, white text. No sound, no other pictures. Here is the text: 'In one week, you'll see:' '144 murders' '143 attempted murders' '13 cases of drug use' '48 robberies' '13 kidnappings' 'We're not talking about violence on the streets.' 'We're talking about violence on your television.' 'Wake up.' 'Canadians Concerned About Violence in Entertainment (905) 545–1111.'

59 *Inquisitive Kids,* NATPE, 1996.

60 *Kids,* Cannes 1996.

61 Richard Lacayo, 'Teen Crime,' *Time,* 21 July 1997, 14.

62 Cannes 1995 and 1996.

7 Appropriations: Benetton and Others

1 See Krishan Kumar, *From Post-Industrial to Post-Modern Society: New Theories of the Contemporary World* (Oxford: Blackwell 1995), 37–65, particularly 44–5 and 61–2. Other sources for this paragraph are Patrick Spain and James Talbot, eds, *Hoover's Handbook of World Business 1995–1996,* (The Reference Press, 1995), 132–3; a background report on Benetton for *Consider the Issues,* available at *http://www.tcom.ohiou.edu/OU_Language/book-CTI.html#publicity* in November 1997; plus two sources made available on Benetton's own Web site (*www.benetton.com*), the 1994 annual report and a 1995 corporate backgrounder.

2 Sales cited in *Hoover's* reports online, available at the Time/Warner news site, *http://pathfinder.com/money/hoovers,* in March 1999.

3 Spending on all forms of publicity became significant as the company grew. 'The Benetton Group today invests four percent of sales in communication: we are present in 300 magazines, on 70,000 billboards, 40,000 posters in

our outlets, and two million catalogs.' *Benetton Group Corporate Backgrounder 1996* (19), available on Benetton's Web site at *http://2061517193.global.net/benetton/pdf/Corporate.pdf* in April 1996.

4 Cited on the Benetton Web site as the title of a discussion of the advertising.

5 The comment appears in an interview of April 1992 photocopied as part of a media package made available when a collection of Toscani's photographs were on display at the Joseph D. Carrier Art Gallery, Columbus Centre, Toronto, 23 January 1994.

6 Cited in a discussion of the 1985 or 'Flags' campaign on the Benetton Web site.

7 Witness the jaundiced comments of two critics, Les Back and Vibeke Quaade, who assessed the campaign much later in *Third Text 22*: 'Throughout the campaigns, human difference is reduced to a set of simplified caricatures which are presented as archetypes. In fact, what we find in Benetton advertising is a parade of racial essences. Thus, the "whites" have blue eyes and blond hair, the "blacks" are Negroid, and the "Orientals" are likewise locked in a crass image of facial traits.' Cited in Henry A. Giroux, 'Consuming Social Change: The United Colors of Benetton,' in *Disturbing Pleasures: Learning Popular Culture* (New York: Routledge 1994), 7.

8 Part of a commentary called 'Contrasts in Black and White 1989' which appeared on Benetton's Web site in April 1996.

9 The comment appeared in Desmond O'Grady, 'The Shocking Adman,' *Toronto Star*, 20 August 1995, E1.

10 Roland Barthes, 'Written Clothing,' in Chandra Mukerji and Michael Schudson, eds, *Rethinking Popular Culture: Contemporary Perspectives in Cultural Studies* (Berkeley: University of California Press 1991), 439. Barthes was dealing specifically with the imagery of clothing.

11 'We decided to use pictures already published by other magazines just to prove our intention was not to shock,' claimed Luciano Benetton; 'nobody had complained about these photographs when they first appeared, so why should they complain when we use them?' Cited in Leslie White, 'Blood, Sweaters and Designer Tears,' *Marketing*, 9 March 1992.

12 'Advert Ruling,' *The Times* (London), 20 February 1992.

13 Cited in Serra A. Tinic, 'United Colors and Untied Meanings: Benetton and the Commodification of Social Issues,' *Journal of Communication* 47, no. 3 (Summer 1997): 8.

14 See Juergen Brandstaetter, 'The Benetton Campaign,' paper given at a New Delhi Conference, 6 November 1997, 'Legal and Cultural Issues in the Advertising and Marketing of Consumer Products – East Meets West,' available at *www.fdblawyers.com/library/benetton.com* in July 1998.

15 Cited in Nancy Millman, 'Controversy Ad Infinitum,' *Tempo*, Chicago *Tribune*, 31 December 1992, 1.

16 This appeared in an interview, dated April 1992, that formed part of the media kit distributed at the Carrier gallery. It should be noted that the family of the deceased had agreed to Benetton's use of the picture.

17 Hence the comment of Peter Fressola, a company spokesperson: 'We're trying to show the literal and figurative branding of AIDS victims in our society and the damage it can do. We want to provoke discussion on the subject.' Cited in the New York *Post*, 17 September 1993.

18 *AA*, 7 July 1995. Made available on the *Advertising Age* Web site.

19 'Rights Groups Attack Ad that Shows Dead Soldier,' *Toronto Star*, 21 February 1994, E8.

20 Cited in 'Benetton Ads Spark Strong German Backlash,' *Globe and Mail* (Toronto), 6 February 1995, B9.

21 The retailers had refused to pay for the goods they received from Benetton, which is why the matter ended up in the courts. There were three press releases dealing with the matter on the Benetton Web site, April 1996.

22 Noted in Toronto *Star*, 20 August 1995, E1.

23 Jennifer DeCoursey, 'Benetton Illustrates New Battles on Ads,' *AA*, 24 July 1995, 28. Other images included a crucified Jesus and a crying Madonna.

24 The letter appeared in *Harper's* and then on the World Wide Web. My copy is from the Flummery Digest at *http://www.ora.com/people/staff/sierra/flum/96.04.htm*. There was also a report in the Detroit *News*, dated 16 April 1996, on the web at *http://detnews.com/menu/stories/44086.htm*, which delved into this story.

25 Cited in the Toronto *Star*, 20 January 1994, E3.

26 Cited in Ann Moline, 'Advertising Blind Spots,' *Sportswear International*, at *http://sportswearnet.com/stealth.html* in July 1998.

27 From the statement on advertising on Benetton's own Web site.

28 Cited in the *Toronto Star*, 20 August 1995, E1.

29 Oliviero Toscani in *The World's Best Sellers, or The Fine Art of Separating People from Their Money*, a film documentary. The script was available at *http://www.worlds-best.com/txt/* in July 1998.

30 An unnamed company official cited in a sympathetic editorial of the *Globe and Mail*, 24 February 1992, A12.

31 '"It's very rare for entrenched values to be challenged by advertisers," says [Dan] Wieden. "But one reason it could be occurring is this growing urge for people to belong. A lot of people have lost their sense of roots, and I think brands have caught on to that fact. They are creating an opportunity to carve out a specific set of values, like a club, and customers can sign up

and express those same values through the purchase of the product.'" Wieden was famous as one of the masters of Nike advertising. The quotation appeared in the *Los Angeles Times*, 30 August 1991, E1.

32 Cited in Helen Fielding, 'Cashing in on a World of Woe,' *The Times* (London), 29 September 1994, 4.

33 From a company document that was part of the media package supplied by Joseph D. Carrier Art Gallery in Toronto.

34 From a company document, 1992, cited in Tinic, 'United Colors and Untied Meanings,' 8.

35 These figures were made available on the Benetton Web site in April 1996 in the form of a graph at *http://2061517193.global.net/benetton/gifs/Revenue.gif*.

36 David Jones, 'Italy: Benetton Ponders Its Cash Pile,' a Reuters story made available on the World Wide Web at *http://www.textilenet.org.tw/citis/tnews/970304-1.html* in July 1998.

37 Cited in Brandstaetter, 'The Benetton Campaign.'

38 Kadu story: Laurel Wentz and Geoffrey Lee Martin, 'Cheaply Made Gore Scores,' *AA*, 4 July 1994, 38.

39 Business in the Community. This was part of an executive summary of a special report made available at *http://www.bitc.org.uk/crm/* in July 1998.

40 Monci Jo Williams, 'How to Cash in on Do-Good Pitches,' *Fortune*, 9 June 1986, 72.

41 Patricia Caesar, 'Cause-Related Marketing: The New Face of Corporate Philanthropy,' *Business and Society Review* 59 (Fall 1986): 15–19.

42 Cited in 'Just Cause,' an article placed on the World Wide Web by EMMI Inc., publishers of *Inside PR* and *Reputation Management*. The address was *http://www.prcentral.com/fmjf97cause.htm* in July 1998.

43 Business in the Community report.

44 International Advertising Association, *Controversy Advertising* (New York: Hastings House 1977), 26.

45 Eugene Mahany, 'Boost Your Image Promoting Good Causes,' *AA*, 11 November 1974, 46.

46 Figures from Karen Singer, 'Has Doing Good Become Overdone?' *AA*, 21 September 1987, 16.

47 The phrase appears in a CRM Report of Cone Communications Inc., available on the World Wide Web at *http://www.iprex.com/News/c_press1.html* in July 1998.

48 'Just Cause' article.

49 'Just Cause' article. The figures in this paragraph are taken from this article

and the Cone CRM Report of 1998 and 1999, the latter made available in summary form at *www.prcentral.com* in March 1999.

50 IS 1995.

51 Ken Riddell, 'Kids' Fair Play Rewarded,' *Marketing*, 24 June 1991.

52 'Just Cause' article.

53 A list of 'Program Accomplishments,' updated to 22 March 1996, was available on Avon's Web site in July 1998.

54 See 'Just Cause' article.

55 The examples of problems are taken from Bruce Silverglade, 'Regulatory Practices for Communicating Health Information,' in Charles Atkin and Lawrence Wallack, eds, *Mass Communication and Public Health: Complexities and Conflicts* (Newbury Park, Calif.: Sage 1990), 93; Fielding, 'Cashing in on a World of Woe,' 4; and 'Hard Lesson in AMA Folly,' *AA*, 1 September 1997, 16.

56 See Charles Atkin and Elaine B. Arkin, 'Issues and Initiatives in Communicating Health Information,' in Atkin and Wallack, eds, *Mass Communication and Public Health*, 17; William Novelli, 'Controversies in Advertising of Health-Related Products,' in Atkin and Wallack, eds, *Mass Communication and Publich Health*, 84–5; Silverglade, 'Regulatory Practices,' 92–3.

57 *Toronto Star*, 26 January 1995, E2.

58 Cone CRM Report.

59 This is the comment from Toscani (available on the Benetton Web site in July 1998) about the image, apparently deemed pornographic by some critics: 'Benetton's white and black horses show us nature's spontaneity, in our artificial world where nothing is authentic. Because of maliciousness sometimes the human mind sees ugliness in beauty and censors not only the expressions of freedom but is also against the Will of Creation. The Benetton horses take us back to innocence and truth, because they are authentic and beautiful.' Sometimes it is hard to take Toscani seriously.

60 The concept of the 'carnivalesque' rests on the work of the literary theorist Mikhail Bakhtin. Jackson Lears applied the concept to explain the origins of American advertising in *Fables of Abundance: A Cultural History of Advertising in America* (New York: Basic Books 1994). Although often denounced or repressed, the carnivalesque has remained a part of the world of advertising, a resource that admakers can draw upon to shape the sell. The tradition enjoyed a new heyday, for example, during the Creative Revolution of the late 1960s.

61 Bruce Horovitz, 'Shock Value Helps an Obscure Jeans Maker Be Not So Obscure,' 11 May 1993, Business Section, *Los Angeles Times*.

62 The Diesel commercials, called 'Guides to Successful Living,' were made available on its Web site in July 1998. The later commercials went on to spoof other common types of advertising and entertainment, from the Japanese taste for demonstrations to the American taste for slasher movies.

63 On Perrier see 'Global Gallery,' *AA*, 27 June 1994, 38; on Pepe see 'Choice of a Nihilist Generation,' *AA*, 19 June 1995, I-2; on RJR Tee Budann Tollack, 'RJR Takes Brazen Tone in New Camel Campaign,' *AA*, 11 May 1998, 2. The quoted words in the last sentence are from Pollack, not the RJR spokesperson.

64 Cited in Sunday *New York Times*, 17 August 1997, E1.

65 Cannes 1986. French authorities employed a more direct parody to combat smoking. In 1992 a French coalition of public and private authorities employed the style of the famous Marlboro ads, opening on a 'limitless plain lit by the yellowish glow of dawn,' to set the scene for an anti-smoking message. After riding back to the ranch at sunset, the virile cowboy, complete with 'a three-day stubble' and a Stetson, confronts the viewer and delivers, deadpan, the message: 'Smoking is against my nature.' Dilip Subramanian, 'Anti-Smokers Stole Myth, Marlboro Says,' *Marketing*, 16 March 1992, 22.

66 The Guerrilla Girls had their own Web site, complete with interviews and samples of their posters, from which comes the information in this paragraph.

67 Bob Mackin, Jr, 'AdBusters Gains Right to Air "TV Addiction" Commercial,' *Marketing*, 11 February 1991, 4.

68 Bob Mackin, Jr, 'Tuning out TV,' *Marketing*, 15 June 1992, 3.

*A 'Risk' Technology?

1 Cited in Steven Holmes, 'Good Times Are Bad for Interest Groups,' *New York Times*, 26 July 1998, WK 3.

2 Ulrich Beck, *Risk Society: Towards a New Modernity*, trans. Mark Ritter (London: Sage 1992).

3 See especially François Ewald, 'Insurance and Risk,' and Daniel Defert, '"Popular Life" and Insurance Technology,' both in Graham Burchell, Colin Gordon, and Peter Miller, eds, *The Foucault Effect: Studies in Governmentality* (Chicago: University of Chicago Press 1991), 197–210 and 211–34.

4 Michael Fitzpatrick, 'A Mad, Mad, Mad, Mad World,' reproduced from *Living Marxism* 87 (February 1996), accessed on the Web at *http://195.40.123.20/LM/LM87_Mad.html* in August 1997.

5 This version of risk theory relies heavily upon the excellent account in

Richard Ericson and Kevin Haggerty, *Policing the Risk Society* (Toronto: University of Toronto Press 1997), 83–130.

6 Cited in M.M. Davis and Brian Clifford, 'Fallacious Images,' *The Listener*, 15 January 1987, 25.

7 John Greyson, *The ADS Epidemic* (1987: 5 minutes) on the compilation 'Video against AIDS,' curated by John Greyson and Bill Harrigan, Video Data Bank, School of the Art Institute of Chicago, and V Tape, Toronto.

8 See Tim Rhodes and Robert Shaughnessy, 'Compulsory Screening: Advertising AIDS in U.K., 1986–89,' *Policy and Politics* 18, no. 1 (1990): 55–61.

9 Steve Rabin, senior vice-president at Ogilvy and Mather in the United States, cited in Janet Meyers, 'Learning To Deploy a Strategic Weapon,' *AA*, 9 November 1988, 148.

10 The ad was made available online in the Boursicot library (*www.adeater.com*) in Paris in December 1998.

11 Cited in Pat Sloan and Joe Mandese, 'TV Nets Warming to Condom Ads,' *AA*, 16 November 1991, 47.

12 'Durex-Truth for Youth Campaign,' a report available online at *www.prcentral.com* in March 1999.

13 Available online at the Boursicot library, December 1998.

*Ricoeur: Utopia

1 Arthur Herman, *The Idea of Decline in Western History* (New York: Free Press 1997), 2.

2 Indeed he may cite a few too many thinkers, from Foucault to Chomsky to Albert Gore to the Unabomber; their numbers suggest that declinism does not constitute a coherent tradition. On the other hand, the coming end of the millennium has provoked a number of sour reflections on the future history of the West and the world, notably Samuel Huntington's *The Clash of Civilizations and the Re-Making of the World Order*, a book published at roughly the same time as Herman's, that being, presumably, why it doesn't figure in his account. See Adam Burgess, 'The Decline of the West Revisited,' *Living Marxism*, issue 101, June 1997, made available at their Web site *http://195.40.123.20/LM/LM101/LM101_Books.html* in August 1997, for a discussion of the phenomenon.

3 Frank Manuel, 'Toward a Psychological History of Utopias,' in Frank Manuel, ed., *Utopias and Utopian Thought* (London: Souvenir Press 1973), 71.

4 George Kateb, 'Utopia and the Good Life,' in Manuel, ed., *Utopias and Utopian Thought*, 242 and 240.

5 Barbara Goodwin and Keith Taylor, *The Politics of Utopia: A Study in Theory and Practice* (London: Hutchinson 1982), 9.

6 Northrop Frye, 'Varieties of Literary Utopias,' 25, and Crane Brinton, 'Utopia and Democracy,' 50, both in Manuel, ed., *Utopias and Utopian Thought.*

7 Jan Relf, 'Utopia the Good Breast: Coming Home to Mother,' in Krishan Kumar and Stephen Bann, eds, *Utopias and the Millennium* (London: Reaktion Books 1993), 108.

8 'Utopia, then, is first and foremost a work of imaginative fiction in which, unlike other such works, the central subject is the good society.' Krishan Kumar, *Utopianism* (Minneapolis: University of Minnesota Press 1991), 27.

9 See Frank Manuel and Fritzie Manuel, *Utopian Thought in the Western World* (Cambridge, Mass.: Harvard University Press 1979). The Manuels' survey is the definitive work on literary and philosophical utopias.

10 The page references in the text are to Paul Ricoeur's *Lectures on Ideology and Utopia*, ed. George Taylor (New York: Columbia University Press, 1986). The lectures were actually delivered in the fall of 1975 at the University of Chicago.

11 Thus: 'the only way to get out of the circularity in which ideologies engulf us is to assume a utopia, declare it, and judge an ideology on this basis' (172).

12 Karl Mannheim, *Ideology and Utopia: An Introduction to the Sociology of Knowledge*, trans. Louis Wirth and Edward Shils, (London: Routledge and Kegan Paul 1936), 183.

13 The whole passage bears repeating: 'what single-minded critics of utopia appear to miss is the "double metaphor," the ambivalent and often dialectical character of the utopian inspiration. Utopias are written out of both hope and despair. They are models of stability conceived in the spirit of contradiction. They are actions – a kind of "action dreaming" – in the name of ideal values: neglected or betrayed in the present, once enjoyed in the past, or yet to be fulfilled in the future. They are interpretations of the existing order, and as often as not programs for change. Utopia's hortatory implication, in the form of a secret injunction, is always there, for all political ideals are implicitly revolutionary: their critical elements lead to dissent, their perfect projections to longing to construct anew. The utopian dream of the future, with its sources in fantasy and alienation, implies the nightmares of the present. And yet ... the conceivable and desirable future is never free of this nightmarish escape.' Melvin J. Lasky, *Utopia and Revolution* (Chicago and London: University of Chicago Press 1985; first published 1976), 9.

14 I am referring specifically to A.-J. Greimas's famous 'semiotic square,'

where the presence of a value creates oppositions of various kinds, including its negation. See A.-J. Greimas and J. Courtés, *Semiotics and Language: An Analytical Dictionary* (Bloomington: Indiana University Press 1979), 308–11 and A.-J. Greimas, *Structural Semantics: An Attempt at a Method*, trans. Daniele McDowell, Ronald Schleifer, and Alan Velie (Lincoln: University of Nebraska Press 1983).

15 Cited in Krishan Kumar, *Utopia and Anti-Utopia in Modern Times* (Oxford and Cambridge, Mass.: Basil Blackwell 1987), 291.

16 Fredric Jameson, *The Political Unconscious: Narrative as a Socially Symbolic Act* (Ithaca, N.Y.: Cornell University Press 1981). Jameson's politics embraces utopianism, and so belongs to that marvellously inventive tradition of Marxism developed by Ernst Bloch – see, for example, Vincent Geoghegan, *Ernst Bloch* (London: Routledge 1996).

17 A modernized version of the poem is provided as an appendix in A.L. Morton, *The English Utopia* (Berlin: Seven Seas Publishers 1968), 279–85.

18 For example, the twentieth-century American folk song 'The Big Rock Candy Mountain' (with its 'ham and egg trees' and its 'lake full of beer'). Cited in Kumar, *Utopia and Anti-Utopia in Modern Times*, 9 and 7, respectively.

19 That recognition came very early. See Gary Steiner's *The People Look at Television: A Study of Audience Attitudes* (New York: Knopf 1963) on the response to commercials in the late 1950s.

20 I have explored this cultural role in my *The New Icons? The Art of Television Advertising* (Toronto: University of Toronto Press 1994), esp. 38–44.

21 See Umberto Eco in *Travels in Hyperreality* (London: Picador 1986).

8 Technopia and Other Corporate Dreams

1 The company's Web site (then *http://www-eu.philips.com/*) offered a justification: 'We were looking for a theme – not just an advertising slogan or isolated corporate statement – that expressed the new mentality of Philips as a whole. A theme that should be aspirational but credible, staking out a winning position without making promises consumers will not believe and we can't keep. Furthermore, the new theme should also be sufficiently flexible to serve as a platform for all Philips communications – at corporate and product level as well as a powerful internal motivator. In short: every appearance of the brand at every level should reinforce the overall image of Philips. The solution was a simple statement: "Let's make things better."'

2 For a discussion of the activities of Grace, see Barbara Mehlman, 'Speaking

out Can Be Good for Your Corporate Health,' *Madison Avenue* 25 (February 1983): 76.

3 Lisa E. Phillips, 'LM, Grace Press Nets,' *AA*, 5 May 1986, 4, and 'Networks Nix Deficit Ad,' *Broadcasting* 110 (3 February 1986): 40.

4 *Deficit Trials* is available in Cannes 1986 and IS 1987. The agency worried that the spot was too powerful, so a softer version was prepared to calm these fears, and both were shown to focus groups to test the response of viewers. 'Yet the focus groups reported the original, intensely dreary version of "Deficit Trials" most effectively drove home the message. They said the cleaner, high-tech setting introduced in the alternate commercial "seemed too orderly,"' according to art director Steve Ohman. 'They didn't feel it in their gut.' The company went with what a critic referred to as the 'Kafkaesque spot.' Cited in 'Grace's Spot Couldn't Be Saved,' *Marketing and Media Decisions* 21 (April 1986): 20–1.

5 'INTV Members to Air Grace Deficit Spot,' *Broadcasting*, 11 August 1986, 60.

6 According to NBC, *Deficit Trials* 'expressed the view that the national deficit is a cataclysmic threat to the very existence of American society and drastic cuts in the federal budget are an economic and moral imperative. This is certainly not the unanimous view, and surely goes beyond merely indentifying [*sic*] or calling attention to a problem.' Reported in 'INTV Members to Air Grace Deficit Spot,' 60.

7 Janice Steinberg, 'Advocacy Approach Past Its Prime,' *AA*, 6 October 1987.

8 Statistics can provide only an estimate of the investment: around $2.5 to $3 billion, maybe up to 3 per cent of total ad spending in 1984, according to one review; or, on the low end, something over $1.25 billion, or 1.06 per cent of total ad spending, in 1988, according to another survey. What the statistics do indicate is that most of the spending was by the majors, very large entities like AT & T ($72 million in 1984) or General Motors ($52 million). It should be noted, however, that the amounts invested in image advertising had slowly increased during the 1970s, though the trend was overshadowed by all the noise generated by issue advertising. Statistics from David Schumann, Jan Hathcote, and Susan West, 'Corporate Advertising in America: A Review of Published Studies on Use, Measurement, and Effectiveness,' *Journal of Advertising* 20, no. 3 (September 1991): 35–56; Thomas Garbett, 'Today's Trends in Corporate Advertising,' *Business Marketing* 70 (August 1985): 64, 66, 70, 72; and Ed Fitch, 'Image Ads More Than Glad Tidings,' *AA*, 10 March 1986.

9 Bessies 1994.

10 Strictly speaking, the term should be 'technotopia,' if I followed the form of the basic term 'topos.' But 'technopia' has a more pleasing rhythm.

11 See Howard Segal, 'The Technological Utopians,' in Joseph Corn, ed., *Imagining Tomorrow: History, Technology, and the American Future* (Cambridge, Mass.: MIT Press 1986), 119–36.

12 See Krishan Kumar, 'Science and Utopia: H.G. Wells and a Modern Utopia,' *Utopia and Anti-Utopia in Modern Times* (Oxford: Basil Blackwell 1987), 168–223

13 See Carol Willis, 'Skyscraper Utopias: Visionary Urbanism in the 1920s,' and Folke T. Kihlstedt, 'Utopia Realized: The World's Fairs of the 1930s,' both in Corn, ed., *Imagining Tomorrow*, 164–87 and 97–118.

14 David Gelernter, *1939: The Lost World of the Fair* (New York: Free Press 1995).

15 Roland Marchand has pointed out how this was just part of a long search for legitimacy, in which corporate America had often made claims that it was crafting the world of tomorrow. See Marchand's *Creating the Corporate Soul: The Rise of Public Relations and Corporate Imagery in American Big Business* (Berkeley: University of California Press 1998), esp. his ch. 7, 'The Corporations Come to the Fair: The Visit to the Factory Transformed.'

16 Witness, for example, the marvellous article of prophecy, and dogma, by Zbigniew Brzezinski, 'America in the Technetronic Age,' first published in 1968, and republished in George Kateb, ed., *Utopia* (New York: Atherton Press 1971), 127–50.

17 Max Horkheimer and Theodor Adorno, *Dialectic of Enlightenment* (New York: Continuum 1995), 3.

18 Ibid., 19.

19 Perhaps they should have. Already corporate films made much of the link between capitalism and technology, even before the World's Fair. And during World War II many a corporation used its advertising dollars to proclaim the glories of the coming world of tomorrow. For an exploration of these phenomena, see Richard Prelinger, curator, *To New Horizons: Ephemeral Films 1931–1945* (New York: Prelinger Associates; Los Angeles: Voyageur Press 1987).

20 IS 1994.

21 Specifically, an IBM ad with the peculiar title, in English anyway, *Computer Theory of Evolution* (IBA 1982) and an Apple ad with the much more appropriate title *Industrial Revelation* (IBA 1991).

22 Walter Benjamin, 'Theses on the Philosophy of History,' in his *Illuminations: Essays and Reflections*, ed. Hannah Arendt (New York: Schocken Books 1968), 253–64.

23 Cannes 1982.

24 *Italian Farmers* was part of 'Solutions for a Small Planet,' on the IBM Web

site in 1996. Likewise *Vision* ... was available on the Bates Advertising Web site, in April 1996, at *http://www.asiaconnect.com.my/bates/advertising/ portfolio/index.html*, while the Singapore Airlines spot was on the Batey Advertising site, *http://bateyads.com.sg/htmlpages/batey/showreel.mov/ sia.megatop.mov*, also April 1996.

25 Bessies 1985.

26 The two Electricity Council ads NMPFTV; ITT was at *http://www.imageg.com/ home/ITT.MOV* in May 1996.

27 The three ads were in IBA 1994 and also available for some years after on the AT & T Web site.

28 *Daddy*, Cannes 1994; the Nynex ad was available at *http://advert.com/toaa/ nynex.mov* in April 1996; Ameritech's series were available on its Web site, *http://www.ameritech.com/news/testtown/movies/*, in March 1996; the hospital ad was at *http://206.210.64.96/ppi_qt_movies/agh.mov* in May 1996.

29 There were others, though these did not appear on the main Web page. One, called *Surfers*, pushed the AS/400 System, using the lingo of surfers in southern California.

30 A series of three ads appearing in *Time* magazine in the spring of 1995 gave special emphasis to the way computer technology could enhance creativity. These have been analysed by Kirsten Hall in 'Are You Connected?' *Critical Mass: The Webzine of Communications Issues* 2, Issue 3, available, in February 1996, at *http://hoshi.cic.sfu.ca/-cm/issue6/contents.html*.

31 *Light On*, Cannes 1979; *A Day in the Life*, Cannes 1985; and *Life Cycle*, IS 1995.

32 Horkheimer and Adorno, *Dialectic of Enlightenment*, 3–4.

33 Francis Bacon, *The New Atlantis*, Internet Wiretap edition, 1993.

34 *Tribute*, IBA 1994; *Wedding*, IBA 1989.

35 This ad appeared on the Lockheed Martin Web site in February 1996. It celebrated the union of Lockheed and Martin Marietta.

36 This was, at least initially, a print campaign with 'ads in The Wall Street Journal, The Economist, Barron's, Pensions and Investments, Business Week, Forbes, Fortune, and Institutional Investor.' The information and the ads were made available on the company's Web site in February 1996.

37 *Voice Recognition*, Cannes 1991.

38 Respectively, *Fiber Optics*, ITT, U.S.A (Cannes 1978); *CN Group of Companies*, Canadian National, Canada (Bessies 1985); *Firemen*, Du Pont, U.S.A (IBA 1990), and *Introducing the Star 2*, Nippon Telephone and Telegraph (NTT), Japan, 1996 (available on the NTT Web site in June 1996).

39 Bessies 1988.

40 Cannes 1987.

41 For instance Esso's *Tiger-Technology* (1975), Shell's *Tempest* (1981), and British Petroleum's *Pub* and *Stars and Stripes* (1980).

42 Available at *http://www.lilly.com/movies/sarah.mov* in February 1996.

43 This type of presentation of corporations is also commonplace, and particularly so among companies, such as financial institutions, railways, automobile manufacturers, retail outlets, and so on, which could not readily employ the imagery of technopia. For that reason, I leave this aside in a discussion devoted to the corporate appropriation of the utopian tradition.

44 The ad appeared on the Web site of Lockheed Martin in February 1996. Not many such commercials appear on television. Another in a similar vein, though, was United Technologies, *F15* (IBA 1983). There was the occasional British version as well, such as *Up Where We Belong*, from British Aerospace, 1986 (NMPFTV).

45 Cannes 1990.

46 Bessies 1974.

47 Under the title *Landscape*, Cannes 1982.

48 Jolyon Jenkins, 'Who's the Greenest?,' *New Statesman and Society*, 17 August 1990, 18.

49 I did have a strange sense, though, when assessing this commercial, of another reading: the possibility that the worried viewer might feel alarmed is linked to the images of placid and stupid cattle; might form a protest group, to a startled collection of crows; might call for an inquiry, to a little bird squeaking; and might write to your MP, to an owl closing its eyes. It is as if the company were mocking the public for taking any stand.

50 Cannes 1992.

51 Cited on the Nature Conservancy Web site at *http://www.tnc.org/crm/about.htm* in July 1998.

52 Southern California Edison and *Nature* in IBA 1994.

53 The ad at NMPFTV. The campaign is discussed in David White, 'The Selling of Sellafield,' *New Society*, 7 March 1986, 410–11.

54 Ibid.

55 This from a report by EMMI Inc., a publisher of public relations magazines, that investigated the nuclear industry: available on the Web at *http://www.prcentral.com/rmja95voice.htm* in August 1997.

56 'A cursory examination of a fistful of corporate image advertising would lead most people to assume those who create it are refugees from some positive mental attitude symposium. Nowhere else in advertising – admittedly an upbeat information forum – can so many glad tidings be found.' Ed Fitch, 'Images Ads More Than Glad Tidings,' *AA*, 10 March 1986, 42.

57 'Marketing Greenery: Friendly to Whom?,' *Economist* 315 (7 April 1990): 83.

58 Cited in Ed Zotti, 'Corporate Image Advertising: Reading between the Lines of Corporate Ads,' *AA*, 24 January 1983, M10.

59 Paul Ricoeur, 'Weber (1)' and 'Weber (2),' *Lectures on Ideology and Utopia* (New York: Columbia University Press 1986), 181–215.

60 These statistics are taken from measure-of-trust surveys which were part of Decima Quarterly Reports (September 1982–September 1989). The cumulative chart is published in Allan Gregg and Michael Posner, *The Big Picture: What Canadians Think about Almost Everything* (Toronto: Macfarlane Walter and Ross 1990), 61.

61 Surveys done in Canada and the United States show a consistent, though slight, difference in the responses to the argument, 'There's too much power concentrated in the hands of a few large companies for the good of the nation.' The ten-year (1977–87) average stood at 68 per cent for Canada, 76 per cent for America. Cited in Seymour Martin Lipset, *Continental Divide: The Values and Institutions of the United States and Canada* (New York: Routledge 1990), 131.

62 Big labour occasionally tried. But, at least recently, it has never found a way of positioning itself that can resell the idea of unions, except as a means of protecting the self-interest of workers. For a criticism of one American campaign, see *AA*, 1 September 1997, 37.

9 Green Nightmares: Humanity versus Nature

1 David Gelernter, *1939: The Lost World of the Fair* (New York: Free Press 1995), 53.

2 See Raymond Williams, 'Utopia and Science Fiction,' in *Problems in Materialism and Culture* (London: Verso 1980), 196–212.

3 Respectively *A Clockwork Orange* (1962), *Earthworks* (1965), *Make Room! Make Room* (1966), *Colossus* (1966), *Do Androids Dream of Electric Sheep* (1968), *Past Master* (1968), *Bug Jack Barron* (1969). There was a tradition to build on, however: in 1953 two classic examples of dystopian science fiction appeared, Ray Bradbury's *Fahrenheit 451* and the Frederick Pohl / C.M. Kornbluth attack on advertising called *The Space Merchants*.

4 John Brunner, *The Sheep Look Up* (New York: Ballantine Books 1972), 456.

5 For a discussion of these authors and the origins of the crusade, see Donal Fleming, 'Roots of the New Conservation Movement,' in D. Fleming and B. Bailyn, eds, *Perspectives in American History* 6 (1972): 7–91.

6 The quotation is taken from Peter Singer's own description, as listed on the Eco Books Web site, September 1997.

7 *The Times* (London), 16 November 1990, 6. The Advertising Standards Authority vigorously criticized the picture, charging that it caused 'unjustified shock and distress.' The picture was used in a campaign to put 'an end to the long-distance transport of live animals for slaughter.'

8 Boxer was associated with the Captain Planet Foundation, which was controlled by the Turner Broadcasting System in the United States. Boxer's comments had purportedly been made to the Environmental Protection Agency. The quotation was made available on the Web in January 1997 at *http://www.turner.com/planet/tune-in/psa.html.*

9 IS 1988.

10 The unnamed spot was available on the Web site of Greenpeace International in November 1996.

11 IBA 1992.

12 The Sierra Club episode presumably occurred in the 1970s – it is cited in David Paletz, Roberta Pearson, and Donald Willis, *Politics in Public Service Advertising on Television* (New York: Praeger Publishers 1977), 102. On the IBA: Brian Rotman, 'Political Advertising,' *The Listener*, 11 September 1986, 27. On the CBC: *Globe and Mail* (Toronto), 14 June 1990, A7. On the anti-meat issue: *Editor and Publisher*, 7 September 1991, 21.

13 Cannes 1990 and 1991.

14 Cannes 1978 and 1985.

15 The self-description comes from one page of its Web site, *http://www.foe.org/ptp/PtP.html,* in October 1997.

16 IS 1993.

17 Frances Kelley, 'Hong Kong Is Slow to "Green,"' *Marketing*, 17 February 1992, 42.

18 Cannes 1993.

19 Lürzers 1989. The ad may well have been retooled for use elsewhere. In 1996 it was present on the Greenpeace Web site as the 'Ozone Shield PSA,' where the warning 'Save the Ozone Shield / Stop Making CFCs / HCFCs and HFCs/ NOW' had been added at the end of the action.

20 *Precious Water*, IBA 1986; *Piggy*, IS 1987; *Apple*, IBA 1989.

21 Ad Council 1988; the second ad was available on the EDF Web site (*http://www.edf.org/index.html*) in January 1997.

22 These figures and quotations are taken from a 'History of WWF,' made available on its Web site (*http://www.panda.org/wwf/history.htm*) in September 1997.

23 Here is a list of some of the commercials sponsored by the WWF: *Noah's Ark* (Canada, Bessies 1982), *Life on Earth* (U.K., NMPFTV 1990), *Woonruimte* (Holland, Lürzers 1992), *Child and Puppy* (Spain, Cannes 1994). In addition the WWF sponsored a British campaign in 1991 which drew upon the

memory of Tarzan and Skippy (the Kangaroo) to drive home the lessons of ecology.

24 Ad Council 1986.

25 IBA 1991.

26 Available on the ECO Web site (*http://www.earthcomm.org/abouteco/econewsroom/neighborsdebut.html*) in January 1997.

27 The paragraph is based upon a story by James Jackson, 'Greenpeace Gets Real,' in *Time International*, 10 June 1996.

28 IS 1988.

29 Bessies 1991.

30 Ad Council 1982

31 Or, rather, one influential version of Arcadia. The memories of Arcadia are various and splendid, according to Simon Schama: 'shaggy and smooth; dark and light; a place of bucolic leisure and a place of primitive panic' (517). See his marvellous account in *Landscape and Memory* (Toronto: Random House of Canada 1996).

32 Bessies 1975.

33 This is a composite of a selection of ads: *Baby Seals*, NBC, U.S.A, Cannes 1984; *Animal Abandonment*, WWF, Italy, IBA 1988; *Slaughter*, American Wildlife Federation, U.S.A, Cannes 1989; *Scream*, Whale and Dolphin Conservation Society, U.K., IS 1991; *Rhino*, Faith Foundation, U.K., IS 1991; *This Message*, Noah's Friends, U.S.A, Lürzers 1991; *Big Cats*, The Nature Conservancy, U.S.A, IBA 1993; *Think*, RSPCA, Hong Kong, IBA 1993.

34 Respectively *Baby Seals*, U.S.A, Cannes 1984; *Vampire*, Finland, Cannes 1980; *Insects*, U.K., IS 1988; *A Hunting We Will Go*, U.K., Lürzers 1989.

35 Andrew Lycett, 'Hope and Charities,' *The Times* (London), 23 December 1987, 25.

36 IS 1986.

37 Cited in Ronald Rice and Charles Atkin, eds, *Public Communication Campaigns*, 2nd ed. (Newbury Park, Calif.: Sage 1989), 215–17.

38 James Jackson, 'Greenpeace Gets Real,' *Time International*, 10 June 1996 (from Web site, hence no page reference).

39 *The Times* (London), 13 August 1989, D5.

40 *New York Times*, 28 March 1991, D7.

41 *The Big Picture: What Canadians Think about Almost Everything* (Toronto: Macfarlane Walter and Ross 1990).

42 Angus Reid Group, 'The Public Agenda,' a survey of national priorities made available on the company's Web site in September 1997. The survey carried material dating back to February 1988. The 1989 ranking was out of twenty separate issues. People were allowed to mention up to three issues. Some of these issues were linked: for instance 'Unemployment/Jobs,' 'Defi-

cit/Debt/Spending,' 'The Economy (general),' 'Taxes/Tax Reform/GST,' and 'Trade Issues' had a much higher combined rate of mention than the lone issue of the environment. Even so, the finding did indicate the priority of saving nature, and it was confirmed by a similar kind of finding of September 1989 mentioned in *The Big Picture* (92).

43 Cited in Michael Valpy, 'The March against Nature,' *Globe and Mail* (Toronto), 9 September 1997. The column I used was made available on the newspaper's Web site.

44 A Time/CNN poll of December 1995, for example, found that 42 per cent of American respondents believed environmental laws should go farther (down from 63 per cent in November 1990), 29 per cent thought the laws adequate (up from 19 per cent), and 23 per cent thought they had gone too far (up from 12 per cent). The poll results were made available on the *Time* Campaign 96 Web site in September 1997.

45 The material on ECO, the Captain Planet Foundation, and Planet Ark comes from material on their Web sites. *The Power of One* was available on the Web in January 1997 at *http://www.itnet.com-80/avi/eco3.avi*. *Dolphin 2*, the Brosnan spot, was available from Planet Ark, also in January 1997.

46 See, for example, *Earth First! Journal: The Radical Environmental Journal*, Eostar 1995.

47 James Berger, 'Ends and Means: Theorizing Apocalypse in the 1990s,' *Postmodern Culture* 6, no. 3 (May 1996), para. 4 (at *http://128.143.200.11/pmc/text-only/issue.596/review-1.596* in December 1997).

48 Cited in Stephen Cook, 'Reflections on Apocalypticism at the Approach of the Year 2000,' *Union Seminary Quarterly Review* 49, nos. 1–2 (at *http://www.uts.columbia.edu/~usqr/COOK.HTM* in December 1997).

49 Rev. Jerry Falwell, one of the leaders of American fundamentalism, was reported as saying to his actual and television audiences, in 1992, 'I do not believe there will be another millennium ... or another century.' Cited by Gary DeMar, ' The Year 2000 or Bust,' at *http://www.avision1.com/bwview/opin0997.html* in December 1997. See as well Randall Balmer's '"Thy Kingdom Come": Apocalypticism in American Culture,' part of the same issue of the *Union Seminary Quarterly Review* cited above.

50 Arthur Herman, *The Idea of Decline in Western History* (New York: Free Press 1997), 400–40.

*Baudrillard and Company: Image, Spectacle, Simulacrum

1 Foucault, *Discipline and Punish: The Birth of the Prison*, trans. Alan Sheridan (New York: Vintage Books 1979), 217.

2 Where the citation is obvious, given the context, I have referenced quoted material in the body of the text.

3 Of course Habermas did not talk about the role of torture, focusing instead on the display of the noble body. 'The staging of publicity involved in representation was wedded to personal attributes such as insignia (badges and arms), dress (clothing and coiffure), demeanor (form of greeting and poise) and rhetoric (form of address and formal discourse in general) – in a word, to a strict code of "noble" conduct.' Jürgen Habermas, *The Structural Transformation of the Public Sphere: An Inquiry into a Category of Bourgeois Society*, trans. Thomas Burger (Cambridge, Mass.: MIT Press 1991), 8.

4 Tony Bennett, *The Birth of the Museum: History, Theory, Politics* (London: Routledge 1995). Bennett's work is a novel and provocative addition to the literature on discipline. It is clearly based on Foucault's work (note the title's similarity to the subtitle, 'The Birth of the Prison,' of *Discipline and Punish*). Indeed, he argues that he has set out to write a 'genealogy,' an account of the origins that determine the present of an institution, borrowing from the vocabulary of Foucault.

5 Walter Benjamin, 'The Work of Art in the Age of Mechanical Reproduction,' in his *Illuminations: Essays and Reflections*, ed. Hannah Arendt (New York: Schocken Books 1968), 217–51.

6 'An image is a sight which has been recreated or reproduced.' John Berger, *Ways of Seeing* (London: Penguin Books 1972), 9.

7 By 'aura' Benjamin referred to the unique existence of the original in a particular place and time which gave the art work an authenticity. By 'cult value' he evoked the idea that art once existed in the context, and the service, of ritual.

8 One among many investigations of the political significance of spectacle, long before the so-called modern era, is Roy Strong's *Splendour at Court: Renaissance Spectacle and Illusion* (London: Weidenfeld and Nicolson 1973).

9 Peter Kenez, *The Birth of the Propaganda State: Soviet Methods of Mass Mobilization, 1917–1929* (Cambridge: Cambridge University Press 1985).

10 Modris Eksteins, *Rites of Spring: The Great War and the Birth of the Modern Age* (Toronto: Lester and Orpen Dennys 1989), 313 and 312.

11 David Welch, *The Third Reich: Politics and Propaganda* (London: Routledge 1993). See also Ian Kershaw, '"The Hitler Myth": Image and Reality in the Third Reich,' in David Crew, ed., *Nazism and German Society, 1933–1945* (London: Routledge 1994), 197–215. Another source of information for this paragraph were the essays posted on the Web that resulted from Professor Bill Eddelman's class, 'Nazi/Weimar Cultural Reconstructions,' at the Stanford Program in Berlin, especially Scott Van Winkle's 'Political Iconog-

raphy in Nazi and Weimar Germany' at *http://wwwosp.stanford.edu/ drama258/van_winkle/default.html* in May 1996.

12 Daniel Boorstin, *The Image: A Guide to Pseudo-Events in America* (New York: Vintage Books 1962).

13 See Christin J. Mamiya, *Pop Art and Consumer Culture: American Super Market* (Austin: University of Texas Press 1992).

14 James B. Twitchell, *Carnival Culture: The Trashing of Taste in America* (New York: Columbia University Press 1992), 6.

15 The views of Foucault and Debord have been elaborated and discussed in a fascinating chapter of Martin Jay's *Downcast Eyes: The Denigration of Vision in Twentieth-Century French Thought* (Berkeley: University of California Press 1993), 381–434.

16 Guy Debord, *The Society of the Spectacle*, trans. Donald Nicholson-Smith (New York: Zone Books 1994).

17 Sadie Plant's *The Most Radical Gesture: The Situationist International in a Postmodern Age* (London: Routledge 1992) makes clear how the ideas of SI survived the demise of the movement and continued to provoke comment in the postmodern heyday of the 1980s.

18 That essay appears in Baudrillard, *Simulacra and Simulation*, trans. Sheila Faria Glaser (Ann Arbor: University of Michigan Press 1994), 1–42. The essays date from the 1970s. The French version of the collection was published in 1981. 'The Precession of Simulacra' was published in English by Semiotext(e) in 1983 in Jean Baudrillard, *Simulations*, trans. Paul Patton and Philip Beitchman (New York: Semiotext[e] 1983).

19 Jean Baudrillard, *Forget Foucault* (New York: Columbia University, Semiotext[e] 1987), 16. The piece was first published in French in 1977.

20 'In Baudrillard, the catastrophe is the end of the whole apocalyptic hermeneutic itself. There can be no unveiling because there is nothing under the surface: there is only surface; the map has replaced the terrain.' James Berger, 'Ends and Means: Theorizing Apocalypse in the 1990s,' *Postmodern Culture* 6, no. 3 (May 1996), par. 4 (at *http://128.143.200.11/pmc/ text-only/issue.596/review-1.596* in December 1997).

21 Baudrillard had been concerned with the consuming capacity of advertising even as a kind of Marxist. One section of *Le système des objets*, published by Gallimard in 1968, dealt with advertising. See Jean Baudrillard, *The System of Objects*, trans. James Benedict (London: Verso 1996), 164–96.

22 From selections cited in *Love for Sale: The Words and Pictures of Barbara Kruger*, text by Kate Linker (New York: Harry N. Abrams 1990), 75. Baudrillard had written an essay in an earlier catalogue of Kruger's work.

23 Jean Baudrillard, 'Absolute Advertising, Ground-Zero Advertising,' in his *Simulacra and Simulation*, 87.

10 When Politics Becomes Advertising

1 The Federal Elections Commission lists the percentage as 49.08 per cent, or a turnout of 96,456, 345 out of a possible 196,511,000. This was made available in July 1998 on their Web site (*http://www.fec.gov/pages/htmlto5.htm*). That percentage has been disputed in Peter Bruce, 'How the Experts Got Voter Turnout Wrong Last Year,' *The Public Perspective* (October/November 1997), 39–43, who argues that the voting-age population is inflated with people ineligible to vote (because they are illegal aliens, legal but not naturalized citizens, felons, etcetera). Bruce prefers a smaller figure that he calls the eligible electorate – but, from the point of view of democratic theory, the voting-age population is actually more suitable when evaluating the political status of the republic.

2 Jean Baudrillard, 'The Precession of Simulacra,' *Simulacra and Simulation*, trans. Sheila Faria Glaser (Ann Arbor: University of Michigan Press 1994), 6.

3 Cited in 'Political Ads Make Local Switch,' *AA*, 3 February 1997, 24.

4 What made this chapter possible was the fact that so many different sources placed political ads on the World Wide Web: individual candidates, the parties, and some media. The single most valuable source was the All-politics Campaign 96 page of *Time* and CNN. This I have supplemented with two collections of political ads, 'Prime-Time Politics' and 'The Classics of Political TV Advertising,' available for purchase from the American magazine *Campaigns and Elections*.

5 John Underwood, 'A Run for Their Money,' *Marketing* (U.K.), 12 November 1996, 16.

6 These figures were made available in September 1997 at Gallup's Web site.

7 A national sample of 1,517 people was asked, via the telephone, to rank certain institutions and individuals on a scale of 10, where 10 represented complete trust and 1 complete distrust. Then the total rankings of 1, 2, or 3 were subtracted from the total ranks of 8, 9, or 10. That produced a deficit of −4.6 per cent for Bill Clinton, −17.7 per cent for Bob Dole, and fully −22.8 per cent for the federal government (note as well that the media stood at −19.2 per cent). The poll was carried out by Angus Reid Group and Bloomberg Business News. It was made available on the Web site of Angus Reid in September 1997.

8 See Edwin Diamond and Stephen Bates, *The Spot: The Rise of Political Advertis-*

ing on Television, 3rd ed. (Cambridge, Mass.: MIT Press 1992), 213. Diamond and Bates discuss at much greater length the populist style of Jimmy Carter.

9 Tim Luke uses this term to describe the presentation of Reagan in 'Tele-visual Democracy and the Politics of Charisma,' *Telos* 70 (Winter 1986–7): 78.

10 Phillip Niffenegger, 'Strategies for Success from the Political Marketers,' *Journal of Consumer Marketing* 6, no. 1 (Winter 1989): 48.

11 'An Interview with Jean Baudrillard,' conducted by Ted Colless, David Kelly, and Alan Choldenko, trans. Philippe Tanguy, in Jean Baudrillard, *The Evil Demon of Images,* Power Institute Publications no. 3 (Sydney: University of Sydney 1987), 47.

12 Bob Graham, 'Campaigns Are for the Public,' *AA,* 9 February 1987, 18. He and his opponent had spent more than $13 million, mostly on television advertising, in the 1986 campaign.

13 Cited in Elizabeth Kolbert, 'Campaign Mechanics Become Issue of Campaigns,' 20 February 1996, *New York Times* News Service.

14 Mentioned by John Mashek, 'The Political Advertising War of 1996,' Tracking the Media Feb 96 Letter 2, available in October 1997 at *http://www.fac.org/publicat/track/ FEB96/FB_SIDE2.HTM.*

15 Kathleen Hall Jamieson, *Dirty Politics: Deception, Distraction, and Democracy* (New York: Oxford University Press 1992), 128–35.

16 Noted in David Hoffman, 'The Frictionless Presidency,' *Gannett Center Journal* 4, no. 2 (Spring 1990): 83.

17 The Political Action Committee was an independent player which could use funds to support and attack individuals, at no cost to the partisan beneficiary. Conservative PACs had pioneered a new wave of negative advertising in 1980 to bring down liberal-minded senators.

18 Randall Rothenberg, 'The Journalist as Maytag Repairman,' *Gannett Center Journal* 4, no. 2 (Spring 1990): 101–2.

19 Jamieson, *Dirty Politics,* 15–42.

20 The Center for Public Integrity, *Well-Healed: Inside Lobbying for Health Care Reform* (Washington, D.C.: Center for Public Integrity 1995 [*http://epn.org/library/ cpwehe.html*]).

21 The transcript appeared in FX/'Under Scrutiny' with Jane Wallace, show: Tuesday, 27 September 1994, *http://delphi.com/fx/jane0927.html*

22 Aired on CNN, 30 August 1994.

23 See Craig Lefebvre, ' Health Reform in the United States: A Social Marketing Perspective,' *Journal of Public Policy and Marketing* 13 (09-01-1994), made available on the World Wide Web in February 1996 at *http://www.elibrary.com/cgi-bin/hhweb/hhfetch? 29899753x0y852:Q001:D002*

24 Witness this comment from one reporter, Chitra Ragavan:

'And so the Harry and Louise folklore was created by reporters who loved the ease of relating to the difficult topic of health reform through the simple image of a suburban couple worrying. That's why every time the Health Insurance Association of America unveils a new Harry and Louise ad, the room is packed with reporters like me.

'Commercials are appealing to us because they jazz up our TV or radio piece, and they express conflict in simple, yet dramatic, terms.' Cited in 'Advertisement Campaigns Distort Health Care Reform,' National Public Radio's *Morning Edition*, 23 August 1994, made available on the World Wide Web in February 1996 at *http://www.elibrary.com/cgi-bin/hhweb/ hhfetch?29899753x0y852:Q002:D007.*

25 Cyndee Miller, 'Ads Are Huge Weapon in the Battle of Health Care Reform,' *Marketing News* 28 (09-12-1994), made available on the World Wide Web in February 1996 at *http://www.elibrary.com/cgi-bin/hhweb/ hhfetch?29899753x0y852:Q001:D008*

26 Beth Bogart, 'Politicians Campaign for Pretested Ads,' *AA*, 13 February 1986, 21.

27 See Stephen Ansolabehere and Shanto Iyengar, *Going Negative: How Political Advertisements Shrink and Polarize the Electorate* (New York: Free Press 1995), 139–41.

28 Ken Bode in *Prime Time Politics*, a video produced by *Campaigns and Elections.*

29 Jean Baudrillard, *America*, trans. Chris Turner (London: Verso 1988), 97.

30 The poll results were available in September 1997 on the World Wide Web at *http://www.lib.uconn.edu/RoperCenter/!85c.pdf.*

31 Malcolm MacDougall, cited in 'Tackle Hard Issues in Ads, Insurance Exec Says,' *AA*, 10 October 1977, 84.

32 Niffenegger, 'Strategies for Success from the Political Marketers,' 49.

33 Described by Bruce E. Gronbeck in 'Negative Narratives in 1988 Presidential Campaign Ads,' *Quarterly Journal of Speech* 78 (August 1992): 339.

34 The executive summary of the report was available on the World Wide Web in September 1996 at the University of Virginia's Web site (*http:// minerva.acc.Virginia.EDU/~postmod/Survey_ Home.html*). The Postmodernity Project later became the Institute for Advanced Studies in Culture.

35 See, for instance, the discussion of schizophrenia in David Harvey, *The Condition of Postmodernity* (Cambridge, Mass.: Blackwell 1990), 53, and elsewhere: the index contains thirteen references to this term, and there are other places in the book where it echoes.

36 See Fredric Jameson, *Postmodernism or, The Cultural Logic of Late Capitalism* (Durham, N.C.: Duke University Press 1991), 26–9.

37 The 1985 essay appeared in Mark Poster, ed., *Jean Baudrillard: Selected Writings* (Stanford, Calif.: Stanford University Press 1988), 219.

38 Witness the contempt in this comment by Zygmunt Bauman: 'We are now being told that the bovine immobility of the masses is the best form of activity we have, and that their doing nothing is the most excellent form of resistance.' In 'The World According to Jean Baudrillard,' *Intimations of Postmodernity* (London: Routledge 1992), 153. Even Mark Poster, the American scholar who has popularized Baudrillard's views, seemed doubtful and apologetic about this conclusion of Baudrillard. See Poster, 'Introduction' to the collection he edited, *Jean Baudrillard: Selected Writings*, 7.

Conclusion: Postmodern Democracy

1 The exhibition and text were available on the web at *www.arts.monash.edu.au/visarts/globe/issue4/bkrutxt.html* in July 1998.

2 Barbara Kruger, 'Arts and Leisures' in her *Remote Control: Power, Culture, and the World of Appearances* (Cambridge, Mass.: MIT Press 1993), 5.

3 Jürgen Habermas, 'Further Reflections on the Public Sphere,' trans. Thomas Burger, in Craig Calhoun, ed., *Habermas and the Public Sphere* (Cambridge, Mass.: MIT Press 1992), 421–61. Citations to this article are referenced in the text as FR. I have also quoted material from Habermas, 'The Public Sphere,' a 1973 essay reprinted in Chandra Mukerji and Michael Schudson, eds, *Rethinking Popular Culture: Contemporary Perspectives in Cultural Studies* (Berkeley: University of California Press 1991), 398–404: referenced as TPS. His classic *The Structural Transformation of the Public Sphere: An Inquiry into a Category of Bourgeois Society*, trans. Thomas Burger with Frederick Lawrence (Cambridge, Mass.: MIT Press 1991) is referenced as *STPS*.

4 Nancy Fraser, 'Rethinking the Public Sphere: A Contribution to the Critique of Actually Existing Democracy,' in Calhoun, ed., *Habermas and the Public Sphere*, 111.

5 'Publicity,' *Gannett Center Journal* 4, no. 2 (Spring 1990).

6 Cited in Barry Ries, 'Up against Big Brother,' *Front and Centre* 2, no. 5 (September 1995), available on the Web at *http://www.ccp.ca/information/documents/fc60.htm* in July 1998. This was in addition to an estimated $175 million in space and time donated by the media: Gail Chiasson, 'Participaction Calls on the Inactive,' *Marketing*, 9 July 1990, 34.

7 Figures cited in Jonathan Rose, 'Government Advertising in a Crisis: The Quebec Referendum Precedent,' *Canadian Journal of Communication*, 1997, on its Web site in July 1998.

8 The following discussion of the council is based on information made available at *http://www.ncpc.org/* in August 1997 and July 1998.

9 In mid-1998, for example, its Web site carried the storyboards of *Wrong Guess* and *Misperceptions*, which told adults to realize that whatever teens looked like (spiked hair, casual dress, etcetera) the good ones had worked to drive crime out of their neighbourhoods. McGruff appeared with his nephew, Scruff, in the animated *Scruff's Adventures II*, aimed at pre-teens, which offered a mildly scary drama (what should Scruff do when menaced?), to sell a 'new comic activity book' to explain how to deal with 'bullies ... drugs ... and guns.' Yet another PSA, *Where Have All the Children Gone?*, presumably meant for everyone, amounted to a national lament about dead kids ('Every day, ten children are killed by gunfire').

10 Alan Travis, 'Whitehall's Soft Soap Embrace,' *Guardian*, 11 May 1989, 23. However, this judgment depended on how ad spending was counted; for example, a second source had government standing second. Margaret Scammell, 'Political Advertising and the Broadcasting Revolution,' *Political Quarterly* 61 (April/June 1990): 203.

11 Cited in Murray Dobbin, *The Myth of the Good Corporate Citizen: Democracy under the Rule of Big Business* (Toronto: Stoddart 1998), 47.

12 Ann Reilly Dowd, 'Winning One from the Gipper,' *Fortune*, 9 November 1987, 125, 128. The Bork nomination was defeated in the Senate.

13 He denied the charge, of course. The exchange is contained in Madelaine Drohan, 'The Meltdown of Cool Britannia,' *Globe and Mail* (Toronto), 8 August 1998, D4.

14 Jenny Hontz, 'DeMoss Foundation Ad Tests Broadcast Limits,' *AA*, 12 September 1994, 37.

15 The rest of this paragraph is based on Dick Morris's *Behind the Oval Office: Winning the Presidency in the Nineties* (New York: Random House 1997), esp. 142–53.

16 Described by Judann Dagnoli, 'Sokolof Keeps Thumping Away at Food Giants,' *AA*, 9 April 1990, a boxed insert in Kathleen Hall Jamieson and Karlyn Kohrs Campbell, *The Interplay of Influence: News, Advertising, Politics, and the Mass Media* (Belmont, Calif.: Wadsworth Publishing 1992), 237.

17 The reference to dissent is a direct steal from Thomas Frank and Matt Weiland, *Commodify Your Dissent: The Business of Culture in the New Gilded Age* (New York: W.W. Norton 1997). This is a collection of essays which originally appeared in a journal of opinion called *The Baffler*. It argues, among much else, that business has successfully marketed rebellion as a lifestyle choice to a large number of American consumers in the 1990s.

18 The ad was available on a *Campaigns and Elections* video entitled 'Best Foreign Spots.'

19 IBA 1994.

20 Jackson Lears, *Fables of Abundance: A Cultural History of Advertising in America* (New York: Basic Books 1994).

21 See Bob Garfield, 'Foundation's Ad Skirts Tough Abortion Issues,' *AA*, 20 April 1992, 40, and Hontz, 'DeMoss Foundation Ad Tests Broadcast Limits,' 37.

22 So the announcer explains that the 'execution procedure starts by puncturing the head with a sharp instrument. Next the brain is suctioned out. After the head collapses, the body is discarded.' The soundtrack is a dirge and the visuals show a condemned man being carried off to face execution. *Death Penalty* identified the procedure as execution. Another in the series, *Three Inches of Separation*, spoke of murder. These ads were available on the Child Protection Fund Web site, *www.nrlc.org/multimedia/index.html*, in August 1998.

23 Robin Room, acting president of the Addiction Research Foundation, cited in Lisa Priest, 'Smoking Increase Is First in 30 Years,' *Toronto Star*, 21 June 1994, A3.

24 Leonard Shyles and John E. Hocking, 'The Army's "Be All You Can Be" Campaign,' *Armed Forces and Society* 16, no. 3 (Spring 1990): 369–83.

25 The Procter and Gamble story is discussed in Zachary Schiller and Mark Landler, 'P&G Can Get Mad, Sure, But Does It Have to Get Even?' *Business Week*, 4 June 1990, 63. See also 'Coffee Boycott Boils Over,' *AA*, 21 May 1990.

26 Respectively, James S. Murphy, 'Marketing "From the Hip" Is No Public Service,' *Marketing News* 23, no. 16 (1989): 4–5; 'Smoke and Spend,' *The Economist*, 28 April 1990, 31; Sandra Porteous, 'N.S. Gasoline Dealers Upset by Anti-Drug Ad,' *Marketing*, 7 January 1994, 4; Scott Hume, 'Anti-gang Ad Effort Stirs Cries of Racism in Chicago Suburb,' *AA*, 7 September 1992, 9; Dianne Allen, 'Drunk Driving Ads Work Better Than Planned,' *Toronto Star*, 1 June 1991, G10.

27 'MediaTelevision,' original air date: Saturday, 18 March 1995, CityTV (but available on their Web site in May 1996).

28 Stephen Kline, 'Image Politics: Negative Advertising Strategies and the Election Audience,' in Mica Nava, Andrew Blake, Iain MacRury, and Barry Richards, eds, *Buy This Book: Studies in Advertising and Consumption* (London: Routledge 1997), 147.

29 Published by the Free Press in New York and elsewhere. All references in brackets in this paragraph are to this book.

30 Walter Benjamin, 'The Work of Art in the Age of Mechanical Reproduction,' in his *Illuminations: Essays and Reflections*, ed. Hannah Arendt (New York: Schocken Books 1968), 241. The article first appeared in 1936.

31 See the series of articles by Robert D. Putnam, esp. 'The Prosperous Community: Social Capital and Public Life,' *The American Prospect* no. 13 (Spring 1993): 35–42; 'Bowling Alone: America's Declining Social Capital,' *Journal of Democracy* 6, no. 1 (January 1995): 65–78; and 'The Strange Disappearance of Civil America,' *The American Prospect* no. 24 (Winter 1996): np (WWW acquisition). *The American Prospect* has carried various responses to Putnam under the general title 'UNSOLVED MYSTERIES: The Tocqueville Files I and II' in 1996. These were available on its Web site, *http://epn.org/prospect/*.

32 Putnam, 'The Strange Disappearance of Civil America.'

33 Cited in Peter Bruce, 'How the Experts Got Voter Turnout Wrong Last Year,' *The Public Perspective* (October/November 1997): 40.

34 See, for example, Michael Schudson, 'Was There Ever a Public Sphere? If So, When? Reflections on the American Case,' in Calhoun, ed., *Habermas and the Public Sphere*, 143–63.

35 Italics in original. Jean Baudrillard, 'Absolute Advertising, Ground-Zero Advertising,' in his *Simulacra and Simulation*, trans. Sheila Faria Glaser (Ann Arbor: University of Michigan Press 1994), 91.

Select Bibliography

The books and sources listed below may be useful for further study of the phenomenon of civic advocacy.

A. Theory

Baudrillard, Jean. 'The Masses: The Implosion of the Social in the Media.' In Jean Baudrillard, *Selected Writings*, edited by Mark Poster, 209–10. Stanford Calif.: Stanford University Press 1988).
– *Simulacra and Simulation*. Translated by Sheila Faria Glaser. Ann Arbor: University of Michigan Press 1994.
Bauman, Zygmunt. *Intimations of Postmodernity*. London: Routledge 1992.
Beck, Ulrich. *Risk Society: Towards a New Modernity*. London: Sage 1992.
Benjamin, Walter. 'The Work of Art in the Age of Mechanical Reproduction.' In Walter Benjamin, *Illuminations: Essays and Reflections*, edited by Hannah Arendt, 217–51. New York: Schocken Books 1968.
Burchell, Graham, Colin Gordon, and Peter Miller, ed. 'Government Rationality: An Introduction.' *The Foucault Effect: Studies in Governmentality*. Chicago: University of Chicago Press 1991.
Calhoun, Craig, ed. *Habermas and the Public Sphere*. Cambridge, Mass.: MIT Press 1992.
Eagleton, Terry. *Ideology: An Introduction*. London: Verso 1991.
Foucault, Michel. *Discipline and Punish: The Birth of the Prison*. New York: Vintage Books. 1979.
– *Power/Knowledge: Selected Interviews and Other Writings 1972–1977*. Edited by Colin Gordon. New York: Pantheon 1980.
– *The History of Sexuality. Volume I: An Introduction*. Translated by Robert Hurley. New York: Vintage Books 1990.

Gramsci, Antonio. *The Modern Prince and Other Writings*. New York: International Publishers 1957.

Habermas, Jürgen. *The Structural Transformation of the Public Sphere: An Inquiry into a Category of Bourgeois Society*. Translated by Thomas Burger with Frederick Lawrence. Cambridge, Mass.: MIT Press. 1991.

Hall, Stuart, Chas Critcher, Tony Jefferson, John Clarke, and Brian Roberts. *Policing the Crisis: Mugging, the State, and Law and Order*. London: Macmillan 1978.

Horkheimer, Max, and Theodor Adorno. *Dialectic of Enlightenment*. New York: Continuum 1995.

Marcuse, Herbert. *One-Dimensional Man: Studies in the Ideology of Advanced Industrial Society*. 2nd ed. Boston: Beacon Press 1991.

Ricoeur, Paul. *Lectures on Ideology and Utopia*. Edited by George Taylor. New York: Columbia University 1986.

Williams, Raymond. *Marxism and Literature*. Oxford: Oxford University Press 1977.

B. Advertising and Propaganda

Ansolabehere, Stephen, and Shanto Iyengar. *Going Negative: How Political Advertisements Shrink and Polarize the Electorate*. New York: Free Press 1995.

Atkin, Charles, and Lawrence Wallack, ed. *Mass Communication and Public Health: Complexities and Conflicts*. Newbury Park, Calif.: Sage 1990.

Diamond, Edwin, and Stephen Bates. *The Spot: The Rise of Political Advertising on Television*. 3rd ed. Cambridge, Mass.: MIT Press 1992.

Ellul, Jacques. *Propaganda: The Formation of Men's Attitudes*. New York: Alfred A. Knopf 1965.

Ewen, Stuart. *PR! A Social History of Spin*. New York: Basic Books 1996.

Frank, Thomas. *The Conquest of Cool: Business Culture, Counterculture, and the Rise of Hip Consumerism*. Chicago: University of Chicago Press 1997.

Kotler, Philip, and Eduardo Roberto. *Social Marketing: Strategies for Changing Public Behavior*. New York: Macmillan 1989.

Lears, Jackson. *Fables of Abundance: A Cultural History of Advertising in America*. New York: Basic Books 1994.

Paletz, David, Roberta Pearson, and Donald Willis. *Politics in Public Service Advertising on Television* New York: Praeger 1977.

Pratkanis, Anthony, and Elliot Aronson. *Age of Propaganda: The Everyday Use and Abuse of Persuasion*. New York: W.H. Freeman 1991.

Rice, Ronald E., and William J. Paisley, ed. *Public Communication Campaigns*. Beverly Hills, Calif.: Sage 1981.

Rutherford, Paul. *The New Icons? The Art of Television Advertising.* Toronto: University of Toronto Press 1994.

Sethi, S. Prakash. *Advocacy Advertising and Large Corporations.* (Lexington, Mass.: D.C. Heath 1977.

Taylor, Philip M. *Munitions of the Mind: A History of Propaganda from the Ancient World to the Present Era.* Manchester: Manchester University Press 1995.

Wernick, Andrew. *Promotional Culture: Advertising, Ideology and Symbolic Expression.* Newbury Park, Calif.: Sage 1991.

C. Sources of Commercials

Ad Archives, CNN/Time AllPolitics. A selection of presidential election ads available for viewing online (*cnn.com/ALLPOLITICS/1996/candidates/ad.archive/*).

Advertising Age (New York). BEST Awards (available for sale).

Campaigns and Elections (Washington D.C.). Various collections of American and foreign political ads (available for sale).

Cannes Lions. These awards are available for sale through different distributors in various countries (in Canada the source is Adfilms, Toronto). There is also a Web site (*www.canneslions.com*) where some material is online.

Clio Awards (U.S.A.). Some award winners for 1995–8 available online, and more promised (*www.clioawards.com*).

Hollywood Radio and Television Society. International Broadcasting Awards (available for sale).

Jean-Marie Boursicot Film Library (Paris). A huge collection of ads available for viewing online (*www.adeater.com*).

Museum of Television and Radio (New York City). Ad Council and Young and Rubicam collections.

National Archives of Canada (Ottawa). Bessie Awards.

National Museum of Photography, Film and Television (Bradford, U.K.). An extensive collection of British ads plus some Lürzers tapes of the late 1980s and early 1990s.

Television Bureau of Canada (Toronto). Bessie Awards and Kodak International Showcase (available for sale).

Index

The dates attached to the ads are only approximations, plus or minus one year, because of the ways in which they have been preserved on tapes or on Web sites.